Keeping THE Traditions

A Multicultural Resource

Phyllis J. Perry

illustrated by **Joe Pancake**

fulcrum resources
Golden, Colorado

For David

Library of Congress Cataloging-in-Publication Data
Perry, Phyllis Jean.
    Keeping the traditions : a multicultural resource / Phyllis J. Perry.
        p.   cm.
    Includes bibliographical references (p.   ).
    ISBN 1-55591-975-8 (alk. paper)
    1. Human geography—Juvenile literature. 2. Manners and customs—Juvenile literature. 3. Immigrants—United States—Juvenile literature. I. Title.
GF48.P47 2000
306—dc21   99–085965

Designer: Patty Maher
Cover and interior illustrations © 2000 Joe Pancake, aka Samuel Austin

Printed in the United States of America
0 9 8 7 6 5 4 3 2 1

Fulcrum Publishing
16100 Table Mountain Parkway, Suite 300
Golden, Colorado 80403
(800) 992-2908 • (303) 277-1623
www.fulcrum-resources.com

Contents

Preface • vii
Introduction • ix

Canada • 3
A Legend From Canada • 3
Background Information • 4
History • 6
Government • 7
Religion • 7
Education • 8
Immigrants • 8
Language • 9
The Arts and Sciences • 9
Food • 10
Recreation • 10
Customs and Traditions • 10
Suggested Activities • 12
Suggested Reading • 14

China • 15
A Legend from China • 15
Background Information • 17
History • 18
Government • 19
Religion • 20
Education • 20
Immigrants • 21
Language • 21
The Arts and Sciences • 21
Food • 22
Recreation • 23
Customs and Traditions • 24
Suggested Activities • 25
Suggested Reading • 26

Colombia • 29
A Legend from Colombia • 29
Background Information • 31
History • 33
Government • 34
Religion • 34

Education • 34
Immigrants • 35
Language • 35
The Arts and Sciences • 35
Food • 35
Recreation • 36
Customs and Traditions • 36
Suggested Activities • 37
Suggested Reading • 39

Cuba • 41
A Folktale from Cuba • 41
Background Information • 42
History • 44
Government • 45
Religion • 46
Education • 46
Immigrants • 47
Language • 47
The Arts and Sciences • 47
Food • 48
Recreation • 49
Customs and Traditions • 49
Suggested Activities • 50
Suggested Reading • 52

The Dominican Republic • 53
A Folktale from the Dominican Republic • 53
Background Information • 55
History • 57
Government • 58
Religion • 59
Education • 59
Immigrants • 60
Language • 60
The Arts and Sciences • 60
Food • 61
Recreation • 61
Customs and Traditions • 62
Suggested Activities • 62
Suggested Reading • 64

France • 67

A Legend from France • 67
Background Information • 69
History • 70
Government • 71
Religion • 72
Education • 72
Immigrants • 72
Language • 73
The Arts and Sciences • 73
Food • 74
Recreation • 75
Customs and Traditions • 75
Suggested Activities • 76
Suggested Reading • 78

Germany • 79

A Legend from Germany • 79
Background Information • 82
History • 83
Government • 85
Religion • 85
Education • 85
Immigrants • 86
Language • 86
The Arts and Sciences • 87
Food • 88
Recreation • 88
Customs and Traditions • 89
Suggested Activities • 89
Suggested Reading • 91

Hungary • 93

A Tale from Hungary • 93
Background Information • 95
History • 97
Government • 98
Religion • 98
Education • 98
Immigrants • 99
Language • 99
The Arts and Sciences • 99
Food • 100
Recreation • 101
Customs and Traditions • 101
Suggested Activities • 102
Suggested Reading • 104

India • 105

A Legend from India • 105
Background Information • 108
History • 109
Government • 110
Religion • 110
Education • 111
Immigrants • 111
Language • 112
The Arts and Sciences • 112
Food • 113
Recreation • 113
Customs and Traditions • 113
Suggested Activities • 115
Suggested Reading • 117

Ireland • 119

A Legend from Ireland • 119
Background Information • 122
History • 123
Government • 124
Religion • 125
Education • 125
Immigrants • 125
Language • 125
The Arts and Sciences • 126
Food • 126
Recreation • 127
Customs and Traditions • 127
Suggested Activities • 127
Suggested Reading • 129

Italy • 131

A Legend from Italy • 131
Background Information • 134
History • 134
Government • 135
Religion • 136
Education • 136
Immigrants • 136
Language • 137
The Arts and Sciences • 137
Food • 138
Recreation • 138
Customs and Traditions • 138
Suggested Activities • 139
Suggested Reading • 140

Japan • 143

A Legend from Japan • 143
Background Information • 145
History • 145
Government • 146
Religion • 147
Education • 147
Immigrants • 148
Language • 149
The Arts and Sciences • 149
Food • 150
Recreation • 151
Customs and Traditions • 152
Suggested Activities • 152
Suggested Reading • 154

Mexico • 155

A Legend from Mexico • 155
Background Information • 157
History • 158
Government • 159
Religion • 159
Education • 160
Immigrants • 160
Language • 161
The Arts and Sciences • 161
Food • 161
Recreation • 162
Customs and Traditions • 162
Suggested Activities • 163
Suggested Reading • 165

The Philippines • 167

A Folktale from the Philippines • 167
Background Information • 168
History • 170
Government • 171
Religion • 171
Education • 172
Immigrants • 172
Language • 173
The Arts and Sciences • 173
Food • 174
Recreation • 175
Customs and Traditions • 175
Suggested Activities • 176
Suggested Reading • 178

Poland • 179

A Tale from Poland • 179
Background Information • 182
History • 183
Government • 184
Religion • 185
Education • 185
Immigrants • 185
Language • 186
The Arts and Sciences • 186
Food • 186
Recreation • 187
Customs and Traditions • 188
Suggested Activities • 189
Suggested Reading • 190

Russia • 191

A Legend from Russia • 191
Background Information • 195
History • 196
Government • 198
Religion • 198
Education • 198
Immigrants • 199
Language • 199
The Arts and Sciences • 199
Food • 200
Recreation • 201
Customs and Traditions • 201
Suggested Activities • 202
Suggested Reading • 203

Senegal • 205

A Legend from Senegal • 205
Background Information • 208
History • 211
Government • 212
Religion • 212
Education • 212
Immigrants • 212
Language • 213
The Arts and Sciences • 213
Food • 214
Recreation • 214
Customs and Traditions • 214
Suggested Activities • 215
Suggested Reading • 217

South Korea • 219

A Legend from Korea • 219
Background Information • 221
History • 222
Government • 223
Religion • 223
Education • 224
Immigrants • 224
Language • 225
The Arts and Sciences • 225
Food • 226
Recreation • 227
Customs and Traditions • 227
Suggested Activities • 228
Suggested Reading • 230

The United Kingdom • 231

A Legend from England • 231
Background Information • 234
History • 236
Government • 236
Religion • 237
Education • 237
Immigrants • 238
Language • 238
The Arts and Sciences • 238
Food • 239
Recreation • 240
Customs and Traditions • 240
Suggested Activities • 241
Suggested Reading • 242

Vietnam • 243

A Legend from Vietnam • 243
Background Information • 246
History • 247
Government • 249
Religion • 249
Education • 249
Immigrants • 250
Language • 250
The Arts and Sciences • 250
Food • 251
Recreation • 252
Customs and Traditions • 252
Suggested Activities • 253
Suggested Reading • 255

Bibliography • 256
Index • 258

Preface

Keeping the Traditions celebrates the contributions of the peoples of twenty countries of the world: Canada, China, Colombia, Cuba, the Dominican Republic, France, Germany, Hungary, India, Ireland, Italy, Japan, Mexico, the Philippines, Poland, Russia, Senegal, South Korea, the United Kingdom of Great Britain and Northern Ireland, and Vietnam.

As people immigrated to the United States from these countries throughout the world, they brought their culture, beliefs, history, art, music, cooking, inventions, and religions with them. These many contributions enriched the United States of America.

Each of the twenty chapters in this book might be of interest to a general reader, to a student, or to a teacher of grades 4 through 8 in studying language arts or social studies. At the end of each chapter, a dozen suggested activities involving writing, reading, vocabulary, math, social studies, geography, music, art, drama/movement, dress, cooking, and a culminating activity are included. Each chapter also contains an illustrated folktale, a recipe for a popular ethnic food, and a bibliography.

I would like to acknowledge assistance on this project from the following people who supported me in so many ways: David Perry, C. J. Cassio, Eileen Edgren, Jay Fernandez, Marie Desjardin, Claire Martin, Claudia Mills, Ann Nagda, Leslie O'Kane, Ina Robbins, Elizabeth Wrenn, Mary Jane Holland, Peter Arnold, Jeni Brice, and Anne Stackpole-Cuellar.

Introduction

Between 1892 and 1954, approximately twelve million people passed through the Ellis Island processing station on their way to a new life in the United States of America. These people brought with them hopes and ideas, skills and determination, dreams and beliefs that added to the richness of our country.

Some people thought that this island, not far from New York City, which was the stepping stone into America for immigrants from all over the world, should be commemorated in some significant way. Completed in 1990 is The American Immigrant Wall of Honor, a waist-high wall that runs along Ellis Island's eastern seawall. It contains almost two hundred thousand names, a small but representative number, of immigrants from Europe, Asia, Africa, Australia, and Central and South America who left their homelands and settled in North America. Two of those names belong to my mother and my father.

Like so many others, my parents left the life they had known in Cornwall, England, to make a new home in a new land. They arrived at Ellis Island, crossed the American continent, and settled in the small gold mining community of Grass Valley in northern California.

Why did they come? What causes emigration—the going from somewhere—and immigration—the coming to somewhere? For each person, the reasons are complex and unique. Some came because they were persecuted in their homeland. Some sought religious or political freedom. But many, like my parents, came for the opportunity to work and make a better life for themselves and for their children. America was a land of promise and opportunity.

Why did they choose to go to a tiny community in northern California called Grass Valley? Like many other immigrants seeking a new life, they wanted to keep some of the "old country" too. In the small town in which they settled were other people, originally from Cornwall, skilled in hard rock mining. So as my parents learned new ways and studied to become citizens of a new country, they also celebrated the traditions of the past and shared memories and stories with friends and relatives in this Cornish community. Their customs and traditions lingered on and found expression in their new country.

No town is more famous for the Cornish pastry, a meat and potato pie, which could be picked up and eaten in the hand by hungry miners during the noon break. During the Christmas season, the Cornish miners sang their carols deep underground, carols that were recorded and shared around the world. At the miners' yearly picnic (attended by all the Cousin Jacks and Cousin Jennys from the old country and the new country) the throwing of horseshoes was a serious competition.

These California Cornish and millions of others contributed to the vitality of the United States. Upon the talents of these millions of immigrants, the United States of America was built. The art, literature, music, architecture, language, foods, and festivals of their home countries enrich us.

This book celebrates twenty countries of the world. For each, there is a very brief description of the home country, its geography and history, and a look at its folktales, government, religion, education, language, arts, and all that made an impact on the United States.

If space were available, these twenty countries might be joined by dozens of others. In 1980, for the first time, the U.S. Census asked people about their ethnic background. To complete the census form, Americans could choose from more than 100 groups. More than 100 million Americans claimed ancestry from Great Britain. Almost as many had a German background. The Irish-American population was third, and the fourth largest group was African-Americans.

But dozens of other groups added to the ethnic mix, including French, Italian, Poles, Mexicans, Hungarians, Russians, Canadians, Colombians, Native Americans, Koreans, Chinese, Japanese, Filipinos, Vietnamese, Cubans, Dominicans, and many more.

And immigrants are still coming. The migration of people is not over. To even begin to know the richness of our country, we must try to understand something about the diverse people who came from other lands to make up the United States of America. The intent of this book is to add in some small way to that understanding.

Notes

A bibliography at the end of each chapter and an annotated general bibliography at the end of the book suggest other sources of information for those who want to read more widely and dig more deeply into *Keeping the Traditions*.

There are always differences in reference books about the estimate of the size and populations of countries. The figures used here all come from the 1998 *The World Almanac & Book of Facts*, published in Mahwah, New Jersey, by World Almanac Books.

Data on immigration come from the 1997 *Statistical Abstract of the United States*.

Keeping THE Traditions

Her husband was so upset, he pushed her off the floating island.

Canada

A Legend from Canada

The Native Americans in Canada have a rich tradition of myths and legends. There are many versions of a Native American story about how the world was created. An Ojibway tale about Sky Woman appears in Bobbie Kalman's *Canada, The Culture*. John Bierhorst retells the tale in *The Woman Who Fell from the Sky: The Iroquois Story of Creation*.

The Woman Who Created Earth

Long, long ago, our world was completely covered with water. Sky People lived high above the sea on a floating island in the heavens. On this floating island, no one was ever born and no one ever died. Sky Woman lived there with her husband. She was kind and good and beautiful, and all the Sky People loved her.

One day Sky Woman told her husband she was going to have a baby. She was very happy at the thought of being a mother, but her husband grew very angry with her. Nothing like this had ever happened to Sky People before. Her husband was so upset, he pushed her off the floating island.

When the other Sky People saw Sky Woman falling down, down toward the waters below, they quickly changed into different creatures and hurried to help her. Some became birds who cushioned her fall. Others became water animals who greeted her when she reached the water.

Sky Woman stood in the waters on the back of a turtle. She looked out at the sea and asked the creatures if one of them could bring her some dirt from the sea bottom. Several animals tried without success.

"I am sorry, but it is too deep," said the beaver as he came up struggling for breath after a dive into the depths.

"Much too deep," agreed the otter after his unsuccessful try.

When the little muskrat dived, the others were sure that he would fail, too, but when he surfaced, gasping for air, he brought with him a tiny paw full of soil.

"Thank you, Muskrat," Sky Woman said. She spread the dirt on top of the turtle's shell and breathed upon it. This soil grew into a small island, then a large island, and finally into an enormous continent.

Sky Woman looked into the empty heavens and created the sun, moon, and stars. The birds and water animals looked up and were amazed.

When her twin sons were born, she named one Sapling and the other Flint. Sapling was as happy as his mother. He created trees, bushes, and land animals to inhabit the new earth. Flint was as angry as his father. He created enormous rocks and changed mild breezes into tornadoes and hurricanes.

Flint also created cold and blanketed the new land with ice and snow. But Sapling created spring and warmed the earth again. He created humans and taught them how to make houses and build fires to keep warm during the winter.

After all of the plants and animals of the earth were created, Sky Woman and her two sons returned to the island in the sky where they could look down happily on their creation. Sky Woman's husband looked down, too. Seeing the beauty of what she had created, he welcomed her back to their home in the clouds.

Background Information

There is probably no country in the world more important to the United States than Canada. These two countries share the same continent, have a common language, share a common 5,525-mile border, and had a common colonial parent. The current economies of the two countries are closely intertwined.

Canada is located in North America, with Alaska and the Pacific Ocean forming the western boundary, and the Atlantic Ocean, Davis Strait, and Baffin Bay on the east. The United States borders the country to the south, and the Arctic Ocean borders Canada to the north. Canada covers an area of 3,849,674 square miles and has a population of 29,123,194 people.

Canada is a land of several regions. The Canadian Shield (sometimes called the Laurentian Shield) is a 700-million-year-old bedrock that spans half of Canada in a swath that covers parts of Quebec, northern Ontario, Manitoba, and Saskatchewan and continues on into the Northwest Territories. It covers about 1.5 million square miles. Most of Lake Superior, the largest freshwater lake in the world, lies within the region.

This area was created during a glacial retreat that left behind lakes, bogs, swamps, and a few pockets of arable soil. A boreal forest of mixed evergreens covers much of the land. The Shield, though not suitable for farming, is rich in nickel, platinum, cobalt, uranium, gold, silver, copper, and iron. It yields 40 percent of Canada's mineral production.

West of the Shield are the interior plains of Canada. Retreating glaciers ground this area flat and left rich deposits of topsoil. The Arctic region of Canada's far north is dominated by tundra. There are hundreds of islands in this area. In eastern Canada, the most prominent features are the Appalachian Mountains, which cover most of the four Atlantic Provinces. The region around the Great Lakes, sandwiched between the Appalachians and the Canadian Shield, has rich agricultural land. About 60 percent of all Canadians live in this small region.

Canada is the second-largest country in the world and east to west, spans six of the world's twenty-four time zones. Canada currently has ten provinces: British Columbia, Alberta, Saskatchewan, Manitoba, Ontario, Quebec, Nova Scotia, New Brunswick, Prince Edward Island, and Newfoundland. It also has three northern territories called the Northwest Territories, Nunavut, and the Yukon. These three vast territories cover more than 40 percent of Canada.

The Atlantic Provinces of Canada (Nova Scotia, New Brunswick, Prince Edward Island, and Newfoundland) at the extreme eastern end of Canada make up only 6 percent of the area of Canada and have only 10 percent of the country's population. This area is beautiful and rural with green hills and tiny communities. There are few factories and there is high unemployment in this area. The federal government spends considerable money to further economic activity in the poorer Atlantic Provinces.

The capital of Nova Scotia is Halifax, which is the chief winter Atlantic port for Canada. This is the largest of the Atlantic Provinces in terms of population. Nova Scotia has fishing, manufacturing, mining, tourism, forestry, and agriculture as its major industries. The Christmas tree industry is economically important. One tree farm near Halifax covers 30,000 acres. Among the minerals produced in this province are coal, gypsum, sand, and gravel.

The largest of the Atlantic Provinces in terms of area is New Brunswick. Forests cover 90 percent of New Brunswick. Its capital, Fredericton, is on the St. John River. The major industries of this province are fishing, manufacturing, mining, forestry, pulp, and papermaking. The minerals produced here are zinc, silver, lead, coal, copper, and stone. The port of St. John on the Bay of Fundy is free of ice all year-round. Daily tidal variations in the bay average more than twenty feet.

The capital of Newfoundland is St. John's, and Churchill Falls is the chief city of Labrador. Major industries include fishing, pulp and paper, hydroelectric production, mining, and manufacturing. Minerals produced include iron, asbestos, zinc, copper, silver, gold, sand, and gravel. Newfoundland was discovered by John Cabot in 1497 and was Great Britain's first overseas colony. A major attraction is Gros Morne National Park, named for Newfoundland's highest mountain, which rises 2,633 feet.

The smallest of the Atlantic Provinces in terms of population and size is Prince Edward Island. Its capital is Charlottetown. Major industries are tourism, fishing, agriculture, and light manufacturing. The only minerals produced are sand and gravel.

To the west of the Atlantic Provinces and just up the St. Lawrence River is Canada's largest province, Quebec. This province is home to most of Canada's French-speaking population. The Laurentian Mountains with their many beautiful lakes are in Quebec Province.

The major industries of the province are manufacturing, agriculture, mining, meat processing, petroleum refining, and hydroelectricity generation. Among the minerals produced in the province are gold, asbestos, copper, zinc, and iron ore. The two principal cities are Quebec City and Montreal. Montreal is a major commercial center of Canada.

West of Quebec is the province of Ontario. This province shares the Great Lakes with the United States. Its capital is Toronto, which is a 244-square-mile city and is the center of Canadian business and finance.

Rainbow Bridge connects the United States with Canada at Niagara Falls. At one end is Niagara Falls, Ontario, and at the other end is Niagara Falls, New York. The two countries share the electric power that is generated by the falls.

Northern Ontario is mostly empty country, while southern Ontario is filled with lush green farms and industrial communities that produce about half of Canada's manufacturing output. The major industries are manufacturing, finance, tourism, construction, agriculture, and forestry. Nickel, gold, copper, uranium, and zinc are produced here.

The capital of Canada, the Federal District, is Ottawa in the province of Ontario. This city has government buildings on Parliament Hill, overlooking the Ottawa River. During the last two weeks in May, the Canadian Tulip Festival is held here.

To the west of Ontario are the Canadian prairies, flat and fertile. The three prairie provinces are Manitoba, Saskatchewan, and Alberta. Wheat, rye, barley, and oilseeds are grown and transported from these provinces by train.

Winnipeg is the capital of Manitoba. It is famous as a cultural center. The Royal Winnipeg Ballet and the Winnipeg Symphony Orchestra are very popular. In addition to agriculture, slaughtering and meat processing, manufacturing, and mining are major industries. Minerals produced are nickel, copper, oil, zinc, and gold. Although it is called a prairie province, Manitoba has thick forests and many rivers and lakes. The International Peace Garden is located here, with half of the garden in Manitoba and the other half in North Dakota.

Regina is the capital of Saskatchewan. In addition to agriculture, meat processing, petroleum refining, and hydroelectric generation are major industries. Minerals produced include oil, uranium, natural gas, coal, and sulfur.

Immediately west of Saskatchewan is the province of Alberta. This province was once noted for its cattle and grains, but in 1947 the focus shifted when huge quantities of oil and gas were discovered in the province. Its capital is Edmonton. Calgary, one of its major cities, is now known as an oil center. In addition to oil production, mining, agriculture, beef ranching, manufacturing and construction are major industries. In addition to oil, there are also deposits of gas, sulfur, and coal.

The most westerly province in Canada, cut off from the rest of the country by mountains, is British Columbia. Offshore islands make up part of this province. On Vancouver Island is Victoria, the capital of British Columbia, which is sometimes referred to as a "bit of England" and where afternoon tea is a popular tradition. The cut-flower industry is very important in Victoria, and the area is famous for its beautiful gardens.

Major industries of the province include forestry, mining, tourism, fishing, agriculture, and manufacturing. Coal, copper, natural gas, oil, lead, zinc, and gold are produced. Vancouver, one of the major cities in the province, is the busiest port on the West Coast of North America.

Britain did not give up its North American Arctic land holdings to Canada until several years after Canada's independence in 1867. North of British Columbia is the Yukon Territory. It is between Alaska and the Northwest Territories. Near the Alaska border is the highest peak in Canada, Mt. Logan, at 19,850 feet. Whitehorse is the territory's capital. This territory has a total area of 186,660 square miles. Mining and tourism are its major industries. Gold, silver, lead, zinc, and copper are produced in the province.

The Northwest Territories make up the rest of Canada, one-third of its land mass. The total area in the Northwest Territories is 1,322,903 square miles. Its capital is Yellowknife. The major industries are mining, oil and gas exploration and extraction, and trapping. Minerals produced here are lead, zinc, oil, and natural gas. The Mackenzie River Delta is in the Northwest Territories. This river is one of the largest in the Western Hemisphere.

The Northwest Territories divided into two areas on April 1, 1999. One is called Nunavut, which means "our land" in the language of the Inuit. The new capital of Nunavut is on Baffin Island. For the time being, the western end of the territory will retain the name of Northwest Territories, although increasingly residents there are beginning to refer to it as the Western Arctic. This western section will have a population that is 50 percent aboriginal and 50 percent white. Proposals are being made to draft a new constitution that will be put to a plebiscite.

History

More than 10,000 years ago, bands of nomads are believed to have crossed from Asia to North America via a narrow land bridge where the Bering Strait now lies. Recent findings suggest that the migrations may have started much earlier as some ancient peoples traveled south by boat along the Pacific coast. Over time, they wandered south and east, developing languages and customs.

The first Europeans to reach Canada were the Vikings, who established a settlement in Newfoundland around A.D. 1000. They found aboriginal people in three linguistic groups.

It was in 1497 that John Cabot landed either in Newfoundland or Cape Breton and laid claim to the land for Great Britain. Jacques Cartier discovered the Gulf of St. Lawrence in 1534 and made a claim for France.

Samuel de Champlain established the first successful permanent settlement in 1608 in Quebec City. He called the area New France. Champlain began fur trading with the Indians in the area, Hurons and Algonquins, and supported these tribes against the Iroquois.

Meanwhile the British continued to explore, hoping to find a Northwest Passage over the top of North America to the Orient. Sir Martin Frobisher sailed into the arctic area in 1576, 1577, and 1578. Henry Hudson sailed into the region in 1610.

In 1663, France's King, Louis XIV, made New France a crown colony. But England had its own settlements along the East Coast of North America and also gained land claimed by merchants in the Hudson Bay Company.

The French and English eventually clashed over ownership of the lands, and there were a series of wars between 1689 and 1763. The Treaty of Paris in 1763 turned Canada over to Great Britain but allowed France to retain the islands of St. Pierre and Miqulon just off Newfoundland.

During the American Revolution, colonists in the Atlantic Provinces who wanted to maintain their loyalty to the British throne emigrated in large numbers into Quebec. As a result of more than 30,000 Loyalists moving into the Atlantic region, in 1784 the colony of New Brunswick was created. Another group of about 10,000 American colonists settled along the northern bank of the St. Lawrence.

During the War of 1812, Americans thought that Canadians would sympathize with their cause. The Americans were forced to surrender when they retreated to Detroit, chased by the British and their Indian allies. In 1813, Americans successfully raided what is now Toronto. The British retaliated from Halifax by burning down the White House in Washington. After what seemed like an impasse, the British and Americans finally ended the war by signing the Treaty of Ghent in December 1814.

Britain then encouraged immigration to Canada, and from 1815 to 1855, about 1 million Britons arrived. With the 1841 Act of Union, Upper and Lower Canada came together under one legislature. The Dominion of Canada was created in Great Britain's Parliament in 1867, and consisted of four provinces, Ontario, Quebec, Nova Scotia, and New Brunswick. Its population at that time was 3.4 million.

Other provinces were eventually added: Manitoba in 1870, British Columbia in 1871, Prince Edward Island in 1873, Alberta and Saskatchewan in 1905, and Newfoundland in 1949. The province of Quebec has for a number of years sought to separate from Canada. So far, this attempt has been defeated, but the matter has certainly not been settled.

As Europeans arrived from France and Great Britain, they found small communities of native peoples throughout Canada. Many of these native groups were hunters. Eight major woodland tribes lived in eastern and parts of central Canada, including the Micmacs, the Cree, and the Ojibway.

The Iroquois (an alliance of several tribes such as the Mohawk, Oneida, Cayuga, and Seneca) lived in southern Ontario. They farmed corn, beans, and squash. Canada's plains Indians (Blackfoot, Blood, Piegan, Plains Cree, and Sioux) sometimes migrated into what is now the United States. They lived in tipis and hunted buffalo.

Fish played a major role in the diet of the coastal Indians of western Canada. This group included the Interior Salish, Lillooet, Shushwap, Okanagan, Koutenay, Haida, the Tsimshian, Gitskan, Nootka, Coast Slish, and Bealla Coola. About ten groups of Inuit with many different dialects live in Canada's far north. They fish and hunt larger sea animals and caribou.

Government

On November 5, 1981, Canada's federal government and the premiers of every province except Quebec agreed on a Canadian Constitution and Charter of Rights and Freedoms. On April 17, 1982, the Canada Act formally went into effect. The legislative powers were removed from the British Parliament and placed in Canada although Canada remains a member of the British Commonwealth.

Canada is a democracy governed by a parliamentary system. There are two houses in the Parliament: the Senate, which has 104 members appointed by the governor-general on the advice of the prime minister, and the Commons, which has 295 members elected by plurality from districts (called ridings) around the country.

The national government controls such areas as transportation, immigration, defense, banking, postal services, and native affairs. Laws for the country are made by the House of Commons and are approved by the Senate.

Each active party has members in the Commons. Five parties are currently represented in Parliament. Each party has a leader elected by party conventions. The leader of the party that controls a majority of members becomes prime minister and the political leader of Canada. The prime minister appoints a cabinet from his or her party's parliamentary members. Much like the president's cabinet in the United States, the Canadian cabinet members oversee various departments. When one party does not have a majority in the Commons, a coalition is made with another party.

Terms of office are for five years, but a prime minister can call an election at any time, usually picking a time when the government leader believes his or her party will do best. If the party in power loses a vote in the Commons, the prime minister is forced to call another election.

There is also a governor-general, the representative of the Queen, who is considered the formal chief-of-state in Canada. This is a mostly ceremonial office. The governor-general is appointed by the Queen or King of England to represent the monarch.

Each province and territory has its own one-house parliamentary system with members elected from local districts. The various provinces have laws protecting their citizens, while the federal government has a complex system of laws to try to equalize opportunities for all Canadian citizens. The Royal Canadian Mounted Police is Canada's national police force. There is a Supreme Court, Federal Court, and Provincial Courts.

Religion

About 46 percent of the population of Canada is Roman Catholic. Another 36 percent is Protestant. A little over 1 percent is Jewish. There are also Canadians who practice Sikhism, Islam, Buddhism, Hinduism, and various native religions.

Depending on the religion, various holy days are observed. The Jewish community celebrates Passover as a festival of freedom during the first full moon of spring. Christians celebrate Easter. Various native tribes celebrate the Sun Dance in late spring or in summer. On November 2, many Canadians celebrate All Soul's Day by visiting cemeteries and placing flowers on graves. Canadian Sikhs celebrate the birthday of Guru Nanek in November, meeting in temples and singing hymns. Canadian Muslims observe a month of prayer called Ramadan.

St. John Baptiste (John the Baptist) is the patron saint of Quebec. On the night of June 23, fireworks and bonfires light up the city. It is the eve of Fete Nationale honoring the patron saint. The following day there are parades and celebrations.

Education

About 89 percent of Canadians between the ages of six and twenty-three attend school. This is the highest rate in the world. Schooling in Canada is compulsory until the age of sixteen.

In Canada, the majority of children attend kindergarten followed by eight years of elementary school. These are publicly funded schools. Students study reading, math, science, and social studies, learn about computers, and take field trips to museums and historic sites.

In high school, students prepare for the university or community college or for a job. They study a variety of subjects and also take part in sports, clubs, concerts, and dances. These schools are paid for through taxes. In Ontario, high schools have one more grade than American schools. A high school graduate in Ontario has completed thirteenth grade.

There are also private and religious schools in Canada for which parents pay to send their children. One popular type of private school in Canada is the Montessori school, which has multi-aged groupings of children taught in the same room.

Perhaps more than in most countries, geography and climate affect schooling in Canada. For example, each Arctic school can schedule its 190 days of classes whenever it wants. This allows schools to recognize local traditions and hunting patterns.

Language is also a complication for Arctic schools. Inuit children speak English in school, but at home they may speak Inuktitut. Some local radio and television stations use the native language while the majority use English. Once these schools tried to stamp out native languages, but today many Native children learn their native language and traditional skills and crafts in addition to English and more typical school subjects.

Young Canadians who wish to do so can continue their education in one of Canada's 69 universities or 203 colleges.

Immigrants

Most of Canada's regions were settled directly from abroad. A family would come by boat from a country such as Scotland and take a train to a town where a Canadian immigration agent placed them. In this way, they joined similar families and continued to speak the same language that they did in their "old country." These settlers had little sense of the country of Canada as a whole.

When Canada was founded in 1867, its population was 3.4 million. It now has more than 29 million people. Much of this growth is due to immigration. Canada accepted more than 8 million immigrants in the eighty years between 1901 and 1981. In the early 1900s, the government offered settlers cheap farmland.

Before 1960, most immigrants to Canada came from Europe and especially Britain. In the 1960s, immigration policies were liberalized and many immigrants from Africa, Asia, and the Caribbean moved into Canada. These newcomers tend to live in enclaves in cities and to keep their native language.

Throughout its history, there has been considerable movement of people from the United States into Canada. Loyalists moved into Canada during the American Revolution. Since Britain had outlawed slavery, hundreds of American blacks fled to Canada and established agricultural communities before and after the Civil War. About a million Americans moved to Canada around the turn of the century when they were offered free land by the Canadian government. In the mid-1900s, thousands of Americans fled to Canada to avoid the military draft for the war in Vietnam.

There has also continued to be a small but steady immigration of Canadians into the United States. From 1981 to 1990, 119,200 Canadians immigrated to the United States. During 1991 to 1995, another 74,900 came.

Language

Canada has two official languages: English and French. In addition, there are many native languages.

The Arts and Sciences

Because so many different groups of people came to Canada, the arts of the country are diverse. And the native peoples have a highly developed art that includes totems, sculptures, and masks. At first, many Europeans simply used the forms with which they were familiar in their "old countries." Only gradually did a sense of real Canadian art emerge.

In recent years, Canadians have contributed in many ways to the cultural life of North America. From Canada's popular music industry came Neil Young, Steppenwolf, and Prism. In country music, big names have included Anne Murray, Don Williams, and Gordon Lightfoot. Others well known in the music field include Paul Anka, Joni Mitchell, Oscar Peterson, Glenn Gould, Guy Lombardo, Percy Faith, and the Canadian Brass.

In the theater and cinema, Canadian stars include Hume Cronyn, Kate Nelligan, Walter Pidgeon, Raymond Burr, Glenn Ford, Christopher Plummer, Arthur Hill, Leslie Nielsen, John Candy, Jack Carson, Rod Cameron, Lorne Greene, Raymond Massey, Donald Sutherland, and William Shatner. Mary Pickford, Margot Kidder, and Genevieve Bujold are other Canadian film stars.

News reporters and television stars such as Peter Jennings, Marley Safer, Robert MacNeil, Art Linkletter, and Alan Thicke are Canadians as well.

A little community of about 350 people in the Yukon Territory was home to Robert Service, the writer who made famous such characters as Dangerous Dan McGrew and Sam McGee. Hugh MacLennan and Margaret Atwood are well known Canadian novelists, while Farley Mowat has focused his writing on a deep love of the land and a sense of the unity of life.

Other popular writers include Saul Bellow, Arthur Hailey, Will Durant, Ross Macdonald, Alice Munro, and Robertson Davies. Lucy Maude Montgomery wrote a famous series of books about "Anne of Green Gables," which followed the young redhead's adventures on Prince Edward Island.

Canadian poetry reached a high point during the 1930s. Among the dominant English-Canadian poets of that period were E. J. Pratt, A. J. M. Smith. F. R. Scott, A. M. Klein, and Dorothy Livesay. Roch Carrier is a leading Quebec playwright and novelist.

Two early experimenters in the arts were Ozias Leduc and James Wilson Morrice. On these early experiments, a group of seven painters based their practice. In 1920, the Group of Seven was formally founded and have succeeded in producing enduring works of modern art. The original members were J. E. H. MacDonald, Lawren Harris, A. Y. Jackson, Franklin Carmichael, Arthur Lismer, Frederick Horsman Varley, and Franz Johnston. Earlier, Tom Thomson, who died in 1917, was a part of their artistic group.

Inventions and discoveries are also contributions of Canadians to the world. One important invention from Canada is the snowmobile. J. Armand Bombardier was born in Quebec in 1908. In 1937, he created the first models of his Ski-doo or snowmobile. The original company, Bombardier, Incorporated, remains the world's largest snowmobile manufacturer.

Sir Frederick Banting, Charles Best, James Collip, and J. R. Macleod, a team of Canadian scientists, discovered insulin in 1921. It is used to control a disease called diabetes. Bunting and Macleod were awarded the Nobel Prize in 1923 for their discovery.

Alexander Graham Bell moved to Canada from Scotland when he was twenty-three. He did much of his research in Baddeck, Nova Scotia. His most famous invention was the telephone. He founded Bell Canada, Canada's largest telephone company.

The first Canadian astronaut is Roberta Bondar, who was selected in 1992 to be part of the crew of the space shuttle *Discovery*. While in orbit, she conducted experiments on the effects on the human body of being in space.

Food

Because people from many countries have settled in Canada, there are a wide variety of specialty foods. Among the famous French Canadian foods are *poutine* and *tourtiere*. *Poutine* are french fries served with gravy and curds. *Tourtiere* is a kind of meat pie.

This is a Canadian food favorite from Quebec.

Pork Pie

2 pounds pork

1 clove of garlic

1 medium onion

$^1/_2$ cup water

$^1/_4$ teaspoon celery salt

$^1/_4$ teaspoon ground cloves

salt & pepper

$^1/_4$ cup dry bread crumbs

double 9-inch pastry pie shell

Mix together in a saucepan 2 pounds of pork, chopped fine, along with 1 crushed clove of garlic. Peel and finely chop and add 1 medium onion. Add $^1/_2$ cup water, $^1/_4$ teaspoon of celery salt, $^1/_4$ teaspoon of ground cloves, salt and pepper to taste. Simmer for about 20 minutes. Then stir in $^1/_4$ cup of dry bread crumbs and let the mixture cool.

Make a double 9-inch pastry pie shell. Roll out one layer of pastry on a floured surface and line a 9-inch pie pan with it. Fill the pastry shell with the pork filling. Cover the pie with the top layer of dough, crimping the two layers of dough together around the edges. Cut a small vent hole in the middle and bake in a 350°F preheated oven for about 35 minutes until browned. Let the pie sit for several minutes before serving. Makes four dinner portions.

Another Canadian food specialty is maple syrup. It is served on pancakes for breakfast and also used in making ice cream and candy.

Quebec is famous for its pea soup, which was a favorite dish of early settlers. Native peoples make *bannock,* a pan-fried bread. Yogurt and cucumber recipes are used to cool the mouth while eating a hot curry with exotic spices from India.

Recreation

Canadians enjoy many of the same sports that Americans do, including baseball, volleyball, and soccer, but hockey is Canada's national sport. There are countless minor-league hockey teams as well as professional teams. Approximately 85 percent of all the professional players in the National Hockey League are Canadians.

Football is also popular in Canada, and to make sure that the Canadian Football League is not dominated by foreign athletes, there is a limit as to the number of foreign players each team can field. Canadian football fields are wider and longer than those in the United States and there are other major rule differences.

Because of the long winters and availability of snow and ice, winter sports, such as skiing, are common throughout Canada. Figure skating is a demanding sport in which skaters perform a routine set to music to which they glide, spin, and jump. Canada is famous internationally for its figure skaters and speedskaters.

Scottish immigrants brought curling to Canada. The object of curling is to slide a large smooth stone across the ice to a target. Canada's curlers are among the world's best.

Because of the network of lakes, rivers, and inlets in Canada, rowing is a favorite summer sport. Canadian athletes have won many Olympic awards in rowing events.

Inuit children in Canada's far north play a game much like Cat's Cradle. They stretch a circle of sinew, instead of string, between a player's two hands, and using their fingers, create a series of loops and designs.

Customs and Traditions

One of the main festivals held in Canada is the Quebec Winter Carnival. It is the biggest winter festival in the world, with more than one million people coming to join in each year. It has been held yearly since 1954. The symbol for the carnival is a plump snowman wearing a red hat and sash.

One event of the carnival is the *Soiree de la Bougie,* which means "night of the candle." The whole city is lit up by thousands of candles on this special evening. There is also a crowning of the Festival Queen and a formal ball in her honor. Sculptors from all over the world come to compete in the annual Ice Sculpting Competition.

Each of the Canadian Provinces holds special festivals. In Banff, Alberta, for four days in July there is an Indian Days Celebration. Indians come from nearby reservations and hold rodeo events, races, ceremonial dances, and singing.

In Caraquet on the Acadian coast, a peninsula in northern New Brunswick, people gather for the annual blessing of the fishing fleet. On the day before their fishing fleets set sail, there is a dockside festival. Women throw flowers on the water. A priest offers thanks for the bounty of the sea.

Many African Canadians live in Ontario. During February they celebrate Black History Month in many of the same ways in which it is celebrated in the United States. People participate in workshops to learn more about their heritage.

African Canadians and others who came from the Caribbean islands also celebrate during *Caribana*, a weeklong festival that is held in Toronto each summer. There are parades, floats, and bands. Similar celebrations are held in Montreal and Winnipeg, where they are called *Carifesta* and *Caripeg*.

Montreal is also famous for the *Cirque du Soleil* or "Circus of the Sun." This is a theater production and circus all in one. A special school, *The Ecole Nationale de Cirque,* in Montreal trains students from all over the world to be acrobats, trapeze artists, dancers, and actors.

Maple Syrup Festivals are held in many small Canadian towns in the spring. In the small town of Warkworth in the province of Ontario, two of the most popular events during the maple syrup festival are going on sleigh rides and taking part in square dances. Other events include log-sawing contests and snowshoe racing.

Another spring festival is Victoria Day. It is celebrated on the Monday before May 25, in remembrance of the birthday of Queen Victoria. It is a day for fireworks and has been celebrated in Canada since 1952.

Celebrating the Fourth of July is a big occurrence in many towns in the United States. In Canada a similar celebration is held on their country's birthday, which is July 1. July 1, 1867, is when four provinces joined together and first formed the country of Canada. Fireworks are set off over the Parliament Buildings in Ottawa, and the Royal Canadian Mounted Police put on a special show. Their Musical Ride is a routine on horseback set to music.

Other cities celebrate Canada Day, too. Halifax, Montreal, Winnipeg, Edmonton, and Vancouver hold special parties for the citizens. Toronto, Canada's largest city, holds a big parade and hosts a free picnic. People of different ethnic groups wear their national dress for the parade.

There are lots of special activities for children on Canada Day, such as soapbox derbies, face painting, sack races, and watching clowns and magicians.

Also during the month of July, the city of Calgary in western Canada holds The Calgary Stampede. It is a rodeo where cowboys come to show their skills in taming wild horses and bulls, roping, racing, and wrestling young steers. The Calgary Stampede lasts for ten days, and in addition to rodeo events includes activities such as pancake breakfasts, country music concerts, and square dancing.

Each year in August, thousands of Ukrainian Canadians gather at Riding Mountain National Park in Manitoba and celebrate their heritage with traditional dancing, singing, and feasting. The feast features a bread called *kolach* that represents life as well as salt, which adds spice to life.

Another big summer event is held in Nova Scotia in the cities of Halifax, Antigonish, and Sydney. Their Highland Games celebrate their Scottish heritage. Many people wear kilts and tams. There is highland dancing, and contestants take part in the caber toss, trying to throw a heavy pole the farthest.

During the month of August, Icelandic Canadians take part in *Islendingadagurinn*. This is a three-day festival of food and fun held in Gimli, Manitoba, which is home to Canada's largest Icelandic-Canadian community. One of the big events is a pillow fight fought by two contestants sitting on a pole over water.

People of the First Nations also hold festivals called *Powwows.* A Powwow usually begins with the Grand Entry, which is a parade of people in native dress coming to a special circle where dancing and drumming take place. Many of the dances that are performed are thousands of years old. The leaders carry the Eagle Staff, the oldest of the First Nation symbols. Others carry flags from the nations that are taking part in the Pow-wow. There is drumming, singing, and prayer.

In the United States, we celebrate Labor Day. This holiday is also celebrated in Canada. It takes place on the first Monday of September and was set aside in 1894 as a national holiday to honor Canada's workers.

In October a festival is held in the Kitchener-Waterloo area of Ontario. It is called Oktoberfest and features a parade, polka bands, and German foods such as sausages, sauerkraut, and strudel.

Canadian Thanksgiving is held on the second Monday in October. Much as in the United States, families gather to give thanks. The traditional meal is turkey, cranberries, potatoes, squash, and pumpkin pie.

Another holiday celebrated by Canadians that is similar to a holiday celebrated in the United States is Remembrance Day, which is celebrated on the eleventh hour of the eleventh day of the eleventh month. In the United States, November 11 is called Armistice Day. Veterans and others participate in memorial services.

Christmas is celebrated in many different ways throughout Canada. Some children hang stockings for gifts, while others hang an empty pillowcase at the foot of their beds. In Newfoundland, some people go *mumming*. They wrap themselves up in clothes and blankets and visit friends and relatives, who try to guess their identity.

Some Canadians celebrate the New Year at a New Year's Eve party very similar to parties in the United States. But the Iroquois nation celebrates after the first new moon in January. Chinese Canadians celebrate at the end of January or beginning of February. Canadians of Middle-Eastern origin celebrate New Year at the time of the spring equinox in a festival called No Ruz. The Jewish New Year, Rosh Hashanah, is held in early autumn. Canadian Hindus celebrate New Year in October or November depending on the lunar calendar.

Suggested Activities

Writing

1. Beluga whales are the most common whale in Arctic waters. These whales grow up to 15 feet long, weigh more than a ton, and are capable of making many different sounds. Invite a group of students to prepare a report on Beluga whales. They should include a bibliography of at least three sources. Post the finished reports on a classroom bulletin board.

Reading

2. North America's largest gold rush occurred in 1898 when gold was discovered in the Yukon Territory near the Klondike River. Have a pair of students do some reading about this gold rush and report orally what they learn to their classmates.

Vocabulary

3. In 1969 the Official Languages Act declared French and English the two official languages of Canada. Signs are usually given in both languages. As they read magazines and books, have students be alert to pictures of businesses and resorts in Canada in which signs appear in both languages. With permission, photocopy these. On a bulletin board, post pictures and write out these signs in both French and English.

Math

4. Using the data below, show the percentages and make an accurate pie chart to reflect the percentage of the total population contributed by each of the provinces and territories of Canada at the time when the total population of Canada was 28,435,600 people.

Alberta 2,632,400
British Columbia 3,451,300
Manitoba 1,113,100
New Brunswick 749,100
Newfoundland 581,100
Northwest Territories 62,300
Nova Scotia 920,800
Ontario 10,609,800
Prince Edward Island 130,300
Quebec 7,150,700
Saskatchewan 1,004,500
Yukon 30,200

Social Studies

5. With the division of the Northwest Territories and the creation of Nunavut, Baffin Island will be in the news. Invite students to learn more about William Baffin and Baffin Island and to share what they learn with the class. Students may want to acquire some of their information from the World Wide Web. To see the route of the early explorers, William Baffin and Robert Bylot in 1615 and 1616, students should consult http://www.schoolnet.ca/collections/arctic/explore/baffin.htm. For pictures of various gulfs, lakes, and mountains in Eastern Baffin Island, see http://sts.gsc.emr.ca/page1/landf/ne/baffin/east.htm.

   For general data about Baffin Island, the fifth largest island in the world, students could go to http://www.pondtour.com/baffin.html.

   A website with information about tours, flying to Nunavut, etc., is http://www.arctic-travel.com/noframes/index.html#get.

Geography

6. On a large wall map of Canada, use pins with colored flags coded to a legend to show the placement of the major national parks in Canada. The map should show the locations of South Moresby, Gwaii Haanas National Park Reserve, Banff National Park, Jasper National Park, Grasslands National Park, Riding Mountain National Park, Point Pelee National Park, La Mauricie National Park, Fundy National Park, Kejimkujik National Park, Prince Edward Island National Park, Gros Morne National Park, Kluane National Park, and Wood Buffalo National Park.

Music

7. Quebec and Montreal have cafe theaters and cabarets that showcase a distinctive class of artists known as *chansonniers.* They are poet-singers who often perform with simply a piano or guitar accompaniment. It would be interesting for students to listen to one of these performers on a CD or record. Perhaps a music specialist could obtain the works of Pauline Julien, Gilles Vigneauli, Felix Leclerc, or Robert Charlebois.

Art

8. With the help of an art educator, students might want to make a dreamcatcher. This is a traditional decoration of the people of the First Nations. Usually hung in a sleeping area, it is supposed to catch bad dreams while letting good dreams reach the person who is sleeping.

   You will need yarn, beads, feathers, and a metal circle the size of an embroidery hoop. Loop yarn around the hoop and across it, making a design like an uneven sort of spider web. Thread wooden beads on the yarn so that there are beads within the circle at irregular intervals. Tie feathers to the dreamcatcher wherever you wish.

Drama/Movement

9. Canadian drama was somewhat slow to develop. One play, which makes good use of its Newfoundland setting, is a 1970s drama, *Leaving Home,* by David French. It is a realistic play about a young man coming to terms with his father. Interested students might like to secure a copy of this play and present a brief scene from it for the class.

Dress

10. Many of the Native American tribes in Canada perform dances in which they wear special masks or headdresses. Among these are the Haida from the Queen Charlotte Islands off the coast of British Columbia. The thunderbird was often used in Kwakiutl dance ceremonies, with the dancer imitating the movement of a bird in time to the beating of drums. Ask a group of students to research dance masks and (with permission) to photocopy pictures that they find and bring them in to share with the class.

Cooking

11. A pancake breakfast is popular in Canada at many festivals and is popular with students, too. With the help of volunteer parents, you could organize a pancake breakfast for the class. You could make the pancakes from scratch or use a mix. You will need to adjust the recipe to make enough for the number of students in the classroom. Be sure to top the pancakes with maple syrup. Depending on where you live, you might be able to get Canadian maple syrup!

Culminating Activity

12. Canada is a remarkable example of multiculturalism. Perhaps your own classroom has representatives from many different ethnic groups. If so, you might plan a classroom multicultural fair. There could be tables set up to represent the different countries and cultures. At each table feature examples of ethnic clothing, arts, and simple finger foods to sample. Parents would be helpful in both planning and participating in the event. Could some share music or dances of their countries?

Suggested Reading

Barlas, Bob and Norm Tompsett. *Festivals of the World, Canada.* Milwaukee, Wisc.: Gareth Stevens, 1997.

Bierhorst, John. *The Woman Who Fell from the Sky: The Iroquois Story of Creation.* New York: William Morrow, 1993.

Editors of the Book Division, National Geographic Society. *Exploring Canada's Spectacular National Parks.* Washington, D.C.: National Geographic Society, 1995.

Editors of Time-Life Books. *Canada.* London, England: Time-Life Books, B. V., 1987.

Hillyer, V. M. and E. G. Huey. *The Americas.* New York: Meredith Press, 1966.

Kalman, Bobbie. *Canada Celebrates Multiculturalism.* New York: Crabtree, 1993.

———. *Canada, The Culture.* New York: Crabtree, 1993.

———. *Canada, The Land.* New York: Crabtree, 1993.

———. *Canada, The People.* New York: Crabtree, 1993.

Malcolm, Andrew H. *The Land and People of Canada.* New York: HarperCollins, 1991.

Melham, Tom, Thomas O'Neill, Cynthia Russ Ramsy, Gene S. Stuart, and Jennifer C. Urquhart. *Canada's Incredible Coasts.* Washington, D.C.: National Geographic Society, 1991.

Sylvester, John. *Canada.* Austin, Tex.: Raintree Steck-Vaughn, 1996.

Woodcock, George. *The Canadians.* Cambridge, Mass.: Harvard University Press, 1979.

China

A Legend from China

The story of a stonecutter is a popular one and appears in both Chinese and Japanese folktales. One version appears in *The Stonecutter* by Demi, and another appears as *The Stonecutter, A Japanese Folk Tale* by Gerald McDermott.

The Wishful Stonecutter

Once upon a time there lived in China a happy and contented stonecutter who worked hard each day. With his chisel, he hewed pieces of rock and transformed them into dragons, horses, and camels. Sometimes he chiseled out huge stones that were used in building tall, beautiful temples. The spirit in the rock was pleased with this stonecutter who contentedly worked so hard and so well.

Then one day a rich man came by and admired the stonecutter's work. He asked the stonecutter to come to his house and work for him. The stonecutter went, and he was amazed when he saw the beautiful home and the fine clothes and other possessions of the rich man.

The stonecutter felt something he had never felt before. It was envy. "Oh, dear," said the stonecutter. "This rich man is much more powerful than I. I wish I were a rich man." The spirit in the rock heard, and being very fond of the stonecutter, granted the wish. The stonecutter became a rich man in a fine house.

One day, as he was being carried around the countryside in a fine cart, the former stonecutter saw a field of beautiful white horses. He decided he must have those beautiful horses and sent his servants to collect them. The farmers were furious that the rich man had taken their horses. They ran after the rich man, caught him, and beat him severely.

"Oh, dear," said the rich man. "Those farmers are much more powerful than I. I wish I were a farmer." The spirit in the rock heard him and granted his wish. For a time, the man was happy as a farmer, but as he toiled in the sun, and felt its heat, the man realized that the sun was more powerful than he.

"Oh, dear," said the farmer. "The sun is much more powerful than I. I wish I were the sun." Again the spirit in the rock granted his wish. For a time, all was well. The stonecutter was so proud of being the sun, that sometimes he shone too long and burned the crops.

One day a cloud came along and covered up the sun. "Oh, dear," said the sun. "The cloud is much more powerful than I. I wish I were a cloud." The spirit in the rock granted his wish.

As a cloud, the stonecutter was happy, until one day the wind came and blew him apart. "Oh, dear," said the cloud. "The wind is much more powerful than I. I wish I were the wind." The spirit in the rock granted his wish.

The spirit in the rock was pleased with this stonecutter who contentedly worked so hard and so well.

One day the wind blew hard at the mountain but could not budge it. "Oh, dear," said the wind. "The mountain is much more powerful than I. I wish I were the mountain." The spirit in the rock granted his wish.

One day as the mountain sat in the sun, stonecutters came and began to chisel pieces away. "Oh, dear," said the mountain. "The stonecutters are much more powerful than I. I wish I were a stonecutter." The spirit in the rock granted his wish.

Once again the man was a stonecutter. He was happy and contented and never again wished to be other than what he was.

Background Information

The Republic of China is located in East Asia, and is the third largest country in the world, surpassed only by Russia and Canada. Almost all of China lies within the Temperate Zone, north of the Tropic of Cancer. In area, it covers 3,849,674 square miles.

China is bordered by Mongolia, Kazakhstan, Kyrgyzstan, Tajikistan, and Russia to the north; by North Korea, the Yellow Sea, and the East China Sea on the east; by the South China Sea, Hong Kong, Macau, Vietnam, Laos, Myan-mar, and Bhutan on the south; and by Nepal, India, Pakistan, and Afghanistan on the west. Its population is over 1,210,004,956 and is growing at the rate of 1.1 percent per year.

China's mountains and rivers extend from west to east, dividing the country into three regions. The western region includes the highlands of Xizang (Tibet). The average height of the Plateau of Tibet is 13,000 feet. It is rimmed by mountain ranges. Mt. Everest, the highest peak in the world, is located on the border between Tibet and Nepal. Its summit is 29,029 feet high.

Much of the Tibetan plateau is desert, and there is a short growing season. Barley is most important, but many different kinds of crops are grown in Tibet, including millet, rapeseed, peanuts, tea, and tobacco.

In addition to those who live in towns and cities, approximately half a million nomads live in Tibet. In the fall they herd animals from pasture to pasture. These nomads, who herd yaks, goats, and sheep, live in yak hair tents.

North of Tibet is the Xinjiang Autonomous Region (Sinkiang), and to the west is the Nei Mongol Autonomous Region (Inner Mongolia). These regions comprise about half of China's land area. There are mountains and deserts, including the great Gobi desert. Only about 5 percent of China's enormous population lives in these two regions.

The third major region is Eastern China, where 95 percent of the population is concentrated. There are fertile plains in this area so there is a great deal of farming. This area also contains the major industrial centers. Eastern China is further divided into three regions: the Northeast (Manchuria), the North, and the South.

Cutting across the mountains and plains of northern China is the Great Wall, which was ordered built by China's first emperor to keep out invading Mongols. The Wall is 30 feet high in places and wide enough to handle five or six horses abreast. It took tens of thousands of workers years to build in the third century B.C. Today, some sections of the wall still stand while other sections are in ruins. Once the wall may have been over 6,000 miles long.

China is an agricultural economy. About two-thirds of the population is engaged in farming, fishing, and forestry. China leads the world in the production of rice, and ranks third in the world in the production of wheat. Corn is also grown, though it is used mainly for animal food.

Tea was introduced in China during the Han dynasty, first as a medicine and later as a common drink. The hilly country south of the Yangtze is well suited for growing tea, which eventually became a trade item. Tea drinking spread to England and its colonies in the late 1600s. By the end of the eighteenth century, tea was China's chief export. China is the largest producer of cotton in the world and one of the world's major producers of oil and coal.

Today, China is divided into twenty-three provinces (including Taiwan), the three large municipalities of Shanghai, Beijing, and Tianjin, and the five autonomous regions of Xinjiang-Uygur, Xizang, Nei Mongol, Guangxi-Zhuang, and Ningxia Hui.

Hong Kong has a deep harbor located at the mouth of the Pearl River estuary on China's southeastern coast. The peninsula is about 30 square miles. It is hilly and rugged. Hong Kong also includes about 235 small islands on many of which no one lives.

Britain acquired Hong Kong in 1841. Over the years it became a heavily populated and important center of business and trade. During World War II, the Japanese occupied Hong Kong. The end of World War II brought renewed fighting between Chinese Nationalists and Chinese Communists. The Communists claimed victory in 1949 and many refugees flooded into Hong Kong.

Many of these new immigrants were skilled workers. By the 1960s, there was a boom in manufacturing. Then on July 1, 1997, the colony became a special Administrative Region of the People's Republic of China.

Shanghai is the largest Chinese city, with a population of around 13 million people. It is a port on the East Coast of China and has become the main center of commerce, trade, banking, and industry. Beijing is China's capital and is its second largest city, with a population of about 8 million people. It is located in the North China Plain and is a center of learning and culture.

The daily temperature in China varies from region to region. In northern Manchuria, the temperatures may fall to -17°F in winter, while at the same time it may be 68°F in the more tropical south. In the north, rainfall occurs during the summer months. In the south, there is some rain every month, with the heaviest rains falling in the southeast.

China is rich in mineral resources. It is the world's largest producer of antimony and tungsten, and is one of the largest producers of coal. There are also on-shore and offshore reserves of oil and natural gas.

Eighty percent of the Chinese people live in the countryside, but more than 200 million live in cities. China is taking steps to slow its population growth. Between 1950 and 1990, China's population doubled.

History

China has a very long history. The Upper Cave People who lived about fifty thousand years ago were probably the first modern human beings in China. These people fished, hunted, and gathered roots and fruits.

Over the next four hundred centuries these people improved their tools and weapons, developed speech, and began using fire. About 5000 to 4000 B.C., they began farming. Remains of a Neolithic village can be seen today in Shenai Province.

Neighboring clans chose chiefs. Huang-ti was a powerful leader in the Yellow River area around 2500 B.C. Rulers formed dynasties where a ruling family stayed in power for a long time. One dynasty or another ruled China for the next four thousand years.

In the eighteenth century B.C., the Shang dynasty came into power. It represented the beginning of documented Chinese history. The Shang dynasty lasted 500 years and was followed by the Chou dynasty, whose rulers were in power for nine centuries (1122–256 B.C.).

Ch'in was a country located in a West River valley in northwest China. The Ch'in people built a strong state and gradually conquered the other six Chinese kingdoms, which had been fighting among themselves. The Ch'in set up a central government under Emperor Shih Huang-ti. It was this emperor who built the Great Wall of China and who ruled a state that reached from the Mongolian Plateau to the Yangtze River basin.

The Ch'in dynasty lasted only fifteen years, but the imperial system of government it established survived for 2,000 years. The Ch'in divided China into provinces and counties. After China became a unified empire in the third century B.C., there were a series imperial dynasties.

The approximate dates of the ten major dynasties are as follows: the Shang dynasty (1766–1122 B.C.), the Chou dynasty (1122–256 B.C.), the Ch'in dynasty (221–206 B.C.), the Han dynasty (202 B.C.–A.D. 220), the Sui Dynasty (581–618), the T'ang dynasty (618–907), the Sung dynasty (960–1279), the Yuan dynasty (1279–1368), the Ming dynasty (1368–1644), and the Ch'ing dynasty (1644–1912).

Confucianism was a unifying factor in China. Those who became government officials were tested in the four key Confucian texts. Women were not allowed to compete in these examinations. Another unifying factor was written language. Although people from one part of China may not understand the speech of those from another part of China, they can read one another's newspapers. Chinese written language has been the same since the third century B.C.

In the early 1800s, China was still an isolated empire. Then Great Britain used force in the Opium War of 1839 to open China to trade. In addition to foreign wars, there were internal rebellions. There were a number of short-term leaders and warlords. Revolutionaries overthrew the Manchu dynasty and established a republic in 1912.

Sun Yat-sen was sworn in as the first president of the Republic of China. He was a Christian who had studied in Hawaii and Hong Kong and traveled to London. He had traveled widely trying to raise money to support the revolution. After a short time, he resigned as Yuan Shih-K'ai took power and tried to set up his own dynasty.

World War I brought Japanese troops into China once again. Various warlords took over provinces, and the Japanese made many demands on China.

The Communist Party, founded in 1921, challenged the national government. After Sun Yat-sen's death in 1925, Chiang Kai-shek took over the leadership of the Nationalist Party and turned against the Communists in 1927. He defeated a number of warlords and established a national government, the Republic of China, in Nanking.

Chiang Kai-shek tried to root out Communism. Many Communist Chinese had taken to the mountains in Kiangsi and Hunan. In 1931, Japan invaded Manchuria.

In 1934, Mao Tse-tung (Mao Zedong) led the Chinese Communists on the "Long March," more than 6,000 miles, from South Kiangsi to the Shensi Province in the north. He won the support of millions of peasants on the way.

The Japanese occupied the northern province of Manchuria and attacked again in 1937. This caused the Nationalist and the Communist Chinese to form a sort of temporary alliance to fight against the Japanese.

Before World War II broke out in 1939, Japan controlled most of eastern China. After the end of World War II, the Communists took control of mainland China, and Chiang Kai-shek retreated to the island of Taiwan (Formosa). The Communists then founded the People's Republic of China. Its capital was Beijing, and their leader was Mao Tse-Tung (Zedong). After Mao's death in 1976, Deng Xiaoping assumed leadership.

Government

The People's Republic of China is, in theory, a socialist state governed by workers and peasants. In reality, leaders of the Communist Party and the army share power.

After the death of Mao in 1976, China underwent numerous changes. In 1982, the National People's Congress adopted a new state constitution. It provided a legal framework for reform. Article 1 of the Constitution describes China as a "people's democratic dictatorship."

The Constitution sets up a legislature called the National People's Congress. It has approximately 3,000 members elected by provincial congresses to serve five-year terms. There is a Standing Committee of 150 members. The Congress meets for about two weeks a year to approve or reject policies, laws, and the budget. At other times of the year, the Standing Committee carries out the functions of the Congress.

Executive power rests in the State Council. The Council is somewhat like our president's cabinet. Members of the Council include the premier, 5 vice-premiers, and the heads of other agencies. The Council takes its orders from the Communist Party Secretariat.

Within the Chinese Communist Party, the highest source of authority is the National Party Congress, made up of about 1,500 people. The Congress meets at least once every five years and basically approves the decisions of the top Party leadership and then communicates those decisions to local governments.

The Party Congress elects a Central Committee of 175 full members and 110 alternate members. This group delegates authority to still smaller bodies. The Politburo Standing Committee has 6 members who hold the most important posts. The Politburo has 17 members and one alternate. The Secretariat consists of the Party's general secretary and 10 other secretaries.

Religion

Traditional Chinese worshipped many different gods and did not recognize one supreme god. Ancestor worship was also practiced in traditional China. When China became Communist, many religions were suppressed. Only recently has religious practice returned to parts of China. The major religions in China today are Confucianism, Daoism, Buddhism, Islam, and Christianity.

Traditional Chinese values come from Confucius, who lived from 551 to 479 B.C. Confucianism was not a religion with deities and priests. It stressed a harmonious social order, respect for human dignity, and strict ethical rules.

In the sixth century B.C., Taoism began as a philosophical system, advocating harmony between man and nature. It grew into a religion with temples and priests but diminished in importance as Buddhism grew.

Buddhism came to China from India at the beginning of the Christian era and became the predominant religion in China. Gautama Buddha, the founder of the religion, was a prince of northern India, born about 563 B.C.

The branch of Buddhism that is the basis of Lamaism is Mahayana. It resembles Christianity in some ways. Mahayana Buddhism teaches that the souls of good people go to Paradise, but only after living through several incarnations.

When Kublai Khan became emperor of China in the late 1200s, he made Lamaism the state religion and appointed a high-ranking lama as priest king of Western Xizang (Tibet). Many years later that priest-king was given the title of the Dalai Lama. At one time, the Potala Palace, a thirteen-story castle overlooking the capital city of Lhasa in Tibet, was a religious center. Now it is a museum.

The fourteenth Dalai Lama fled Tibet in 1959 for India after a failed uprising against Chinese rule. The Tibetans are followers of the Lamaist version of Buddhism, and the Mongols are also followers of Lamaism.

Islam existed in China as early as the 700s. It is based on the belief in one god, named Allah, whose prophet was Muhammad. Islam grew and spread slowly. Today it is estimated that there are 25 million Muslims in China. Most of the 7 million Uygurs practice the religion of Islam, and the Hui are descendants of Chinese who adopted Islam.

Christianity arrived in China with the Jesuit missionaries in the 1500s. It is estimated that today there are 11 million Christians in China.

Education

When the Communists took over China in 1949, it is estimated that only about 20 percent of the children attended school. In 1985, the People's Republic of China set the goal of having all children attend school for nine years.

In 1987, more than 95 percent of all Chinese children of primary-school age went to school. Classes are crowded with as many as 50 students in each. The dropout rate is high, especially in rural areas where parents need their children to work on farms. Only about 60 percent of those enrolled in primary school actually graduate.

Some children in China begin kindergarten at age three. Most begin primary school at age six or seven. They attend school six days a week. Primary schools have a five- or six-year course of study. The school year has two semesters and includes a vacation in July and August.

The curriculum in rural areas is different from urban areas. Urban schools tend to prepare young children for further education and skilled jobs. Students study mathematics, Chinese, physical education, history, geography, drawing, and music. English is usually added to the curriculum in third grade. Rural schools prepare students for manual labor. Rural students study Chinese and mathematics.

Secondary schools in China are called middle schools. They are divided into junior and senior levels. Students begin the junior level at age twelve and take a three-year course of study. Senior middle schools offer a two- or three-year course that a student begins at age fifteen. Many middle school students take vocational courses related to industry, services, business, or agriculture.

Higher education was almost shut down during the Cultural Revolution in China. This resulted in a critical shortage of teachers and other highly trained people. Beginning in 1976, emphasis was placed on restoring institutions of higher education, and scores on entrance exams were used to determine admission.

There is still a shortage of teachers, and many students who wish to do so cannot attend school. Some take university courses offered through television. The government also sponsors correspondence schools and workers' colleges in factories.

Immigrants

Tens of millions of people have left China over the centuries and settled abroad, usually in English-speaking parts of the world. The largest emigration was during the nineteenth and twentieth centuries. Many immigrants come from two provinces on the southern coast of China: Guangdong and Fujian.

As trade opened up between China and the rest of the world, many Chinese moved to the coast and lived in port cities where there was work. From these ports, thousands began emigrating all over the world seeking better opportunities.

One method of emigration was the credit-ticket system. A Chinese person received free passage on board a ship and carried a piece of paper, or ticket. When that person arrived at his or her destination, the cost of the passage was paid by a friend or relative or by a new employer. Others emigrated by the "coolie" system, as indentured laborers. Thousands of Chinese were given contracts to travel and then work abroad for a fixed number of years, much like slaves.

Many Chinese emigrants came to California, Australia, and other parts of the world to search for gold. In 1852, it is estimated that 20,000 Chinese passed through San Francisco on their way to the goldfields. Other Chinese workers became involved in building railroads across the United States in the 1860s and in Canada during the 1870s.

About 70 percent of the inhabitants of Hong Kong either came from Mainland China or have a parent who did. As the date drew near for Hong Kong to be returned to Chinese control, Chinese began emigrating from Hong Kong to the United States, Australia, and England. In the three years between 1986 and 1989, 5.7 million Chinese left Hong Kong.

During the last thirty years, an enormous number of Chinese have emigrated to the United States so that now there is one Chinese person for every hundred people in the United States. Between 1981 and 1990, 388,800 people from China and Taiwan immigrated to the United States. From 1991 to 1995, another 227,000 emigrants arrived.

Language

Mandarin is the official language in China, but many other dialects are spoken.

About 94 percent of the people in China are known as Han Chinese. They use a common written form of Chinese and are mostly agricultural people. There are also 4 million Hui, descendants of Chinese who adopted Islam, who are almost indistinguishable from the Han. Most live in northwest China where the Ningxia Hui Autonomous Region was created in 1958.

There are more than 8 million Zhuang, who are concentrated in southern Central China in the Guangxi Autonomous Region. The Zhuang are also agricultural, but their spoken language is different from the Han.

Scattered all over Asia, including China, are the Miao or the Hmong. In China there are 7.4 million Miao. Most live in the Guizhou and Yunnan provinces. They speak varying languages.

The Uygurs who live in the Xinjiang-Uygur Autonomous Region number about 7 million. Their language is related to Turkish. They are also primarily farmers.

There are 5 million Tibetans. Some live in Xizang (Tibet), but the majority live under Chinese rule elsewhere in China. The Tibetan language existed for a long time before being written down. It was based on the Indian Sanskrit alphabet. Today Tibetan is only taught as a second language. Chinese is the language used in high schools and universities.

The Mongols live in the Nei Mongol Autonomous Region (inner Mongolia). There are about 3 million Mongols, some of whom are settled while others are nomadic moving with their herds of sheep, goats, horses, and cattle.

The Arts and Sciences

The Chinese have contributed to the world inventions and manufacturing techniques as well as rich legacies in the arts.

The Chinese taught the world how to make paper, and they also invented printing with movable type in 1045, four hundred years before Gutenberg invented it in the West.

Many people in all parts of the world, including the United States, use acupuncture as a means of relieving pain and treating illness. The Chinese, during the Han dynasty (202 B.C.–A.D. 220), perfected acupuncture. During acupuncture, needles are inserted at certain points of the body.

Chinese counting rods were the first decimal system. And the Chinese, along with Arab and Indian thinkers, helped to develop algebra.

Chinese made huge, flat, cast iron pans to boil brine water. They piped natural gas mixed with air through bamboo pipes to use in heating the brine water to get salt. Villages near the salt works piped in natural gas for lighting or cooking in 100 B.C.

According to Chinese legends, the Empress Hsi Ling-shi discovered silk around 2,700 B.C. She is also credited with inventing the first loom for weaving silk fabric. The art of painting on silk in China can be traced back to the third century. Silk was highly valued and traded throughout the world.

Chinese potters produced elegant porcelain in shades of green, blue, gray, and ivory. This was also exported to the West. Others did not discover the secret of making this special "chinaware" until the eighteenth century.

Chinese traditional theatre is highly stylized, with spoken dialogue, song, dance, pantomime, and acrobatics. There is often an accompaniment of drums and stringed instruments. The Beijing Opera has a repertoire of more than 1,000 works. Many of these operas trace military and political struggles.

Traditional literature in China dates from the Eastern Zhou dynasty (770–256 B.C.) and includes Confucian texts and poetry. In 1918, Lu Xun wrote a short story called "Diary of a Madman." This was the first real break with the traditional writings of the past. In the 1930s, Ba Jin wrote a novel called *Family*, deploring the practice of arranged marriages.

After the Communist revolution in 1949, literature served the goals of the party, and there was a decline in literary activity. After Mao's death, and the arrest of his wife, Jiang Qing, writers in China became more active again.

Movies were also brought under the control of the Ministry of Culture under Communist China and were expected to support the government and its policies. Radio and television began expanding their services rapidly in the 1980s.

Two important contemporary Chinese writers are Jung Chang and Amy Tan. Jung Chang was born in Szechwan Province in China in 1952 and now lives in London. Her best selling book is *Wild Swans*. Amy Tan was born in California after her parents immigrated to the United States. Her first novel, *The Joy Luck Club*, was published in 1989 and was made into a successful movie.

Other famous Chinese emigrants include the novelist Betty Bao Lord, Tsung-dao Lee, winner of the Nobel Prize, I. M. Pei, an architect who designed the glass pyramid in front of the Louvre in Paris, and the cellist Yo-yo Ma. An American, Maya Lin, whose parents were Chinese immigrants, designed the famous Vietnam Veterans Memorial in Washington, D.C.

The best known Tibetan art form is the thangka, which is a cloth banner with scenes painted on it. These wall hangings are draped like tapestries in temples. After the scene is painted, strips of silk are sewn around the edges to form a border. On many thangkas, there is a figure of Buddha.

Food

Different foods are popular in different parts of China. Food from the province of Szechwan is famous throughout the world. Breakfast may consist of bean milk and crullers. A late meal, served after lunch and dinner, may consist of noodles, dumplings, or stewed rice. Most dishes from the southwestern province are spiced with pepper and small red chilis.

In the north, which includes Beijing, dishes contain a lot of ginger and garlic. Beijing is famous for its crispy duck. In the east, people eat a lot of fish and enjoy sweet dishes. Cooking in the south features a good deal of fish too. Southern foods include those from Canton. Cantonese food is usually sweeter and more colorful than food from other regions. It includes sweet-and-sour-pork and dumplings called dim sum. Shanghai is known for its salty foods.

One famous Chinese dish is bird's nest soup. The nest of a small swift, fashioned with moss and feathers and stuck to the roofs of caves, is considered a great delicacy. These nests can be served in different kinds of sweet or savory soups.

Depending on the part of the country, the midday or evening meal will consist of rice or noodles. There may be fish or meat. Fresh vegetables such as onions, peppers, and mushrooms are very popular. Instead of using knives and forks, people use chopsticks, invented at least 3,000 years ago. People drink tea with all meals.

In Tibet, yak milk is used in making yogurt, cheese, and butter. Yak-butter is an ingredient in Tibetan style tea. Yak meat is dried and smoked. A dish of lamb dipped in sauces is popular in Inner Mongolia.

Tang Yuan is a sweet dessert that is served at the Chinese Winter Solstice Festival. The following recipe serves four.

Tang Yuan

2 cups glutinous rice flour

water

2 cups brown sugar

red, green, and yellow food coloring

In a medium-sized bowl, mix together 2 cups of glutinous rice flour and sufficient water to make a dough. Knead the dough for a few minutes.

In a saucepan on the stove, add 2 cups of brown sugar into 5 cups of water. Stir until you have a smooth sugar water mixture.

Divide the dough into three parts. Use several drops of red food coloring to one piece of dough and work the dough until the coloring is mixed evenly throughout the dough. Repeat this process with the other two parts of dough, adding green food coloring to one lump of dough and yellow food coloring to another lump.

Take each piece of colored dough and form it into small balls the size of marbles. Drop all the balls into the sugar water and cook them until the balls of dough rise to the top.

Serve balls in small bowls with some of the syrup. Tang Yuan may be served hot or cold.

Recreation

Common toys in the United States such as POGS, kites, tops, stilts, and yo-yos have their origins in China. Many children in schools in the United States and at home have enjoyed making patterns using tangram pieces. The tangram was invented in China over 1,500 years ago.

Although not as popular today as it once was, many children in the United States still enjoy playing Pick Up Sticks. This game had its origins in China. It is played with thirty ivory or bamboo sticks.

Adults in the United States enjoy playing mah-jongg, which in China is called *majiang*. United States craftspeople enjoy doing macrame. The Chinese perfected the art of macrame over the centuries. It involves using intricate knots with various types of threads and cords.

The ancient game of weiqi is still played today in China. Two players each have approximately two hundred pieces arranged on a large board divided into squares. The object of the game is to surround the other players' pieces.

The game of Chinese chess is played on a board that looks much like a western checkers board. The chessmen are round, rather than carved figures like western chessmen, and they are placed on the intersections on the board.

Chinese checkers is played on a board with two overlapping triangles that form a star. The Chinese call this game *tiaoqi* or jumping chess.

There are many different types of puppets that are used in China today. The oldest type of puppet used in China is the marionette, which is controlled by strings. The most popular is the hand puppet. The puppets have removable heads so that, with a change of head, they can be used for more than one part in the play. Chinese puppet theatres are intricate and elaborate.

Almost everyone in China engages in daily athletics. It may be calisthenics or team sports. Athletics has value in Communist China because participants are keeping themselves in condition to defend their country.

Soccer is among the most popular sports played in China. The first women's world soccer championship was held in China in 1991. During the 1996 Olympic Games held in Atlanta, Georgia, the Chinese women's team won the silver medal.

Polo is another popular game and one that requires skillful horsemanship. There are paintings from the Han Dynasty showing Chinese nobles playing polo. Two competing teams use mallets with flexible handles to drive a wooden ball across the field. Shooting the ball across the other team's goal line makes scores.

Badminton is played throughout Asia. Badminton became an Olympic sport in 1992. During the 1996 Olympic Games, China's women's teams won a gold and bronze medal in doubles play, and China's mixed doubles team won a bronze medal.

Martial arts, popular in China, have also had a big effect in the United States, caused partly by the influence of the movie star, Bruce Lee. Gongfu, as it is used today, includes the martial arts of boxing and weapon wielding. The origin of gongfu goes back to the Shaolin Temple in Henan Province.

Acrobatics are also very popular, including tightrope balancing, juggling, and tumbling. Some of China's acrobatic groups have toured the United States to widespread acclaim.

Gymnasts from China have built upon their long tradition of excellence in acrobatics. During the 1996 Olympic Games, China's men's gymnastic team won the silver medal in the team competition.

Chinese athletes are famous for their abilities as swimmers and divers. In some Olympic swimming and diving competitions, both the men's and women's teams from China have won all the medals.

Customs and Traditions

China uses two types of calendars. The Gregorian calendar (like the one used in the United States) is used for work and school. A Lunar calendar is used for most festivals.

In spring, there are five main festivals. Chinese New Year is the biggest festival of the year. It lasts three days and is celebrated with firecrackers, drumming, and feasting. Dai people celebrate the Water Splashing Festival on the second day of the first month. People splash water on one another to shower blessings and happiness. The Great Prayer Festival, Monlam Chemno, begins three days after the New Year celebrations. People pray for good harvests and peace.

On the fifteenth day of the first month, there is a Lantern Festival known as the Feast of the First Full Moon, which celebrates the light and warmth of sun after winter. The Chinese Lantern Festival traditionally marks the end of New Year celebrations and the beginning of spring. Lanterns are hung from poles and carried in processions.

Part of the celebration is the parade of the dragon. The dragon is made on a long framework of bamboo and may be as much as 100 feet long. Its body is covered with bright paper or silk.

In Tibet, the New Year festival, which occurs sometime in February or early March, is called Losar. The first day is a religious holiday. Offerings are made at temples or at home altars. Prayer flags are flown. The second day is a day of feasting. On the third day, prayer services are held on rooftops.

The Qing Ming Festival is one of the few holidays that appears on the Gregorian calendar. It falls on April 4 each year. This Festival is for remembering ancestors. People go to cemeteries to offer food and burn paper money and other offerings to the dead.

On the twenty-third day of the third month, many people celebrate the birthday of Tian Hou, Goddess of the Sea. This holiday is especially popular with sailors. There are lion dancers, stiltwalkers, acrobats, and parades. This holiday is often celebrated where Chinese have moved away from the mainland to places like San Francisco, Hong Kong, and Taiwan.

The biggest summer festival, the Dragonboat Festival, is held on the fifth day of the fifth month. It may have originally been used to celebrate the planting of the rice crop. Today the highlight of the festival is boat racing. Dragonboats have a carved dragon's head at one end and a tail at the other.

In autumn, five Chinese festivals are celebrated. The Cowherd and the Weaving Maid Festival is held on the seventh day of the seventh month to honor women's work. A sewing competition is featured. The Hungry Ghosts Festival is the fifteenth day of the seventh month. It is something like Halloween in that people believe spirits are wandering the earth that night. Food and incense are left by the road for the hungry ghosts.

The Mid-Autumn Festival is the fifteenth day of the eighth month. It began as a day of thanksgiving for the rice harvest. It is celebrated outdoors, and people eat mooncakes. Many mooncakes are round, and some are sweet with a paste filling.

The Double Ninth Festival is celebrated on the ninth day of the ninth month. People hold picnics, climb in the hills, and celebrate the coming of winter.

National Day is a celebration held on October 10 in Beijing to celebrate the birthday of the People's Republic of China. The Winter Solstice Day is celebrated with feasting, much like our Thanksgiving.

Suggested Activities

Writing

1. Astronomers held important positions in China during the Han dynasty. Between A.D. 78 and 139, the royal astronomer was Zhang Heng. He built a model called an armillary sphere. Invite a pair of students to research astronomy in ancient China and to write a report to share with the class. In their report, they should discuss the armillary sphere and how it worked. The report should contain a bibliography showing at least three sources of information.

Reading

2. Chinese immigrants have sometimes been discriminated against in their new countries. A pair of students might want to study the problems these immigrants faced, and in an oral report, share what they learn with the class. Suggested reading would include *The Chinese American Struggle for Equality* by Franklin Ng (Rourke, 1992) and *New Kids on the Block: Oral Histories of Immigrant Teens* by Janet Bode (Franklin Watts, 1989).

Vocabulary

3. One of the challenges of studying Chinese is that names are sometimes given in contemporary spelling and sometimes in the previous Romanization. This can cause considerable confusion. Students would benefit from learning both names of the provinces and autonomous regions of China. Two students might want to prepare and display

these on a wall map: HEILONGJIANG (Heilungkiang), JILIN (Kirin), NEI MONGGOL (Inner Mongolia), LIAONING (Liaoning), HEBEI (Hopeh), SHANDONG (Shuntung), SHANXI (Shansi), NINGXIA (Ningsia), GANSU (Kansu), XINJIANG (Sinkiang), QINGHAI (Tsinghai), SHAANXI (Shensi), XIZANG (Tibet), SICHUAN (Szechwan), HENAN (Honan), JIANGSU (Kiangsu), ANHUI (Anhwei), HUBEI (Hupeh), ZHEJIANG (Chekiang), YUNNAN (Yunnan), GUIZHOU (Kweichow), HUNAN (Hunan), JIANGXI (Kiangsi), FUJIAN (Fukien), GUANGXI (Kwangsi), GUANGDONG (Kwangtung), and TAIWAN (Formosa).

Math

4. A Chinese abacus has 5 beads on each of the 12 rods below the bar, and 2 beads on each rod above the bar. The abacus is used for counting and calculating. To operate the abacus, you use the thumb, first, and middle finger. Bring in a Chinese abacus, and someone who is skilled in using it, and demonstrate how to use an abacus to quickly add, subtract, multiply, and divide.

Social Studies

5. One area of China that will fascinate students is Inner Mongolia. A good deal of information on this topic is available on the World Wide Web. Invite a pair of students to research the topic on the Web and report back to the class what they learn. At http:/www.citsusa.com/mongolia.html, students will find information on Mongolian cities such as Hohhot, Chengde, Changchun, Harbin, Datang, Shenyang, and Jilin. A photo gallery is available at http://www.alumni.caltech.edu/~pamlogan/gallery/monggal.htm. A virtual library on Mongolia with links to other sites is at http://bvoice.com/vl.html.

Geography

6. Mount Everest is located at the border of Tibet and Nepal. There have been many expeditions to climb the mountain, some successful and some disastrous. Ask a pair of interested students to research this mountain. What different routes are used to climb it? What were

the most famous expeditions? Which countries of the world are represented among those climbers who have successfully ascended Everest? Ask these students to make an oral report to the class sharing what they learn.

Music

7. Invite a group of students to research the bronze bells used to make music by the Zhou people and to share what they learn in an oral report to the class. These bells did not have clappers inside. They were struck by musicians. Each bell was tuned to ring two different pitches, one when it was hit high and another when it was hit near the bottom. Sets of bells were tuned to match each other's tones.

Art

8. Bright paper lanterns could be used to decorate a classroom area. To make a simple lantern, begin with a rectangular piece of paper. Make a sharp fold in the middle the length of the paper. Cut through the fold to within 2 cm. of the open edge. (The cuts may be straight but are more interesting if they are wavy.) Open out the paper. Bend the paper to make a cylinder and glue the short edges together. Use another strip of paper to make a handle.

Drama/Movement

9. Among the most common shows at Chinese theatres are acrobatic troupes. These troupes sometimes tour the United States. Invite a student to research acrobatics in China and orally report to the class.

Dress

10. After the Communist revolution in 1949, people throughout China wore plain clothes, but a group of students might be interested in Chinese clothing of an earlier period. They could find illustrations of Chinese clothing, and with permission, photocopy and share them with the class, explaining what they had learned about Chinese dress.

   Color was significant in Chinese clothing. Because blue dye was cheap, poor people often wore blue. Yellow was worn by the upper classes. Brides wore red, and white was worn during mourning.

Cooking

11. The traditional meal served on Chinese New Year ends with a sweet cake. The belief is that all those who eat this sweet cake will have good fortune in the year ahead. Here is a recipe for cake that yields ten slices.

Nin Go Cake

1 cup sugar
2 cups water
2 $\frac{1}{2}$ cups glutinous rice flour
$\frac{1}{2}$ cup raisins
$\frac{1}{2}$ cup candied cherries

Stir together 1 cup sugar and 2 cups water in a large mixing bowl. Add 2 $\frac{1}{2}$ cups glutinous rice flour a cup at a time, mixing until it forms a smooth batter. Stir in $\frac{1}{2}$ cup raisins and $\frac{1}{2}$ cup candied cherries. Pour the batter into a greased 10-inch round cake pan. Place the cake pan on a steamer basket that has been set over boiling water. Steam for 45 minutes, until the Hin Go has risen and is translucent. Allow the cake to cool, then cut into slices and serve.

Culminating Activity

12. Over several months' time, students might want to create their own "Great Wall of China." This would be a large bulletin board on which students would place clippings of articles and pictures from magazines and newspapers dealing with important places, people, animals, and events in China. These could include meetings and visits of politicians, art events, natural disasters, the loan of panda bears, the opening or closing of businesses and factories, etc. The Great Wall should serve to show how often China is in the world news.

Suggested Reading

Bradley, John. *China, A New Revolution?* New York: Gloucester Press, 1990.

Cheong, Colin. *Festivals of the World, China.* Milwaukee, Wisc.: Gareth Stevens, 1997.

Croft, Jennifer, Anne Johnson, Barbara Miller, Eugene Murphy, Roger Rosen, Steven Rubenstein, Colleen

She, Jeanne Strazzabosco, and Pegi Vail. *Miao.* Danbury, Conn.: Grolier Educational, 1995.

Davies, Kath. *A First Guide to China.* Winchester, England: Zoe Books, 1995.

Demi. *The Stonecutter.* New York: Crown Publishers, 1995.

Dramer, Kim. *Games People Play, China.* Danbury, Conn.: Childrens Press, 1997.

Fisher, Leonard Everett. *The Great Wall of China.* New York: Macmillan, 1986.

Hacker, Jeffrey H. *The New China.* New York: Franklin Watts, 1986.

Kalman, Bobbie. *Tibet.* New York: Crabtree, 1990.

Kendra, Judith. *Chinese Migrations.* New York: Thomson Learning, 1995.

Ling, Bettina. *Maya Lin, Award-Winning Architect, Artist.* Austin, Tex.: Raintree Steck-Vaughn, 1997.

McDermott, Gerald. *The Stonecutter: A Japanese Folk Tale.* New York: Viking, 1975.

McLenighan, Valjean. *China, A History to 1949.* Chicago, Ill.: Childrens Press, 1983.

———. *People's Republic of China.* Chicago, Ill.: Childrens Press, 1984.

Pitkanen, Matti A. with Reijo Harkonen. *The Children of China.* Minneapolis, Minn.: Carolrhoda Books, 1990.

Reynolds, Jan. *Mongolia, Vanishing Cultures.* San Diego, Calif.: Harcourt Brace, 1994.

Riehecky, Janet. *China.* Minneapolis, Minn.: Carolrhoda Books, 1999.

Schell, Orville and Joseph Esherick. *Modern China: The Story of a Revolution.* New York: Alfred A. Knopf, 1972.

Stein, R. Conrad. *Hong Kong.* Chicago, Ill.: Childrens Press, 1985.

Stewart, Gail B. *China.* New York: Crestwood House, 1990.

Waterlow, Julia. *China.* Austin, Tex.: Raintree Steck-Vaughn, 1997.

Williams, Suzanne. *Made in China, Ideas and Inventions from Ancient China.* Berkeley, Calif.: Pacific View Press, 1996.

They had heard stories about a huge serpent with glowing red eyes
that lived in the lake.

Colombia
A Legend from Colombia

Many stories from South America mention a gilded king and a land of emeralds. Some of these have found their way into the folklore of Colombia. Beatriz Vidal tells the story of this golden king in *The Legend of El Dorado*. She traces her story to the chronicles of Sebastian de Benalcazar, dated 1541. The story also appears in Lulu Delacre's work, "El Dorado, A Colombia Legend, Sixteenth Century" found in *Golden Tales, Myths, Legends, and Folktales from Latin America*. Delacre used as a source of her material *Los Muiscas Antes de la Conquista* by Jose Perez de Barradas, Madris: Consejo de Investigaciones Cientificas. Instituto Bernardino de Sahaguin, 1950.

El Dorado and the Lake of the Moon

Long ago, the Sun and the Moon shone down on an earth where there were no people. The pale Moon, almost blinded by the brightness of the Sun, shed a single tear. This teardrop became a gorgeous lake named Lake Guatavita.

Many, many years later, a group of Chibcha Indians settled not far from this magnificent lake. It was deep blue and round, and the Chibchas honored it but were afraid. They had heard stories about a huge serpent with glowing red eyes that lived in the lake. According to the stories, anyone who touched the waters would enter its depths and never return.

Not far from the lake, in the village of the Chibchas, lived the king with his beautiful wife and their lovely little daughter. This was a lush land of plenty. They were surrounded by mountains filled with emeralds and streams filled with gold. The Chibchas made and wore many lovely ornaments.

One morning the Queen and her daughter went for a long walk. The child ran on ahead and when she reached Lake Guatavita she took a stick and plunged it into the shimmering lake before the Queen could stop her. At that moment, the Sun dipped behind a cloud.

The Queen hurried to her child and picked her up in her arms. But as the Queen looked into the ruffled waters of the lake, she spied the ruby eyes of a dazzling emerald-colored serpent. Transfixed, the queen and her daughter stared down into the depths until the sun reappeared, and glared upon the water, causing the image in the lake to disappear.

When the queen got back to the village, she told the king what had happened. She no longer felt afraid. The queen described the beautiful serpent and confessed to her husband that she longed to be with it forever.

The king worried over what had happened. He warned the queen and his daughter to never again go to the shores of Lake Guatavita.

The queen would never knowingly disobey her husband whom she loved dearly, but that night she had a dream. In her dream she saw two ruby eyes that beckoned her into the darkness. The queen wrapped her sleeping daughter in a cloak, picked her up, and followed the glowing eyes through the moonlight to the lake.

In the morning, when the king found his wife and daughter gone, he had his men search everywhere for them. But deep in his heart, the king knew where they must be. After the search parties reported that they could find no trace of the queen and the little girl anywhere near the village, the king took his men and walked to Lake Guatavita.

Looking into the water, the king thought he caught a glimpse of his wife and daughter, but a breeze ruffled the surface of the lake, and the image disappeared. Then, floating on the lake, the King saw the Queen's royal scarf and his daughter's tiny cloak.

Sadly, the king returned to his village and sat upon his throne day after day, speaking to no one. The Chibchas began to worry. If their mighty king did not bestir himself, they knew that their enemies would soon encroach upon their lands. Their farms and treasures would be taken from them.

The priest met with the troubled people and spoke. "At the full moon, we must all gather on the shores of the lake. There we will listen to the words of the serpent and be guided by them."

On the eve of the full moon, the king, the priest, and all the Chibchas gathered near the shores of the lake. They built a fire, beat their drums, sang, danced, and prayed. The moon rose and shone on the lake, making a full circle of light. Then the moon slipped behind a cloud. All was darkness. Suddenly waves violently tossed across the lake, and a noise like thunder came from the depths.

The frightened Chibchas waited silently. Then the moon came out again and formed a circle of light in the center of the lake.

"The serpent has spoken," said the priest to the king. "Your wife and child are happy in the palace of the great serpent. One day, he promises, if you have ruled your people wisely, you will be allowed to join them."

The king went back to the village. Because he believed the serpent's promise that in time he would be reunited with his wife and daughter, the king's vigor was restored. He ruled wisely and his people prospered. But once a year, the king held a ceremony at Lake Guatavita, because he did not want the serpent to forget his promise.

The king declared a fasting period to purify their bodies and souls. Then the villagers prepared delicate foods and exquisite drinks, cleaned their masks and headdresses, and polished their musical instruments.

On the chosen day, the Chibchas rubbed their king's body in fragrant oil. Then they covered him with gold dust and carried him on a throne to the shores of the lake. There they made a raft and on it they put heaps of flowers as well as necklaces and bracelets of emeralds and gold. Finally, they seated their King, El Dorado, the golden one, on the raft, and pushed it out into the lake just as the sun set.

As the moon rose, the Chibchas beat drums and played flutes until the raft reached the middle of the lake. Then they stopped, and all was still. The king called upon the serpent to guard his wife and daughter. He threw the flowers and jewels into the lake and then dove in himself and rubbed his skin, so that a circle of gold dust surrounded him. Then the king swam back to shore. They all returned to the village and took part in feasting and festivities.

This ceremony was performed year after year. The king grew old, and one year as he stood on his raft, throwing jewels into the lake, he saw the ruby eyes of the serpent beckoning him to follow. The king dove into the water and down into the depths of Lake Guatavita to be joined at last with his wife and daughter.

Background Information

The Republic of Colombia, located on the northwest corner of the continent, is the fourth largest country in South America. Colombia's border to the northwest is the Isthmus of Panama. On Colombia's northern coast is the Caribbean Sea, and its western coast abuts the Pacific Ocean. To the northeast is Venezuela and to the southeast are Brazil and Ecuador. To the south is Peru. The area of Colombia is 440,762 square miles. Its population is 37,418,290.

Two-thirds of Colombia's land is made up of the humid plains of the Amazon River Basin and one-third of the land is covered in mountain ranges. Almost all Colombians live in the high, western third of the country. Only a few Indians live on the humid plains.

The Amazonia of Colombia is nearly one-third of the land surface of the country. Most of Colombia's Amazonian tributaries have countless waterfalls and rapids and are not navigable. This has helped keep settlers out of this large southern area of the country. There are few population centers, but the Amazonia is home to a large number of Indian tribes who speak several different languages.

Many of the tributaries of the Amazon flow over rocky beds. The black water Vaupes River in Colombia has many rapids such as the Devil's Cataract. These rapids limit navigation. Decaying vegetation in the river discolors the water and gives it the name "black water." Indians make traps of vines and leaves and catch fish on the Vaupes River as the fish leap the rapids struggling upstream to spawn.

Colombia has three major mountain ranges that fan out northward from its Ecuadorian border. The most westerly range is the Cordillera Occidental. The middle range is the Cordillera Central, and the eastern range is the Cordillera Oriental. Colombia's major river, the Magdalena, runs between the central and eastern mountains to the Caribbean.

The climate in Colombia is not determined as much by seasons as by elevation. The lower elevations, from sea level to 3,000 feet, are warm and tropical. Above 9,000 feet is a cold, treeless area, known as the *paramo*.

Because communication and travel through the mountainous areas are difficult, the dress, foods, folklore, customs, and music of the various areas and cities in Colombia differ greatly. Even the Spanish accent varies, just as in the United States, a New Englander sounds very different from a southerner. Road and rail building has been difficult, but air travel has started to bring the country together.

The chief export from Colombia is coffee, which is sold all over the world. Colombia's coffee production is second only to that of Brazil. Coffee is raised on plantations, and young coffee plants are grown beneath great shade trees. More than 2.6 million acres of land on about 300,000 farms are in use to cultivate this crop. It is estimated that there are about 2 billion coffee trees in Colombia, and each needs to be harvested twice a year.

In addition to coffee, other agricultural exports include bananas, cotton, and tobacco. Beef cattle are raised on large ranches in the eastern part of the country, and lumber is being cut in the Amazon basin.

Colombians used to import most of the goods that they needed. When World War I cut off European supplies, Colombians began to develop their own manufacturing of furniture and clothing. An oil industry also began to develop.

Colombians have rich deposits of iron ore in their country and make their own steel. Colombia also produces gold, iron, platinum, and lead and is the world's largest producer of emeralds.

One of the less attractive sides of South America is the international drug trade. While Bolivia and Peru are also cocaine-producing countries, Colombia is the center for growing, refining, and distribution. The city of Medellin is the control center for most of the exporting operations to the United States.

Drug barons are sometimes referred to as the Medellin cartel. They have made enormous profits. Approximately 3 million dollars spent in refining chemicals and coca leaves can yield 1 billion dollars in sold cocaine.

At various times the United States has declared a "war on drugs," but most efforts have failed. When the Colombian government tried to crack down on drug gangs, violence broke out, and thousands died. Drugs remain a major problem.

Although much of its population is still engaged in agriculture, manufacturing is increasing and cities are growing. Bogota, the capital of Colombia, is home to over four million people. Gonzalo Jimenez De Quesada, who, accompanied by 800 Spanish soldiers, was seeking gold, founded it on August 6, 1538. He founded the city on a high plain, ringed with mountains. It is thought that the city's name was to honor the Chibcha Indian chief, Bacata.

Although near the equator, it is cool in Bogota, with temperatures never rising above 60°F all year long, because the city is located at 8,600 feet above sea level. On the plains around Bogota today are orchards, wheat fields, and coffee plantations. There are also eucalyptus trees, which were originally brought here from Australia. The city still has a few remaining old churches and palaces, but for the most part is filled with tall buildings and new residential areas.

Famous spots in Bogota include The National Museum and the Institute of Anthropology. The Gold Museum holds more than 29,000 interesting gold objects made by pre-Columbian Indians. The Colonial Museum, which was once a Jesuit monastery, houses silverwork and religious statues.

Two hours north of Bogota is the famous Cathedral of Zipaquira, which is carved out of solid salt. The salt mines in this area have been worked for centuries. A tunnel leads down into the cathedral, which is 75 feet high and capable of holding 10,000 people.

Colombia has two old seaports that were early Spanish settlements: Cartagena and Santa Marta. Cartagena, founded in 1533, is one of the oldest towns in the Western Hemisphere. It still has some fortress-like walls that are 40 feet high and 50 feet thick. Santa Marta, which was founded in 1535, is a leading banana port. From here, bananas are shipped to harbors around the world.

During the nineteenth century, another seaport began to develop in Colombia. Barranquilla is located between Cartagena and Santa Marta. It is located near the mouth of the Magdalena River. It has become the country's leading port and is a busy city with modern office buildings, factories, and residential areas.

The main city in central Colombia is Medellin, founded in 1675. It is situated at an altitude of 5,000 feet in a steep valley of the Cordillera Central. Medellin is a manufacturing center for textiles. Its plants and machinery are very modern.

The city is noted for its famous Joaquin Antonio Uribe Botanical Gardens. Every March the Gardens feature an exhibit of orchids. Tourists who come to Medellin often take a side trip to visit El Ruiz, an 18,000-foot-high peak, where they can ski on snow-covered slopes.

The city of Cali lies in the Cauca Valley. It is the home of several universities and is experiencing rapid economic growth.

The small village of San Agustin is located in the mountains near the border of Ecuador. It is famous for its ancient stone statues. Some resemble masked monsters while others are images of eagles, jaguars, or frogs.

Leticia is a small port and Colombia's only access to the Amazon. A Greek-American from Florida put this little port on the map. Using Avianca Airlines, Mike Tsalickis built up a business of collecting, housing, and shipping a variety of wildlife from Colombia to zoos and medical research laboratories. He collects such creatures as squirrel monkeys, freshwater dolphins, and electric eels.

In 1822, the islands of San Andres and nearby Providencia came under Colombian rule. These islands had been taken from the Spanish by an English pirate, Henry Morgan, and were largely uninhabited for 100 years. Since being ruled by Colombia, the islands have become a popular vacation spot for Colombians and North Americans. The islands also supply coconuts to the United States. The people living on these islands speak English rather than Spanish and are mostly Protestants, rather than Roman Catholics.

The people of Colombia are diverse and include whites, Indians, blacks, and people of mixed blood. People of mixed Indian and Spanish blood are called *mestizos*, while people who are part black and part Spanish are called *mulattos*. The largest group, mestizos, make up about two-thirds of the total population. Africans tend to live in the lowland areas on the Pacific and Atlantic coasts and along the Cauca and Magdalena rivers. In Choco, Africans and mulattos make up 80 percent of the population.

History

Indian civilizations developed in the mountains of Colombia. The *Muisca* were the most advanced of perhaps as many as eight existing Indian groups. Their principal god was called Chibchachum, and most historians refer to this group of Indians as the *Chibcha*.

The Chibcha settled in the basins of the Cordillera Oriental. Legends were told about their holy lakes, among them Lake Guatavita, where gold, silver, and jewels were thrown in as gifts to the gods. The Chibcha Indians hunted and fished and raised corn and potatoes. They traded goods for gold and were expert craftsmen.

Alfonso de Ojeda first landed on the Caribbean coast of Colombia in 1499. He met the local Tairona Indians. These Indians and others from the Muisca, Sinu, and Quimbaya cultures often wore objects of gold for religious and decorative purposes.

When Spaniards arrived in Colombia early in the sixteenth century, they had already heard the myth of El Dorado and thought they would find an empire of gold and emeralds. They established settlements at Santa Marta in 1525 and at Cartagena in 1533. They forced the Indians to work in their mines and on their plantations. When they needed more labor, they brought in blacks from Africa.

Gonzala Jimenez de Quesada traveled up the Magdalena River in 1536. He defeated the Chibcha Indians and founded the city of Bogota in 1538. Other expeditions from Ecuador reached Bogota not long after.

What the Spaniards called Nueva Granada (made up of present day Colombia, Ecuador, Panama, and Venezuela) was ruled by a high court of officials appointed by Spain. In 1550, gold was discovered in Antioquia. As soon as gold shipments to Spain started, English and Dutch pirates began attacking Spanish ships.

In 1781, Antonio Galan led an uprising against Spanish rule. Eventually the uprising was put down and Galan was executed. The movement for independence continued in the 1790s after the French Revolution.

In May 1810, Cartagena declared independence, and Bogota followed on July 20. Six years of independence followed. Spain regained the territory in 1816. In August 1819, Simon Bolivar defeated the Spanish at the Battle of Boyaca. Bolivar's comrade, Francisco de Paula Santander, set up and helped to organize the new republic that was finally independent of the Spanish Empire. Santander pushed for a federation of states called the Republic of Colombia that included Panama, Venezuela, and Ecuador.

Bolivar was elected president of Gran Colombia but continued to fight for Ecuador's liberation and the independence of Peru. Santander, as vice president, ruled the nation. Gran Colombia lasted from 1819 to 1830. Then in 1830, Colombia and Panama formed a separate nation.

For the first half of the nineteenth century, the progressive liberal party led Colombia and Panama. In 1863, these Liberals adopted a constitution that protected civil liberties and abolished the death penalty. Then in 1886, the Conservatives came to power and declared the 1863 constitution dead. They named the country the Republic of Colombia in honor of Columbus.

Miguel Antonio Caro framed a new constitution for the country in 1886 that remained in effect for many years. Between 1899 and 1902 there was bitter fighting between the Liberals and the Conservatives with a great loss of life and property. The government during this period would not agree to lease to the United States the land it needed to build the Panama Canal.

In 1903, the United States helped Panama to revolt and become independent of Colombia. Not until 1921 did the United States make reparations for its actions to Colombia.

During the first half of the twentieth century, power in Colombia rotated back and forth between the Liberals and the Conservatives. In 1953, General Gustavo Rojas Pinilla declared a military dictatorship that continued for four years.

In 1957, former president Alaberto Lleras Camargo, united the Conservatives and Liberals to overthrow the dictatorship. Camargo was elected president in 1958, and a new constitution was drawn up. The Liberals and Conservatives agreed to alternate the presidency every four years. Representation in assemblies, Congress, and councils would be equally divided. This arrangement lasted until 1974. A new constitution was drawn up in 1991. It provided for the popular election of state governors.

Government

Colombia has a limited democracy based on the Constitution of 1991. A president heads the government. The president and members of the two-house Congress are directly elected.

The president is elected for four years and after serving a term of office, must wait at least four years before being eligible to run for office again. He has the power to approve or veto legislation. To assist him, the president appoints 13 ministers for such functions as public works and defense. The president is assisted in decision-making by a consulting body of 10 members called the Council of State.

The legislative branch of government is the National Congress which consists of two houses: the Senate and the Chamber of Representatives. Each department or state has two senators-at-large and an additional senator for every 200,000 people. There are two representatives for each department and an additional one for every 100,000 people. Currently there are 102 senators and 161 representatives. All members of Congress are elected for four-year terms.

Colombia is divided into twenty-three *departmentos*. These departments are similar to states in the United States. Departmentos are divided into municipalities, each of which has a mayor appointed by the departmental governor. There are also four territorial districts, five special districts, and the special district of Bogota. The president appoints governors of each department.

Colombia also has a Supreme Court consisting of 20 members. It is divided into civil, criminal, and labor divisions.

To be eligible to vote, a citizen must be eighteen or older, must register to vote, and have a citizenship card. In 1957, an act was passed allowing women to take part in voting.

Religion

Colombia's constitution guarantees freedom of religion. The principal religion of Colombia is Roman Catholicism. Catholics in Colombia tend to be conservative and traditional, with the parish church the center of a town's activities.

The concordat of 1887 defined a special role for the Catholic Church in civil matters. This remained in effect until 1973 when a new concordat was issued and the Church lost its special influence in education, Indian territories, and in marriage regulation.

While about 94 percent of the people are Catholic, the other 6 percent are Tribal Religionists, Protestants, Jews, Baha'is, Muslims, Buddhists, and Hindus.

Education

At least 10 percent of the national budget must be spent on education. Elementary education in Colombia is free, but wealthy and middle class Colombians often send their children to private schools. The public schools are called *escuelas* while the private elementary and high schools are called *colegios*.

Most children attend school from the age of five until they are sixteen. For the poorest families, education is not a priority, and children may miss school because parents need the income that their children can earn from working to keep the family going.

A typical school program is two years of kindergarten followed by five years of elementary education, and six years of secondary schooling. A few students continue to study at a university. A new movement in vocational training in high school programs is growing to help prepare students to meet the country's need for skilled labor.

There are 73 universities and approximately 60 additional institutes of higher learning in Colombia. Among these are *The Universidad Nacional de Colombia* in Bogota, the school of medicine in the *Universidad del Valle* in the Cauca Valley, and the *Universidad Industrial de Santander* in Bucaramanga. Bogota is also home to the *Universidad de los Andes* and the *Instituto Caro y Cuervo*, which draws scholars for the study of Spanish.

Immigrants

Steadily increasing and significant streams of Colombians continue to immigrate to the United States. From 1961 to 1970, 70,300 entered. From 1971 to 1980, the number increased just slightly to 77,600. From 1981 to 1990, 124,400 Colombians immigrated to the United States. During 1991 to 1995, another 67,300 came.

Language

Spanish is the official language of Colombia. About 4 percent of the people speak a native Indian language, although some of these native speakers speak Spanish as well.

Castillian Spanish was spoken by the early explorers and still predominates, although variations of Spanish are spoken in the various regions. A few Indian words still exist, especially in the names of native fruits such as *guayaba* and *zapote*.

When greeting people, the verbal greeting is almost always accompanied by at least a handshake.

The Arts and Sciences

Colombia is well known for its writers. The earliest historical and descriptive writings date back to Gonzala Jimenez de Quesada who, among other things, was an explorer.

Among famous Colombian writers of the nineteenth and twentieth centuries are Jose Eusebio Caro, Jorge Isaacs, Jose Eustacio Rivera, Tomas Carrasquilla, and German Arciniegas. Jose Asuncion Silva and Guillermo Valencia are recognized as famous poets of the literary movement known as *modernismo*. A well-known contemporary playwright is Isaac Chocron.

The best known Colombia artist of the nineteenth century, concerned with the portrayal of customs and lifestyles, was Ramon Torres Mendez. Other artists of note include the painter Enrique Grau and the sculptor Edgar Negret. Negret has exhibited throughout the world. Among contemporary painters, the works of Fernando Botero, Ramirez Villamizar, Judith Marquez Montoya, and Alejandro Obregon stand out.

The music and dance of Colombia have also made an impact outside the country. Regional dances tell familiar stories. The *meringue*, which is also common in Caribbean islands, has become a well known dance throughout the world.

Blacks and Indians have an influence on the dance and music of the coastal regions. *Fandangos, porros,* and *mapales* are African-Colombian rhythms that have gained attention outside the country. Well-known folk dances include the *bambuco* (which is the national dance), the *salsa,* and the *cumbia.*

Instruments used in Colombian music include the *flauta,* which is an Indian flute; the *tiple,* which is a many-stringed guitar; and the *raspa,* which is made from a gourd and is played like a washboard.

The Museum of Folk Arts and Tradition in Bogota is filled with fine craftwork, including intricate goldwork and pottery made in Boyaca.

Food

In Colombia, the food that is served varies from region to region. Generally, Colombians eat starchy foods such as potatoes, rice, and noodles. Most families do not eat together at breakfast, but eat according to their varying schedules. A typical breakfast would include fruit, juice, jam, and coffee.

Lunch is the most important meal of the day. Fathers may come home to eat this meal with their families. Soup, rice, meat, and vegetables are usually served. The evening meal, served around 7:00 P.M. is similar to lunch but usually soup is not served.

At almost every Colombian meal, *arepa*, a bread made of corn flour, is served. With adult volunteers to assist, students might want to make the following "corn pancakes."

Tortillas de Maíz
1 cup fresh corn kernels cut from 2 large ears
    of corn
    or 1 cup of defrosted corn kernels
$^1/_3$ cup vegetable oil
8 eggs
2 tablespoons flour
1 $^1/_2$ teaspoons salt
$^1/_2$ teaspoon black pepper
5 tablespoons butter
$^1/_2$ cup sour cream
2 tablespoons finely chopped fresh parsley

Use paper towels to pat the corn kernels completely dry. In a heavy 10-inch skillet, heat the oil over moderate heat until a light haze forms above it. Drop in the corn, and cook, stirring frequently, for 10 minutes or until the corn is golden brown. Drain the corn on a double thickness of paper towels.

Make the pancake batter in a large bowl, beating the eggs until they are well combined and foamy, and then beating in the flour, salt, and pepper.

Melt 1 tablespoon of butter in a heavy skillet or crepe pan set over moderate heat. When the foam subsides, pour in 1/3 cup of the batter. As soon as the edges begin to set, sprinkle the tortilla with 2 tablespoons of corn. Then with a fork, push the edges of the tortilla toward the center of the pan and tip it slightly, allowing the uncooked batter to run and cover the exposed areas of the pan.

When the tortilla is set and the bottom is a light brown, turn it over with a spatula and cook for 1 minute to brown the other side.

Slide the tortilla onto a heated platter and proceed similarly with the remaining batter, stirring the batter before making each tortilla. Add a teaspoon of the remaining butter to the pan for each one. As they are done, stack the pancakes one on top of the other. Serve them on individual plates topped with a tablespoon of sour cream and a sprinkling of chopped fresh parsley. Makes 8 pancakes.

Stews and thick soups are popular in Colombia. *Mazamorra* is a thick soup of corn flour, beans, and vegetables. An onion soup, *cuchuco*, is also common. Another hearty dish is *sobrebarriga*, or beef stew. *Bandeja paisa* is a dish made of ground beef, sausages, beans, rice, plantain, and avocado.

Sundays are often times that families gather to have a meal together. In addition to *frijoles* and *arepas*, there may be treats of *mogollas*, whole-wheat muffins with raisins. And on special occasions children may get a *roscon*, a bun filled with guava jelly with sugar sprinkled on top.

In Bogota, *ajico*, a soup of chicken, potatoes, and vegetables is frequently served, as is *puchero*, a broth of chicken, beef, potato, and pork. A specialty along the coast is *arroz con coco*, rice cooked in coconut oil, *and cazuela de mariscos*, a seafood stew.

After a day's work on a coffee plantation, a typical Colombian family may have *sudado*. It's made with chicken, tomatoes, onions, potatoes, and a vegetable called yukka. This is served on rice with a sauce made with onions and tomatoes.

Coffee is very popular among Colombians, and it is estimated that the average Colombian drinks 20 cups a day. Coffee is served with every meal. A cup of black coffee is called a *tinto* and usually contains a lot of sugar. *Cafe perico* is coffee with milk. *Cafe con leche* is a cup of warm milk with coffee added. *Agua de panela* is another drink enjoyed by Colombians. It is made of brown sugar and water.

Recreation

The favorite sport in Colombia is soccer. Baseball, basketball, and table tennis are also popular. In cities, there are local auto racing events on Sundays and holidays. Boxing tournaments are held in Bogota's *Coliseo El Salitre*.

Many Colombians engage in water sports such as fishing for marlin, tarpon, and sailfish, surfing, swimming, water skiing, scuba diving, and snorkeling. The Rosario Islands off of Cartagena are famous for skin diving.

Many Colombians are mountain climbers, skiers, and cyclists. Wealthy hunters hunt tapirs, deer, and boar and go on safaris into the Amazon Basin.

Bullfights and cockfights are popular spectator events. Bullfighting takes place year-round on Thursday and Sunday afternoons. There is always considerable betting at bullfights and cockfights.

In rural areas, there are sports clubs and leagues often affiliated with churches. Favorite activities include chess, soccer, bicycle races, volleyball, and the old Indian disk-throwing game of *Tejo*. This traditional game is played something like horseshoes. A stone or smooth metal piece is thrown at a mound built around pipes that contain small amounts of gunpowder. Almost every town has a tejo court.

Customs and Traditions

Because the major religion in Colombia is Roman Catholicism, twelve of Colombia's eighteen national holidays are religious. In addition to Easter and Christmas, the nine religious holidays are: Epiphany (January 6), St. Joseph's Day (March 19), Maundy Thursday, Good Friday, Corpus Christi, Saints Peter and Paul Day (June 29), Assumption Day (August 15), All Saints' Day (November 1), and Immaculate Conception Day (December 8).

Many towns are famous for their religious celebrations. In Baranquilla, for example, parades and carnivals mark the pre-Lenten season. These often include a procession of men wearing brightly colored masks and long robes. There are floats and symbolic dances. One of the ritual dances is the *coyongo,* where several birdmen circle around a man dressed as a fish who tries to escape from them.

Medellin is known for several festivals. During the annual flower festival in May there are parades with floats and arches over the intersections featuring fragrant blossoms. In June, Medellin is also home to the tango festival. Tangos are sung and danced. This festival honors a famous tango singer from Argentina, Carlos Gardel.

Other cities also recognize special festivals. In January, Manizales hosts an Inter-American Festival of Folklore. Popayan holds two special days during the first week in January. On *Dia de Negritos,* boys run about trying to blacken girls with shoe polish. And on *Fiesta de los Blanquitos,* the next day, boys chase the girls with white flour.

On June 8, Bogota holds a special ceremony honoring students who lost their lives during various uprisings. In July, Santa Marta holds a festival of the sea. In late December, Cali celebrates with a sugarcane festival that includes dancing, parades, horse racing, and bullfights.

The feast of Saint John is celebrated by lighting fires in the hills around the villages. Special celebrations are held for Saint Francis' Day at Quibdo and for Saint Isidore at Cauca.

On April 4, the image of San Isidro is carried through the town of Rio Frio. April marks the end of the dry season and San Isidro is responsible for bringing rain to the farmers. It is hoped that the first shower of the season will take place during the celebration.

An annual carnival is held on November 11, the anniversary of the Declaration of Independence. This is a four-day celebration attended by thousands of costumed participants. There are parades, floral displays, and fireworks. The culmination is a National Beauty Contest to select the young woman to represent Colombia in international beauty pageants.

Often there is dancing as part of a religious fiesta. Ritual dances may be performed in the church courtyard. Fiestas that last a week or more are called *ferias.*

Suggested Activities

Writing

1. One of the most interesting creatures to be found in Colombia is the three-toed sloth. Some sloths spend years in a single tree. Invite a pair of students to research sloths and prepare a written report to share with the class including a bibliography of their sources of information.

Reading

2. A small group of students might enjoy reading and discussing a book set in Colombia. As part of their discussion, they might examine the setting with particular care. How does the fact that the setting is Colombia affect the story? One fiction book that might be of interest is *So Loud a Silence* by Lyll Becerra de Jenkins (Lodestar Books, 1996). The central character of this story is 17-year-old Juan Guillermo, who examines family ties while with his grandmother in rural Colombia during fighting between guerillas and the army. For those students who prefer nonfiction, Ronald Syme's *Quesada of Colombia* (William Morrow, 1966) might be a good choice.

Vocabulary

3. Establish a bulletin board where students can pin up 3 x 5-inch cards with words and phrases and translations that they encounter during the unit of study. The following are a few to use as "starters": *cafeteros*—coffee farmers, *arepas*—corn griddle cakes, *frijoles*—refried kidney beans, *llanos*—flat grasslands, and *tierra calinete*—hot zone.

Math

4. As students read books and articles during their study of Colombia, ask them to collect facts and figures and

turn them into math problems for the class. For example, on a typical coffee plantation, there are 50,000 coffee plants growing. In one year, the workers pick 12,000 sacks of coffee beans. Each sack weighs 12.5 kilograms. How many pounds of coffee beans are produced on this plantation in a year?

A typical picker of coffee beans picks about 50 kilograms (110 pounds) a day. Using this "typical" rate, how many worker days would it take to pick the 12,000 sacks of coffee beans described above?

Social Studies

5. Coffee production and exportation is very important to the country of Colombia. Coffee was introduced to South America from Europe in the 1700s. The Europeans had been drinking coffee for a hundred years prior to that, having borrowed the drink from Arabia and Turkey. The hillsides of Colombia proved a perfect place for growing a mild *arabica* type of coffee.

Invite a pair of students to trace the spread of coffee from Turkey and Arabia to Europe and then from Europe to South America. Have them prepare a written report with bibliography to share with the class.

Geography

6. Secure a topographic map of Colombia for students to study. It will reveal the dramatic differences in the land, which includes low-lying zones along the sea on both the Pacific and Caribbean seacoasts; a "temperate zone" between 4,000 and 7,500 feet where most of the coffee is grown; the *tierra fria* from 7,500 to 10,000 feet where it is cool and moist; the *paramos*, which are barren hills and plains along the crests and in the valley of mountains; and finally the *nevado*, or snow country over 15,000 feet high.

Music

7. With the help of a music teacher or media specialist, try to locate music from the peoples of the rainforest to share with students. One source is *The Spirit Cries: Music of the Rainforests of South America and the Caribbean*, RCD-1-250. This is a release of the Endangered Music Project and presents digitally re-mastered recordings from four decades. Included is music of the endangered rainforest peoples of Colombia and elsewhere. It is available from Multicultural Media, RR3, Box 6655, Granger Road, Barre, Vermont, 05641. Offerings can be seen at http://www.worldmusicstore.com.

Art

8. With the help of the school's art educator, try to secure books with reproductions of famous modern Colombian artists so that students might study these. Painters might include Alejandro Obregon, Fernando Botero, Judith Marquez Montoya, and Ann Mercedes de Hoyos.

Drama/Movement

9. With help from the school music educator, explore whether or not a dance group would be willing and able to come to school and demonstrate some typical Colombian dances for the class. Of special interest are the *bambuco,* which is the national dance, and the *fandango* and *salsa.*

Dress

10. Invite a pair of students working with a media specialist to find, and with permission photocopy, pictures of traditional Colombian dress. These items of clothing might include *alpargates,* which are sandals; a *ruana,* which is a short woolen cloak worn by men of the highlands; and the *panolon,* which is a woman's shawl made of bright cotton or silk.

Cooking

11. With adult help and supervision, students will enjoy making and eating a favorite Colombian dish of boiled potatoes in a tasty sauce.

Papas Chorreadas

8 large potatoes, peeled and boiled
2 tablespoons butter
4 scallions
$^1/_2$ cup finely chopped onions
5 tomatoes, peeled, seeded, and chopped
$^1/_2$ cup heavy cream

1 teaspoon coriander

$^1/_4$ teaspoon dried oregano

pinch of cumin

$^1/_2$ teaspoon salt

1 cup grated mozzarella cheese

Peel and boil 8 large potatoes. Heat butter over moderate heat in a 10-inch skillet. Add scallions and onions, cooking them while stirring frequently, for about 5 minutes until the onions are transparent. Add the tomato pieces and cook, stirring often, for 5 minutes. Add the cream, coriander, oregano, cumin, and salt, stirring constantly. Continue stirring and drop in the cheese, stirring until the cheese melts.

Serve the sauce over the boiled potatoes.

Culminating Activity

12. Post Card Day could make a very interesting culminating activity. As a result of this unit of study, each student should choose an event important in the history or daily life of Colombia, depict it in a colorful post card drawing, and write on the back of the card from the point of view of a participant in the event describing it to a friend.

One student might describe the terrifying volcanic eruption in 1985 that wiped out the town of Amero. Another might describe being in Popayan during the first week in January and participating in the Day of the Black Ones or the Festival of the White Ones.

Students should have time to show their cards and read their messages, and then add them to a class bulletin board.

Suggested Reading

Delacre, Lulu. *Golden Tales, Myths, Legends, and Folktales from Latin America.* New York: Scholastic, 1996.

DuBois, Jill. *Colombia.* New York: Marshall Cavendish, 1991.

Hintz, Martin. *Living in the Tropics, A Cultural Geography.* New York: Franklin Watts, 1987.

Jacobsen, Peter Otto and Preben Sejer Kristensen. *A Family in Colombia.* New York: Bookwright Press, 1986.

Kline, Harvey F. *Colombia: Portrait of Unity and Diversity.* Boulder, Colo.: Westview Press, 1983.

McLeish, Ewan. *South America.* Austin, Tex.: Raintree Steck-Vaughn, 1997.

Parnell, Helga. *Cooking the South American Way.* Minneapolis, Minn.: Lerner Publications, 1991.

Perrottet, Tony, ed. *Insight Guides, South America.* Boston, Mass.: Houghton Mifflin, 1997.

Reichel-Dolmatoff, Gerardo. *Colombia.* New York: Frederick A. Praeger, 1965.

Rodman, Seldon. *The Colombia Traveler.* New York: Hawthorn Books, 1971.

Schreider, Helen and Frank. *Exploring the Amazon.* Washington, D.C.: National Geographic Society, 1970.

Schultes, Richard Evans. *Where the Gods Reign: Plants and Peoples of the Colombian Amazon.* Oracle, Ariz.: Synergetic Press, 1988.

Syme, Ronald. *Quesada of Colombia.* New York: William Morrow, 1966.

Vidal, Beatriz. *The Legend of El Dorado.* New York: Alfred A. Knopf, 1991.

von Hagen, Victor W. *The Golden Man: A Quest for El Dorado.* Farnborough, England: Saxon House, 1974.

A handsome rooster was walking along the path one day
on the way to attend the wedding of his uncle.

Cuba

A Folktale from Cuba

One version of the Cuban folktale *The Bossy Gallito* includes Spanish and English texts and is retold by Lucia M. Gonzalez and illustrated by Lulu Delacre. An old Spanish version of the tale is called "El Gallo," and similar versions of the story appear in different cultures throughout the world using various animals, including Eric Kimmel's *The Old Woman and Her Pig,* Anne Rockwell's *The Old Woman and Her Pig, and 10 Other Stories,* Paul Galdone's *Old Woman and Her Pig,* and Rosanne Leitzinger's *The Old Woman and Her Pig.*

The Bossy Rooster

A handsome rooster was walking along the path one day on the way to attend the wedding of his uncle, *Tio Perico.* The rooster looked very fine and was spotlessly clean.

Seeing two golden kernels of corn on the muddy ground, the rooster paused to think. "If I stop to eat this tempting treat, I'll dirty my beak." But the rooster could not resist. He ate the corn and dirtied his beak, his *pico.*

The rooster had not gone far when he saw some lush green grass. "Aha!" he thought. "I'll tell the grass to clean my *pico* so I'll be neat for the wedding of *Tio Perico.* Grass," he said, "I order you to clean my beak." But the grass would not.

Very out of sorts, the bossy rooster continued until he met a goat. "Goat," he ordered, "eat that clump of grass back there by the fence. It would not clean my *pico* so that I can look fine at the wedding of my *Tio Perico.*"

But the goat, which did not like to be bossed about, would not eat the grass.

The bossy rooster continued until he saw a stick. "Stick," he ordered, "strike the goat who won't eat the grass that won't clean my *pico* so that I can look fine at the wedding of my *Tio Perico.*"

But the stick would not.

A little farther on, the bossy rooster found a fire burning in a bush. "Fire," he ordered, "burn the stick that won't strike the goat who won't eat the grass that won't clean my *pico* so that I can look fine at the wedding of my *Tio Perico.*"

But the fire would not.

Not far away, the bossy rooster found a small stream rushing by. "Water," he ordered, "put out the fire that won't burn the stick that won't strike the goat who won't eat the grass that won't clean my *pico* so that I can look fine at the wedding of my *Tio Perico.*"

But the water would not.

The bossy rooster was very unhappy. It seemed that no one would follow his orders. Then he noticed the sun shining brightly down on him. The bossy rooster loved the sun and greeted it by crowing loudly every morning. He was sure the sun would help him. "Sun," he ordered, "dry out the water that won't put out the fire that won't burn the stick that won't strike the goat who won't eat the grass that won't clean my *pico* so that I can look fine at the wedding of my *Tio Perico.*"

And the sun said, "With pleasure, my dear friend."

Hearing the sun's response, the water quickly said, "Oh, no need, I'll gladly put out the fire." And the fire said, "Oh, no need, I'll gladly burn the stick." And the stick said, "Oh, no need, I'll gladly beat the goat." And the goat said, "Oh, no need, I'll gladly eat the grass." And the grass said, "Oh, no need, I will clean the rooster's *pico.*" And he did.

Very happy, and once again looking handsome and spotlessly clean, the rooster first crowed a thank you to the sun, and then hurried along so he would not be late for the wedding of his *Tio Perico.*

Background Information

Cuba is one of a long, narrow island chain located in the Caribbean Sea. This whole group of islands, called the Antilles, are summits of submerged mountains. They curve in an arc from Florida to Venezuela. These islands are divided into two groups, the Greater Antilles and the Lesser Antilles. The Greater Antilles lie to the northwest and include Jamaica, Hispaniola, Puerto Rico, and Cuba.

The Republic of Cuba consists of the biggest single island located in the West Indies and an archipelago of over 1,600 smaller islands and keys. The Isle of Youth (formerly known as the Isle of Pines), which lies south of Cuba, is popular as a recreation spot. At one time it was a haven for pirates. Robert Louis Stevenson used this island for his novel *Treasure Island.*

Cuba is long and narrow. It measures slightly more than 750 miles in length and averages 60 miles in width. It is in a strategic location, between the Atlantic Ocean and the Caribbean Sea, close to both the United States and Mexico. Havana, the capital of Cuba, is only 100 miles from Key West, Florida, and Cuba's Cape San Antonio is only 120 miles from the Yucatan Peninsula of Mexico.

Near neighbors are the Dominican Republic and Haiti, 85 miles away to the east, and Jamaica, less than 50 miles to the south. The population of Cuba is 10,999,041, and Cuba covers 42,804 square miles.

Because Cuba is located south of the Tropic of Cancer, it is a subtropical country with two major seasons. The rainy season runs from May to October and the dry season from November to April. Gentle northeastern winds blow in from the Atlantic in winter and summer, and the warm Gulf Stream current keeps the temperature along the shoreline constant.

The average annual temperature is about 78°F. In January, the temperatures are often in the 60s, while in August temperatures may reach the 90s. The annual rainfall in Cuba is 60 inches. Each autumn, hurricanes move across Cuba and often strike the mainland of the United States. These hurricanes are accompanied by heavy rainfall that often floods areas of Cuba and causes death and destruction.

Cuba has about 200 rivers, but most are shallow and unnavigable. *The Rio Cauto* (Cautious River), in the east, is about 230 miles long and is the island's main waterway. During hurricane season, the Rio Cauto often floods. There are many spectacular waterfalls on the island, including Caburni Falls, Toa Falls, and Agabama Falls. On the south coast is the Zapata Peninsula, which is an enormous swamp and an excellent place to see some of the 300 species of native birds.

Mountains cover about a quarter of Cuba. There are four major mountain ranges. These include the Sierra de los Organos and the Sierra del Rosario in the west, the Sierra de

Trinidad Mountains in the south central part of the island, which include the Trinidad range and the Sierra del Escambray, and the chief range, the Sierra Maestra. The Sierra Maestra, over 100 miles long, rise steeply from the southeastern coast and contain the highest peak on the island, Pico Real del Turquino, at 6,540 feet.

In the hot eastern provinces, Cubans grow sugarcane. In the savannas of the west and central portions of Cuba, there are tobacco farms and cattle ranches. Spanish settlers introduced domestic cattle to Cuba. Cuban farmers also raise swine and chickens.

Cuba is made up of fourteen provinces, and each of these provinces has at least one major city. The provinces, from west to east, are Pinar del Rio, City of Havana, Havana, Matanzas, Villa Clara, Cienfuegos, Sancti Spiritus, Ciego de Avila, Camaguey, Las Tunas, Holguin, Granma, Santiago de Cuba, and Guantanamo.

Havana, located in the northeast of the main island, is the capital of Cuba. With over 2 million people, it is the largest city in the West Indies. It is also one of the oldest cities in the Western Hemisphere. Havana is a busy port from which sugar, tobacco, rum, and minerals are shipped. It is built along a curving harbor guarded by El Morro, a fortress built by the Spanish in the sixteenth century.

Old Havana, or *Habana Viejo,* looks like a Spanish city with villas, castles, and churches. One old building is the Castle of the Moors, built by the Spaniards between 1589 and 1630. The castle is surrounded by a moat. In 1844, a lighthouse was added to the castle. The lighthouse beacon can be seen 19 miles out to sea. Old Havana also contains the Plaza de Armas, Havana's oldest square.

The Castle of the Point, which was a low, sturdy fortress, has been turned into a museum. The Castle of the Force is the oldest surviving building in Cuba. It was built in 1538 after a pirate attack on the city of Havana.

New Havana houses a government center, with a capitol resembling the capitol of the United States, and many other government buildings. The newer section of Havana once was filled with luxury hotels, but many of these have been converted to other uses since the Castro revolution.

Cuba's second largest city, Santiago, is situated in the southeastern end of the island. It has almost half a million residents and lies at the foot of the Sierra Maestra next to a deep bay. Some of the residents work at the United States naval base at Guantanamo Bay.

Other major cities include: Camaguey, which is inland and a center for the cattle and sugar industry; Holguin, an industrial city; Santa Clara, a manufacturing center; Guantanamo, which produces Cuba's salt; Cienfuegos, a harbor town; Pinar del Rio, a center for tobacco raising; and Matanzas, the center of the sugar industry.

The sugar industry in Cuba was nationalized in 1959. During the 1970s this industry underwent massive mechanization. It provides the bulk of Cuba's foreign exchange earnings. Tobacco was a source of income until the late 1970s, when a disease wiped out much of the tobacco harvest. Cuban factories also turn out textiles, shoes, cigarettes, and processed food.

Because the United States has an embargo against trade with Communist Cuba, Cuba trades mainly with Mexico, Canada, and Spain. Cuba's major exports are sugar, nickel, fruit, fish, tobacco, and coffee.

Cubans raise potatoes, sweet potatoes, rice, and poultry for home consumption. Fish is both a mainstay of the regular diet of Cubans and it is exported. Oysters, crabs, shrimp, crawfish, and langosta are all harvested for food.

Cuba's major imports are machinery, oil, steel, food, and pharmaceuticals. One of Cuba's exports is nickel, of which it is one of the world's main suppliers.

Since the collapse of the Soviet Union in 1989, which brought about a tremendous economic hardship, there have been many changes in Cuba. Prior to that time in Communist Cuba, the government had nationalized almost all jobs, so the government employed almost 100 percent of the work force. After the collapse of the Soviet Union, private ownership of small businesses in Cuba was allowed. Farmers are allowed to sell their crops at farmers' markets. The tourist industry is being promoted.

The growth of Cuban industry has been slow because Cuba lacks oil, natural gas, and coal deposits on the island from which to make fuel. Local industries involve food preparation, sugar refining, meatpacking, canning, and milk processing.

Cubans are issued books of ration cards, which they use to purchase consumer goods. Basic foods are sold at markets, and the government subsidizes this food to keep it low enough so that everyone can afford to eat properly. If a customer wants to buy more than the limit of his ration card, the customer must pay a higher price. When they buy milk, many Cubans bring in their own milk bottles to be refilled. In stores there are long lines that people must stand in to purchase whatever goods are available.

History

It is believed that the first people on Cuba were the Ciboney and Guanahacabibe Indians, who lived in the western half of the island. They probably came by canoe to the Antilles as long ago as 3500 B.C. A third group, the Taino Indians, originally from South America, came to Cuba much later, around A.D. 1100. The Tainos gradually occupied most of the island except for the far West. The Tainos, also called *Arawak,* spoke a language called Arawakan.

These Taino Indians were living on Cuba when Christopher Columbus arrived in 1492. The Indians lived in permanent villages and raised maize, cassava, beans, and tobacco. They also hunted and fished. They farmed with tools made of seashells, stone, and wood.

In 1511, Diego Velazquez landed on the northeastern tip of Cuba, founded Baracoa, Cuba's first Spanish colony, and took control of the land. Very quickly Spanish explorers began building cities and towns. On their arrival, the Spaniards found the Taino Indians, who offered them little resistance.

The Spanish used the Tainos like slaves to work on farms and in mines. Through overwork, poor treatment, and diseases brought in by the Spanish, the natives died in large numbers. Almost the entire Indian population died out. By 1524, the Spaniards were importing African slaves from the West African tribes of Bantu, Congolese, Dahoman, Mandingo, and Yoruba to take over the work previously done by the Indians.

Spain and its allies were defeated by the British in the War of the Spanish Succession, and as a result, in 1713 in the Treaty of Utrecht, Spain was forced to end its trade monopoly over Cuba.

Spanish rule of Cuba continued until 1762, when the British captured Havana. The next year, they traded it back to Spain in exchange for Florida, and Spanish rule continued until the end of the nineteenth century. By then, many Cuban patriots wanted independence from Spain, and there were signs that the Spanish Empire was breaking up.

In 1791 there was a massive slave revolt on Saint Domingue. There was a long and bloody war, and in 1804, the colony declared itself the independent nation of Haiti. During the fighting, many left the island and fled to Cuba. In the years that followed, other Spanish colonies became independent from Spain. By 1825, Cuba and Puerto Rico were the only remaining colonies in the Americas.

The United States worried about Cuba being so close to its mainland. There was a fear that an enemy nation could take over Cuba and use it as a base from which to attack the United States. Many people in Cuba and the United States wanted to annex Cuba to the United States.

In the late 1800s, there were many uprisings in Cuba by rebels who were seeking Cuban independence. Some planters freed their slaves. Others resisted this movement. In general, American sympathies were with the rebels. This fighting, often referred to as the Ten Years' War, was lost by the rebels. But the uprisings did not end.

Jose Marti and Maximo Gomez launched the second war for Cuban Independence in the spring of 1895. Marti was killed in one of the early battles. By late spring 1987, the Liberation Army was near victory. But the Cuban revolutionary movement was splintered into three groups with different ideas about Cuba's future.

The U.S. diplomatic envoy in Cuba worried about the interests of American citizens in Cuba and requested that a battleship be sent to show intent to protect them. On February 15, 1898, the United States battleship *Maine* mysteriously blew up in Havana harbor. This precipitated the Spanish-American War. When the United States won this war, it took Cuba, Puerto Rico, the Philippines, and Guam.

When the United States Congress declared war on Spain, it also passed the Teller Amendment. This amendment stated that the United States would not maintain a permanent jurisdiction over Cuba. But a provisional military government was set up that lasted until 1902.

Cuba found that it had exchanged Spanish rule for American control. Marti's visions of land reform and labor rights were not carried out. Although Cuba was granted independence in 1902, it was forced to accept the Platt Amendment as part of its new constitution. The Platt Amendment made Cuba a dependency of the United States. It provided that the United States could buy or lease Cuban land for military bases and that the United States could intervene on behalf of Cuban independence.

Many struggles took place as Cuba coped with its new independence. In the 1920s, Cuba was under the dictatorship of Gerardo Machado y Morales. Revolutionaries overthrew this government, and Ramon Grau San Martin became president. Fulgencio Batista y Zaldivar took over the government as a dictator in 1934. In 1934 the Platt Amendment was terminated. In 1944, Cuba briefly had a representative democracy, but a strong middle class did not develop. Batista returned to power in 1952.

In 1953, Fidel Castro attempted to storm the Cuban army barracks in Santiago. He was captured, jailed, and later released. He went to Mexico and organized an invasion of Cuba.

Castro landed in Oriente Province. Peasants, students, and liberals joined him in guerilla warfare. Some of his chief supporters had strong sympathies for Communism.

In two years, Castro brought about Batista's downfall. In January 1959, Castro took over the government in Havana. For the first few months, Cubans seemed happy with their new government. But elections were postponed, and before long, Castro allied his government with the Communist world. Under Castro, Cuba began trading with the U.S.S.R.

In 1960, Cuba began to nationalize sugar plantations, factories, and industries. Americans who had invested in Cuban businesses suffered losses. Foreigners were barred from ownership. By 1962, the United States had imposed a complete embargo against Cuba.

Cubans who owned small businesses found them taken over by the government. Many Cubans left the island, some coming to the United States. Miami, Florida, especially became home to thousands of Cuban exiles.

Some of these exiles attempted to land on the southern coast of Cuba and set up a rebel government. Their efforts, known as the Bay of Pigs, failed, and the exiles were killed or captured.

In 1962, the Soviet Premier, Nikita Khrushchev, agreed to install in Cuba defense weapons, including nuclear missiles. More than 40,000 Soviet troops were to accompany the weapons.

President Kennedy sent aircraft carriers to prevent any more weapons shipments. He also demanded that any missiles in place should be removed. Khrushchev agreed to these demands on the condition that the United States would never invade Cuba.

Cuba received massive amounts of economic aid from the Communists, which allowed Cuba to survive after severing its ties with the United States.

Castro created a police state to assure there would be no opposition to his revolution. In 1976, the Cuban government adopted a new constitution based on the Soviet model.

In 1980, Castro announced that those who wished to leave Cuba were free to do so. Between March and October of that year, thousands of Cubans fled Cuba, most of them coming to the United States.

Since the Cuban revolution, conditions have improved for the peasants. They receive better salaries, live in better homes, and their children attend free public schools and have access to medical care. Conditions in many cities, however, have deteriorated and the standard of living has fallen.

Government

Under Castro's leadership, Cuba got a new constitution in 1976. This constitution recognizes the leadership role of the Cuban Communist Party. Fidel Castro has been head of state since 1959 and is the first secretary of the Cuban Communist party and the president of the Council of State. His brother, Raul Castro, serves as second secretary.

The Cuban constitution, which was drawn up in 1976, was based on the Soviet Union's 1936 constitution. The Cuban constitution was revised in 1992, and the revisions included secret ballot elections, tolerance for religion, ending the state monopoly on trade, and allowing some private investment in companies.

The top three bodies of the Communist party in Cuba are the Central Committee, the Political Bureau, and the Secretariat.

Cuba is divided into fourteen provinces, which in turn are divided into 169 municipalities. The provincial and municipal assemblies oversee local services such as schools, hospitals, utilities, and transportation.

Cubans vote for their municipal delegates and these delegates do not have to be members of the Communist party. The municipalities elect delegates to attend higher assemblies, but the assemblies meet only occasionally. Most of the power is exercised by executive committees controlled by boards dominated by the Communist party.

The chief legislative body in Cuba is the national assembly. In 1993, there were 589 members. These members are elected every five years by voters aged sixteen and older. Eighty percent of the members belong to the Communist party.

The National Assembly holds two sessions a year and may be called to sit for special sessions. This assembly elects from its members and is guided by a 31-member Council of State. The Council of State is made up of the president, 5 vice presidents, 1 secretary, and 23 members.

The National Assembly selects the president, who serves as both head of state and head of government. Fidel Castro has held this position since the constitution first went into effect. His brother, Raul, is first vice-president.

The president selects the heads of all the government ministries and these top officials make up the Council of Ministers. This group conducts foreign policy and trade and draws up the budget. Fidel and Raul Castro lead the Council of Ministers. Raul Castro is minister of the armed forces and Fidel Castro is commander in chief.

There is a People's Supreme Court, the members of which are appointed by the National Assembly. There are a Criminal Court, a Civil and Administrative Court, a Labor Court, a Military Court, and a Court for State Security. Beneath these high courts there are provincial and municipal courts.

Religion

Until Fidel Castro came to power, the majority of people in Cuba were Roman Catholics. Under Castro's Communist government in 1961, all religious processions and holidays were banned. Many priests and nuns were expelled. The government claimed that Cuba was an atheist state.

The 1992 constitution brought about some changes. Religious believers were allowed to belong to the Cuban Communist party, and discrimination for religious beliefs was outlawed.

It is estimated that about half of Cubans consider themselves nonreligious. Another 40 percent are Roman Catholics and about 3 or 4 percent are Protestants. Only about 80,000 Cubans regularly attend Catholic Church services.

Many Cubans subscribe to Afro-Cuban beliefs, and a small number of Cubans practice a secretive religion called *Santeria.* This was first practiced in Africa and was brought to Cuba by slaves. It involves the worship of saints as well as the casting of spells.

Other beliefs include Voodoo, widely practiced on Haiti and also practiced by some Cubans, which involves invoking the voodoo spirit world through magical prayers and rites, and *Palo Mante,* which also relies on the power of black magic. A small number of people adhere to a religion open to men only, *Abakua,* which originated in Africa.

Education

One of the achievements of the regime of Fidel Castro is the improvement of schooling throughout Cuba. The literacy rate rose from 75 percent in 1955 to 96 percent in 1996. The state provides transportation, textbooks, equipment, and school meals.

Education is free from the elementary to the university level. School is in session from September through June. Most students wear uniforms provided by the government. Common uniforms are khaki or blue trousers or skirts, with a white blouse or shirt and a red neckerchief.

The state operates day-care and preschool centers to encourage mothers to work. Babies are admitted at forty-five days old.

Children begin school at age six and most attend school through the age of fifteen. In the rural areas, thousands of children attend boarding schools and return home only on the weekends. Part of the school curriculum is to learn about soil and cultivation. Students spend time planting and growing crops.

After elementary school, students may attend a vocational technical school to prepare for work, attend an elementary teacher-training school, or attend a basic school. Secondary students study both English and Russian languages. Science and math are stressed. Before being graduated, all students are expected to perform public service as part of their studies.

Good work in a basic secondary school may lead to attendance at a college or university. Cuba has 4 universities, the largest of which is the University of Havana.

All students attending school in Cuba from the elementary to the university level work half a day without pay. Students may work in agriculture, on assembly lines, or on other industrial tasks. All students study Marxist philosophy and economics.

All men must serve three years in a branch of military service. Civilians are also mobilized in semi-military forces, such as the Militia of Territorial Troops.

Immigrants

Spanish colonists introduced sugarcane to Cuba, and as the sugar industry grew, Cuban plantation owners needed labor. Between 1600 and 1886, hundreds of thousands of Africans were brought to Cuba to work on plantations.

In addition to the Africans who were brought as slaves to work on plantations, Chinese indentured labrorers were brought to Cuba in the middle of the 1800s. There remains today a small Chinese segment of the Cuban population. Large numbers of Spanish immigrants came to Cuba from the Canary Islands at the beginning of the twentieth century.

Today whites make up almost 66 percent of the population, blacks make up 12 percent, and people of mixed white and black races make up about 22 percent. About 1 percent are Chinese.

Many exiles fled Cuba for the United States after 1959 when Fidel Castro established a Communist government there. Between 1959 and the end of 1980, it is estimated that more than a million Cubans left the country and came to the United States, Spain, and other Latin American countries. Many of the immigrants did not intend to stay permanently in the United States but expected to return to Cuba.

From 1981 to 1990, 159,200 Cubans immigrated to the United States. During the period of 1991 to 1995, another 68,400 Cubans came. Although Cubans branched out throughout the United States, huge numbers stayed in Miami, Florida. They established a neighborhood known as "Little Havana."

This immigration of Cubans into Miami revitalized the city. The Cuban Refugee Emergency Center in Miami helped many of these people get started in their new lives. Cubans found low-paying jobs at first but gradually worked their way into middle-class professions. Many established businesses of their own and hired other Cubans.

Some of these immigrants were "boat people." In 1994, thousands of Cubans set to sea in small rafts or boats trying to make the dangerous trip to the United States. U.S. Coast Guard ships picked up thousands of these rafters, kept them for a time at Guantanamo Bay, and eventually admitted them into the United States.

Language

Regardless of their backgrounds, Cubans all speak Spanish, which is the nation's official language. Because many early explorers and seafarers were Spanish, we also find Spanish names throughout the United States, such as Arizona and Florida.

The first Spaniards in Cuba came from Andalusia and this has influenced the way Spanish is spoken in Cuba. There is a relaxation of consonants at the ends of words and a tendency to drop the pronunciation of "s" at the ends of words.

Because at one time before the revolution Cuba had close relations with the United States, many older adults in Cuba also speak English. English is also taught in the schools and is required for entrance into the university.

The Arts and Sciences

Cuban music is a unique blend of Spanish guitar and African drums. It has had a profound effect on the music and many musicians in the United States. Many dances such as the congo, rumba, and cha-cha have Cuban origins. Popular bands and groups have included Xavier Cugat, Celia Cruz (called the Queen of Salsa), and Gloria Estevan and the Miami Sound Machine.

In addition to conventional musical instruments, some Cuban instruments are original and peculiar to Cuban music groups. The *guiro* is made out of oval-shaped dried fruit and is rubbed with a stick, *maracas* are dried round fruits filled with dried seeds that are shaken rhythmically, and the *bongo* is a pair of drums bound together on which goatskins are tightly stretched.

Ignacio Cervantes (1847–1905) was a Havana-born concert pianist and a well known composer. Later Cuban composers include Leo Brouwer and Aurelio de la Vega. Ernesto Lecuona (1896–1963) wrote serious works as well as popular songs. Horacio Gutierrez made his piano debut with the Havana Symphony Orchestra in 1959, and in 1970 won a silver medal in the Tchaikovsky Competition held in Moscow.

Cuban rhythms influenced other composers, too. George Bizet wrote a Cuban-influenced "Habanera," and George Gershwin wrote a "Cuban Overture." American jazz musicians such as Stan Kenton, Artie Shaw, and Dizzy Gillespie were influenced by the rhythms of mambo.

The Great Theater of Havana (sometimes called the Garcia Lorca Theater) was built in 1837. In its early history, foreign companies performed plays there. Many plays are now organized by the Casa del Teatro under the sponsorship of the International Institute of Theatre.

The Opera, Light Opera, and National Ballet Companies also perform in the Great Theater of Havana. Alicia Alonzo was prima ballerina and founded the National Ballet of Cuba. Havana also supports a symphony orchestra, *The Orquesta Sinfonica Nacional.* Two other dance companies in Cuba are Camaguey Ballet and Cuban National Dance.

Many filmmakers in Cuba have made a name for themselves internationally, but films and literature are heavily controlled and influenced by the government.

In the late 1700s, a Cuban artist, Vicente Escobar, was noted for his portraits, and in the 1800s, Esteban Chartrand gained a reputation for landscapes. In the early twentieth century, well-known artists such as Amelia Pelaez, Carlos Enriquez, and Wilfredo Lam, dealt with native subjects in Cuba. Wilfreda Lam's work, *La Jungle,* is in the Museum of Modern Art in New York. Raul Martinez introduced pop art into Cuba. One of his well-known works, painted in 1970, is *The Island.*

Literature in Cuba is often tied with the revolution. The revolutionary leader, Jose Marti, for example, is known as both a patriot and as a poet. Poetry is regularly published in newspapers and magazines. In the twentieth century, two Cuban writers who have been praised internationally are the poet Nicolas Guillen and the novelist Alejo Carpentier.

Although he was born in the United States, the writer Ernest Hemingway spent much of his life just outside Havana at an estate called Finca Vigia. Today Finca Vigia is preserved as a museum.

Food

Cuban cooking is a combination of traditional Spanish foods and Caribbean fruits and vegetables. Although many spices are used, Cuban food is milder than that of most neighboring Latin American countries. It is spicy but not hot. Popular dishes include *moros y cristianos,* which is rice with black beans; *arroz con pollo,* which is rice and chicken; *ropa vieja* or shredded flank steak; and *cerdo asada,* which is roast pork. Crocodile meat is sometimes eaten, and turtle meat is used in stews and soups. The most basic Cuban food is rice. It is often served with beans.

Common side dishes served with a Cuban meal include fried plantains, sweet potatoes, cassava, and malanga. Guava pastries and *flan,* a custard topped with burned sugar, are popular desserts.

When Cuban children come home from school, they often enjoy a snack. A popular one is *pan con timba,* a bread roll that has guava and cheese inside.

Cuba is famous for its rum, which is a liquor distilled from sugarcane. Light and dark rum are made. Cubans also enjoy a sweet drink called *guarapo,* pure sugarcane juice on ice. *Batidos* are nonalcoholic beverages made with any of the tropical fruits found on the island.

With parental help and supervision, students might enjoy preparing Cuban's unofficial national dish, *moros y cristianos.*

Moros y Christianos

2 tablespoons olive oil

1 chopped onion

1 minced clove of garlic

1 sliced green pepper

2 chopped tomatoes

8 oz. cooked black beans

6 oz. rice

$^3/_4$ pint water

salt and pepper

Heat the olive oil in a saucepan. Add onion, garlic, and green pepper. Sauté until tender. Add the tomatoes and stir until a thick consistency is reached. Season with salt and pepper and add the cooked black beans. Then add the rice and water. Cover the saucepan and continue cooking until the water has been absorbed. Cubans often serve this over plantains.

Recreation

Many Cubans vacation along their beautiful beaches and like to snorkel, water-ski, surf, and scuba dive. The most famous of Cuban beaches is Varadero, a ten-mile beach along the north coast, in the province of Matazas. The sand here is white and very fine.

Sport fishing is popular along Cuba's coasts. The warm seas off Cuba contain snapper, tarpon, muttonfish, swordfish, bonito, barracuda, mackerel, marlin, and shark.

The favorite national sport is baseball. The Cuban national baseball team has won over 20 world championships, including the gold medal at the 1992 and the 1996 Olympics. Cubans have made a positive impact on many major league baseball teams in the United States, giving us such players as Rafael Palmeiro of the Baltimore Orioles and Tony Oliva of the Minnesota Twins.

The government encourages sports programs beginning in primary schools. Secondary students may study fencing in school, and Cuba has a national fencing team.

Other popular sports include boxing, gymnastics, basketball, volleyball, golf, tennis, track and field, and jai alai. Cycling is one of the newer organized sports in Cuba, and several competitive cycling races are held throughout the year.

Dominoes is another popular Cuban pastime. Cuban dominoes do not stop at double sixes, but go on until double nines. Having more pieces makes the game more challenging.

Individuals representing Cuba have done well in Olympic competition. They have won Olympic medals in running, high jumping, heavy weight boxing, and track.

Customs and Traditions

Many holidays in Cuba are different now from the way they were prior to Cuba becoming a Communist country. For example, Christmas is no longer a public holiday. The first of January is no longer celebrated as New Year's Day but it is celebrated as Liberation Day. It commemorates President Batista's flight from office and the coming to power of Fidel Castro.

There are ten national holidays and each has a political significance. January 1 is the anniversary of the victory of the revolution, January 28 marks the birthday of Jose Marti, February 24 celebrates the beginning of the 1895 revolution, and March 13 is the anniversary of the attack on the presidential palace.

April 19 marks the Bay of Pigs Victory and May 1 is International Labor Day. On July 25–27, Cubans celebrate remembrance of the national revolution. October 8 marks the anniversary of the death of Che Guevara, and October 10 is the anniversary of the start of the 1868 War of Independence. December 2 is celebrated as the anniversary of the landing of the Granma.

Cuba's major annual festival takes place on July 26. This carnival is a national holiday and celebrates the anniversary of the 1953 revolt when Fidel Castro tried to capture the Moncada army base during the Santiago festivities. As part of the celebration, there are fantastic costumes, floats, and parades.

The July 26 Remembrance of the National Rebellion holiday coincides with historical traditional carnival days. It represents a blending of Spanish and African cultures. It began as the celebration of Catholic holidays, but over the years slaves joined in parades with dancing, music making, drumming, and costumes celebrating their African folklore. The original carnival marked the time after the sugarcane was cut and was marked by feasting, music, and dancing. In Santiago de Cuba there is a museum dedicated to preserving artifacts associated with the old July carnival days.

Some families continue to celebrate religious holidays. Children in Cuba used to receive their holiday gifts on January 6 at the feast of the Dia de Reyes. But nowadays, gifts are given and received on July 26.

In Cuba, as in Spain, towns celebrate the feast of the town on its own special day, depending on the town's patron saint. In Camaguey, for example, the Feast of San Juan is celebrated on June 24. Because the Feast of Saint Peter and Saint Paul is celebrated on June 29, the Feast of San Juan is extended from June 24 through June 29.

Indeed, the whole month of June is part of the carnival celebration in Camaguey. During the first week of the month, decorations go up as neighborhoods compete to be the best decorated in the city. Flame tree and palm tree branches, paper flowers, and colored lights are used. People dress in costumes and parades of floats pass through the town at night. At the end of the parade, people dance through the streets to the rhythm and music of drums.

African gods or *orishas* may be honored today on a Catholic saint's day. People celebrate the African *orisha* Babalu Aye on December 17, which is also the Catholic St. Lazarus' day. These days are celebrated with music and dancing and crowds often wear colorful costumes.

Suggested Activities

Writing

1. At various points in history, the world has seemed close to nuclear war. One of these times was the Cuban Missile Crisis of 1962. With the help of a media specialist, have two interested students research this crisis. Who was involved? What provoked the crisis? What concessions ended the crisis? How did Cuba benefit from this? Ask the two students to write a report for the class sharing what they learned. They should include a bibliography of their sources of information.

Reading

2. Books are helpful in the study of any country, but they become out of date. Current information can be found in newspapers and magazines. Invite a small group of interested students to research what has been in the news about Cuba during the past year. Have them gather information, take notes, and share their information with the class. Two useful resources for students to use are *Readers' Guide to Periodical Literature* and *Children's Magazine Guide*.

Vocabulary

3. During the unit of study on Cuba, encourage students to add 3 x 5-inch cards to a bulletin board giving words in Spanish and their English equivalents. Students may collect their Spanish words and phrases as they do reading.

Here are a few words to use as "starters": *barco*—boat, *calle*—street, *castillo*—castle, *escuela*—school, *helado*—ice cream, *hola*—hello, *adios*—goodbye, *playa*—beach, *primaria*—elementary school, and *secundaria*—secondary school.

Math

4. The unit of money in Cuba is the *peso*. The peso is divided into 100 units called *centavos*. There is a rate of exchange between American dollars and Cuban pesos. Have a student find out through calling a local bank what the current rate of exchange is. Using that rate of exchange, have students determine what one dollar, ten dollars, and twenty dollars are worth in Cuban centavos.

Social Studies

5. During the time that the United States maintained a provisional military government over Cuba, a medical battle was fought over yellow fever, an often-fatal virus. Many people played a role in successfully combating this disease. Among them were Carlos Juan Finlay, George M. Sternberg, and Walter Reed.

Invite a small group of interested students to read about this disease and the development of an effective treatment for it. They should present their findings to the class in the form of a paper, that includes a bibliography of resources. Students can find useful information about Walter Reed at http://wrair-www.army.mil/welcome/reedHistory.htm, and additional information on George M. Sternberg at http://www.med.virginia.edu/hs-library/historical/yelfev/pan8.html.

Geography

6. Cuba is the world's seventh largest island and the largest of the Antilles. Ask a pair of students to make a large scale map of the islands in the Caribbean, label each one, and show the capital of each. Post the map on a classroom bulletin board to share with the class during this unit of study.

Music

7. The music of Cuba is a combination of Afro-Cuban rhythms. With guidance from the school music educator, find tapes, CDs, or records of Cuban music to share with the class. Two possibilities, both available from Multicultural Media, RR 3, Box 6655, Granger Road, Barre, Vermont, 05641, are *Cuba: I Am Time* and *El Camino de La Salsa. Cuba: I Am Time* (4CD Order #BJE-500) is a 4-CD collection including a 112-page booklet of notes, histories, and essays. *El Camino de La Salsa* (CD Order # WDR-30) features Afro-Cuban music through six selected groups originally recorded in Havana.

Art

8. Cuba has a beautiful coat-of-arms known as the royal palm. Ask a student who is interested to find a colored picture of this coat-of-arms and to draw it to share with the class. The student should be able to describe the various parts and what they stand for. (It is flanked on the left and right by oak and laurel branches. A seascape represents the mouth of the Gulf of Mexico. There are a key, blue and white diagonal bars, a royal palm, two mountains, a liberty pole, and a red wool cap with a lone white star.)

Drama/Movement

9. Dance is integral to Cuban culture, with origins partly in Africa and partly in Spain. Perhaps a local dance school could send an instructor or students with CDs or tapes to school to demonstrate Cuban dances such as traditional rumba, mambo, conga, tango, or danzon, which is related to the cha-cha-cha.

Dress

10. There is really no national costume in Cuba. People wear light cotton clothes. The closest thing to a national costume is the *guayabera*. This is a cotton top that is a cross between a shirt and a jacket. It dates back to the eighteenth century. The guayabera is decorated with embroidery and is worn by both sexes. Ask an interested student to try to locate such a garment or a picture of a guayabera and bring it to class to share.

Cooking

11. *Batidos* are a Cuban version of our milkshakes. They are very popular and are often served as a refresher in the middle of the day. The following is one version of this cool and refreshing drink, which could be served to the class. Makes two glasses.

Batidos

1 cup milk
$^1/_2$ cup peeled, diced, ripe mango
$^1/_2$ cup sliced bananas
$^1/_2$ cup peeled, diced, ripe peach
$^1/_2$ cup crushed ice

Place the milk, mango, bananas, peach, and ice in the container of a blender. Process until smooth, and serve.

Culminating Activity

12. The smallest amphibian in the world, the banana frog, is found in Cuba. Also found in Cuba is the tiniest mammal in the world, a shrewlike creature called the Almiqui. Among Cuba's flowers and trees are flame trees, African tulip trees, the Flor San Pedro orchid, and the frangipani. Nine-hundred species of fish are found in Cuban waters,

including the clown fish and queen angelfish. Invite each student to choose and research a favorite from the flora and fauna of Cuba to share with the class. Students should draw (or with permission photocopy) a picture to show and should write a brief report including a bibliography of their information sources. After the oral presentations, the reports and pictures could be gathered into a class book.

Suggested Reading

Appel, Todd M. *Jose Marti.* New York: Chelsea House, 1992.

Crouch, Clifford W. *Cuba.* Philadelphia, Pa.: Chelsea House, 1997.

Cummins, Ronnie. *Cuba.* Milwaukee, Wisc.: Gareth Stevens, 1991.

Galdone, Paul. *Old Woman and Her Pig.* New York: Whittlesey House, 1960.

Gernand, Renee. *The Cuban Americans.* New York: Chelsea House, 1988.

Gonzales, Lucia M. *The Bossy Gallito.* New York: Scholastic, 1994.

Kimmel, Eric A. *The Old Woman and Her Pig.* New York: Holiday House, 1992.

LaFray, Joyce. *Cuba Concina, The Tantalizing World of Cuban Cooking—Yesterday, Today, and Tomorrow.* New York: Hearst Books, 1994.

Leitzinger, Rosanne. *The Old Woman and Her Pig.* San Diego, Calif.: Harcourt Brace Jovanovich, 1993.

Marvis, Barbara. *Rafael Palmeiro, A Real-Life Reader Biography.* Childs, Mass.: Mitchell Lane, 1998.

Morrison, Marion. *Cuba.* Austin, Tex.: Raintree Steck-Vaughn, 1998.

Rockwell, Anne. *The Old Woman and Her Pig, and 10 Other Stories.* New York: Crowell, 1979.

Selsdon, Esther. *The Life and Times of Fidel Castro.* Philadelphia, Pa.: Chelsea House, 1998.

Sheehan, Sean. *Cuba.* New York: Marshall Cavendish, 1995.

Vasquez, Ana Maria B. and Rosa E. Casas. *Cuba.* Chicago, Ill.: Childrens Press, 1987.

The Dominican Republic

A Folktale from the Dominican Republic

Most of the folktales of the Dominican Republic are derived from European origins, but a few also have African parallels. Tales of tricking Death and the Devil appear in *The Types of the Folktale in Cuba, Puerto Rico, The Dominican Republic and Spanish Speaking South America* by Terrence Leslie Hansen. Dorothy Sharp Carter, in *Greedy Mariani and Other Folktales of the Antilles*, has adapted "How the Clever Doctor Tricked Death" from a tale retold by Manuel J. Andrade in his *Folklore de la Republica Dominicana*.

Tricking Death Twice

There was once a charming young man, filled with ideas and a desire to be rich. He told wonderful stories to all who would listen, but never troubled himself to find work. One day, Death appeared before him and said, "I've taken a fancy to you, and I'm willing to make you a very good bargain. You can be a famous and rich doctor. I will help you, and you will be able to cure anyone that you lay your hands upon."

"What is the trick?" asked the young man.

"When you see a patient," explained Death, "if you see me standing at the foot of the bed, you can be certain of a cure. But, if you see me standing at the head of the bed, don't waste your time. There will be no cure, for that patient is mine."

The young man agreed. He went to the nearest town and opened up an office. When a patient came, the doctor had him lay down on a bed. The doctor glanced at the head and the foot of the bed. Death always stood at the foot.

The doctor would smile and then put his hands first on the patient's head and then over his heart and the patient would be cured. Word spread quickly of the great *medico*. The doctor cured thousands of people and became very rich.

One day two armed messengers came running to the doctor's office. "Come quickly," one said. "The king commands you to come to the palace at once and cure his beautiful daughter who is deathly ill. If you succeed," the messenger continued, "the king promises you half his wealth and his daughter's hand in marriage. If you refuse to come or if you fail, the punishment is death."

The young doctor hurried with the messengers to the palace. As he went, he thought how glorious his life would be, married to the princess and with enormous wealth.

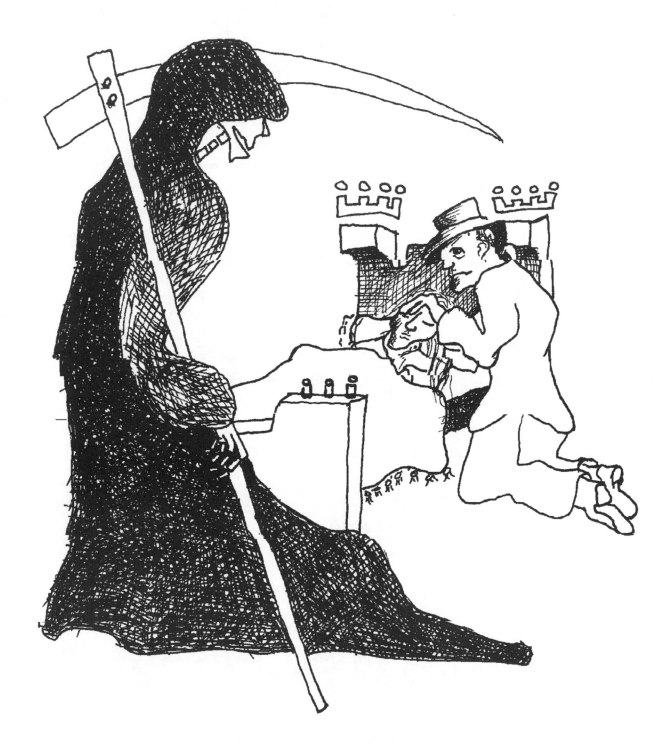

"When you see a patient," explained Death, "if you see me standing at the foot of the bed, you can be certain of a cure."

Once he reached the palace, the doctor went to the room of the princess. Near death, she lay on her bed. As usual, the doctor glanced at the foot of the bed. Death was not there! The doctor turned to look at the head of the bed, and there stood Death.

Although astonished, the doctor kept his wits. He quickly picked up the bed and swung it around so that the foot of the bed was toward the wall where Death stood. Quickly the doctor put his hands on the head of the princess and then over her heart. Cured, the beautiful girl sat up in bed and gazed lovingly at the doctor.

The wedding was to take place in one week. But the night before the wedding, Death came to call. He took the doctor with him into the heavens and showed him millions of oil lamps that were burning.

"Each of these lamps stands for a life on earth. When a light goes out, a life goes out," Death explained. "Here is your lamp. See, the oil is almost all gone. Because you tricked me, you will die within five minutes."

The quick-witted doctor said, "Please give me enough oil to last fifteen minutes, and I will tell you one last wonderful story."

The young man watched as Death dipped out oil into his lamp, enough to last for fifteen minutes. Then the young man began to weave his tale. As he talked, Death fell asleep. Quickly the young doctor filled his oil lamp to the very brim and then stole back to earth to marry and live a long and happy life with the beautiful princess.

Background Information

The Antilles islands curve in an arc from Florida to Venezuela. These islands are actually the summits of a submerged mountain range. There are two main groups of islands, the Greater Antilles to the north, and the Lesser Antilles to the south.

The Dominican Republic is part of the Greater Antilles. The four islands in the Greater Antilles are Cuba, Jamaica, Puerto Rico, and Hispaniola. Hispaniola lies about 600 miles southeast of Florida and is shared by the nations of Haiti and the Dominican Republic. The Dominican Republic occupies the eastern two-thirds of the island. Cuba is to the northwest and Puerto Rico is to the east.

The Dominican Republic has 977 miles of coastline. Located just south of the Tropic of Cancer, it is bordered by the Atlantic Ocean to the north and the Caribbean Sea to the south. The Mona Passage lies between the eastern tip of the Dominican Republic and Puerto Rico. After Cuba, the Dominican Republic is the largest nation in the Caribbean.

All of these islands in the Greater Antilles are in the tropics and are cooled by the northeast trade winds. Although they receive considerable rain, most days are sunny. The average annual temperature in the Dominican Republic is 77°F. Temperatures in the valleys, however, may go above 100°F, and temperatures in the high mountains may reach lows of 32°F. The Dominican Republic receives an average of 60 inches of rain per year, but this varies with the region.

The most dangerous weather time is from July to October, which is hurricane season. Hurricanes are formed over warm tropical seas and develop in the trade winds. About once every two years, hurricanes hit the island with winds up to 125 miles per hour. Most strike the southern part of the island along the Hoya de Enriquillo.

The population of the Dominican Republic is 8,228,151. It occupies 18,792 square miles. Other than being located on the same island, the people in the Dominican Republic have little in common with the people of Haiti. They speak different languages and have a different culture and different racial heritage.

The Dominican Republic contains rugged mountains and fertile valleys. Valuable woods grow in these mountains, including mahogany and pine. The highest peak in the West

Indies, Pico Duarte at 10,370 feet, is located in the Dominican Republic.

The largest mountain range, the Cordillera Central, divides the country in half. These mountains run from the Haitian border westward almost the length of the island. An extension in the east is called the Cordillera Oriental, and in the north there is a smaller, parallel range called the Cordillera Septentrional.

The northern region of the Dominican Republic along the Atlantic Ocean consists of a coastal plain running from the city of Montecristi to the city of Nagua. Below the southern slopes of the Cordillera Septentrional is the rich Cibao Valley. Located here on the Yaque del Norte River is the city of Santiago de los Caballeros.

To the east of the city, the plain is called the Vega Real or Royal Plain. This flood plain is the most prosperous part of the Dominican Republic. The farms in this rich agricultural area produce food for home consumption such as rice, corn, and beans, and crops for export including coffee, cacao, and tobacco.

In the middle of the Dominican Republic are the Cordillera Central mountains. East and south of them is the Caribbean coastal plain. There are limestone terraces here near the foothills of the Cordillera Oriental. The western edge of the central region has poor agricultural land.

In the southwest region are more mountains, the Sierra de Neiba and the Sierra de Bahoruco. Between these ranges is Lake Enriquillo, the largest lake in the Caribbean Islands. It is a salt-water lake and contains crocodiles.

The most important river in the Dominican Republic is the Yaque del Norte, which is approximately 184 miles long. It rises in the Cordillera Central mountains at an elevation of 8,462 feet, crosses the Cibao Valley, and empties into the Atlantic Ocean on the northwest coast.

The Yaque del Sur River rises at an elevation of 8,900 feet in the Cordillera Central, comes through the mountains, and empties in Neiba Bay on the southern coast. Other rivers include the Artibonite along the Haitian border, the San Juan River, which joins up with the Yaque del Sur, the Ozama and the Isabela in the Caribbean coastal plain, and the Yuna River, which empties into Samana Bay.

The Dominican Republic has more than 1,000 miles of beaches. Many of these are famous resorts favored by tourists. The Caribbean's longest stretch of white sand is Punta Cana, located on the easternmost coast.

The northern coast of the Dominican Republic is often called the Amber Coast. Amber jewelry is very popular with tourists. This island has the world's largest deposits of amber and these translucent, semi-precious stones range in color from pale yellow to dark brown. Especially valuable are amber, pieces containing tiny insects or small leaves.

The largest cash crop in the Dominican Republic is sugar. Sugarcane is grown on plantations in the southern and southeastern parts of the country. The Dominican Republic is the fourth largest sugar producer in the world and exports half its sugar to the United States.

Parts of the Dominican Republic are suited to livestock raising and dairy production. There is a well-established cattle industry along the coastal plain. The Dominican Republic produces enough livestock to be self-sufficient and to do some exporting. About 10 percent of the cattle are exported to the United States.

The importance of mining in the Dominican Republic grew in the 1970s. Although it employs less than 1 percent of the labor force, in 1989 mining generated 47 percent of export earnings. The primary minerals are ferronickel, bauxite, and a gold-silver alloy. Other minerals include iron, limestone, copper, gypsum, mercury, salt, sulfur, onyx, and travertine.

Tourism is of growing importance to the country. It is currently centered on a very few cities and beaches. The Dominican Republic has national parks and nature reserves that cover more than 10 percent of the country's area. Many of these are hidden in remote areas and are not currently easily accessible.

The capital of the Dominican Republic is Santo Domingo, which is the country's largest city and is also the oldest city in the Western Hemisphere. Santo Domingo has a population of more than 2 million people and is the nation's principal port.

There are buildings still standing today in Santo Domingo that were built in the sixteenth century. This section is referred to as the Colonial Zone and covers about a 12-block area. Among the famous buildings here is the

Cathedral of Saint Mary the Minor. Although it is disputed, some believe that the tomb there houses the remains of Christopher Columbus. Another old surviving building is the Alcazar de Colon, which was the headquarters for Christopher Columbus's son, Diego Columbus, when he served as governor of Hispaniola.

After a hurricane destroyed large portions of Santo Domingo in 1930, much of the city was rebuilt and is quite modern and new. Santo Domingo is home to the University of Santo Domingo, the main institution of higher learning in the nation.

The second largest city in the Dominican Republic is Santiago de los Caballeros, which is in the Cibao region. It is the agricultural center of the country. The initial settlement of this city dates to 1504. Because many wealthy families live here, it has a reputation as a center of culture.

La Romana is a provincial capital located on the southern coast. It is one of the most important medium-sized cities in the country. A popular resort area, it is also the center of the sugar industry.

Bonao is located halfway between Santo Domingo and Santiago. It is the nation's mining center. In the early 1970s rich deposits of nickel, bauxite, silver, and gold were found in this region. Since then, there has been rapid growth.

Christopher Columbus settled Puerto Plata in 1494 as the town of Isabela. Today it is the center of the hotel and tourist resort boom. It is located north of Santiago.

History

Archaeologists have tried to piece together the history of the early peoples in the West Indies. The Siboneys probably settled on the Caribbean Islands after having sailed there from the mainland of Northern America. They appear to have lived off the land and had simple tools of stone, bone, or wood.

The Arawaks came to the Caribbean from the South, moving from one island to another. They farmed and fished. It is thought that as many as 500,000 may have lived on the island of Hispaniola. Caribs came to the Caribbean from South America using Trinidad as a stepping stone. Caribs were primarily fishermen.

Christopher Columbus discovered the island of Hispaniola on December 5, 1492. His ship, the *Santa Maria*, wrecked on the Atlantic shore. Columbus claimed the island for Spain and named it La Isla Española. When he landed, he found friendly native Indians called the Tainos.

The Tainos cultivated crops such as corn, sweet potatoes, and cassava (also called *manioc*). From the cassava they made flour for bread. The Tainos grew squash, beans, peppers, and peanuts. Near their homes they also grew small amounts of tobacco with which they made cigars. It is believed that this is the first contact Europeans had with tobacco.

These early Indian villages housed about 2,000 inhabitants each. The Indians worshipped deities called *zemis*. The chief of each village might be a man or a woman. These Indians traveled in canoes that could carry up to 150 people.

After Columbus sailed back to Spain in the *Pinta*, his brother, Bartholomew Columbus, along with Nicolas de Ovando, founded Santo Domingo in 1496. This settlement became the seat of Spanish colonial government.

The Spaniards took what gold they could find from native Indians who belonged to the Taino tribe. Many Indians were forced to work as slaves. By 1524, most of the island's native population had disappeared. Spaniards replaced their native workers with slaves from Africa.

Santo Domingo declined during the sixteenth and seventeenth centuries as Spain paid more attention to Mexico and Peru. There were occasional battles with French and English pirates. In 1586, Sir Francis Drake captured the city of Santo Domingo and demanded ransom from the Spanish government for its return.

In 1696, Spain ceded to France the western third of Hispaniola through the Treaty of Ryswick. The new colony, which is present-day Haiti, was renamed Saint Domingue. In 1791, the slaves, under the leadership of Francois-Dominique Troussaint, revolted against the white landowners.

In 1797, Spain surrendered the entire island of Hispaniola to Troussaint. From 1804 to 1809, the Haitians, French, and Spanish fought for control of the island. The British aided the Spanish in driving the Haitians back to the west. In 1809 Spanish rule was reestablished in Santo Domingo.

In 1821, the Dominicans declared their independence, but within a few weeks they were taken over by neighboring Haitian armies. The Dominicans remained under the control of Haiti for twenty-two years, from 1822 to 1844.

During this time, many families fled to the mainland and the long-established clergy lost power. Fugitive slaves came from the United States and more immigration from Africa was welcomed. An attempt was made to stamp out Spanish speech and customs.

Many patriots began to plan for freeing the Dominican Republic from the Haitians. Among these was Juan Pablo Duarte. He founded a secret society, "La Trinitaria," and organized a revolt. On February 27, 1844, with financial backing from Venezuela, the Dominicans overthrew the Haitians and proclaimed the Dominican Republic. That date is now celebrated as Independence Day.

Duarte was soon exiled, and political power was placed in the hands of two generals. The new Republic had tremendous problems with corruption, coups, and assassinations. The country was reannexed by Spain in 1861, but proclaimed its independence again in 1865. A treaty in 1869 offered the Dominican Republic to the United States, but the treaty was not ratified.

Although the Dominican Republic did not become a part of the United States, the U.S. took an active interest in the country. U.S. marines occupied the Dominican Republic in 1916 and continued the occupation until 1924. During this period, the U.S. military fostered public works projects, such as roads and port facilities. Then Horacio Vasquez became president, and for six years there was relative peace and democracy.

In 1930, Rafael Trujillo became president and ruled the Dominican Republic as a dictator for thirty-one years. During this period, the capital was renamed Trujillo City. After Trujillo was assassinated in 1961, the name Santo Domingo was restored to the capital.

A democratic election was held in 1962, and Juan Bosch became president. A military group overthrew this new government within seven months. More power struggles and fighting broke out. The Organization of American States (OAS) sent a peacekeeping force, including a large number of Americans, to Santo Domingo. Under OAS auspices,

another election was held in 1966. Joaquin Balaguer became president.

In 1978, Balaguer ran against a moderate candidate, Antonio Guzman. Guzman won the election and took office in August 1978. Under Guzman's leadership, there was more political freedom. Human rights and social programs for the poor were stressed.

The United States continues to have a strong influence on life in the Dominican Republic. The country has been fairly stable since the 1970s and the various administrations have been supporters of the United States.

The majority of people who populate the Dominican Republic today are descendants of Spaniards and African slaves. About 16 percent of the population is white, 11 percent of the population is black, and about 73 percent of the population is of mixed ancestry. And in the Constanza Valley, there is a community of rice farmers descended from Japanese laborers.

There remains in the Dominican Republic a small landowning upper class, a middle class made up of shopkeepers, teachers, clerical employees and professionals, and a lower class made up of the rural poor and the urban poor.

Government

Throughout its history, the Dominican Republic has had unstable governments with many military coups and assassinations. Because a high rate of poverty remains today, there is still considerable social unrest.

Voting in the Dominican Republic is compulsory for all citizens aged eighteen or older and for any married individual regardless of age. But this requirement is not enforced. Members of the police and armed forces are not allowed to vote. And candidates for president must not have been on active duty with the armed forces or the police within one year prior to the election.

The Dominican Republic is governed under its twenty-fifth constitution, which was ratified in 1966. A president and vice-president, elected by popular vote, carry out the executive branch of government. They are elected to four-year terms but may run for re-election. The president appoints a cabinet of 15 secretaries and has authority to appoint and dismiss almost all public officials.

The president reports annually to Congress on his administration. He receives the representatives of foreign governments, directs diplomatic negotiations, and concludes treaties.

The legislative branch of government is carried out by the National Congress, which is composed of a Senate and a Chamber of Deputies. Members are elected directly for four-year terms. The senate has 30 members, one from each province and one from the national district government of Santo Domingo. The chamber of deputies has about 120 members. These members provide proportional representation from provincial districts. One member represents 50,000 people, and each district gets a minimum of two deputies.

The Congress meets for two 90-day sessions, one that begins in February and one that begins in August. It can levy taxes and determine the method of tax collection and expenditure. It can also determine the number of courts of appeal, and it can legislate on immigration.

A Supreme Court heads the judicial branch of government. There are nine members who are elected by the Senate and serve renewable four-year terms. The civil and criminal codes that form the legal system were adopted in 1884.

Below the Supreme Court of Justice are courts of appeal located in various cities. Each court has five judges, including the president. Each of the provinces and the National District form judicial districts and in each there is a court of first instance. There are also a series of special courts such as land courts, juvenile courts, labor courts, and military courts.

Religion

The predominant religion in the Dominican Republic is Roman Catholicism. Although it is estimated that 95 percent of the population is Catholic, few Dominicans attend mass regularly, and some people sometimes mix elements of Catholicism with folk spirituality. The Dominican Republic has 1 archdiocese, 8 dioceses, and 250 parishes.

The Catholic Church lost much of its power when Haitians occupied the Dominican Republic. When Trujillo came to power in the Dominican Republic, he persuaded the Vatican in Rome to send many new priests to his country. And in 1954, Trujillo established Roman Catholicism as the official religion of the Dominican Republic. After Trujillo's dictatorship ended, the power of the Catholic Church decreased again.

The Catholic Church carries a major responsibility for public health and education. The church manages hospitals, clinics, orphanages, convalescent homes, and nursery schools. It also runs many elementary and secondary schools, colleges, and technical institutes.

About 2 percent of Dominicans are Protestants. Protestantism gained a foothold when migrant Protestants came from North America in the 1820s. Evangelical Protestants also gained influence in the rural parts of the country during the 1960s and 1970s. The major Protestant groups are Seventh Day Adventists, and members of the Dominican Evangelical Church and the Assemblies of God.

About 0.02 percent of the population is Jewish. Most of these people immigrated just before World War II to escape Hitler. Almost all settled in Santo Domingo and Sousa.

A few Dominicans practice folk religions such as Voodoo, which was introduced to the Republic by Haitian descendants of African slaves.

Education

About 83 percent of the population of the Dominican Republic is literate. Children must attend school beginning at age seven for a minimum of six years of primary education. In reality, not all rural schools offer all six grades of education, and some children do not attend because they go to work, lack transport, or lack the money to purchase needed uniforms. It is estimated that while three-fourths of Dominicans begin school, only one-third finish.

English is taught to students in the fifth, sixth, seventh, and eighth grades and in the secondary schools.

Secondary education is not required, and only about 45 percent of the students attend secondary school beginning at age thirteen. At the secondary level, students must buy their own textbooks. Secondary students may attend a six-year school geared toward university admission or attend a school geared toward teacher training or other vocations.

Many urban families who can afford it send their children to private secondary schools. The Roman Catholic Church operates most of these.

There are 8 universities, some public and some private, in the Dominican Republic. Wealthy families often send their children to attend schools in the United States.

Immigrants

Many people from the Dominican Republic and the rest of the West Indies left their islands and helped in the building of America's railroads and in the construction of the Panama Canal in the early twentieth century. In the 1950s, thousands of West Indians migrated to the United Kingdom where they found jobs in hospitals, restaurants, and public transportation.

Between 8 and 15 percent of the Dominican population lives abroad. From 1981 to 1990, 251,800 people immigrated to the United States from the Dominican Republic. During 1991 to 1995, another 218,500 came.

Many come to avoid the high unemployment rate in their country. Others come for higher income, to pursue their education, or to join family members. Many retain strong ties to relatives back in the Dominican Republic and regularly send money to their families.

Dominicans migrate primarily to New York. And although some have made headlines as drug dealers, many more are skilled workers such as doctors and teachers. Others have opened small businesses such as stores, bars, and restaurants. Some work in factories. Today, Dominicans are the seventh largest immigrant group in the United States.

C-Town is a Dominican success story. It is a chain of owner-operated supermarkets created in 1975 in New York to fill the void in chain stores after many city dwellers left for the suburbs. Roughly half of these stores are owned by Dominicans. The group does more than 1 billion dollars in sales a year.

Language

Spanish is the official language of the Dominican Republic. In the Cibao region, where many of the country's oldest and most powerful families live, the spoken language contains Medieval and Renaissance words and phrases which long ago dropped out of modern Spanish. Many Dominicans are also fluent in English.

The Arts and Sciences

The arts of the Indians of the Caribbean were at first neglected. But the Institute of Anthropology, with cooperation from the University of Santo Domingo, made significant finds. They excavated a ceremonial plaza along the bank of the river Chacuey. Neighboring rocks show the traces of earliest bas relief sculpture in the Antilles. Some of the art work, mostly miniatures, of the Arawak-Taino peoples, has since been displayed.

The city of La Vega is famous for its devil masks, *diablos cojuelos.* Many crafts are also available in El Mercado Modela, a covered market place in Santo Domingo.

Among well known contemporary artists and sculptors from the Dominican Republic are Ernesto Scott, Clara Ledesma, Dario Suro, and Enrique Martinez Richiez.

Santa Domingo from its beginnings was eager to receive European culture. Poets, writers, and dramatists came to the colony and wrote and also founded a theatre movement. Soon native-born talent added to the literary scene. There were poets, essayists, and a strong early emphasis on ecclesiastic writers. Among the best known literary figures of the colonial period was Bartolome de las Casas, who recorded the early history of the Caribbean area.

In colonial times, Dominicans adapted the Spanish *romancero* or romantic ballad. Many of these ballads have been collected by specialists in folkloric art, including *Don Albertos y Don Carlos* or "The Unfaithful Wife," and *El Marinerito* or "The Little Sailor." A Dominican Folklore Society was founded in January 1946 and attempts are being made to preserve dances, roundelays, and games from the past.

During the period of Haitian control, French literary style became prominent, while many local writers fled and became literary refugees. After this period, writing began to flourish again on the island. Felix Maria del Monte earned the name of "the father of independent Dominican literature." Other literary leaders of that period were Javier Angulo Guridi, Nicolas Urena Mendoza, and Jose Joaquin Perez.

Another leading figure was the poet Fabio Fiallo. Manuel de Jesus Galvan wrote an account of early colonial times called *Enriquillo.* Many regard this as the greatest novel by a Dominican writer in the nineteenth century. Federico

Garcia Godoy wrote about the era when Santo Domingo was occupied by the U.S. Marines in *El Derrumbe,* "The Downfall." In *Canas y Bueyes* "Sugarcane and Oxen," Francisco Eugenio Moscosco, described the sugar industry. Other noted writers include Arturo Freites Roque, Dionisio Pieter, Horacio Read, Jayme Colson, and Enrique Agular. The former president of the Dominican Republic, Juan Bosch, is also known for his novels and short stories.

The major dramatists from the Dominican Republic have been Rafael A. Deligne (1863–1902), Virginia Elena Ortea (1866–1903), Arturo Pellerano Castro (1865–1916), and Ulises Heuriquez (1876–1913).

Dominican music is a mixture of native and Spanish rhythms colored with French and African influences. Out of this an authentic Dominican dance evolved, called the *merengue.* It has become the most popular dance today in the Dominican Republic and is well known worldwide.

The Dominican Republic has had an effect on world fashion. This is the homeland of designer Oscar de la Renta, and his influential creations are known throughout the world.

Food

Dominicans generally eat a light breakfast, *Desayuno,* of coffee and bread, although in the country there may be a more filling breakfast of boiled plantains. The evening meal, *Cena,* often consists of leftovers, but it may also include eggs, bread, and boiled roots. The main meal of the day, *comida,* is served at mid-day. Most meals feature large amounts of rice along with beans, *habichuelas,* and cassava, *yuca.* The national dish is *arroz con habichuelas,* beans and rice.

Plantains and bananas are plentiful. Like potatoes, plantains can be cooked in a variety of ways. *Mangu,* for example, is made from mashed green plantains fried with onions.

Locally grown mangoes, papayas, pineapples, guavas, avocados, passion fruit, coconuts, and star fruit are eaten in season. Although it is expensive, people may eat small amounts of chicken, beef, pork, or goat. Fresh fish is a popular food all along the coast.

A favorite dish throughout the nation of the Dominican Republic is *sancocho.* This is a rich stew made with meat, potatoes, plantains, and yucca. The most common meat used is goat, but pork, beef, and chicken are also used. The stew is cooked for several hours in a big iron pot.

Another common native dish is *sopa criolla dominicana* or Dominican creole soup. It contains stew meat, carrots, peppercorns, vermicelli, onions, potatoes, cabbage, and herbs. *Pastelon de vegetables,* baked vegetable cake, is a rich mixture of green beans, carrots, eggs, Parmesan cheese, peas, cabbage, beets, onions, tomatoes, pickles, and spices.

At Christmas time, Dominicans often serve *lechon asado* or roasted pig. It is frequently served with rice and beans cooked with pigeon peas.

A sweetened drink popular at Easter is *Habichuelas con dulce,* made from beans. Many fruits are grown in the Dominican Republic. In various combinations, they make delicious drinks, too. Students may enjoy making and drinking a typical West Indies punch.

Dominican Fruit Cocktail

2 peeled star fruit

8 oz. pitted cherries

1 guava, peeled, seeded, and quartered

$^1/_4$ pineapple

3 cups water

sugar to taste

Puree separately the star fruit, cherries, guava, and pineapple. Strain each through a fine sieve. Combine the juices in a large pitcher. Add the water and then sugar to taste. Serve over ice cubes.

Recreation

The United States has had a marked effect on sports in the Dominican Republic. Dominicans avidly follow major league baseball in the United States, and some of their players, such as Ramon Martinez and Felipe and Matty Allou, came to the United States to play. Juan Marichal, who played for the San Francisco Giants, became the first Dominican in the Baseball Hall of Fame.

In 1998, homerun hitter Sammy Soso from the Dominican Republic, who played for the Chicago Cubs, passed the long-standing homerun record of Roger Maris.

Baseball can accurately be called the national pastime in the Dominican Republic, where there is a Professional Winter League that runs from late October through January. Boys start playing baseball almost as soon as they can walk and join baseball teams by age six or seven.

Although baseball has the largest following, volleyball, basketball, and soccer are popular too. Wealthy people belong to clubs where they can sail, play polo, and play tennis. Water sports of all kinds, including sailing, scuba diving, windsurfing, boating, and deep-sea fishing, are popular.

Many people of the Dominican Republic enjoy hiking, cycling, and horseback riding. Children play games much like those played in the United States. *La gallinita ciega* is like blindman's bluff and *escondido* is like hide and seek.

A very popular game is dominoes. There are outdoor tables in front of homes and markets where, especially on Sundays, people may play for hours.

Customs and Traditions

National holidays include New Year's Day (January 1); *Dia de los Reyes* (day of Kings, January 6); *Nuestro Sonora de la Alta Gracia* (Our Lady of High Gratitude, January 21); Durate's Day (January 26); Independence Day (February 27); Easter; Labor Day (May 1); Corpus Christi; Restoration of Independence (August 16); *Nuestra Señora de las Mercedes* (Our Lady of Mercies, September 24); Columbus Day (October 12); and Christmas (December 25). Gifts are not exchanged at Christmas but are commonly given on January 6, Epiphany, traditionally the day the Magi arrived with gifts for the Christ child.

Catholic feasts and saints' days are often celebrated with festivals and parades. Major religious holidays include the Feast of the Circumcision, the Feast of the Epiphany, Our Lady of Altagracia Day, Saint Joseph's Day, the Feast of the Assumption, Our Lady of Mercedes Day, All Saints' Day, the Feast of the Immaculate Conception, as well as Christmas and Easter.

It is common for urban families to go to the beach or mountains during *Semana Santa,* Holy Week before Easter.

Carnival is celebrated for several weeks in the early spring. There are costume parades and other festivities. One of the most famous carnivals is the 10-day Merengue Festival in late July, which features entertainment from outdoor bands and orchestras.

People from the Dominican Republic observe many special customs when there is a death in the family. After a person has died, all water receptacles in the house are emptied. The front of the house is closed for nine days and everyone must come and go through the back door. All mirrors are covered or turned toward the wall. The family members dress in black or gray and sit with the body until the funeral the next day.

At the end of the ninth day, the mourners hold a special ceremony called *la vela de muerto,* or the vigil for the dead. Mourners may pray and sing. They make a small altar with candles and place a crucifix or picture of a saint on the altar. They also place a glass of water there for the ghost. On the first anniversary of the death, a similar ceremony is held.

Suggested Activities

Writing

1. It is estimated that the Dominican Republic has over 5,600 plant species. Invite a group of students to research the flora of this country and to write a report to share with the class on what they learn. They should find pictures of some of the unusual plants and trees and (with permission) photocopy these to accompany their report. Among some of the possible topics are: manioc, papaya, tobacco, the calabash tree, the Dominican magnolia, the bija, and the cieba or silk-cotton tree.

Reading

2. Students, with the assistance of a media specialist, may want to read books and magazine articles about the fauna of the Dominican Republic. Once they have information, they should share it in an oral report to the class. Possible topics include caiman, found around Lake Enriquillo; the rhino iguana; the palmthrush, which is the national bird; flamingos in the Rio Una Delta and in Lake Enriquillo; the *cotorra* or local parrot; the solenodon, an insectivore found only on Hispaniola and

in Cuba; the *hutia,* an endangered rodent; the manatee; and four species of sea turtles.

Vocabulary

3. Many words and phrases used in the Dominican Republic are Spanish, and some are Taino words adopted by the Spanish to describe unfamiliar objects. As students read about the Dominican Republic during their unit of study, have them put up 3 x 5-inch cards on a bulletin board giving the Spanish and/or Taino words and their English equivalents. Among these might be *hamaca*—hammock, *tabaco*—tobacco, *huracan*—hurricane, *canoa*—canoe, *cibao*—plain, and *Mi casa, su casa*—my house is your house.

Math

4. Invite a group of students to prepare story problems about traveling in the Dominican Republic for classmates to try to solve. Make some initial assumptions, such as that a car rental is $75 a day in the Dominican Republic. You will travel from place to place at 45 miles an hour and will get an average of 30 miles per gallon of gas. Gasoline will cost $1.50 per gallon. Then, using a road map, compute how much it would cost and how long it would take to drive a car from Santo Domingo to Monte Cristi; from Punta Cana to Enriquillo; and from Santiago to Rio San Juan.

Social Studies

5. In the Dominican Republic, as in most countries, there are "folk beliefs" or "remedies." One such belief is that if an owl lands on the roof of a house, it announces the death of someone in the family. Another folk belief is that opening an umbrella inside a house causes misfortune. Invite a pair of interested students to make a listing of some of the more interesting folk beliefs from around the world and post it on a classroom bulletin board. Where available, have the students indicate the name of the country in which the folk belief is common.

Geography

6. The largest lake in the Caribbean Islands, Lake Enriquillo, is located in the Dominican Republic. Invite two interested students to do some research on this lake. Exactly where is it located? How big is it? Why is it a salt lake? What kinds of creatures live in the lake? Ask the students to make an oral report to the class sharing what they learn. One source of information is http://www.nando.net/prof/caribe/Caribbean_Adventures.html.

Music

7. The most popular and influential music worldwide from the Dominican Republic is the *merengue.* The following book and CD would be useful in tracing the background of this music, which is often called the "national dance" of the Dominican Republic: *Merengue: Dominican Music and Dominican Identity* by Paul Austerlitz, Book Order # TUP-484, and *Merengue: Dominican Music and Dominican Identity* CD Order # RDR-1130. Both are available from Multicultural Media, RR 3, Box 6655, Granger Road, Barre, VT 05641. You can also visit their Web page at http://www.worldmusicstore.com.

Art

8. Invite a pair of students to research the coat-of-arms of the Dominican Republic and to draw a colorful representation of it to share with the class as they report on what they learned. Both the Bible and the cross are displayed prominently in this coat-of-arms.

Drama/Movement

9. If there is a dance troupe in your town or city that performs for schools, this would be an excellent time to invite them. If not, perhaps a film or video showing dances famous in the Dominican Republic would be available to share with students. The featured dances should include the *merengue,* the *yucca,* the *Sarambo,* the *guarapo,* the *zapateo,* and the *fandango.*

Dress

10. Carnival is celebrated as the final merrymaking before the 40 days of Lent. In the Dominican Republic, Carnival reaches a climax on February 27, Independence Day. Many Dominicans dress in fantastic masks and costumes, including designs of African origins. One of

the characters is often a horned devil, *diablo cojuelo.*

Invite a group of students, working with a library media specialist, to locate pictures of some of the costumes and especially masks that are seen in Santo Domingo, Santiago, and Monte Cristi at Carnival time. Students should make copies of these (with permission), or bring in books and magazines with photos, or make drawings of them to share with the class.

Cooking

11. The following recipe would require some adult volunteers to assist in the preparation and cooking of a simple treat from the Dominican Republic.

Frituras de Name (Fried Yam Cakes)

1 pound fresh yams, peeled and finely grated

1 tablespoon butter, melted and cooled

1 tablespoon finely grated onion

1 tablespoon finely chopped fresh parsley

Salt

Freshly ground black pepper

2 egg yolks

$^1/_4$ cup vegetable oil

In a deep bowl, combine the yams, butter, onion, parsley, salt, and a liberal grinding of pepper. Mix well. Drop in the egg yolks and beat vigorously with a large spoon until the mixture is fairly smooth and thick enough to come away from the sides of the bowl in an almost solid mass.

Preheat the oven to the lowest setting. Line a large shallow baking dish with paper towels and place it in the oven. In a heavy skillet, heat the oil over moderate heat until a light haze forms above it. For each cake, drop about a tablespoon of yam mixture into the hot oil. Cook 4 or 5 at a time, leaving space between them so that they can spread into 2 to 2$^1/_2$-inch rounds. Fry the cakes for about 4 minutes on each side, or until golden and crisp around the edges. As they brown, transfer the *frituras de name* to the lined dish to drain and keep warm. Serve at once. Makes about 20 two-inch round cakes.

Culminating Activity

12. Working in committees, the class might plan a trip to the Dominican Republic. One group might investigate the journey. How would a group of thirty people most economically get from your town or city to the Dominican Republic? What city would you arrive in? How much would a round trip ticket cost? How would you travel around the Republic? How much would that cost?

Another group might plan the sights you would want to see during a two-week visit. Where would you go? How long would you stay in each spot? What hotels or other facilities are available? How much do they cost? What are the highlights in each town or region?

A third group might investigate travel needs. Do you need a passport or visa? How do you get one? What money would you use? How much money would each person need per day in addition to the actual travel expenses? Are shots required from your doctor? When each group has finished researching, have a sharing of the information among the students.

Suggested Reading

Andrade, Manuel J. *Folklore de la Republica Dominicana.* Santo Domingo, Dominican Republic: University of Santo Domingo Press, 1948.

Anthony, Suzanne. *West Indies.* Philadelphia, Pa.: Chelsea House, 1999.

Barlow, Genevieve. *Stories from Latin America, Historias de Latinoamerica.* Lincolnwood, Ill.: Passport Books, 1995.

Carter, Dorothy Sharp. *Greedy Mariani, and Other Folktales of the Antilles.* New York: Atheneum, 1974.

Creed, Alexander. *Dominican Republic.* New York: Chelsea House, 1987.

Dawson, Mildred Leinweber. *Over Here It's Different, Carolina's Story.* New York: Macmillan, 1993.

Foley, Erin. *Dominican Republic.* New York: Marshall Cavendish, 1995.

Gordon, Ginger. *My Two Worlds.* New York: Clarion Books, 1993.

Haberfeld, Carolyn V. *Fodor's 98 Caribbean.* New York: Fodor's, 1997.

Hansen, Terrence Leslie. *The Types of the Folktale in Cuba, Puerto Rico, the Dominican Republic, and Spanish South America.* Berkeley, Calif.: University of California Press, 1957.

Harding, Bertita. *The Land Columbus Loved, The Dominican Republic.* New York: Coward-McCann, 1949.

Haverstock, Nathan A. *Dominican Republic in Pictures.* Minneapolis, Minn.: Lerner Publications, 1988.

Hodge, Alison. *The West Indies.* Austin, Tex.: Raintree Steck-Vaughn, 1998.

Johnson, Sylvia A. *Tomatoes, Potatoes, Corn, and Beans: How the Food of the Americas Changed Eating around the World.* New York: Atheneum, 1997.

Lalbachan, Pamela. *The Complete Caribbean Cook Book.* Boston, Mass.: Charles E. Tuttle, 1994.

Logan, Rayford W. *Haiti and the Dominican Republic.* New York: Oxford University Press, 1968.

Mayer, T. W. *The Caribbean and Its People.* New York: Thomson Learning, 1995.

Pariser, Harry S. *Adventure Guide to The Dominican Republic.* Edison, N.J.: Hunter Publishing, 1993.

———. *Explore the Dominican Republic.* Edison, N.J.: Hunter Publishing, 1998.

Tucker, Jack and Ursula Eberhard. *Hippocrene Insiders' Guide to Dominican Republic.* New York: Hippocrene Books, 1993.

Weil, Thomas E., Jan Knippers Black, Howard I. Blutstein, Kathryn T. Johnston, Davis S. McMorris and, Frederick P. Munson. *Area Handbook for the Dominican Republic.* Washington, D.C.: U.S. Government Printing Office, 1973.

Wiarda, Howard J. and Michael J. Kryzanek. *The Dominican Republic, A Caribbean Crucible.* Boulder, Colo.: Westview Press, 1982.

Winn, Peter. *Americas, The Changing Face of Latin America and the Caribbean,* New York: Pantheon Books, 1992.

"Get me a sack and a pair of boots, and you will learn
what a valuable cat I am."

France

A Legend from France

Many of the most famous folk tales from France can be traced back to Charles Perrault's work in 1697, *Histoires ou Contes du Temps Passe*. One of these is *Puss in Boots*.

A retelling of this famous story appears in Virginia Haviland's 1959 collection, *Favorite Fairy Tales Told in France*. Still another version is *Puss in Boots* by Fred Marcellino, published in 1990.

A Retelling of *Puss in Boots*

When an old miller died, he left what little he had to his three sons. The oldest received the mill, the second son inherited the donkey, and all that was left for the youngest son was a cat.

The youngest son went out into the world alone except for his cat and complained loudly to himself. "My two older brothers, working together, will surely survive," he said. "All I have is a worthless cat that won't even catch mice. After I've eaten it and made a muff from the fur, I will surely starve."

Hearing this, and having no desire to be eaten, the quick-witted cat spoke up. "I could catch mice if I wished," said the cat. "But there are more important things to do. Never fear, my master. From this moment forward, you will be Lord Carabas. Follow my directions and you will prosper. Get me a sack and a pair of boots, and you will learn what a valuable cat I am."

"Why do you need boots?" asked the young man.

"When he is out and about, a gentleman always wears boots," said the cat grandly.

The young man knew this was a clever cat. He rather liked the grand title of Lord Carabas, and he had little to lose, so he outfitted the cat with boots and a sack, found temporary shelter in an old barn, and waited to see what would happen.

The cat took a handful of bran from the barn, went directly to a rabbit warren, arranged the open sack with bran in it, and waited. Almost immediately, a young rabbit walked into the trap. The cat pulled the strings of the bag tight and killed the rabbit.

The cat took the animal straight to the palace and asked to see the king. When he reached His Majesty's apartment, the cat said, "Your Highness, I've brought you a plump wild rabbit sent to you by the Marquis of Carabas."

"Tell your master that I thank him kindly," said the king.

Next, the cat caught two partridges in a wheat field. He took one to his hungry master and took the other to the king. For two months, the cat took food to his master and daily gifts to the king, declaring them all to be from his master, Lord Carabas.

The day came when the cat learned the king would be driving along the river in his carriage with his daughter, who was the most beautiful princess in the world. Quickly the cat went to his master. "This will be a grand day for you," said the cat, "if you do exactly as I say. You must go to the river and swim, and your fortune will be made. Follow me and I'll show you just where to jump in."

The young man did as he was asked. While he was swimming in the river, the king's carriage came by. Puss, who was standing near the road, began to shout. "Help! Help! My master, the Marquis of Carabas, is drowning!"

Hearing the familiar name, the king stopped the carriage and sent his men to rescue the Marquis. Puss quickly told the king that thieves had come while his master was swimming, had tried to harm him, and made off with his clothes. Actually, the cat had hidden his master's old clothes under a rock.

The king ordered his servants to fetch a fine suit for the Marquis of Carabas. When he was dressed, Puss presented his master to the king and the beautiful princess. Seeing him dressed in his finery, the princess thought the young man very handsome indeed, and the two of them exchanged tender looks.

The king took the Marquis into his carriage. The cat ran ahead to some peasants mowing in a meadow. He drew himself up tall in his boots. "When the king comes by and asks who owns this land, you must say it belongs to the Marquis of Carabas. If you do not, I'll cut you into sausage meat."

Soon after, the king's carriage came riding up. "To whom do these fine lands belong?" demanded the king.

"To the Marquis of Carabas," the peasants replied.

Meanwhile, the cat ran ahead and came to a group of harvesters. Again Puss drew himself up tall in his boots and said, "The king will be coming soon. If he asks who owns this land, you must say it belongs to the Marquis of Carabas. If you do not, I'll cut you into sausage meat."

Shortly after, the king's carriage came by. "To whom do these fine lands belong?" demanded the king.

"To the Marquis of Carabas," the harvesters replied.

The cat ran ahead to a beautiful castle that belonged to the Ogre who owned all these lands. Puss ran in to meet the Ogre. "I have heard," said Puss, "that you have remarkable powers and can change yourself into whatever animal you wish."

"That is correct," said the Ogre, and he promptly changed himself into a roaring lion. Puss trembled and stood very still until the Ogre had changed back into his own shape.

Then Puss said, "That was wonderful. I've heard you can also change yourself into something as small as a mouse. That seems impossible to me."

"Impossible?" said the Ogre. "Nonsense." And quickly he changed himself into a tiny mouse.

Puss leaped on the mouse immediately and gobbled him up.

Just then the king's carriage came riding up. "Welcome, your Majesty," said Puss, running to the front gate. "Welcome to the castle of the Marquis of Carabas."

Now it happens that the Ogre was expecting guests that very evening and already had a fine feast waiting for them. But when the Ogre's guests saw the king's carriage out in front, they dared not interrupt and come into the castle. So they went away hungry.

Puss led the king, the princess, and his master to the dining room where they feasted.

The king said, "I am very impressed with your castle and your lands. You have only to ask, and you may have the hand of my daughter in marriage."

And so it was that the young man and the princess were married that very night. They lived handsomely in the castle and on the lands that Puss had claimed in the name of the Marquis of Carabas.

And as for Puss, he became a great lord, served his master faithfully and never ever bothered to catch a mouse again, because he had far more important things to do.

Background Information

The Republic of France is the largest nation in Western Europe, covering an area of about 213,010 square miles, including the island of Corsica, which occupies an area of about 3,367 square miles. France is divided into twenty-two regions. It borders Spain on the south, Italy and Switzerland on the east, and Germany, Luxembourg, and Belgium on the northeast. About half of France's border is a long coastline with the Atlantic Ocean and the Mediterranean Sea. The English Channel separates France from Great Britain.

France has a variety of climates. On the Mediterranean shore, and in much of southern France, summers are hot and dry. Winters in the south are mild, with the exception of cold winds that sweep down from the Pyrenees and Alps. In the Alps and Juras, the peaks are snow-covered all year-round. France's Atlantic coastline has abundant rain. The warm water of the Gulf Stream brings generally mild temperatures. In the interior, temperatures seldom reach extremes of hot or cold.

France has a population of 58,040,230. The various regions and cities of the country are tied together by a network of rivers. The Seine flows northwest from eastern France, through Paris, and into the Channel at Le Havre. The Loire begins farther south, flows northwest to Orleans, and turns west before emptying into the Atlantic at Saint-Nazaire. The Goronne rises in the Pyrenees, and flows northwest through the Bordeaux wine country. The Rhone flows southwest from Lake Geneva in Switzerland and branches out into a wide delta before reaching the Mediterranean.

Several great mountain ranges surround France; the Pyrenees to the south, and the Alps and the Jura to the east. In the French Alps is Mount Blanc, at 15,781 feet, the highest mountain in Western Europe.

The island of Corsica, in the Mediterranean Sea off the coast of Italy, has been part of France since the eighteenth century. It is a mountainous island, and its chief claim to fame is that it is the birthplace of Napoleon.

Among the famous cities of France is Paris, which is often called "The City of Light." It is the capital of France. The river Seine flows through the heart of Paris, dividing it into the Left Bank and the Right Bank.

Getting around Paris is made easier by the city's fifteen subway lines. Among the special sights for tourists is the Eiffel Tower, which was built for the 1889 Paris Universal Exposition.

The Louvre is the largest royal palace in the world and houses the most famous collection of art, including Leonardo da Vinci's *Mona Lisa.* Just 12 miles outside of Paris is the Chateau de Versailles, built between 1678 and 1682 for Louis XIV. It is now a museum and park.

Other important French cities are Marseilles, on the Mediterranean, which is the chief port of France; Strasbourg, the capital of Alsace and a port on the Rhine; Toulouse, the center of the French aircraft industry; and Bordeaux, a major industrial city and wine center. The Romans, around 123 B.C., founded the ancient city of Aix-en-Provence, located near the resorts of Cannes and St. Tropez.

France has rich agricultural land and produces more foodstuffs than any other Common Market country. Wheat is grown in the north and northwest. Barley, oats, sugar beets, and vegetables are also grown. Various regions produce an abundance of fruits, including apples, oranges, cherries, apricots, and plums.

Livestock production is increasing in France. Farmers raise cattle, sheep, poultry, horses, pigs, and goats. The dairy herds of Normandy produce milk and cream and are the source of many kinds of French cheeses.

France's best-known agricultural export is wine. Wine has been produced in France since Roman times. There is a great variety, including the rose's of Provence and Anjou, the reds of the Rhone, the whites of the Loire and Alsace, and the sparkling wines of the Champagne region.

Modern France is also an industrial country. France has considerable aluminum ore and bauxite. Steel production is booming, and France leads Western Europe in the extraction of iron ore. France has an abundance of hydro-electricity, which powers the French textile industry. France also has a large-scale oil refining industry.

France built the world's first tidal power station on the Rance River near Dinan. Uranium deposits from central France fuel nuclear reactors that run generators. And at Odeillo, there is an experimental solar power station.

History

People have found cave paintings in Lascaux in the Dordogne in southwest France that are thought to be more than 20,000 years old. The pictures show wild animals such as bison, horses, and mammoths.

Standing stones, called *menhirs,* at Carnac in Brittany date from 3,000 B.C. It is thought that these stones may have been used in religious festivals.

It was about 3,000 years ago that the Celtic peoples moved from the Alps into northern and eastern Europe. These people were warriors, farmers, and skilled craftspeople. The Celts settled where they found iron to make axes, swords, and wheels. The Romans moved into southern Gaul in 154 B.C., and by 51 B.C. all of Gaul was part of the Roman Empire under the rule of Julius Caesar. The Romans stayed in Gaul for 500 years.

Missionaries from Greece began preaching Christianity while the Romans occupied Gaul. The Roman Emperor Constantine allowed freedom of religious worship around A.D. 313. After the Roman Empire fell in A.D. 476, Gaul was overrun by many tribes from Scandinavia, England, and Germany. Most powerful was Clovis, chief of the Franks, from Germany. He united the country, which became known as Francia. Clovis and his tribes adopted Christianity.

The empire of the Franks was most powerful during the reign of Charlemagne. King Charlemagne (A.D. 742–814) was a strong military and religious leader. On Christmas Day, A.D. 800, Pope Leo III crowned Charlemagne emperor of western Europe.

After his death, Charlemagne's empire was left to his son Louis, and then to Louis's sons. Central power declined. In A.D. 843, the Treaty of Verdun divided up the empire. The western part became France.

In 1095, Pope Urban II urged Christian knights to fight to free Jerusalem. The First Crusade set out from France. Jerusalem was freed by 1099, and then once again fell under the control of the Muslims. In 1147, King Louis VII of France led a second Crusade to the Holy Land. By 1291, the Crusades had ended.

During the late Middle Ages, there were conflicts between the King of France, Philip IV, and the Catholic Church. In 1305 a Frenchman was elected Pope Clement V and moved the residence of the Pope to Avignon. But in 1378, the Papacy returned to Rome.

For over a hundred years, from 1339 to 1453, France was at war with England. In 1422, when Charles VI of France died, the French throne was given to his grandson, Henry VI of England, instead of to Charles's son, the French Dauphin.

Joan of Arc went to help the Dauphin Charles and led the troops to end the siege at Orleans. The English fled, and the Dauphin was crowned King Charles VII in 1429.

By 1453, the French had driven the English out of France except for the port of Calais, which the English held for another hundred years.

King Francois I (1494–1547) ruled France during the Renaissance. During this time, protests against the Church, known as the Reformation, led to the creation of many different branches of Protestant churches throughout Europe. Many French nobles became Protestants in the 1500s.

The conflict between Catholics and Protestants (or Huguenots) resulted in sporadic civil war from 1562 to 1629. In 1593, Henri IV, who was a Protestant, was forced to accept the Catholic religion. This temporarily ended the fighting, and in 1598, he issued a royal command, The Edict of Nantes, which gave the Protestants some religious freedoms.

Henri IV was assassinated in 1610, and his son became King Louis XIII. Louis's prime minister was Cardinal Richelieu (1602–1674), who strengthened the power of the king and brought an end to the fighting that had broken out again between Catholics and Protestants.

King Louis XIV was known as the Sun King. He became king in 1643 when he was only five years old. He reigned for seventy-two years, and during that time tried to stamp out the Protestants. He is remembered for the construction of the Palace at Versailles, which stands outside Paris.

By the eighteenth century, many were speaking and writing about the terrible inequalities between rich and poor. This period, called the Enlightenment, eventually led to the French Revolution (1789–1799), when the people rose up against the king, and France became a Republic.

A Reign of Terror began in 1792, when anyone considered an enemy of the Revolution was ordered executed. This lasted until 1794, when a new government, called the Directory, was established. On November 9, 1799, a young general, Napoleon Bonaparte, overthrew the Directory.

Napoleon set up a government of three men, called a consulate, with himself as first consul. He did a great deal to reform government, including setting up the Napoleonic Code, which is the basis of modern French law. Then in 1804, Napoleon was declared emperor of France. He invaded Russia in 1812 and marched into Moscow. When he and his army were caught in the Russian winter, only one-sixth of Napoleon's men returned to France. An army of European nations, including Russia and Great Britain, occupied Paris in 1814. Napoleon was sent into exile on the island of Elba. Louis XVIII was made king.

Napoleon escaped and tried to win back the throne. He became emperor of France again for 100 days. He was defeated at the battle of Waterloo in Belgium by the European armies led by the Duke of Wellington. Napoleon was exiled to a remote island, St. Helena, and Louis XVIII was put back on the throne.

In 1824, Louis XVIII's brother, Charles X, came to the throne during a period of general unrest in the country that led to rioting. Charles X gave up the throne, and Louis Philippe

was proclaimed king. He was overthrown by revolution in 1848. The Second Republic was declared. Louis Napoleon Bonaparte became president. He soon dissolved the National Assembly and declared himself emperor. Napoleon III ruled from 1852 to 1870.

In 1870, Napoleon III declared war on Prussia. The French suffered heavy losses, and the Prussian troops marched into France. Napoleon was taken prisoner and surrendered. France gave up two rich provinces, Alsace and Lorraine, to the German empire.

When World War I began, the French and English fought together against Germany. The United States entered the war on the side of the French, British, and Russians. In the Treaty of Versailles, the provinces of Alsace and Lorraine were given back to France.

Peace did not last long. Germany, under the leadership of Adolf Hitler, began to expand Germany's territory. German troops took Czechoslovakia and Poland. On September 3, 1939, France and Great Britain declared war on Germany. World War II had begun. Again the United States entered the war on the side of France and against Germany.

The Germans marched into Paris on June 14, 1940, and divided France into two parts. The Germans occupied the northern part. The southern part, which had its capital in Vichy, set up a new French government that cooperated with the Germans. Many were against collaborating with the Germans, and General Charles de Gaulle led the resistance to the Vichy government.

At the end of World War II in 1945, General Charles de Gaulle became head of the provisional government. In 1968, there was again unrest in France. The government was on the verge of collapse. President de Gaulle resigned in 1969.

Later presidents governed France along conservative lines until the election of a Socialist, Francois Mitterand, in 1981. He nationalized some banks and industries. He was reelected in 1988. In the 1993 elections, the Socialists were defeated, and there was a shift toward the right for the National Assembly.

Government

France is a republic and is governed under the 1958 constitution. According to that constitution, governmental power is shared among the president, the prime minister, and his cabinet, and Parliament, which consists of the National Assembly and the Senate.

The president is the head of state and is elected directly by the people for a period of seven years. Citizens who are at least eighteen years of age are eligible to vote. The president appoints the prime minister, who leads the government and recommends to the president the 26 ministers of the cabinet.

Parliament is made up of the National Assembly and the Senate. The people elect the 577 members of the National Assembly. An Electoral College elects the 321 senators for a term of nine years. One-third of the Senate is renewed every three years.

For administrative purposes, France is divided into 96 departments, which are similar to states in the United States. A general council administers the affairs of each department. A municipal council, elected by the people, governs each township or commune. A mayor is elected from the council members.

France's judicial system is administered by a number of different courts. Civil courts rule on disputes between private parties. Criminal courts deal with violations of the law. Judgments may be appealed to higher courts. The Republic's highest appellate court is the Court of Cassation.

Religion

The main religion in France is Roman Catholicism. More than 80 percent of the people are Catholics.

There are many people who live in France who follow other religions. Some of these people came to France from colonies in different parts of the world. Those who come from North Africa may follow the religion of Islam. Muslims make up about 7 percent of the population. Others are Protestants or practice the Jewish religion.

Education

France has a literacy rate of 99 percent, making it one of the most literate countries in the world.

French children must attend school between the ages of six and sixteen. There are government-run and private nursery schools. After nursery school, most pupils attend state schools, which are free, although there are a few private schools, mostly run by the Catholic Church.

The students who go to public school attend primary school between ages six and eleven, then from ages eleven to fifteen students attend a secondary school called a *college*, which is like a junior high school in the United States. They prepare for a classic higher education by studying Greek and Latin, or they may study modern foreign languages. Some go into general education combined with vocational training. Many students leave school at age sixteen after secondary school.

Students who plan to go on to a university next attend a three-year academic high school or *lycee*. They may choose majors from literature, social sciences, mathematics, science, or industrial technology. At the end of three years, they take a difficult examination called the baccalaureate. Those who pass the baccalaureate may go on to study at a university.

A small percentage of students spend an extra two years in a lycee and prepare for the very competitive exams to enter one of the 175 *grandes ecoles*. Classes in these schools are smaller and they offer better student living conditions than in most universities.

A typical school day begins at 8:30 A.M. and finishes at 4:30 P.M. Students have a two-hour lunch break. Each of the classes lasts 55 minutes, with a 5-minute passing period. It is common for students to have a day off on Wednesday and to attend school on Saturday mornings. Students study French, English, mathematics, science, history, and geography.

Immigrants

By the end of the 1700s, French immigrants to Canada numbered 25,000. Between 1846 and 1932 emigration from France totaled 519,000 people. The United States was by far the largest receiving country of emigrants from Europe.

France received refugee white and Muslim immigrants in the early 1960s from its former territory, Algeria.

From 1981 to 1990, 23,100 French immigrated to the United States. During the period 1991 to 1995, another 13,800 came.

Language

French is one of the Romance languages. Although French is the main language of France, several different languages and dialects are spoken, depending on the area. For example, in parts of Brittany, some people speak a language known as Breton. Near the border with Spain, Basque is spoken. In the Alsace and Lorraine regions, a German dialect is common.

It is estimated that over 70 million people use French as their first language. The bulk of these people live in France, Belgium, Haiti, Luxembourg, Monaco, Switzerland, Canada, and the former French and Belgian colonies in Africa. After English, French is the most widely spoken second language in the world.

Written French uses the same Roman alphabet that English does, but it also uses three different accents that show how to pronounce some vowels. It also uses gender to define nouns, something that English does not do.

A law was passed in France in 1977 that banned the use of foreign words in government documents, in ads, and on radio and television in those cases where French words could be used instead.

The Arts and Sciences

One of the contributions France makes to the world is in fashion design. Paris is a fashion center. French designers such as Yves Saint Laurent and Jean-Paul Gaultier set trends and influence fashion throughout the world.

France is also known for its perfumes. Major names include Dior, Chanel, and Givenchy. France has had a thriving perfume industry since the sixteenth century and uses locally grown wild lavender, jasmine, and violets as well as imported flowers such as roses, mimosa, and orange blossoms.

France is one of the world's major car producers. Well known cars are Renault, Peugeot, and Citroen. These cars are exported to many countries, including the United States.

The world is indebted to France for the work of many great scientists, including Louis Pasteur, Pierre Eugene Marcelin Berthelot, Henri Poincaré, and Marie and Pierre Curie.

France has given the world famous painters. Among these are Louis le Nain (1593–1648), Nicolas Poussin (1594–1665), Philippe de Champaigne (1602–1674), Jean-Francois de Troy (1679–1752), Jean Huber (1721–1786), Jean-Pierre Houel (1735–1813), Jacques Louis David (1748–1825), Camile Corot (1796–1875), Gustave Courbet (1819–1877), Edgar Degas (1834–1917), Pierre-Auguste Renoir (1841–1919), Georges Seurat (1859–1891), Fernand Leger (1881–1955), Raoul Duffy (1877–1953), Georges Braque (1881–1963), and Marcel Duchamp (1887–1968).

Eugene Delacrois (1798–1863) is considered the leader of the Romantic School of French painting. His *The Raft of the Medusa* was hung in the Louvre. Many regard Delacroix as the greatest French painter of the first half of the nineteenth century.

In the mid-1800s, Jean Baptiste Camille Corot was the leading French nature painter. Edouard Manet was born in 1832. He was a master of Realism, painting figures and still life, and was a major figure in the Impressionist movement.

Claude Monet was one of the primary inspirations of the Impressionist movement in French art. He was born in Paris in 1840. His painting of the harbor at Le Havre, *Impression, Sunrise,* in 1872, with its pointillist technique, gave the movement its name.

The leading Post-impressionist was Paul Cezanne whose interest in shape and structure marked a major change in the art world. In the 1920s Gorges Braque, along with the Spaniard Pablo Picasso, who was a resident of France, helped develop Cubism.

Paul Gauguin (1848–1903) produced a number of paintings regarded as masterpieces. He eventually traveled to Tahiti and many of his works feature the people and bright colors of the South Sea islands.

One of the world's most famous statues is called *The Thinker.* It is on display in the Rodin Museum in Paris. The statue is the work of a famous French sculpture, Auguste Rodin (1840–1917).

Two great figures in literature from France are Moliere (1622–1673) and Victor Hugo. Moliere wrote comedies based on people's weaknesses. Victor Hugo is remembered for his two most famous novels, *The Hunchback of Notre*

Dame and *Les Miserables.* Other French literary greats include Jean Racine, Voltaire, Jean-Jacques Rousseau, Anatole France, Gustave Flaubert, Emile Zola, Guy de Maupassant, Arthur Rimbaud, Andre Gidet, and Jean Giraudoux.

Another famous French author, mathematician, scientist, and philosopher was René Descarte. His *A Discourse on Method* was published in 1637. Descarte expressed the belief that man was essentially a thinking creature.

In the 1830s, feeling and imagination came to the forefront in French literature. In the mid-nineteenth century, Charles Baudelaire published his poems, *Flowers of Evil,* and was followed by the symbolist poets. Marcel Proust became a major influence on twentieth century writers after the publication of *Remembrance of Things Past.* Other great French philosophical writers of the twentieth century include Albert Camus (1913–1960) and Jean Paul Sartre (1905–1980).

Musical greats also came from France. Claude Debussy composed *The Afternoon of a Faun* in 1892. Cesar Franck, professor of organ at the Paris Conservatory, completed many of his best known works from 1872 to 1890. Camille Saint-Saens wrote his *Third Symphony* in 1886. Igor Stravinsky's ballet, *The Rites of Spring,* debuted in Paris in 1913. The works of Maurice Ravel have become part of the great European musical tradition. Other great French musicians include Hector Berlioz, and Georges Bizet.

Although ballet first appeared in Italy in the 1400s as part of opera, the first ballet to combine action, music, and decoration was presented in Paris in 1581. Many words used in association with ballet are French, including *plie, jete,* and *en pointe.*

Food

French cooking is famous throughout the world. The food varies in each part of France because chefs take advantage of the local produce. In Brittany, seafood is featured in *bouillabaisee,* fish soup, and *moules,* mussels. There are lobsters, crabs, scallops, clams, langoustines, shrimp, mussels, mackerel, monkfish, sole, cod, sardines, and oysters. This area is also famous for its lamb, which is reared in salty meadows around Mont St. Michel. Brittany's national dish is the *crepe,* something like a pancake, that can be purchased from stalls in the street.

Normandy has a variety of seafood as well as rich dairy products. There are also apple orchards here, so many common dishes contain apples. Cider is another chief product of the area. Dishes in Normandy often feature fowl such as duck, grouse, pheasant, and partridge.

Lorraine is famous for its cakes, pastry, preserves, and confectionery offerings. Quiches are another specialty of the region. In Alsace, there is a marked German influence on the cooking. Pork is a specialty here.

France is famous for its cheeses and produces over 400 different varieties. Roquefort, made of sheep's milk, comes from the town of Roquefort in south central France. Other favorite types include Brie, Camembert, Port Salut, and Coulommiers.

Mustard is also popular in France. A study done in 1994 showed that the French use 60,000 tons of mustard per year. For six centuries, Dijon has been the mustard capital of France.

Rolls are a favorite French breakfast food. These include flaky croissants, brioches, and crisp petits pains, often served with cafe au lait. Paris offers some of the best bread in the world.

Countless varieties of fluffy omelets and soufflés are served in France. At different meals, favorite foods include onion soup served bubbling hot with cheese on top, snails prepared with garlic and herbs, and savory stew served with crusty loaves of bread.

Burgundy produces tender, lean beef and a rich selection of vegetables. In Guyenne, Gascogne, and Bearn, tuna, squid, and sardines are abundant. Languedoc and Provence are especially famous for bouillabaisse. Auvergne, Lyonnais, Savole, and Dauphine offer simple country fare, with potatoes and cabbage being favorite vegetables.

Throughout the country there are many delicious desserts ranging from rich puddings to chocolate mousse and *glace,* ice cream.

With a food processor, it is easy to make little butter and nut cakes like those sold in Parisian bakeshops.

Little Almond Cakes

1 cup whole blanched almonds

1 1/2 cups confectioners' sugar

1/2 cup cake flour

Pinch of salt

6 egg whites

1 1/2 sticks unsalted butter, melted

Heat the oven to 350°F. Butter a mini-muffin pan. (Makes about 20 small cakes.) Spread the almonds on a baking sheet and toast in the oven, shaking the pan occasionally, until the almonds are golden, about 12 minutes. Turn the oven up to 450°F.

Put the toasted almonds in a food processor fitted with the metal blade and process until finely ground. Add 1 1/4 cups sugar, the flour, and salt. Process until the mixture is well blended and then transfer to a mixing bowl.

Pour the unbeaten egg whites into the nut mixture and stir to combine. Then stir in the melted butter until well-blended. Ladle the batter into the buttered muffin cups until 2/3 full.

Bake 7 minutes. Reduce the heat to 400°F and bake 10 minutes longer. Turn the oven off and let the pan rest in the oven 5 minutes. The muffins will be golden around the edges with little peaks in the center. Remove from the oven and set aside to cool in the pan 10 minutes. Invert to remove. When the cakes are cool, put the remaining confectioners' sugar through a sifter to sprinkle on the tops. The almond cakes keep up to 4 days.

Recreation

Boules, or *petanque,* is the national game of France. It is played with metal balls and a jack ball. The object of the game is to toss or roll the boules from a circle about 18 to 30 feet in diameter as close to the jack as possible.

Young people in France play other games that are very familiar in the United States. They jump rope, play cat's cradle, enjoy skateboarding, in-line skating, and computer games.

Other popular sporting events include tennis, horse racing, soccer, and rugby. In tennis, the French Open tennis championship held in May is one of the four Grand Slam tennis events. The Prix de l'Arc de Triomphe, run at the Longchamp racecourse in Paris, is one of the most famous horse races in the world. Soccer is the most popular team sport in France, followed by basketball, and the French rugby union team competes each year in the Five Nations' Championship against England, Scotland, Wales, and Ireland.

Among individual sports, skiing is most popular. There are dozens of winter resorts, including Albertville, the site of the 1992 Winter Olympic Games. Other popular sports include judo, sailing, water-skiing, hunting, and fishing.

An event watched throughout the world is the famous bicycle race, the Tour de France, which is held each summer. Professional cyclists from all over the world compete. The race follows a 2,975-mile course.

Customs and Traditions

In France, Bastille Day is celebrated on July 14 in recognition of liberty, national unity, and the beginning of the French Revolution. There is a grand military procession in Paris followed by fireworks and dancing.

At Christmas, many homes in the Alsace and Lorraine region will have decorated Christmas trees. Mistletoe and holly are used as holiday decorations. On Christmas Eve, children put slippers by the fireplace hoping that Pere Noel will come and fill them with toys and goodies. Almost every home in Provence will display a creche. People do not usually give presents on Christmas day but instead give them on St. Nicholas's Day, which is December 6.

Flowers are an important part of the Christmas holiday. There will be a lavish arrangement on almost every holiday table. A favorite flower is hellebore, a small blossom with white petals, which the French call a Christmas rose.

The Christmas Eve supper is called *Reveillon* and is very elaborate. It will include fruits and pastries and may feature a roast of beef, a leg of lamb, or a goose or turkey or duck.

The town of Nice holds a huge carnival each year called Mardi Gras. This marks the two weeks before Lent begins. There are floats, parades, brass bands, fireworks, and people dressed in fancy costumes.

Throughout France there are hundreds of local festivals. Some celebrate harvests and some are celebrations of saints' days. In Brittany, people hold Pardons, which are festivals to honor their local saints. These often include wearing costumes and performing traditional folk dances.

Suggested Activities

Writing

1. Those who study France will certainly read a good deal about the French Revolution. A group of students might choose one major character from that period in history and write a report on that person. These reports could be edited, printed, and finally gathered and bound in a class booklet, *Major Characters of the French Revolution.* In addition to others of interest, characters that might be included are: Louis XVI, Marie Antoinette, Lafayette, Comte de Mirabeau, Madame Roland, Jean-Paul Marat, Robespierre, and Napoleon Bonaparte.

Reading

2. A small group of students might enjoy getting a paperback copy of Arthur Byron Cover's *Blade of the Guillotine* (Bantam, 1986), and read and discuss it together. This story involves traveling back in time to the French Revolution. It is a plot-your-own story, so that readers make decisions that may lead to safety or to their being stranded in time.

Vocabulary

3. A French language bulletin board, giving French/English equivalents, will be of interest to students. They can collect words and phrases through their reading and add words and definitions printed on 3 x 5-inch cards throughout the unit of study.

Here are a few to begin the bulletin board: *le drapeau*—flag, *le timbre*—stamp, *l'argent*—money, *les Francais*—the French, *la carte*—map, *l'ete*—summer, *l'hiver*—winter, *le soleil*—sun, *le chateau*—castle, *le pain*—bread, *la lait*—milk, and *le sucre*—sugar.

Math

4. France is one of the least crowded of the Western European nations. Invite a small group of students to prepare a graph to present to the class, using stick figures to indicate how many people there are per square mile in France if each figure represents 250 people. What would the chart look like in comparing the population per square mile for France, Italy, Great Britain, Belgium, and Holland?

Social Studies

5. Invite a team of students to make a time line showing the major historical incidents in the history of France. Display the time line on a classroom wall.

Geography

6. At one time, the French Empire was second in size only to Great Britain's and covered about 4.7 million square miles. Much of this empire is gone, but France still has many territories around the world.

On a map of the world, have a pair of students locate the French Departements or Territories. These include Clipperton, Wallis et Futuna, French Polynesia, Sainte-Pierre and Miqueton, Guadeloupe, Martinique, French Guiana, Mayotte, Reunion, St. Paul, Kerquelen, New Caledonia, and Terre Adelle.

Music

7. Multicultural Media, RR3, Box 6655, Granger Road, Barre, VT, 05641 is an excellent resource for teachers interested in music from different countries. Students might enjoy listening to *Singers & Musicians in Liomousin—France*, CD # Y225113. This provides a taste of the folk music of France and is compiled on 41 tracks recorded between 1974 and 1991. It includes singers, fiddlers, pipers, and accordionists performing 70 minutes of song and dance. A booklet gives English and French notes on the region, history, instruments, and performers.

Art

8. Fruits are often featured as holiday ornaments and are hung on Christmas trees in France. Students might enjoy making these ornaments. First they should sketch the fruit they wish to make (a banana, strawberry, orange, pineapple) and trace it onto a piece of waxed paper.

Then they should mix in a bowl 1 cup salt, 2 cups flour, and 1/2 teaspoon baking powder. Next, gradually stir in 1 cup of water. Knead the mixture for about 5 minutes until the dough feels like clay. (Flour hands to keep the dough from sticking.) This will yield 3 cups.

Sprinkle flour on a wood cutting board. Take a lump of "clay" and roll it into a ball. Flatten it to 3/8 inch thick. Put the waxed paper fruit pattern on the "clay" and carefully use a knife to cut around the edge. Draw details on the fruit with a toothpick. Make a hole near the top of the fruit so that it can be hung later by putting twine through the hole. Allow the fruits to air dry for 48 hours. Paint the ornaments and let them dry again. Seal with a coat of clear nail polish. When dry, thread an 8-inch cord through the hole, knot it, and hang the ornament.

Drama/Movement

9. Performers such as Charlie Chaplin and Emmett Kelley exemplified modern mime in the United States. It is a silent art whereby meanings are conveyed through gesture, expression, and movement. Foremost among mimes was the French performer, Marcel Marceau.

Ask a pair of students interested in mime to prepare a short program to present to the class.

Dress

10. Among the special pieces of French clothing from the past are the unusual hats worn by women. With help from a research librarian, a group of students may be able to check out books that have drawings of these different hats. This group may share the pictures with the class.

Among the special hats, students might look for the following. On special days in the town of Quimper, the headdress for women was called a *coif*. This is a stiff white cap with a lace over-cap, worn over another little cap. In southern Brittany, women wore the lace cap of *Vannes*. In northern France, women wore a towering headdress called *bourgoins*. These hats are made from starched muslin over stiffened shapes and have velvet chin straps and lace streamers.

The fisherwoman's headdress from Pas de Calais is a cap with a frill starched and pleated into a halo, with tiny lappets at each side. Women in Burgundy wore a wide-brimmed hat with a tiny high crown.

Cooking

11. A hearty lunch could be prepared for a class of students by serving slices of French bread with a Provençal vegetable soup.

Plenty of adult supervision is needed for the activity to go smoothly. The recipe below serves 6.

First, make 1 cup of *Pesto*:

Pesto

2 cups basil leaves

3 peeled garlic cloves

1/2 cup olive oil

1/2 teaspoon coarse salt

1/2 cup plus 2 tablespoons grated Parmesan cheese

In a food processor fitted with its metal blade, or in a blender, combine basil, garlic, olive oil, and salt. Process until a smooth paste is formed. Add the cheese and pulse to combine. Refrigerate.

Pistou

2 medium red potatoes, with skins

2 carrots, peeled

3 leeks, white part only, cut in half lengthwise and washed

2 zucchinis, ends trimmed

1 yellow crookneck squash, ends trimmed

1 15-ounce can white kidney beans

2 large tomatoes, peeled, seeded, and diced

1/4 pound green beans, trimmed and cut in 1/2 inch lengths

8 cups chicken broth

1/2 teaspoon salt

freshly ground black pepper

Finely dice the potatoes, carrots, leeks, zucchinis, and squash. Place the white beans in a strainer to drain and rinse under cold water. Place the potatoes, carrots, and leeks in one bowl and the remaining vegetables with beans and tomatoes in another bowl.

Pour the chicken broth into a stockpot or large dutch oven and bring to a boil. With a ladle, skim and discard any foam that rises to the top. Add the potatoes, carrots, and leeks, reduce to a simmer, and cook uncovered for 15 minutes. Add the remaining vegetables and beans. Bring the stock back to a boil and reduce heat to simmer. Cook uncovered about 15 minutes longer, or until the green beans are done. Add salt and pepper.

Place a generous dollop of pesto in each serving bowl. Ladle in the soup. Serve with crusty french bread.

Culminating Activity

12. Divide the class into four or five groups. Ask each group to independently plan a five-day trip to Paris. The trip should begin and end in your town or city. The final report should include an itinerary, a list of planned daily activities, and an estimated cost per person.

What airlines will be used? What is the current price for round trips per person? What hotel will be the home base in Paris? What are two or three restaurants that will be tried? What buildings, monuments, museums, etc., will be included in the sight-seeing tour?

Students might find that http://paris.org/ would be a good place to begin research for the trip. It gives addresses for tourism offices and provides information about hotels, airports, etc.

Allow time for each of the groups to tell the class about the Paris trip they planned. Compare and contrast the planned trips.

Suggested Reading

Banfield, Susan. *The Rights of Man, The Reign of Terror, The Story of the French Revolution.* New York: J. B. Lippincott, 1989.

Barnes, Rachel, ed. *Monet By Monet.* New York: Alfred A. Knopf, 1990.

Clay, Rebecca. *Kidding Around Paris.* Santa Fe, N.Mex.: John Muir, 1991.

Davidson, Marshall B. *The Horizon Concise History of France.* New York: American Heritage, 1971.

Dunford, Mick. *France.* New York: Thomson Learning, 1995.

Editors of Time-Life Books. *France.* Alexandria, Va.: Time-Life, 1985.

Fisher, Teresa. *France.* Austin, Tex.: Raintree Steck-Vaughn, 1997.

Fox, Lilla M. *Folk Costume of Western Europe.* Boston, Mass.: Plays, 1969.

Ganeri, Anita and Rachel Wright. *Country Topics for Craft Projects: France.* New York: Franklin Watts, 1993.

Haskins, Jim and Kathleen Benson. *Count Your Way Through France.* Minneapolis, Minn.: Carolrhoda Books, 1996.

Haviland, Virginia. *Favorite Fairy Tales Told in France.* Boston, Mass.: Little, Brown, 1959.

Holbrook, Sabra. *Growing Up in France.* New York: Atheneum, 1980.

Marcellino, Fred. *Puss in Boots.* New York; Farrar, Straus and Giroux, 1990.

Olney, Richard. *Simple French Food.* New York: Macmillan, 1974.

Powell, Jillian. *France.* New York: Bookwright Press, 1991.

———. *A History of France Through Art.* New York: Thompson Learning, 1996.

Ross, Corinne Madden. *Christmas in France.* Lincolnwood, Ill.: Passport Books, 1991.

Rubinstein, Helge. *Provincial French Cooking.* New York: Hearst Books, 1981.

Siegel, Helene. *French Cooking for Beginners.* New York: HarperCollins, 1994.

Sookram, Brian. *France.* Philadelphia, Pa.: Chelsea House, 1997.

Waterlow, Julia. *The Seine.* East Sussex, England: Wayland Publishers, 1993.

Wright, Patricia. *Manet.* New York: Dorling Kindersley, 1993.

Germany
A Legend from Germany

For almost 200 years people have enjoyed the fairy tales of Jakob and Wilhelm Grimm, which were collected in Germany and first published in their *Kinder und Hausmarchen* in 1812. One of these tales is *The Bremen Town Musicians*. It was retold by Nancy Garden in *Favorite Tales from Grimm*, which was illustrated by Mercer Mayer; it was retold and illustrated by Ilse Plume in *The Bremen-Town Musicians;* it was retold by Virginia Haviland and illustrated by Susanne Suba in *Favorite Fairy Tales Told in Germany;* and the original Grimm tale was re-printed in *Grimm's Fairy Tales, Twenty Stories,* illustrated by Arthur Rackham.

A Retelling of
The Bremen Town Musicians

A man had a faithful donkey that for years tirelessly carried sacks of corn to the mill to be made into meal. But the donkey had grown old and no longer had the strength to work. Instead, it stood about braying all the time, "Hee-haw! Hee-haw!" proud of its fine voice.

The master began to think perhaps he should do away with the worthless beast, have some peace and quiet, and save the expense of feeding him. But the donkey, sensing trouble in the air, ran away. He thought he might go to Bremen Town and become a great musician.

The donkey had not gone far when he came upon an old dog looking lonely and weary. "Why are you panting so hard, friend?" asked the donkey.

"I've run away from my master who was going to kill me," said the dog. "I am old and can no longer keep up with the pack." He howled, "Ooo-ooo-oo."

"You're in luck!" said the donkey. "I'm on my way to Bremen Town to become a great musician. You have a fine voice for baying at the hounds. You're welcome to come along and join me."

The dog agreed and the two continued on their way. They hadn't gone far when they came upon a sorry-looking cat.

"What's the matter, Puss?" asked the donkey.

"I've run away from my mistress who tried to drown me," said the cat. "You see I've grown so old that I would rather sit by the fire and dream than chase mice. Meeoowwwww."

"You're in luck!" said the donkey. "We are on our way to Bremen Town to become great musicians. You have a fine voice for serenading. You're welcome to come along and join us."

The cat agreed and the three of them continued on their way. They were passing a farmyard when they came upon a rooster who was crowing loudly.

"You're in luck!" said the donkey. "We are on the way to Bremen Town
to become great musicians."

"What's the matter, Rooster?" asked the donkey.

"I'm crowing while I can," said the rooster. "You see, I'm not as young as I used to be. We are having company for dinner tomorrow and I heard my mistress say she would turn me into chicken soup. I must leave here. Er-er-er-er-ooo."

"You're in luck!" said the donkey. "We are on the way to Bremen Town to become great musicians. You have a fine voice for heralding the dawn. You're welcome to come along and join us."

The rooster agreed, and the four of them continued on their way. Although they walked all day, they were still a good ways from Bremen Town when night fell. They decided to sleep in the woods. The donkey and the dog settled down at the base of a tree. The cat climbed up into the lower branches, and the rooster flew clear to the top.

Suddenly the rooster called down to the others. "Not too far off I see a light. We're close to someone's home."

"Why not continue on to it then?" suggested the donkey. "Perhaps they will have something for us to eat."

The four animals approached the house with its brightly lighted windows. The donkey was tall enough to peer through the window, and he reported to the others what he saw. "There are a group of robbers inside," he said. "They have stacks of gold and the table is all set for a feast."

The animals decided to make wonderful music, certain that they would be asked to join the feast. The donkey stood outside the window. The dog jumped on his back. The cat jumped up on the dog. And the rooster flew up and perched on the cat's head.

When the rooster flapped his wings, they began to perform. The donkey brayed, the dog barked, the cat howled, and the rooster crowed. And in the middle of their song, they leaped right through the window.

The robbers were so astonished and frightened by the terrible racket that, without pausing to see what had caused it, they went rushing out the door and into the woods.

The four animals arranged themselves around the table and feasted. When they were finished, they each settled down for the night. The donkey lay down outside in a pile of straw, the dog took a place by the back door, the cat curled up near the fire, and the rooster first fanned his wings to put out the candle and then flew up to the rafters.

The robbers out in the cold woods began to regret their hasty departure from the house. "What frightened us?" asked one.

"It was probably nothing," said another.

"I'll go back for our loot," offered a third.

The robber crept quietly up to the house. He went inside and moved toward the fireplace where he saw the cat's eyes shining and thought they were coals. He came close, stepping on the cat's tail, and tried to blow the coals into flame. The angry cat leaped up, hissed, and scratched him dreadfully.

The robber screamed and tried to leave the house. As he reached the back door, the dog bit him on the leg. Outside, the donkey kicked the robber and sent him flying. All the while the rooster flew about screeching "Er-er-er-er-ooo! Er-er-er-er-ooo!"

The badly frightened robber ran back to his friends.

"What happened?" they cried.

"Our house has been taken over by goblins. A witch hissed and scratched me with her long fingernails. Then a demon with a knife stabbed me in the leg, and a hairy monster outside beat me with a club. All the while, some devil was shouting, 'You know what to do! Run the robber through!' I was lucky to escape with my life."

And so the robbers moved away, never daring to return to their house. The four musicians found it so comfortable that they decided to stay on and never went to Bremen after all. But often in the evening they serenaded one another before they went to sleep, and were well pleased with the result.

Background Information

The Federal Republic of Germany is in the center of Europe, south of the Scandinavian countries, west of the Slavic ones, and east of the Romance nations. It has a small, northern coastline. Its nine neighbors are Denmark, Poland, the Czech Republic, Austria, Switzerland, France, Luxembourg, Belgium, and the Netherlands.

Germany, which has a population of 84,068,216 people, covers an area of 137,830 square miles. It can be divided into three principal regions: the northern lowlands, the central highlands, and the southern alpine region.

The northern region of Germany extends between the North and Baltic Seas. Along the coast, it has a damp, maritime climate. This area is mostly flat plains with marshes and lakes. There is fertile land along the coast and in the river valleys. Parts of this region are sandy heathland, which supports some agriculture and sheep grazing. Rugen, a favorite vacation spot, is separated from the mainland by a narrow channel.

Between the northern plains and the central highlands is an area of rich soil stretching from Cologne on the west to Dresden on the east. This area is densely populated.

The central highlands contain forests, vineyards, fields, and mountains. The Hartz Mountains are in this area and contain peaks of over 3,000 feet.

The third region is the southern alpine area, which receives the heaviest precipitation. This area includes the Black Forest Range in the southwest. The Danube River originates in these heights and flows eastward for about 400 miles. The Bavarian Alps form the border between Germany and Austria.

The country is divided into sixteen states called *Länder*. The Länder make their own laws but also join together under a central government.

Germany has a number of navigable rivers, including the Rhine, Weser, Elbe, and Oder. There is also a network of canals, which connects the various rivers. The River Rhine passes through five European countries. It starts as a small stream in the Swiss Alps, skirts Liechtenstein, and flows towards the North Sea through France, Germany, and the Netherlands. The Middle Rhine, between Bigen and Bonn in Germany, is a tourist attraction. The river flows between the steep sides of a gorge with castles high above.

Duisburg is the largest inland port on the Rhine. It is situated at the junction of the Rhine with the River Ruhr. This is the center of Germany's heavy industry. It is made up of industrial centers like Dortmund, Essen, and Bochum. The region is famous for its coalfields, iron, steel, and chemical plants.

Germany's most important natural resource is coal, which is found in the Ruhr in the western part of the country. Crude oil is found in the Lüneburger Heide and around Schleswig-Holstein as well as offshore in the North Sea. But it is not sufficient to meet domestic needs. Iron ore, lead, zinc, and copper are mined, and Germany is one of the world's largest suppliers of potash salts used as fertilizers.

The heart of German industry is in the state of North Rhine-Westphalia. Here, coal mines and industries employ about three million workers. The capital of this section is Dusseldorf.

Germany exports heavy machinery, cars, machine tools, electrical equipment, chemical products, optical and precision instruments, cameras, and electronic equipment.

About 90 percent of German firms could be described as *mittelstand,* or small to medium-sized businesses. Each state has many small businesses and the regional governments support them. In western Germany, it is estimated that there are 46,700 businesses, and of these only about 2 percent are large companies with more than 1,000 employees. The large companies, though, employ about half of the 7 million people employed in industry.

There has been a movement of people away from the country and into the cities, but about half of Germany's total area is agricultural. Farms tend to be small, with over 90 percent smaller than 125 acres. Crops include wheat, barley, potatoes, and sugar beets. There are big grain farms on the North German Plain, in Lower Saxony, and in Schleswig-Holstein. There are dairy farms in the mountainous area of Bavaria, and pig farms in the north and west of the country such as in North Rhine-Westphalia.

German farmers provide for the country's grains, sugar, butter, pork, beef, and eggs. Most vegetables and fruits, however, are imported.

Winemaking is a small but fascinating part of the national economy. Grapes are grown on the steep slopes of the valley of the Rhine Gorge. Vineyards cover the Rhine valley between Lake Constance in the south and Bonn in the north. The very best wines come from a short section of the river between Mainz and Bingen. The area, called the Rheingau, is famous for its fruity-tasting Riesling wine.

Beer production is another important industry. There are 1,290 breweries in Germany and about 5,000 types of German beers.

About 85 percent of German beer is made with barley malt. Between 5,000 and 6,000 tons of hops are harvested each year.

Almost one-third of Germany is forested. These forests provide about 10,000 acres of timber every year and meet about two-thirds of the domestic demand for lumber. Fishing is also an important industry in the north. Germans fish in the North Sea, the Baltic Sea, and the Atlantic. Bremerhaven on the North Sea is a particularly busy fishing port.

German people from the western and southern regions are mostly Celtic and Mediterranean in composition. The people of the central parts are largely Celtic and Teutonic, while the eastern part has more people with a Teutonic and Slavic background. Many refugees entered Germany in recent years, and there were over 6 million foreigners living in Germany by 1994. A small Danish minority lives in the north and many dependents of American military personnel live in various German cities.

Berlin is Germany's capital and largest city. It covers an area of 342 square miles with a population of over 3 million. During World War II, the city suffered intense bombing.

After the war, the United States, Russia, Britain, and France took over the administration of Berlin. A wall was built across the city by the East German government in August 1961. This wall was not removed until 1989.

Other important German cities include Hamburg, a busy port and the second largest city in Germany; Bonn, a university city on the Rhine River; Potsdam, where the palace of Prussia's King Frederick II is now a popular museum; Cologne, a city on the Rhine famous for its cathedral and university; Leipzig, an important trading center; Dresden, which was the most heavily bombed German city in World War II; Frankfurt am Main, which has one of the largest airports in Europe and is important as a center of banking and insurance; Heidelberg, with its world-renowned university; and Munich, one of the fastest growing cities in Germany.

History

In A.D. 9, Germanic tribes pushed the Roman legions behind the lower Rhine and upper Danube Rivers. In the fourth century A.D., barbarian tribes from the north and east attacked the Romans. As the Roman Empire collapsed, Germanic tribes poured into western Europe.

One of the Frankish kings, Charlemagne, who reigned in 800 A.D., ruled the territories known as the First Reich. After his death, one of his grandsons took the German lands to the east; one took the western part, which is now France; and another took the center section. Germany would remain disunified for over a thousand years.

Within the east kingdom, five great tribal duchies developed—Franconia, Swabia, Bavaria, Saxony, and Lorraine. In the tenth century, Otto, Duke of Saxony, commanded unity in this area. From the tenth century on, the German people moved eastward in search of more land. By the thirteenth century, they were firmly established in Prussia.

In 1517, Martin Luther, a Roman Catholic priest, began the Protestant movement in Germany. He protested the sale of indulgences and what he thought was the misleading teaching that went with them. He made a list of ninety-five arguments against the indulgences and sent them to the Archbishop Albert. He also posted another copy on the door of the Wittenberg church, inviting people to debate the issue.

Religious wars broke out throughout Europe. Most of the south Germans continued as Roman Catholics. In the north, many accepted the Protestant teachings. This religious dissension led to the Thirty Years' War, which was mainly fought on German soil. By the end of the war, there were more than 300 separate units of government, kingdoms, principalities, and free towns.

In the seventeenth century, Frederick William I of Brandenburg took over the duchy of Prussia. His son, Frederick the Great, became king of Prussia in 1740. At the beginning of the nineteenth century, Napoleon I of France annexed much of Germany and defeated Prussia. The German armies pushed Napoleon back across the Rhine in 1813. The peace settlement reached in 1815 made Prussia even stronger by giving it the Rhineland.

There were revolutions in 1848, after which a constitution was drawn up in Frankfurt. This document set up a constitutional monarchy headed by the king of Prussia. The crown was refused by the king of Prussia, and a short time later, his brother succeeded to the throne. In 1862, he called on Otto von Bismarck to become prime minister of Prussia. In 1867, Bismarck achieved German unity by organizing the North German Confederation of German states north of the Main River.

In 1863, Prussia defeated Denmark in a short war and annexed Schleswig-Holstein, which is Germany's northernmost state. After defeating the Austrian armies in 1866, Bismarck drew Hanover, Saxony, and the north German states into the North German Federation. The Franco-Prussian War in 1870 was the first large-scale conflict in which modern weapons were used: breech-loading rifles, machine guns, and rapid-firing fieldpieces. The victorious Prussians then took most of the provinces of Alsace and Lorraine.

In 1871, William I of Prussia was made emperor of Germany's Second Reich with Otto von Bismarck as chancellor. Berlin was the new capital of this constitutional monarchy.

A unified Germany prospered and became an industrial power. In 1888, William II became the new German Kaiser. He forced Bismarck to resign. William II maintained close ties with Austria-Hungary.

When the heir to the Austrian throne was assassinated in 1914, World War I began. Germany and Austria-Hungary fought against Britain, France, Russia, and eventually, the United States. In 1918, having lost the war, Kaiser Wilhelm II was forced to abdicate.

In 1919, a democratic republic was proclaimed in Germany. A national assembly met in Weimar to write the constitution, and the new government was called the Weimar Republic. Alsace and Lorraine were returned to France.

A worldwide depression hit, and by 1932 six million Germans were unemployed. Adolph Hitler came to power as the leader of the National Socialist German Workers Party. In the 1932 general election, the Nazis were the largest party in parliament. In January 1933, Hitler was appointed chancellor of Germany. Soon after, he became leader of the Third Reich and established a dictatorship.

A month later, the Reichstag building burned. Hitler used this as an excuse to round up communists and place them in concentration camps. Hitler became Germany's *Führer* (leader) controlling both the state and the army. More and more Jewish people and others called "undesirables" were placed in concentration camps.

Hitler formed an alliance with Italy and Japan. He quickly took the Rhineland, annexed Austria, and took Czechoslovakia. Hitler formed a nonaggression pact with the Soviet Union in 1939. Eventually Hitler attacked Russia, and Japan bombed Pearl Harbor. World War II was under way.

This war cost 45 million people their lives. The special concentration camps that had been set up massacred approximately 6 million Jews in the Nazi attempt to annihilate European Jewry. The atrocities committed in these camps only became fully known to the world after the war ended

On May 7, 1945, Germany surrendered and was divided into four zones, as was its capital, Berlin. It was occupied by American, British, French, and Soviet forces. The Soviet Union set up a Communist system in its zone. In 1961, they built a wall separating East and West Berlin. The occupation was to continue until the Allies agreed that Germany had become stable and peaceful.

The United States, Britain, and France combined their zones in 1949 and established the Federal Republic of Germany as a self-governing state. It joined the North Atlantic Treaty Organization (NATO) and the European Economic Community. The east section was known as the German Democratic Republic.

West Germany developed as a democracy with several political parties and regular elections. It had a market economy where businesses operated without too much governmental interference. East Germany developed a Communist government with control in the hands of the Socialist Unity Party. East Germany was allied to the Soviet Union and traded with other communist countries of Eastern Europe. This period of separation and hostility between the democratic West and the communist East became known as the Cold War.

In 1990, the first free elections were held in East Germany and there was a mandate for reunification with West Germany. By mid-1990, reunification had become a fact.

Although unified, Germany still faced problems. There was almost a total collapse of east German industry and agriculture. Investment in east Germany was slower than predicted. German taxpayers are still paying many subsidies in the east, and unemployment is climbing steadily.

There are now sixteen German states: Mecklenburg-West Pomerania, Brandenburg, Saxony-Anhalt, Saxony, Thuringia, Schleswig-Holstein, Bremen, Hamburg, Lower Saxony, North Rhine-Westphalia, Hessen, Rhineland-Palatinate, Saarland, Baden-Württemberg, Bavaria, and Berlin.

Government

West Germany developed a constitution, The Basic Law, which was meant to serve only as a transitional document. It is, however, the document that serves a united Germany today.

The head of state in Germany is the federal president, elected for a five-year term by a direct popular vote. The president can succeed himself/herself only once. Most of the president's powers are ceremonial.

The government is a parliamentary system with a legislature consisting of two houses. Members of the *Bundestag,* or lower house, are elected by popular vote of all citizens eighteen years of age and older and serve for four-year terms. This group is also known as the Federal Diet.

The upper house, the *Bundesrat,* or Federal Councils, includes 3 to 6 representatives from each Land (state) depending on population. These representatives are appointed by the Land's parliament.

Real power is in the hands of the chancellor, who is chosen by a majority of the *Bundestag.* He is the leader of the party or the coalition with a working majority in the *Bundestag.* By a majority vote, the *Bundestag* can remove the chancellor from office.

Helmut Kohl provided sixteen years of conservative rule as chancellor. In October 1998, Gerhard Schroeder took power as Germany's seventh postwar chancellor and provided a new direction for the country. He planned to strengthen social services and is committed to a free market.

There are several political parties in Germany. The two major parties currently are the Christian Democratic Union and the Social Democratic Party.

Religion

There are both Protestants and Catholics living in Germany. There are roughly 46 million Protestants and 35 million Roman Catholics. The Lutheran Church was founded in Germany in the sixteenth century. Bavaria has the highest percentage of Catholics.

The largest and most important Protestant cathedral in Germany is in Cologne.

Islam is also practiced in Germany. There are about 2 million Muslims, most of whom are people from Turkey, who practice the religion of Islam. Many mosques have been built where Muslims go to pray.

Education

Germany has a well-developed educational system. School is compulsory from the ages of six to eighteen. Many children attend kindergartens that are run by local government, churches, associations, companies, or private individuals. These kindergartens are not part of the state education system, so parents pay fees.

Children attend a basic primary school for the first four years. They start school at 8:00 A.M. and study until 1:00 P.M. Then they go home for lunch. When they have done their homework, most have the afternoon free. After primary school, students take examinations. Teachers advise parents whether their children should go on to *Hauptschule* until they are fifteen, to *Realschule* until they are sixteen, or to *Gymnasium* until they are nineteen.

About 80 percent continue school until they are fourteen or fifteen. Then they may attend a school part-time while they work and learn a trade.

Those who go on to attend the six-year intermediate schools are trained for a business career. They learn a foreign language, mathematics, science, and business skills.

A student who passes the examination for *Gymnasium* may continue for nine more years. A *Gymnasium* offers classical or modern languages, mathematics, and science. At age nineteen, *Gymnasium* students take another examination, called the *Abitur*, to qualify for the university.

Immigrants

Unremitting warfare was one reason Germans left their country. In 1709, about 15,000 Germans went to Britain, of whom nearly 4,000 settled in Ireland. Another 3,000 crossed the Atlantic to New York.

There were a substantial number of Germans who settled in colonial America. They came not only from Germany but also from Switzerland, Austria, and Russia. Other German immigrants came to North Carolina and to Pennsylvania. By 1745, there were an estimated 45,000 Germans living in Pennsylvania.

As late as 1834, almost all German emigrants came from the southwestern region of Germany. Then emigrants began coming from other regions. About half of the Germans who emigrated from 1816 to 1830 went to South America. Beginning in 1830, and on into the twentieth century, about 90 percent of German emigrants came to the United States.

The early German immigrants were farmers. Later on, German immigrants were often skilled as artisans or came with knowledge of advanced science and technology. They were involved in printing, iron works, and brewing beer. German names such as Budweiser and Coors remain prominent among American beer companies. There was a concentration of German immigrants in Wisconsin and in the middle Atlantic states.

Most of the early German immigrants to the United States came directly from Germany. But by 1920, about 300,000 descendants of Germans from Russia (also known as the Volga-Deutsche) were living in the United States.

Starting with the War for Independence, American military history has a long tradition of famous Americans with German ancestry. Some of these men had Anglicized their names. Among them are von Steuben, General George Custer, General John Pershing, General Dwight D. Eisenhower, Admiral Chester Nimitz, and General Norman Schwarzkopf.

Between 1820 and 1970, approximately 7 million Germans immigrated to the United States. German immigration peaked in the 1880s when more than 1.4 million Germans arrived. Then it dropped off dramatically in the early 1900s. From 1981 to 1990, 70,100 Germans immigrated to the United States. During the period of 1991 to 1995, another 30,900 came.

Over the years Germans have contributed to all fields of endeavor in the United States. The following are a few of the prominent names: Bausch and Lomb in optics; Weyerhauser, wood products; Chrysler, automobiles; Steinway, pianos; Wurlitzer, organs; Heinz, prepared foods; and Hershey, candy.

Language

Latin had a strong influence on the development of German, which is an Indo-European language. German is inflected with changing endings for verbs and nouns. It has three genders and fairly complicated grammatical rules. But many words in English and German share the same roots.

Of the 90 million German speakers in Central Europe, 90 percent live in Germany. The rest are in Austria, Switzerland, Italy, and parts of Belgium, France, and Luxembourg. German is also spoken in parts of Poland, Romania, and the former Soviet Union.

Martin Luther, who is responsible for the Protestant Reformation, also had an effect on the German language. His translation of the Bible into German from Latin was published in 1534. The language Luther used in the translation helped set a standard in the development of modern German.

Although German is spoken throughout the country, there are great differences in local dialects depending on the region. Swabian and Bavarian dialects are widespread in the south. In the north, Low German, which has much in common with English, is spoken. At school, children learn *Hochdeutsch* or High German, which is the language of business, newspapers, and television.

In addition to German, some of the citizens also speak Turkish and Wend. The Kreuzberg district in the middle of Berlin is the largest Turkish community outside Turkey.

The Arts and Sciences

German literature dates back to myths and folklore that were passed on by word of mouth during the wanderings of early Germanic tribes. Monks wrote the earliest literature in Latin. The *Nibelungenlied* is a battle saga that has become a national epic in Germany.

From the seventeenth century on, Germany produced writers of enormous literary stature. Perhaps the greatest of these is Johann Wolfgang von Goethe, who wrote poetry and novels. His greatest recognized masterpiece is *Faust*, a dramatic poem that took him 60 years to finish.

During the eighteenth century, major literary figures included playwright-critic Gotthold Lessing, playwright Friedrich Schiller, the poet Heinrich Heine, and philosophers Immanuel Kant and Friedrich Hegel.

Best known to children are the collection of fairy tales compiled in the early 1800s by Jacob and Wilhelm Grimm.

During the nineteenth century, two important philosophers were Friedrich Nietzsche and Karl Marx. Marx's *Communist Manifesto*, written with Friedrich Engels, along with his *Das Capital*, were the foundations of Communism.

In the twentieth century, the major literary figures in Germany were Thomas Mann and Bertolt Brecht. Mann wrote *Buddenbrooks* and *The Magic Mountain*. Both he and Brecht fled Nazi Germany.

Among well known recent German authors are Wolf Biermann, Reiner Kunze, Manfred Bieler, Uwe Johnson, Gisela Eisner, Heinrich Böll, who won the 1972 Nobel Prize for literature, and Günter Grass, who won the 1999 Nobel Prize for literature.

In the art world, Germany has had many masters including Albrecht Dürer, Matthias Grünewald, Hans Holbein the Younger, Lucas Cranach the Elder, Caspar David Friedrich, and Ernst Ludgwig Kirchner.

More recent major German artists of the nineteenth and twentieth centuries include Ernst Ludwig Kirchner, Kathe Kollwitz, Franz Marc, and Ernst Barlach.

Over the centuries, Germany has contributed greatly to the field of music. Early works include Gregorian chants and the lyric poems of the twelfth and thirteenth centuries. The Meistersingers were popular from the fourteenth to the seventeenth centuries.

In the early part of the eighteenth century, baroque music reached its height in the works of Johann Sebastian Bach. George Frederick Handel was a contemporary but composed most of his work in England. Ludwig von Beethoven began his work, which included nine symphonies, at the end of the eighteenth century and was followed by Johannes Brahms.

Great German composers from the nineteenth and twentieth centuries include Robert Schumann, Felix Mendelssohn, Richard Wagner, Richard Strauss, Paul Hindemith, Hans Werner Henze, and Karlheinz Stockhausen. Two famous German conductors were Bruno Walter and Otto Klemperer.

Perhaps the single most important German invention was the printing press. Johann Gutenberg began experimenting with the process of printing in 1440. He invented the movable type system and printed his first book, the *Holy Bible,* in 1453.

German inventors have had huge successes in science and engineering. In 1851, Hermann von Helmholtz invented the ophthalmoscope used in examining the eye. In 1876, Nikolaus Otto built the first four-stroke gas engine. Werner von Siemens built the first electric tramway in Berlin in 1881. In 1885, Gottlieb Drimler pioneered the first petrol-engined motorcycle, and in that same year Karl Benz produced the first petrol-driven motor car. In 1892, Rudolf Diesel invented the diesel engine. Wilhelm Röntgen discovered X-rays in 1895.

Johannes Kepler (1571–1630) expanded on the work of Copernicus and Galileo with his laws of planetary motion. Max Planck (1858–1947) developed quantum theory. And Albert Einstein (1879–1955) brought forth his theory of relativity that made him internationally famous. He left Nazi Germany for the United States in 1933.

Among German industries, the one that has had the strongest effect on every day life in the United States is the production of automobiles. The Volkswagen is famous around the world. Volkswagen owns Audi, which is the third largest exporter of luxury cars to the United States from Europe. And today's modern Mercedes is the direct descendant of Karl Benz's three-wheeler of 1885.

Food

Germans traditionally have rolls served with cheese, jam, or thin slices of ham for breakfast. Boiled eggs may be served too. The main meal is often served at lunchtime. A full lunch, called *Mittagessen,* may include soup, meat, vegetables, and fruits. Supper is lighter, often including cold meats and breads or an omelet with salad.

Each region of Germany has special foods. Berliners are known for their various sausages, such as Bockwurst, Leberwurst, Blutwurst, and Knackwurst. The most famous German sausage is the frankfurter, which is known around the world. In Germany, however, it is called a *Wiener-Wurschein.*

In the north, near the coast, a lot of fish are eaten. Hamburg is famous for its eel and for its vegetable soups. It is also the biggest area for growing fruit in Germany. Stuttgart is the Spätzle capital. Spätzle are crinkly flour noodles that are served with meat dishes.

Schnapps, a kind of gin with a strong juniper berry aroma, is often served in north Germany. German Hamburg and Bremen beers have been world famous for centuries. Although beer is the national drink, Germany also produces many fine wines. Pale, aromatic German wines are often served with meals.

Other German foods common in the United States and around the world include *Sauerbraten,* which is a pot roast in a sauce, and many varieties of potato salad. Sauerkraut is another well known German food.

Game such as deer, wild boar, rabbit, and pheasant make up many German meals. Game may be roasted with a wine sauce or stewed with mushrooms and berries.

Just as the British take high tea, the Germans at five o'clock in the afternoon have *Kaffee mit Kuchen,* coffee with cakes and tarts. This can be enjoyed at home or in town at a *Konditorei,* or pastry shop. The shops are filled with cakes, cream pies, fruit pies, and chocolate tarts.

The German delicatessen is a unique contribution to good eating. There is a great variety of cold meats and sausages, ready to serve salads, as well as smoked salmon, smoked eel, and Bismarck herring. There is also a wide range of local cheese and breads, often flavored with caraway or poppy seeds. Breads made from rye include the dark, heavy pumpernickel from Westphalia.

Christmas dinner in Germany is a special feast that often includes roast goose along with Christmas fruit bread, or Stollen. Spiced gingerbread and honeybread are part of the Christmas celebration.

The following is a recipe for making *Nürnberger Lebkuchen* or Christmas spice cookies.

Christmas Spice Cookies

2 eggs
1 cup sugar
1 cup sifted flour
$1/4$ teaspoon cinnamon
$1/8$ teaspoon ground cloves
$1/8$ teaspoon powdered cardamom
$1/4$ cup blanched almonds, chopped fine
$1/4$ cup candied lemon peel
$1/2$ teaspoon grated lemon peel

Beat the eggs in a bowl, gradually adding the sugar, and continue beating until thickened. Blend in the flour, spices, almonds, and lemon peels. Drop by teaspoonful on well-greased cookie sheets. Bake in a 325°F oven for 15–20 minutes. Remove from cookie sheet and cool on a rack. Cookies may be sprinkled with powdered sugar. Makes 2 dozen 2-inch cookies.

Recreation

Germans enjoy hiking and camping and have many hostels and camping grounds. Swimming, sailing, winter sports, handball, cycling, tennis, and riding are also popular. About one person in four in Germany belongs to a sports club.

Football (soccer) is the most popular team sport. The German national team won the World Cup in 1990.

As in the United States, computer games of all sorts are popular with German youth.

Customs and Traditions

Germany holds many pre-Lenten carnivals, called *Fasching* or *Karneval.* These usually take place in Catholic parts of the country in the south, such as the Rhineland or Bavaria. The biggest carnival is in Cologne. There a Rose Monday Procession is held. Millions of people line the streets to watch floats.

Oberammergau, a village in southern Bavaria, has become famous for its Passion Play, which is presented every ten years. The story of the first Easter is retold with local people playing all the parts. The Passion Play was first performed in 1634.

In the fall, Munich's famous beer festival, the *Oktoberfest,* is held. The St. Martin's Day procession is held on the eleventh of November. Children parade through the streets with paper lanterns.

In almost every German village, town, and city there is a *Christkindlmarkt,* Christ Child Market. It contains booths selling fruits, candies, sausages, cookies, and toys.

The Christmas tree, which is now universally a symbol of Christmas, is a German creation. Legends abound about the history of the German fir tree. When Prince Albert of Saxony, the husband of England's Queen Victoria, had a tree set up in Windsor Castle in 1841, he began a fashion that spread quickly throughout England and the world.

The carol, as we know it today, was first developed in Germany. One of the earliest carols, *Good King Wenceslas,* is associated with the life of the saint who was ruler of Bohemia in the tenth century. Another popular carol is *Stille Nacht,* or Silent Night.

In Germany the Christmas season extends from Saint Andrew's Night (November 30) to the Octave of Epiphany (January 13). During those 45 days, 18 holidays and festivals are observed. Starting on December 1, the First Sunday of Advent, children open a new window of their cardboard Advent Calendar each day until Christmas.

In rural Bavaria, the three Thursday evenings before Christmas are called *Klopfelnachten,* or knocking nights. Children wear masks and go through the neighborhood ringing cowbells and knocking on doors. Neighbors give them candy, coins, or fruit.

On Christmas Eve, the tree is lit and presents are distributed. In Lorraine, the Yule Log is lighted and will burn for three days. In northern Germany, there are Star of Seven processions. Hundreds of people carrying lighted seven-branch candlesticks march through the fields. At Berchtesgaden, over a thousand people in ancient costumes carry antique firearms and shoot off volleys at midnight.

Carp, a fish that is considered lucky, is often served at the Christmas Eve supper. People attend midnight church services and the manger scene is featured under almost every household Christmas tree.

Suggested Activities

Writing

1. There are many accounts of what happened at midnight on November 9, 1989, when the Berlin Wall, which had stood for 28 years dividing in half the city of Berlin finally came down. Have students read some of these stories from books, magazines, and newspapers.

   Ask students to imagine that they were present that night. Have them write a letter to a friend describing the sights and sounds. Share these letters on a class bulletin board called "When the Wall Came Tumbling Down."

Reading

2. This would be an excellent time to read and discuss *The Diary of a Young Girl* by Anne Frank. As part of the discussion, you might want to include Rian Verhoeven's *Anne Frank, Beyond the Diary* (Viking, 1993). It includes photographs, illustrations, and maps that will clarify many of the entries in the diary. *Anne Frank* by Wayne Jackman, from the "Life Stories" series (Wayland, 1992), also gives a simply written account of Anne Frank's life.

Vocabulary

3. To read and understand the history of Germany after World War II, when it was first divided into an East

and West Germany and later was unified, requires the understanding of many words and terms. Invite each student to contribute to a vocabulary bulletin board. Fill the board with 3 x 5-inch cards on which important words and phrases are defined in a few sentences. Some of these might include: Allies, black market, capitalism, chancellor, Cold War, communism, Communist bloc, Great Depression, Holocaust, immigrant, *Lebensraum*, NATO, Nazi, *Reich*, and scapegoat.

Math

4. World War II was very costly in human lives. For example, 5.3 million Germans, civilian and military, died during the war. Ask a pair of students to research the toll on the other countries that took part in World War II and to display the results of their research in bar graphs.

Social Studies

5. An agreement was reached to bring about the reunification of Germany after discussion between West German Chancellor Helmut Kohl and President Gorbachev of the Soviet Union in 1990. One of the key provisions of the agreement was that a united Germany would be free to join NATO. Ask a small group of students to research NATO. What is it? What does it do? When was it formed? Who are its members? Ask these students to report orally to the class what they learn.

Geography

6. Ask a small group of students to use a projector to project the outline of a map of Europe onto a large sheet of paper. The students should trace on the paper the borders of the various countries. Then, by the use of colors and other markings of their choosing, they should complete a legend showing when and which of the countries were invaded and taken over by Nazi Germany.

Music

7. Ask the music educator to share with students some of Ludwig van Beethoven's music. A small group of students might search the Web for information to share before or after hearing some of his music. For general information

and excerpts from letters that Beethoven wrote see http://classicalmus.com/composers/beethove.html. For pictures, audio midi files, an account of his life, and a listing of his works, see http://magic.hofstra.edu.70003/immortal/index.html. See http://www.cl.cam.ac.uk/users/mn200/music/composers.html for general information about classical composers, including Beethoven.

Art

8. The art educator, with adult volunteers, might be willing to work with a group of students to make "Prune People." These pieces of folk art are sold by the thousands in the Christmas markets in Germany. Although each is unique, a prune person usually has a dried fig for a body, prunes for arms and legs, and raisins for feet and hands. The pieces are threaded over wire. The head is a walnut in its shell. The faces of the Prune People are hand-painted. They are dressed in costumes of every color and description. The completed Prune People might be displayed in a library display case. Among books with pictures of these pieces of true folk art is *Christmas in Germany* (Passport Books, 1991).

Drama/Movement

9. With the help of a media specialist, locate and encourage students to read and discuss an old morality play. A good one would be *Everyman*, an English morality play, which shows how ordinary people thought about God at the end of the fifteenth century. This will be a good introduction to understanding the life and times of Martin Luther.

Dress

10. A pair of students might want to research the clothing worn in the Bavarian Alps in southeast Germany. They should find pictures of these outfits, and with permission, make photocopies that can be hung in the classroom.

Men from this area wear embroidered shorts and braces, often made of leather. In their hats they have a plume of hair from the little deer that live in that part of the mountains. They often wear calf socks with special knitted patterns.

The women wear silver laces and ornaments on their blouses and wear round hats that are often decorated with an eagle's feather. Green is a favorite color, and many of the pieces of clothing may be made of thick, green homespun called Loden.

Cooking

11. Students would enjoy making and decorating a gingerbread house. Many books will offer patterns that can be traced on stiff cardboard and then used to cut the pieces of cake to size. There are also many varieties of recipes for making both the cake and the decorative icing. Adding gumdrops, peppermints, or other candies adds to the fun.

Culminating Activity

12. The term *Holocaust* is most frequently used in reference to the approximately 6 million European Jews who were murdered by the Nazis and their supporters between 1933 and 1945. Others use the term to include the 4 million non-Jewish victims, including Gypsies, homosexuals, Jehovah's Witnesses, and Soviet prisoners of war.

    Much has been written on this topic and there have been dramatic films such as *Schindler's List,* documentaries, and videos. The United States Holocaust Memorial Museum attracts millions of visitors each year.

    Have class members plan and implement activities for a Holocaust Memorial Day in your school. It might include a special bulletin board, inviting a guest speaker, showing a film, etc.

Suggested Reading

Altman, Linda Jacobs. *Forever Outsiders, Jews and History from Ancient Times to August 1935.* Woodbridge, Conn.: Blackbirch Press, 1998.

Born, Wina, Project Editor. *German Cooking, Savory German Dishes Prepared in the Traditional Way.* New York: Garland Books, 1973.

Bradley, Catherine and John. *Germany, the Reunification of a Nation.* New York: Gloucester Press, 1991.

Burke, Patrick. *Germany.* New York: Thomson Learning, 1995.

Chrisp, Peter. *Blitzkrieg!* New York: Bookwright Press, 1991.

Cumming, David. *Germany.* East Sussex, England: Wayland, 1993.

Davies, Kath. *A First Guide to Germany.* Winchester, England: Zoe Books, 1994.

Dolan, Sean. *Germany.* Philadelphia, Pa.: Chelsea House, 1997.

Editors of the NTC Publishing Group. *Christmas in Germany.* Lincolnwood, Ill.: Passport Books, 1991.

Haviland, Virginia. *Favorite Fairy Tales Told in Germany.* Boston, Mass.: Little, Brown, 1959.

Hazelton, Nika Standen. *The Cooking of Germany.* New York: Time-Life Books, 1969.

Jackman, Wayne. *Anne Frank.* Hove, England: Wayland, 1992.

Krensky, Stephen. *Breaking into Print, Before and after the Invention of the Printing Press.* Boston, Mass.: Little, Brown, 1996.

Lace, William W. *The Nazis.* San Diego, Calif.: Lucent Books, 1998.

Mayer, Mercer, illustrator. *Favorite Tales from Grimm.* New York: Four Winds Press, 1982.

O'Neill, Judith. *Martin Luther.* Minneapolis, Minn.: Lerner Publications, 1979.

Plume, Ilse. *The Bremen-Town Musicians.* Garden City, N.Y.: Doubleday, 1980.

Rackham, Arthur, illustrator. *Grimm's Fairy Tales: Twenty Favorites.* New York: Viking, 1973.

Ripley, Elizabeth. *Dürer: A Biography.* Philadelphia, Pa.: J. B. Lippincott, 1958.

Schloredt, Valerie. *Germany.* Englewood Cliffs, N.J.: Silver Burdett Press, 1991.

Smalley, Mark. *The Rhine.* Winchester, England: Zoe Books, Wayland, 1992.

Steele, Philip. *Discovering Germany.* Winchester, England: Zoe Books, 1993.

Stewart, Gail B. *Germany.* New York: Crestwood House, 1990.

———. *Hitler's Reich.* San Diego, Calif.: Lucent Books, 1994.

Werstein, Irving. *The Franco-Prussian War, Germany's Rise as a World Power.* New York: Julian Messner, 1965.

Williams, Brian. *Karl Benz.* New York: Bookwright Press, 1991.

"Great gizzard eat up all these bees."

Hungary

A Tale from Hungary

One source for the retelling of this story from Hungary is *The Valiant Red Rooster* by Eric A. Kimmel, illustrated by Katya Arnold. Another version is found in Kate Seredy's *The Good Master*. And a third version appears in *The Little Cockerel* by Victor G. Ambrus. Other versions are common throughout Europe.

The Brave Red Rooster

A scrawny red rooster lived happily for a long time with a kindly old woman. The rooster scratched contentedly in the yard outside the old woman's cottage. Each morning faithfully, she came outside and threw the rooster some corn. But one morning the old woman did not appear.

After waiting for what seemed like a long time, the rooster crowed loudly. "Er-er-er-er-eee. Please remember me!" Still nothing happened. So the rooster walked up to the open door of the cottage and peered inside. There sat the old woman crying.

"Whatever is wrong?" asked the rooster.

"There is no money to buy food for you or for me," the woman said.

"Er-er-er-er-oo. I'll take care of you!" the rooster said. "Don't worry." And so saying, the rooster left the house,

The rooster stationed himself near the spot where a boulder made a big bump in the road. There he kept a watchful eye on the farmers' wagons as they went by. Some of the grain spilled out of sacks from almost every wagon. The rooster pecked it out of the road, stored it in his gizzard, and when he had enough, went to the miller.

The miller ground the corn into flour, which the rooster took to the baker. The baker turned the flour into bread, which the rooster took to the old woman. The rooster's gizzard grew larger and larger. In this way, the rooster and the old woman lived from day to day.

One morning the brave red rooster found a golden coin that had been dropped on the side of the road.

The rooster crowed, "Er-er-er-er-eee. I'm lucky as can be! I'll take this valuable golden coin to my good mistress and she will be able to buy all kinds of food."

The rooster set off for home with the gold coin sparkling in his beak. He hadn't gone far when a Sultan came riding by in his carriage. The Sultan spied the coin and wanted it for himself.

"Quick," the Sultan called to his guards. "Stop that rooster. Take the golden coin from him and bring it to me."

The guards rushed after the brave red rooster, snatched the coin from him, and took it to the Sultan who was very pleased. The Sultan carefully put the coin in a pocket of his wide yellow silk trousers and rode away.

The brave red rooster called after him. "Er-er-er-er-eee. Give that gold coin back to me!" But it was no use. The Sultan continued on his way. "I will follow you and crow in your window night and day until you return it," promised the rooster.

The rooster set off down the road after the Sultan. When at last the rooster reached the Sultan's palace, he marched up and down in front of the window and made an awful racket crowing. "Er-er-er-er-eee. Give my gold coin back to me!"

The Sultan grew very angry and called his guards to him. "Catch that rooster and drown him in the well," he commanded.

The guards rushed out of the palace, caught the rooster round the neck, and threw him into the deep, dark well.

But the moment that the rooster landed in the well, he began to drink. His great gizzard filled with water until the well was empty. Then the rooster flew out and began to parade again, back and forth, back and forth in front of the Sultan's window.

And as he marched, he crowed. "Er-er-er-er-eee. Give my gold coin back to me!"

The Sultan stared out the window and could scarcely believe his eyes and ears. He called his guards to him again. "I thought I commanded you to throw that rooster into the well?" he said.

"We did, oh mighty one," replied the captain of the guard. "Somehow he has escaped."

"This time," said the Sultan, "throw him into the fiery furnace so that he will be burned to ashes."

The guards marched outside, seized the brave red rooster, and threw him into the furnace.

Feeling the hot flames, immediately the rooster crowed, "Er-er-er-er-ee. My great gizzard will save me!" And all the water from the well came pouring out his gizzard. Immediately the water quenched the flames, and the rooster flew back to the Sultan's window where he began to march back and forth.

"Er-er-er-er-eee. Give my gold coin back to me," he crowded louder than ever.

The Sultan could scarcely believe his eyes and ears. He called his guards to him. "Did I not command you to throw that noisy rooster into the furnace?" he asked.

"We did, oh mighty one," the guards replied. "Somehow he has escaped."

"This time," the angry Sultan demanded, "throw him into the beehive and let the bees sting him to death."

The guards rushed outside again and seized the rooster. They carried him straight to the beehive and threw him into the midst of the buzzing bees.

Immediately the rooster cried, "Er-er-er-er-oo. I know what to do! Great gizzard eat up all these bees." The gizzard ate up all the bees, and the rooster returned to the Sultan's window where he once again began parading up and down, up and down, crowing all the while, "Er-er-er-er-ee. Give my gold coin back to me."

The Sultan could scarcely believe his eyes and ears. Again he called his guards to him. "What's this? What's this?" he demanded. "Did I not command you to throw this rascal rooster to the bees?"

"We did, oh mighty one," responded his captain of the guard. "Somehow he has escaped."

"This time," commanded the Sultan, "there will be no escape. Go get that rowdy rooster. I myself will squash him flat."

The guards rushed out and brought the rooster to the Sultan who thrust him inside his yellow silk trousers and was about to sit down as hard as he could on his throne when a terrible buzzing sound was heard. As soon as he was thrust into the Sultan's trousers, the rooster's gizzard set free all those angry bees. The bees swarmed inside the Sultan's trousers and began to sting.

"Ow! Ow! Ow!" the Sultan screamed, and he began hopping about the room.

The bees continued to sting the mighty Sultan until he cried out and said, "I am justly punished for being a thief. Give the gold coin back to the righteous rooster."

The soldier took the coin and handed it back to the rooster who spread his wings and flew all the way home.

The old woman was there waiting for him. "I've been so worried," she said. "What have you been doing?"

Then the rooster dropped the gold coin in front of her and crowed, "Er-er-er-er-ooo. I'll tell you what to do. Take this gold coin to market. You'll be able to buy all the food we need. Enough to last us for a long, long time."

And that's exactly what the old woman did. She brought home meat, sausages, pies, cakes, fruit, vegetables, cheese, and yogurt.

When the rooster saw what she had brought, he crowed, "Er-er-er-er-eee. Enough for you and me."

Then the brave red rooster and the little old woman ate, and ate, and ate. They were never hungry again and lived happily ever after.

Background Information

The Republic of Hungary is a flat landlocked country in the center of Europe. It shares boundaries with Slovakia to the north, the Ukraine to the northeast, Romania to the southeast, Yugoslavia to the south, Croatia and Slovenia to the southwest, and Austria to the northwest. The population of Hungary is 9,935,774. It covers 35,919 square miles.

Until the end of World War I, the kingdom of Hungary reached from the Carpathian Mountains to the Adriatic Sea. After the 1920 Treaty of Trianon, Hungary lost about 70 percent of its territory and was reduced to its present size.

The Danube River, or Duna, flows south and cuts the country in half. The Danube is an important trade route between Hungary and its neighbors. The main tributary of the Danube, the Tisza River, also crosses the country from north to south. The Ipel in the north, and the Mur and Drava Rivers in the southwest make up part of Hungary's borders.

Most of eastern Hungary is lowland, called the Great Plain or *Great Afold*. This covers more than one-half of Hungary's total land. This area, sometimes called the *puszta*, is filled with farms and cattle ranches. The long-horned gray cattle are descendants of the original animals brought to Hungary by the first nomadic invaders. The Hungarian *pulis*, a breed of rough-coated dogs, are a big help to herdsmen.

West of the Danube are hills, valleys, and woods. In the western part of the country is Lake Balaton, which is the largest lake in central Europe. It is so large that it is sometimes called the Hungarian Sea. This shallow lake, averaging only 10 feet deep with a maximum depth of 35 feet, is a favorite spot for tourists from Western Europe.

To the northwest is the Little Plain or *Kisalfod*. This plain covers about one-third of Hungary. In the northeast are hills and ranges of mountains, and in the north-central portion of the country are mountains of volcanic origin.

The mountains in these north-central highlands include the Borzsony, Cserhat, Matra, Bukk, and Sempleni. They are separated by river valleys, and contain an enormous system of caves. Mt. Kekas, in the Matra Mountains, at 3,330 feet is the highest peak in Hungary.

The climate in Hungary is continental, with seasons of almost equal length. But the climate can vary from year to year because Hungary is located where three climatic zones intersect. Temperatures vary between 25°F to 72°F. The annual mean temperature is 50°F. The average rainfall each year is 25 inches. There is more rain in the west than in the east, and the west has more temperate winters and summers than the east. About 55 percent of the land is suitable for cultivation, so Hungry is nearly self-sufficient in food.

Hungary is not rich in mineral wealth. Copper, lead, zinc, and iron are found in sufficient quantities for mining. There is some hard coal, lignite, and natural gas. Bauxite, the raw material for aluminum, is a major export. Coal, oil, coke, and iron ore are brought into the country on barges that are shipped on the Danube from Russia and the Czech Republic.

Most of Hungary's industrial plants are powered by water-produced electricity or fossil fuels. The first atomic power plant in Hungary began operating in 1982. Because it lacks resources for large industry, Hungary has developed industries requiring skill but limited materials. Hungary manufactures machine tools, electrical appliances, agricultural machinery, trucks, and bicycles. There is also a developing pharmaceutical industry.

About one-fifth of Hungarians work on farms. During the Communist era, farming was done on state farms or cooperatives where farmers were paid fixed wages. They raised wheat, rye, corn, potatoes, sugar beets, and tobacco. Each farmer was also given a small plot of land for personal use and could market the extra produce from these plots. Since the end of Communist rule in 1989, there has been an encouragement of private farmers cultivating private land. Hungarian farms produce paprika, sweet peppers, sunflower seeds, fruits, potatoes, sugar beets, grain, and livestock.

Budapest is the capital city of Hungary. About one-fifth of the total population of the country resides in this city. Budapest is located in north-central Hungary near the border of Slovakia.

The river Danube divides the city of Budapest in half. At one time Buda on the west bank, and Pest on the east bank, were separate cities. They merged into one in 1873 and included at the same time another old city on the riverbank, Obuda. More than half of the country's industry is located close to the capital.

Many things make Budapest a particularly interesting city. It has a series of 8 bridges that cross over the Danube and 123 thermal springs, which make it a great spa. Budapest has many theatres, two opera houses, and three symphony orchestras.

Because it is the seat of government, Budapest has an imposing Parliament and other government buildings. It also contains the rounded domes of ancient Turkish mosques, and, on Castle Hill, a small Turkish cemetery. Since the city has been destroyed and rebuilt several times, many of the buildings are reconstructions of the originals.

The city is filled with statues, monuments, and parks. The statue, "Liberty," stands atop Gellert Hill, marking the Soviet victory over the Nazis and Hungarian fascists. Mellenary Monument in Heroes' Square marks the one-thousandth anniversary of the Magyar conquest of Hungary. The Hungarian National Gallery and History Museum are housed in Buda Castle. The Budapest City Park, with its Zoological Gardens, is a favorite spot for weekend outings.

Located in the Danube are many small islands, including Margaret Island, which is famous for its huge park and luxury hotel.

There are also historical ruins nearby. At the northern border are remains of Celtic settlements from the Copper Age. There are ruins of a Roman capital and Roman amphitheater built to hold 16,000 spectators. There are also the remains of a fourth century Christian chapel.

Famous buildings in or near the city include the Gothic Coronation Church of Matthias, the National Library, which is housed in the rebuilt Royal Palace, and the Parliament Building that was completed in 1903.

Located in the south is the city of Pecs. The country's largest coal and uranium mines are located here. It is also home to Hungary's oldest university, founded in 1367. One of its most famous buildings is an eleventh century cathedral.

Other major cities include Dunaujvaros, about 45 miles south of Budapest. Most people who live here are employed in the Danube Iron Works, which is the largest foundry in the country. Miskoic, an industrial town, is in the north; Debrecen, an old college city, is located in the east; and Szeged, to the west, has Cathedral Square, which is used for open-air drama and opera.

In the Great Plains is the city of Kecskemet, which is in the center of apricot growing in Hungary. Here there are distilleries for making brandy and factories for jams and jellies.

Szeged is the major center for southern Hungary. It is on the banks of the Tisza River. Votive Church, the town cathedral, has an exceptional organ with 1,040 pipes and 5 keyboards.

History

During its earliest history, around 14 B.C., Hungary was part of the Roman Empire and later was overrun by Huns, Slavs, and Germanic tribes. Today's inhabitants of Hungary are descendants of warrior-nomad Magyar tribes led by Arpad that moved into central Europe from Asia in the ninth century. These settlers included horsemen with fur-trimmed caps and leather boots as well as women and children who came in covered wagons.

The Magyars brought with them oxen, agricultural tools, cattle, horses, water buffalo, sheep, and dogs. In about ten years, these Magyars who invaded Hungary conquered the Slavic and other groups who had lived in this region. These tribes formed a medieval kingdom.

Geza introduced Christianity in the late tenth century, and Geza's son, Stephan, became the first Christian ruler. On Christmas Day, A.D. 1000, Stephan I was enthroned with a crown sent by the Pope. Later he was canonized and became the patron saint of Hungary.

The Germans made unsuccessful attempts to take over Hungary, and in the twelfth century, Hungary was threatened by the Byzantine Empire but survived until the thirteenth century when Hungary was over-run by the Mongols.

During the fourteenth century, under Charles Robert and Louis the Great, Hungary became a leading European power. In the middle of the fifteenth century, the Ottoman Turks raided Hungary and were fought off by the Hungarian military leader, Janos Hunyadi. After his death, the country became divided, and the invading Turks defeated the Hungarian army.

Central and southern Hungary were ruled by the Turks for 150 years, while the west and north were ruled by the Habsburg emperors of the Holy Roman Empire. All that remained of Hungary was Transylvania.

In 1686, the Turks were driven out of Hungary and all of the country came under the rule of the Austrian Habsburgs. Then in 1848, Hungarians demanded independence from Austria, but the revolt was put down. Hungarians forced the Habsburgs to compromise and create the Dual Monarchy of Austria-Hungary. Hungary accepted the Austrian Emperor, Franz Joseph, as king but kept an internal autonomy.

During World War I, Hungary fought on the side of Germany and Austria. When the empire collapsed at the end of the war, Hungary lost two-thirds of its territory to Romania, Czechoslovakia, and Yugoslavia. Hungarian minorities continue to live in Slovakia, Romanian Transylvania, and Croatia.

In 1938, under pressure from Germany, Hungary passed its first anti-Jewish laws. In 1941, Hungary entered World War II on the side of Germany. By 1944, the Nazis had killed many of the Jews of Europe, and the largest community of Jews that were left, approximately 750,000, was in Hungary. The Nazis put Adolf Eichmann in charge of exterminating the Hungarian Jews.

The Nazis moved into Hungary in March 1944 and began sending Jews to Auschwitz and other concentration camps. The Jews were forced to turn over their possessions and were then herded into train cars. From May 1944 to July 1944, almost 150 trains left Hungary for the concentration camps, where Jews and Gypsies, among others, would be gassed and killed.

When word of what was happening reached the United States, President Franklin Delano Roosevelt set up a new organization called the War Refugee Board to help the Hungarian Jews. The United States asked Sweden, a neutral country, for help, and Raoul Wallenberg, a Swedish diplomat, was chosen to lead the effort. Wallenberg went to Budapest.

Wallenberg designed a fake passport called the Schutz-Pass and gave these out to Jewish people. Nazis believed those holding these documents were official Swedish citizens and left these people alone. Many buildings in Budapest were turned into "safe houses" where those who had a Schutz-Pass could live and be safe.

After the Hungarian government surrendered to the Allies, a Nazi-Hungarian group called Arrow Cross seized power and still persecuted the Jews. Wallenberg continued his efforts and is credited with saving 100,000 Hungarian Jews.

In January 1945, Soviet forces occupied Hungary and Communists took power. Shortly afterward, Raoul Wallenberg disappeared. Many think he was taken to a Soviet prison.

The Russians set up a provisional government in Hungary in October 1944 that heavily favored Communists. In the 1945 elections, the Smallholders Party, representing farmers and middle class workers, won 60 percent of the vote, while Communists received only 17 percent. The new government began rebuilding the country.

By 1948, the Communist Party took full control of Hungary and arrested many of the leaders of other parties. The new government outlawed all parties and organizations that they did not control. There was a revolt against the Communists in November 1956. The revolt failed, thousands were killed, and the leader of the uprising, Imre Nagy, was executed.

Janos Kadar came to power. Although he was loyal to Communism, he did liberalize the economic system in Hungary and got some autonomy for his country. Eventually, he was removed from power. In October 1989, the Communist Party was dissolved and reconstituted as the Hungarian Socialist Party. Free elections took place in the spring of 1990. Hungary is currently moving toward a market economy and a free political system.

Government

In 1989, a new constitution was endorsed, and it ended the Communist Party's monopoly of power. In the years following, Hungary found itself somewhere between Communism and a real democracy. Its political system is still developing.

The constitution calls for a National Assembly or parliament consisting of 386 deputies to be elected to four-year terms by voters who are eighteen years of age or older. This assembly is called the *Orszaggyules*. Parties must receive at least 4 percent of the vote to be represented in the parliament. At present, several different political parties hold seats in this assembly.

The members of the Parliament are responsible for electing the president of the republic, the prime minister, and the

members of the Constitutional Court. The president of Hungary, who is chief of state, has a mostly ceremonial role. The prime minister is the acting head of government.

Hungary is divided into twenty-four counties and the metropolitan area of Budapest. Local government is responsible for collecting local taxes and passing legislation and providing services including education, health care, and welfare.

A Supreme Court administers justice. There are other courts, including the Budapest Metropolitan Court, county and district courts, and a Constitutional Court that decides on constitutional questions.

Religion

About two-thirds of the Hungarian people are Roman Catholics. There are also many Protestants. Approximately 20 percent of the population are Calvinists and 5 percent are Lutherans. Another 80,000 are Jewish.

When the Communists came to power, religion was strictly controlled. In more recent years, relations between the state and the Catholic Church have improved. Diplomatic relations with the Vatican were established in 1978. In 1990, religious freedom was granted to all Hungarians.

Education

Education in Hungary is free and compulsory for all children ages six to sixteen. The adult literacy rate is 99 percent.

Most children begin school at the age of six. For the first four years, they study reading, writing, math, and basic science, drawing, and singing. During the next four years, they study history, Hungarian language and literature, geography, sciences, and foreign languages. Russian is usually taught from the fourth year of school on. In the elementary grades, it is common to offer two years of English, one year of French, and one year of German.

There are also many after-school activities. Clubs centered on topics such as folkdancing, target shooting, and literature are popular.

After the eighth grade, students in the top 20 percent go on to the *gimnazium*. This is like an academic high school. The next 25 percent go to vocational high schools, where they are trained for middle positions in industry. About 40 percent go to "skilled worker training schools." Here they study specific industries and get on-the-job-training. The rest join the work force.

Less than half of the graduates of the gimnazium go on to university level. To continue, they must have the highest academic qualifications. Open to them currently are 5 academic, 4 medical, and 9 technical universities. Other institutions of higher learning are also available. Education in Hungary is in a period of transition, and the government is allowing the establishment of private schools and church-run schools.

Several thousand people take correspondence courses or go to night school. Adult summer school is also popular. Until 1994, university education was free to those who were admitted, but now students must pay tuition.

Immigrants

The Magyars were the ancestors of today's Hungarians, and there are very few minorities living in Hungary. About 0.5 percent of the population is German, and there are about 400,000 Romanies or gypsies, some of whom speak Romany.

Since the large country that was once Hungary was split into pieces, about 7 million ethnic Hungarians live outside their country. Over 2 million Hungarians live in neighboring Romania, and large numbers of Hungarians are also living in Slovakia and Serbia.

Substantial numbers of Hungarians have immigrated to Western Europe. Others have left Hungary to immigrate to Australia, Canada, and the United States. Between 1890 and 1910, approximately 1.5 million Hungarians came to the United States.

Hungarians have contributed much to the United States. Joseph Pulitzer, who immigrated to the United States, rose to become the owner of the *New York World*, funded the establishment of the Columbia Journalism School, and is remembered for the Pulitzer prize given to outstanding writers, artists, and journalists.

Agoston Haraszty helped to found the California wine industry by importing 200,000 grape cuttings from Europe, including the Hungarian Tokay variety.

In the film industry, Adolph Zukor, who also founded Paramount Pictures, produced the first American full-length film, *The Prisoner of Zenda*.

Many Jews fled Hungary during and after World War II, and other Hungarians fled the Soviet occupation, especially after the failed uprising during 1956. Hungarians have been admitted to the United States under a number of Refugee Acts. From 1981 to 1990, 4,942 were admitted. From 1991 to 1995, another 1,201 came.

Language

The official language of Hungary is Magyar, or Hungarian. Ninety-eight percent of the population speak, Hungarian. Most minority groups speak their own language in addition to Hungarian. German and English are popular courses taught in the schools.

About 5 percent of the total population of Hungary are gypsies. Originally they were a nomadic people from India and they live apart from other Hungarians. They speak a dialect called Romany.

The Hungarian language is not related to Germanic, Romance, or Slavic languages. Hungarian belongs to the Finno-Ugric family of languages, as do Finnish and Estonian.

The stress in Hungarian words is placed on the first syllable, and letters of the alphabet always stand for the same sound. Accents, or the lack of accents, may completely change the meaning of a word. Hungarian is difficult to translate.

Hungarians have made contributions to the English language that we speak. For example, the word coach, meaning a bus, comes from the Hungarian *kocsi*. We get our word "dollar" from the old Hungarian word *taller*, which means gold coins. And the Hungarian phrase *ici-pici*, meaning very little, appears in English as *itsy-bitsy*.

The Arts and Sciences

There have been many fine Hungarian writers, but few are known to the world at large because their works have not been translated. The writings of Mor Jokai from the nineteenth century are still very popular. Imre Madach wrote a well known philosophical drama, *The Tragedy of Man.* The poet Endre Ady wrote in the early twentieth century. Perhaps the greatest modern Hungarian poet is Attila Jozsef.

One of the few Hungarian writers well known abroad is Ferenc Molnar, who died in 1952. His work, *Liliom,* was the basis for the famous Broadway musical, *Carousel.*

Several Hungarian musicians are revered worldwide. Among these is Franz Liszt, the nineteenth century pianist who wrote concerti, sonatas, ballads, rhapsodies, and etudes that influenced many composers who followed him. Liszt became the first director of the Hungarian Academy of Music.

Two other major musicians are Bela Bartok (1881–1945) and Zoltan Kodaly (1882–1967). Both of these men wrote work rooted in Hungarian folk music. Kecskemet is the birthplace of Kodaly, where there is the Kodaly Music Institute, which is internationally known for its intensive course work and lectures.

Among famous Hungarian operettas is *The Merry Widow* by Franz Lehar. Sandor Szokolay has written three full-length operas as well as works for choirs and orchestras.

Hungarians have also made many contributions in the sciences. Lorand Eotvos invented a pendulum used by researchers seeking oil. Janos Csonka produced the first working carburetor. Albert Szent-Gyorgyi received the 1937 Nobel Prize for medicine recognizing his work on vitamin C.

Janos Bolyai worked in the field of relativity and space physics. Ignaz Semmelweis discovered the cause of childbirth fever. World-renowned mathematicians included Gyorgy Alexits, Lazlo Redei, and Alfred Renyi. While working in the United States, Edward Teller and Leo Szilard worked on the development of atomic energy. Hungarian Erno Rubik designed the multi-colored puzzle, Rubik's Cube.

Food

Two groups, influential in the early history of Hungary, that have had a strong effect on Hungarian cooking were the Magyars and the Turks. Since the Magyars were nomads, they preferred flavored food that would travel well without spoiling. They ate *gulyas,* a soup made by drying cubes of meat that had been cooked with onions. Mixed with hot water, it made a nourishing meal. Today's goulash is still a favorite Hungarian dish, but the meat used is no longer dried.

Magyars introduced a special cooking utensil called a *bogracs.* This is a copper or cast iron kettle suspended from a stick over an open fire. On cookouts Hungarians continue to use *bogracs* to make their goulash or fish stew.

Chicken paprikas are famous Hungarian dishes. Peppers are grown in Hungary, and red paprika is the national spice. Paprika first appeared in Hungary during the sixteenth century during the Turkish occupation. The Spice Pepper Museum is located in the city of Kalocsa and is the only museum in the world honoring paprika.

Strudel and coffee are other Hungarian treats introduced during the Turkish occupation. Hungarians fill phyllo dough with sweet fillings such as cherries or poppy seeds to make their strudel.

Hungarians raise fat geese that have been stuffed with corn to enlarge their livers. When these geese are killed, the goose liver pate is highly prized at restaurants throughout the world.

Hungary has native wines and a fine apricot brandy. The wines from Lake Balaton and Mor are the most famous. The town of Hajos is Hungary's famous cellar village. Many of the families have cellars used to make special wines. The grapes are grown on the Hosszuhegy State Farm outside the town.

With parent help, students could enjoy a simple breakfast of Hungarian scrambled eggs.

Hungarian Scrambled Eggs/ Tojasrantotta

8 eggs

$1/2$ teaspoon salt

$1/4$ pound smoked sausage cut into $1/2$ inch pieces

1 medium peeled and chopped onion

1 medium seeded green pepper cut into rings

$1/2$ teaspoon paprika

Beat the eggs lightly in a medium bowl. Stir in the salt and set aside.

In a large frying pan, fry the sausage over medium heat. Add the onion and green pepper and sauté until the onion is transparent.

Add the egg mixture to the frying pan and cook, scrambling with a spoon, until the eggs are set. Sprinkle with paprika before serving hot. Serves 4 people.

Recreation

A large percentage of Hungarians belong to sports clubs. They take part in track and field events, swimming, water polo, soccer, fencing, weight lifting, gymnastics, sport shooting, boxing, and wrestling.

Swimming is a popular sport and is usually a part of a school's physical education program. Most new schools are built with enclosed pools. At the first modern Olympics, Alfred Hajos won the 100-meter and 1,200-meter swim meets.

Canoeing and kayak racing are competitive sports. Many teams train on the Danube River and compete in world championships.

Hungary has many spas and hot springs where people go to relax. At some baths, chess players play on boards fixed at the level of the water.

Football, or soccer, is the favorite sport in Hungary. There are annual countrywide championships for young players. In 1986, the national soccer team made it to the finals of the World Cup soccer championships in Mexico.

Other favorite leisure activities include gymnastics, volleyball, team handball, bicycling, basketball, ice hockey, skating, and cross-country skiing.

Customs and Traditions

When Hungarians meet, they greet each other with a firm handshake. Men allow women to extend their hand first. Except between men, Hungarians also *puszi*, or greet one another with a hug and a kiss.

Many of Hungary's traditional holidays and festivals are related to the religious or agricultural calendars. These include saints' days and planting and harvesting days. During the Communist regime, there were many political holidays that have since been dropped.

Rather than celebrate birthdays, Hungarians prefer to celebrate "name days." The days on the Hungarian calendar are each assigned to a certain Christian name that is commonly used. People with that name celebrate on their "name day." Flowers and small gifts are given, and the family comes together to celebrate.

Major national holidays include the following: New Year's Day on January 1, National Holiday commemorating the 1848 Revolution on March 15, Easter Monday in April, Labor Day on May 1, Whitsun Monday in May, National Day/St. Stephen's Day on August 20, National Holiday for the 1956 Revolution on October 23, and Christmas on December 25.

A popular tourist attraction is the *buso,* which is a pre-Lenten procession held at Mohacs. There are parades throughout the city in which people wear grotesque masks. This tradition dates back to the days of the Turkish occupation, when the masks were supposed to frighten away evil spirits.

On Palm Sunday, Hungarians hold religious processions called *Virag Vasarnap.* This includes having pussy willows blessed. The pussy willows are then placed in a holy corner in their homes. In some of the villages, an effigy made of rags and straw, which they call Prince Cibere, is burned. Hungarian peasants believe that this ceremony keeps away sickness and trouble and hurries along the coming of spring to their towns.

Since the crowning of King Stephen by the Pope, Catholicism has been vitally important to many Hungarians. St. Stephen is the focus of veneration. On August 20, St. Stephen's Day, a great procession of costumed people holding religious banners files through the streets of Budapest.

In the Hungarian countryside, August and September are the months for harvest festivals marked with drinking, eating, and dancing in the open air.

The Hungarian Christmas season begins on December 6, St. Nicholas Day. On the eve of St. Nicholas Day, Hungarian children put boots in the window similar to the way many people in the United States hang stockings by the fireplace on Christmas Eve. The boots are filled with goodies such as chocolate, tangerines, walnuts, dates, and figs, from the Hungarian Santa named Telapo.

On Holy Night, or Christmas Eve, family members in Hungary sit around a Christmas tree and share gifts and eat and drink together. On December 26, family members visit each other and feast and eat special cakes such as the *bejgli,* a rolled pastry covered in walnuts or poppy seeds.

New Year's Eve, or *Szilveszter,* is celebrated with music and dancing and drinking. At midnight, people eat wieners called *virsli.* In Budapest, fancy New Year's Eve balls are held. These often include dancing and full orchestras. Pork is served at the traditional New Year's Day dinner.

Suggested Activities

Writing

1. A small group of students might want to plan what sights they would see if they could make a trip through Hungary. Using pictures from books and magazines, these students could share their imaginary journey with the class. One source of information would be to write for free information from the Embassy of Hungary, 3910 Shoemaker Street NW, Washington, D.C. 20008 or the Hungarian Tourist Office, 150 East 58th Street, 33rd Floor, New York, NY 10155-3398.

Reading

2. Invite a few interested students to participate in a book discussion group. One possible title is *The Fall of the Red Star* by Helen M. Szablya and Peggy King Anderson (Boyds Mills Press, 1996). This book describes Stephen's life when he joins the Resistance movement in Hungary to drive out the Communists. Another possibility is the award-winning novel, *Upon the Head of the Goat, a Childhood in Hungary 1939–1944* by Aranka Siegal (Farrar, Straus & Giroux, 1981). This book tells the story of nine-year-old Piri Davidowitz and her Jewish family in Europe during World War II.

Vocabulary

3. To have a clear understanding of the period of World War II in Hungary necessitates a somewhat specialized vocabulary. Have students discuss the following words and terms and define them: Allied Powers, anti-Semitism, Aryans, death camps, deport, ghetto, Holocaust, Nazi, refugees, Shoah, and Third Reich.

Math

4. It sometimes helps students to get a more accurate idea of the size of a relatively unknown country (such as Hungary) by comparing it with something that is known, such as one of the states in the United States. In size, Hungary covers about 36,000 square miles. Ask a pair of students to investigate and report to the class what they learn. What state or states in the United States are similar in size?

Social Studies

5. The Holocaust that occurred during World War II is one of the darkest periods in human history. It is estimated that the Hungarian Budapest community of Jews now numbers 75,000 people, as compared with 750,000 before the war. It is one of the few large Jewish communities remaining in Eastern Europe.

Divide the class into four to six groups to study the Holocaust. Each group might choose a specific topic or read and discuss a book together. Some possibilities are: *The Holocaust* by R. Conrad Stein; *The Holocaust: A History of Courage and Resistance* by Bea Stadtler; *My Brother's Keeper: The Holocaust Through the Eyes of an Artist* by Israel Bernbaum; *Anne Frank: The Diary of a Young Girl,* by Anne Frank; and *A Nightmare in History: The Holocaust* by Miriam Chaikin.

Geography

6. Ask a pair of students to prepare a detailed map showing Hungary and its immediate neighbors the Ukraine, Slovakia, Romania, Yugoslavia, Croatia, Slovenia, and Austria. The map should indicate major cities, mountain ranges, rivers and lakes. Post the map on a bulletin board to share with the class.

Music

7. With the help of the school music educator, this would be an excellent time to study Bela Bartok and/or Franz Liszt. Possible music includes Bela Bartok's *Concerto for Orchestra,* RCA, 1993, CD, RCA: 09026-61504-2 with the Chicago Symphony Orchestra and Franz Liszt's *Hungarian Rhapsody No. 1,* 1 compact disc, Sony 1992,

with the New York Philharmonic. Websites with further information on Bela Bartok are www.classicalmus.com/composers/bartok.html and www.media.mcmaster.ca/bb.htm. Sites with information on Franz Liszt include www.d-vista.com/OTHER/franzliszt.html and www.futurenet.com/classicalnet/reference/composers/liszt.htm.

Art

8. Hungary has a traditional coat-of-arms that was established in 1848. It was not used during the Communist regime, but was restored in 1990 by the Parliament. Ask a pair of students to research the coat-of-arms, called a *cimer*, draw it in color, and discuss it with the class.

Drama/Movement

9. Two internationally famous Hungarian playwrights are Imre Madach and Ferenc Molnar. Invite a pair of students, with help from a media specialist, to research these two writers and share what they learn with the class.

Dress

10. One of the most interesting forms of dress in Hungary is the long, reversible fur coats worn by shepherds. Working with a media specialist, have a pair of students search out pictures of this traditional garment, and with permission, photocopy or bring them in to share with the class.

Cooking

11. A group of students might want to gather at home in one student's kitchen and made strudel for the class.

Strudel/Retes

(Phyllo sheets may be purchased at most grocery stores.)
6 phyllo sheets
6 tablespoons unsalted butter, melted
6 tablespoons powdered sugar, plus extra for sprinkling

Cherry Filling/Meggyes

2 16-ounce cans unsweetened tart cherries
6 tablespoons sugar
2 teaspoons cinnamon sugar (1 part cinnamon to 3 parts sugar)
1/4 cup finely chopped almonds
2 tablespoons fine bread crumbs

First drain the cherries in a colander. Preheat the oven to 350°F. Butter a 9 x 13-inch pan. Place a damp, clean kitchen towel (not terry cloth) on a clean work surface. Gently place 1 phyllo sheet on the towel. Dip a pastry brush into the melted butter and brush the sheet. Then sprinkle it with powdered sugar. Repeat this with 2 more sheets of dough.

On the top sheet of dough, sprinkle the bottom third with 1 tablespoon bread crumbs. Spread half the drained cherries over the bread crumbs, and over the top sprinkle 3 tablespoons sugar, 1 teaspoon cinnamon sugar, and 2 tablespoons almonds. Leave 1 inch on each side of the pastry free of filling. Fold in the 2 sides and, starting at the bottom, carefully roll up the sheets.

Place the roll, seam side down in a buttered pan and brush with melted butter. Make a second roll in the same way. Bake for 30 minutes or until golden brown. Allow to cool and then cut each roll into 1-inch slices. Place on dessert plates and sprinkle with powdered sugar. (Makes about 24 pieces.)

Culminating Activity

12. Pairs of students might select and present information on an important person from Hungary's history in whatever format they choose on a day given over to this celebration of greatness. Each pair of students might have 2 to 5 minutes to present.

The following names are among those that might be considered. Prior to 1500: Arpad, Bela IV, Matthias Corvinus, Janos Hunyadi, St. Stephen, and Sigismund, King of Hungary.

From 1500 to 1900: Janos Arany, Balent Balassi, Farenc Deak, Gyorgy Dozsa, Theodor Herzl, Franz Liszt, Victor Madarasz, and Prince Ferenc Rakoczi.

From 1900 to the present: Dennis Gabor, Gyorgy Hevesy, Nicholas Horthy, Zoltan Kodaly, Lajos Kossuth, Franz Lehar, Georg Solti, and Aron Tmasi.

Suggested Reading

Ambrus, Victor G. *The Little Cockerel.* New York: Harcourt, Brace & World, 1968.

Daniel, Jamie, Michael Nicholson, and David Winner. *Roaul Wallenberg.* Milwaukee, Wisc.: Gareth Stevens, 1992.

Dobler, Lavinia. *Customs and Holidays around the World.* New York: Fleet Press, 1962.

Esbenshade, Richard S. *Hungary.* New York: Marshall Cavendish, 1994.

Hargittai, Magdolna. *Cooking the Hungarian Way.* Minneapolis, Minn.: Lerner Publications, 1986.

Hill, Raymond. *Hungary.* New York: Facts on File, 1997.

Hintz, Martin. *Hungary.* Chicago, Ill.: Childrens Press, 1988.

Jackson, Livia Bitton. *I Have Lived a Thousand Years: Growing Up in the Holocaust.* New York: Simon & Schuster, 1997.

Kimmel, Eric A. *The Valiant Red Rooster.* New York: Henry Holt, 1995.

Seredy, Kate. *The Good Master.* New York: Viking, 1963.

St. John, Jetty. *A Family in Hungary.* Minneapolis, Minn.: Lerner Publications, 1988.

Steins, Richard. *Hungary: Crossroads of Europe.* New York: Benchmark Books, 1997.

Wolter, Annette and Christian Teubner. *Best of International Cooking.* Tucson, Ariz.: Hamlyn Publishing, 1984.

India

A Legend from India

A story about a potter who blunders his way into wealth and leadership is a favorite folk tale told by mothers to their children in India. It appears as "The Valiant Chattee Maker" in *The Beautiful Blue Jay and Other Tales of India* by John W. Spellman, as well as in the picture book *The Valiant Chattee-Maker* retold by Christine Price. An early source of this tale is *Old Deacon Days; or, Hindu Fairy Legends Current in Southern India*, collected in India by Mary E. Frere and printed by Lippincott in 1868.

The Brave Chattee-Maker

One night there was an awful storm that sent rain gushing into the village. The Chattee-Maker, or potter, wanted nothing more on this night than to stay at home keeping as dry as he could. But the storm had so frightened his old donkey that it had run away.

"Away with you," shouted his wife to the Chattee-Maker. "Find the donkey and bring it home, or you will have no way to take your pottery to market."

So out into the rain went the Chattee-Maker, grumbling as he went.

Meanwhile an enormous tiger had wandered into the village. It took shelter against the outside thatched wall of an old woman's house. The tiger could hear the old woman talking to herself within.

"Oh, dear," she said. "This old house leaks so badly." And she dragged her few sticks of furniture from one side to another trying to find a dry spot. "I would rather face a tiger or an elephant in my house," the old woman continued, "than face this perpetual dripping." And she dragged her furniture across the room again, making a terrible noise.

The tiger kept very still. He wondered about the Perpetual Dripping that so frightened the old woman. He had never heard of one before, and he was sure he did not want to meet one.

Meanwhile, in a flash of lightning, the Chattee-Maker saw a large animal crouched by the old woman's house and thought that it was his donkey. By now the Chattee-Maker was quite wet and very out of sorts.

He went up to the tiger in the darkness, still mistaking it for his donkey, and grabbed the animal by its ear. "You disobedient beast," the Chattee-Maker scolded. "You will come home with me at once." And the Chattee-Maker climbed on the tiger's back, beating him with a stick, and forcing the tiger to carry him.

The tiger, thinking this must be the Perpetual Dripping, meekly took the Chattee-Maker home. When they arrived, the Chattee-Maker bound the tiger's front feet together and tied the animal to the donkey's post in front of the house.

Next morning, the Chattee-Maker's wife looked out and was astonished to find the tiger. She woke her

Meanwhile, in a flash of lightning, the Chattee-Maker saw a large animal crouched by the old woman's house and thought that it was his donkey.

husband who could hardly believe his eyes. Then she rushed through the village sharing the news. Everyone came to stare at the tiger.

One of the villagers sent word to the Rajah telling him what had happened, and the mighty Rajah himself came to view the tiger. He marveled at the great beast and decided to add it to his royal zoo. In return he gave the Chattee-Maker a fine house, servants, money, and gave him the command of ten thousand horsemen.

The Chattee-Maker's wife was overjoyed, but the potter was worried. "I have never ridden a horse in my life," he said. "I am used to my low-to-the-ground, lazy, old donkey who will come wandering back soon. What if I must lead the ten thousand horsemen somewhere? What would I do? I should be a laughing-stock."

The very next week an enemy ruler from an adjoining kingdom threatened war. He marched his huge army of men right to the border. The Rajah called his generals together to decide who would lead the fight against their fierce neighbors.

Since the country was so unprepared, none of his men wanted to assume responsibility for leading the army to defeat. One cleverly suggested, "Why not ask that brave man who captured the tiger? Surely he would make a fine general."

The Rajah sent for the Chattee-Maker and made him head of the army. The Chattee-Maker was terrified. Hoping to gain time, he begged that he first be allowed to go alone to the border and spy out the enemy's strength.

Then the Chattee-Maker went home and told his wife what had happened. Within the hour, the Rajah sent a mighty white steed in full trappings for the Chattee-Maker to ride to war.

The Chattee-Maker could not refuse so fine a gift, so he sent thanks to the Rajah. But to his wife, the Chattee-Maker said, "What shall I do? I cannot ride this horse."

"Wait until evening," said his wife. "When it is dark, you can mount the horse, and I will tie you in the saddle. Then you will not fall off."

When darkness came, the Chattee-Maker tried to mount the dancing and prancing steed. He had a terrible time getting into the saddle, and the horse grew more and more impatient with him. When the Chattee-Maker finally succeeded, his wife tied his feet into the stirrups, tied the stirrups together, and tied the Chattee-Maker firmly into the saddle.

The horse could wait no longer. It sprang off toward the border and the enemy camp. In the early morning, as he came closer and closer to the camp, the Chattee-Maker worried. "Surely they will kill me," he said. He tried to stop the steed by grabbing a banyan tree. But the earth was soft and the tree pulled right out of the ground. Carrying the tree in his arms, the Chattee-Maker raced toward the camp.

The enemy forces saw him coming and went rushing to their Rajah. "We must flee!" they cried. "A fearsome man is leading the enemy troops on a great steed. He is so fierce that he rips trees out of the ground as he comes. His troops must be right behind him, and we cannot stand against such men as these."

The soldiers began to flee, but before he left, the enemy ruler quickly wrote a letter promising peace and left it in his tent.

When the Chattee-Maker finally arrived in camp, the ropes holding him in his saddle broke and he slid to the ground. The exhausted horse stopped, too. The Chattee-Maker was astonished to find the camp empty. He went into the finest of the tents and found the message left for his Rajah.

The Chattee-Maker was too weak to mount the horse, but he picked up the message and led the horse back to his village. That night when they reached his home, his wife came out to greet him.

"Here," said the Chattee-Maker. "I cannot go another foot. Please send this message to the Rajah and send his horse, too. That way I will not have to ride him again. Tell the Rajah that I will call on him first thing in the morning."

In the morning, the Chattee-Maker walked to the Rajah's palace. People lined the streets to see him. "How humble he is to walk to the Rajah," they said. "Most men would have ridden up in fancy trappings."

The Rajah had read the message of peace and was very pleased not to have to go to war. He came out to greet the Chattee-Maker and gave him more gold. "Is there anything else you desire?" asked the Rajah.

"There is one thing," said the Chattee-Maker. "I am a simple man, and I would like to return to my own village to find my favorite donkey, which I prefer to ride."

The Rajah smiled at the strange and modest Chattee-Maker. "Of course," he agreed.

The very next day, the Chattee-Maker returned to his village. He found his donkey that had been wandering about waiting for him near his old house. All of his old neighbors came to greet him, and the Chattee-Maker shared his gold with them. There was enough for the old woman to have the perpetual leaks in her roof repaired and for all to buy food.

They cheered the Chattee-Maker as he rode back to his new home on his old donkey. The Chattee-Maker was honored by all as a brave hero, but he never rode a horse again.

Background Information

India is the seventh largest country in terms of land area in the world. It covers 1,222,243 square miles and has a population of 967,612,804. There are four main regions to India: the mountainous Himalayan North, the Indo-Gangetic plain, the Thar Desert, and the southern peninsula called the Deccan Plateau. The Vindhya Mountains and the Narmada River divide the north from the south.

On the southwest, India borders the Arabian Sea, on the south the Indian Ocean, and on the east the Bay of Bengal. Pakistan is its neighbor to the northwest. To the north China and Nepal border it. And to the northeast it borders on Bhutan, Myanmar (formerly Burma), and Bangladesh. Sri Lanka lies just off India's southern tip.

In the north are the Himalayas, a huge mountain range that separates India and Nepal from China. Three major rivers begin here, the Indus, Brahmaputra, and Ganges.

The Ganges travels 2,500 miles across northern India to the Bay of Bengal in the Indian Ocean. The Ganges delta is a huge area, most of which is now in Bangladesh, with a smaller part in West Bengal, a state in northeastern India.

The major rivers of southern India are the Godavari, the Kistna, and the Cauvery, which flow to the Bay of Bengal. These are fed largely by the monsoon rains from June through September.

At the southern end of India are two more major mountain ranges, the Eastern Ghats and the Western Ghats. In the extreme northeast are the Lushai, Naga, and Chin hills. These form the frontier between India, Myanmar (Burma), and China.

Half of the people in India live in the Gangetic Plains of the north and the plains of the three southern rivers. There are more than 500,000 small villages in India, many with fewer than 1,000 people. About 80 percent of the population live in these villages.

In the northeast, where India adjoins the country of Myanmar, is a hilly borderland. The Naga people live on both sides of the border. Half a million Naga live in the Indian state of Nagaland. They raise crops such as dry rice, millet, taro, maize, ginger, chilies, and cotton.

Ladakh is a region in the far north of India. It is a high-altitude desert that spans about 40,000 square miles and has a population of about 150,000, most of whom are Ladakhi. The majority of Ladakhi are practicing Buddhists.

Bordering Ladakh is the Chang Tang, which is a high plateau on the border between Tibet and India. Only a few crops grow in this cold mountain air, such as barley, peas, turnips, and potatoes. At lower elevations, there are black walnut, apple, and apricot trees. The people here also raise sheep, yak, and goats.

India's major cities are Calcutta, which has 10 million people; Bombay, with 9 million people; and Madras, with 5 million people. These three cities are important ports and industrial centers. Other cities with 2 million or more residents are Hyderabad, Ahmadabad, Kanpur, and Bangalore.

Calcutta, located on the Ganges River, is the capital of West Bengal State. It produces paper, iron, steel, leather goods, and jute, and is a center of Indian cultural and intellectual life. The Maidan is a huge park in the center of Calcutta, and there are also museums and a famous zoo.

Bombay is the capital of the Maharashtra State. It is India's major port on the west coast. There are facilities here for processing raw cotton, which is brought in from the surrounding countryside.

Madras, the principal city of southern India, is the capital of Tamil Nadu. A colorful cloth also called Madras is produced in local factories and shipped throughout the world. This city is noted for its beautiful gardens and temples.

Old Delhi and New Delhi combined form the largest city in northwestern India. Ancient buildings dominate Old Delhi. New Delhi has been the capital of India since 1931. Between Old Delhi and New Delhi lies Raj Ghat, a shrine. The president lives in New Delhi, and the Parliament House is a popular attraction. Industries include the manufacture of cotton and wool cloth, food processing, and flour and sugar mills.

Amritsar is a sacred city for the world's 16 million Sikhs. It is in northwest India in the State of Punjab. There is an enormous pool in the city out of which rises the Golden Temple. Inside the Golden Temple lies the collection of Sikh holy scriptures known as the *Guru Granth Sahib*. First built in the 1570s, the city has been demolished and rebuilt several times, until today it is quite modern.

Near the city of Agra is the Taj Mahal. It is a building showing the great beauty of Islamic architecture and is considered one of the "wonders of the world." It was built by Shah Jahan as a memorial to his wife, Mumtaz Mahal. The chief architect was Ustad Ahmad, a Persian engineer. It took 20,000 workers twenty-two years to complete the Taj Mahal.

About 70 percent of India's population is agricultural workers. Growing food is complicated because of the monsoons, which bring 70 percent of all the rain falling on India every year. Sometimes there are floods and sometimes droughts.

The government has begun programs to modernize farming and to increase output of the food supply. By the early 1970s, surpluses were being stored against times of famine. Leading food crops include grains, oilseeds, peas, beans, and lentils. Farmers produce sugar for export and jute and cotton for use in the textile industries.

The British began the industrialization of India. India has rich resources of iron ore, manganese, bauxite, coal, and zinc. It also has lignite, silver, copper, and gold. India imports most of the petroleum it needs. Many industries are government-owned. The leading industries are textiles and steel. It has also developed atomic energy.

Starting in the 1980s, numerous private companies started up and began producing consumer products such as televisions and computers.

History

Indian history goes back 5,000 years. Archaeologists have discovered prehistoric towns in what is now Pakistan showing the existence of an Indian civilization dating back to 2500 B.C. or earlier.

The Dravidians were the first known inhabitants of India. These indigenous Indians survived by hunting and gathering. They moved from the Deccan plateau in central India to the plains near the river Ganges.

About 1500 B.C., Indo-Aryans from central Asia (possibly Iran) migrated into India. They conquered parts of northern India and developed religious beliefs that eventually evolved into Hinduism. They also developed the Sanskrit language.

The Moguls, from central Asia, attacked India in 1526, and by the end of the century, their emperor, Akbar, ruled an empire stretching across northern India. Much of the population converted to Islam.

In the middle of the sixth century B.C., Persians invaded northwestern India. Alexander the Great led the Greeks into India in the fourth century B.C. and this led to an exchange of ideas between India and the West for the first time.

The Mauryan Empire appeared about 324 B.C. Its ruler was King Ashoka, who reigned from 272 to 232 B.C. Ashoka devoted his life to spreading Buddhism. The Gupta Empire lasted from A.D. 320 to 550. This is often called the Classical Age of India. During this period, Hinduism became firmly established.

For five centuries after the Gupta Empire, small kingdoms fought one another. Arabs and Turks invaded India. The Turks established a kingdom in Delhi in 1206. In 1526, Moguls from central Asia established their empire with capitals in Agra and Delhi. The Mogul Empire lasted until the eighteenth century.

Beginning in 1498, the Portuguese seized ports along the western coast of India. During the 1600s, the English East India Company set up trading posts in India. Then the French set up trading companies.

In the second half of the 1700s, the British emerged as the strongest power in India and in the following century used troops to crush Indian revolt against British rule. In 1860, the responsibility for the administration of India was transferred to the British Parliament. A British governor-general ruled India until 1947, when India became independent.

The Indian National Congress was organized in 1885. In 1920, Mahatma Gandhi became leader of this organization. He believed in *satyagraha*, organized, nonviolent protest. His teaching spread from South Africa to India and then throughout the world.

Gandhi became a leading force in the movement for India's independence from Great Britain. His nonviolent method of protest has been used in many places. Reverend Dr. Martin Luther King, Jr. acknowledged Gandhi's principle of nonviolent protest as the basis for the U.S. civil rights movement of the 1950s and 1960s.

Government

Jawaharlal Nehru became the first prime minister of an independent India. Until 1947, Britain had ruled India indirectly through 500 local princes who had nominal control of their states.

An Indian Constitution, patterned on the government of the United States and of Britain, was adopted in 1950. It guarantees certain rights to individuals, including equality before the law and freedom of speech, assembly, and religion. It sets up a union of twenty-five states and seven federally administered territories. The Constitution has been amended several times, and new states have been created and borders adjusted.

Each state has a legislature, a court system, and a governor who is appointed by India's president. The federal government is presided over by a president and vice-president chosen by an electoral college, which is made up of members of the union and state legislatures. The president also holds the ceremonial post of commander of the Armed Forces.

Most of the union or central government's power rests with a cabinet, called the Council of Ministers, headed by the prime minister. The union legislature has two chambers, the *Lok Sabha* (House of the People) and the *Raja Sabha* (Council of States). The people elect the 545 members of the Lok Sabha every five years. Members of the state legislatures elect the 250 members of the Raja Sabha.

A chief justice heads the federal court system. Beneath it are High Courts, Subordinate Courts, and the *panchayats,* or district and village courts.

Religion

About 83 percent of the people in India are Hindus, but there are also many people of other religions. About 11 percent of the population belong to the second largest religion in India, Islam. Christians make up 2.5 percent of the population and are about evenly divided between Protestants and Catholics. Other religious groups include Buddhists, Jains, Sikhs, Jews, and Parsis.

India also has a large tribal population, about 40 million, whose religion is animism. Rather than a formal religion, they believe in powerful spirits or gods.

The roots of Hinduism go back at least to 1500 B.C. Hindus believe that God is in everything. They call this god Brahma but believe that this one god can be pictured and thought about in many different forms, represented by various gods and goddesses. The three main gods are *Brahma* (the creator), *Vishnu* (the preserver), and *Shiva* (the destroyer).

Hindu society has been divided into a caste system. One is born into a caste, with the *Brahmans* (priest) at the top, followed by *Kshatriyas* (warriors), *Vaisyas* (merchants and bankers), and *Sudras* (farmers, artisans, and laborers.) The caste system was abolished by the Indian Constitution of 1950.

Muslims believe in one god. Their holy book, as revealed to the Prophet Mohammed, is the *Koran*. Muslims worship in mosques. The Jama Masjid mosque in Delhi is especially noted for its beauty.

Guru Nanak started Sikhism in the fifteenth century in the Punjab area of northern India. This area is where the majority of Sikhs live today. Sikhs believe that there is only one God, that all humans are equal, that all religions should be accepted, and that it is good to serve others. The Sikh's place of worship is called the *gurdwara*.

Education

It is estimated that 47 percent of adult Indian men and 33 percent of adult Indian women can read and write. Hundreds of thousands of new schools have been built in recent years. Many children attend free government schools. Others attend private schools where tuition is paid. Classes start at 9:00 A.M. and continue until 1:00 P.M. They continue after lunch for older pupils.

Approximately 85 percent of Indian children aged six through eleven attend primary schools. They learn to read and write in their native language. Those that remain in school learn English and Hindi. But many young Indian children go to work at an early age. Few children complete eight full years of schooling. It is estimated that 48 out of 100 pupils drop out before they complete primary school. In 1991, there were at least 50 million child workers in India.

Many children attend boarding schools away from their villages. Children take an aptitude test to enter these special Navodaya Vidyalaya schools, of which 261 have opened since the mid-1980s. In addition to being taught, students receive a nutritionally balanced diet, free school uniforms and equipment, and guidance.

Children from Sikh families often attend weekend school at the *gurdwara*. They learn Punjabi so that they can read their religious book, the *Guru Granth Sahib*. At Saturday and Sunday school, gurdwaras also offer children classes in the harmonium, tabla, and singing.

Only about one-third of the children in India get a high school education. Indian universities produce more engineers and scientists than any other country except the United States. The largest university of India is in Calcutta.

Immigrants

As of 1981, the number of people born in India but living outside of India was estimated at more than 13 million. Of these, more than 400,000 live in the United States. Another 440,000 live in Trinidad, 500,000 in Britain, 800,000 in South America, 3 million in Nepal, and more than 1 million each in Myanmar and Malaysia.

Between 1946 and 1964, fewer than 7,000 people emigrated from India to the United States. In 1970, it was estimated that there were only 32,000 Indians, Pakistanis, and Bangladeshis living in the United States.

At the beginning of the twentieth century, the British who ruled India took skilled Indians, including Sikhs from the Punjab, to help build railways in East Africa. When the East African countries became independent, Indians had problems. In 1972, General Idi Amin forced all Indians to leave Uganda. At this time, many Indians moved to Britain, Canada, and the United States.

Because of events in South Africa, and due to the less restrictive American laws and policies that went into effect in the late 1960s, significant increases in immigration began. The new wave of people from India were mostly Sikhs and Punjabis, many of whom went into farming. Many Sikhs settled first in Stockton, El Centro, and Yuba City, California. Others moved to big cities like Washington and New York.

By 1980, an American census showed that more than 378,000 people in the United States were born in India or of Indian ancestry. By this time also, more Indians were in professional and technical occupations.

From 1981 to 1990, 261,900 Indians immigrated to the United States. During the period of 1991 to 1995, another 191,500 came.

The 1990 census showed that the Asian Indian population in the United States had grown to more than 786,000 people. Just over a fourth of these were naturalized American citizens.

Many of these relatively new immigrants have occupations in engineering and medicine. Indian students who train in the United States tend to specialize in electronic engineering. Many have also gone into business, owning a large percentage of the small motels in the United States.

Language

At least sixteen major languages are spoken in India and 1,000 dialects. The oldest is Sanskrit, which has not been used by ordinary people for over 2,000 years although scholars still study it. The northern language groups include Hindi, Gujarati, Bengali, Marathi, Oriya, Assamese, Sindhi, Punjabi, and Urdu. The southern group of languages includes Tamil, Telugu, Kannada, and Malayalam. Hindustani, a mix of Hindi and Urdu, is spoken widely in the north.

Today, Hindi is the national language of India and is spoken by about 30 percent of all Indians. Sikhs continue to speak Punjabi. English is used in government and business communication and is spoken by about 2 percent of the people.

The Arts and Sciences

The first of the long epics of Hinduism, the *Mahabharata,* has 100,000 verses and contains stories that form a code of behavior. It dates back to about 800 B.C. The second epic is called *The Ramayana.* Kalidasa's *Shakkuntalam* in Sanskrit and Ilango Adigal's *Silappadigaram* in Tamil are regarded as the most famous secular works of ancient India. There are also a number of books, called the *Puranas,* dealing with Hindu legends and mythology.

Well known names in Indian literature of a more recent period include Anita Desai, Girish Karnad, Dom Moraes, R. K. Narayan, Vikram Seth, and Rabindranath Tagore. Tagore won a Nobel Prize for his work.

There are two distinct styles of music in India, the North Indian, *Hindustani,* and the South Indian, *Karnatak.* Both are based on a system of *raga,* which uses a melodic base to convey an emotion. Indian music follows a rhythm cycle called *tala.* Indians use about 500 different kinds of instruments. Ravi Shankar, a classical musician, made the sitar popular.

India has exerted a major force on dance in Asia. Many Indian dances involve representing or worshipping the gods, while others are for entertainment and fun. *Bharata natyam* is a dance performed by a woman who wears tiny bells on her feet as she moves.

The South Indian *Bharathanatyam* is one of the most popular dance forms. Dancers wear elaborate costumes and use hand gestures and facial expressions. *Kathakali* is a dance of Kerala involving wearing huge headdresses. *Odissi* is a popular dance form of east India, while *Kathak* is a North Indian form.

Traditional Indian theatre includes musical opera, masked theatre, and puppetry and takes the form of dance drama dealing with old world legends. Modern plays are more like those presented in the West, relying on social themes and dialogue.

India has the second largest film industry in the world. Many of today's Indian films are musicals. Some are made for an international audience. The director Satayajit Ray is well known in the west. Bombay is the heart of the film industry.

When Europeans came to India, they found that Indians were far ahead of them in the area of astronomy. For example, in A.D. 500 an astronomer, Aryabyata, knew that the earth was round and that a year lasted 365.3586 days.

Indian mathematicians provided the world with the use of zero and the decimal system. Long before modern day computers were invented, Indians had a method of multiplication used in calculating machines. And India made steel in 325 B.C., long before anyone else.

In the late 1700s, many British visitors traveled to India. The buildings that they saw influenced architecture in Britain. Cockerell's design for Sezincote, which is in Gloucestershire, and Reton and Nash's design for the Brighton Pavilion, were influenced by the Taj Mahal.

Food

In India, as in many countries, food varies from one region to another. In the south, rice is a staple food. Southerners are coffee drinkers and like foods seasoned with peppers. Many orthodox Hindus are vegetarians. In the north, wheat is a staple food. Meat is frequently eaten, and tea is the preferred drink.

Most Indians do not eat with knives and forks. They roll their food into little balls and pop them into their mouths. Sometimes food is eaten off a metal tray called *thali*, on which little bowls with various foods are placed. In the south, banana leaves may be used as plates.

In the north in Amritsar, people eat a flaky fried bread called *paratha* for breakfast with fried eggs and spicy pickles. Most main meals include fresh vegetables. A favorite dish is mustard leaves or spinach with butter and corn bread. People also eat *nan* or *chapatis*, round flat bread. A meal is often completed with buttermilk and sweet rice pudding flavored with almonds and fruits.

A large variety of split peas and beans is generally eaten daily. These are flavored with spices such as turmeric, ginger, garlic, coriander, and cloves. Vegetables are popular throughout India.

Special foods are prepared for big events, such as when the family is invited to attend the naming of a baby. Guests eat rice, special curries, *ladus* (balls of butter and powdered lentils), sweet chapatis bread, salads, crisp wafers, yogurt, and buttermilk.

Indian sweets are very rich and are usually made with butter, milk, and nuts. This is a recipe for a sweet dessert.

Indian Sweet Milk Dessert

1/2 quart milk
2 pounds granulated sugar
3 1/2 ounces butter
1/2 cup dried coconut
1/2 cup chopped almonds and pistachio nuts
2 pounds powdered milk

Heat the milk gently in a nonstick saucepan, stirring with a wooden spoon. Add the sugar and stir continuously while bringing the mixture to a boil. When it is boiling, add the butter, and keep stirring. When the butter has dissolved, add the chopped almonds, pistachios, and dried coconut. Remove the mixture from the heat.

Add the powdered milk and stir thoroughly. Pour the mixture onto a lightly greased baking tray, and spread evenly. Wait for the mixture to cool (approximately 4 hours). Cut the dessert into small squares and diamond shapes. This dessert is best if eaten the same day it is made.

Recreation

In cities in India, games introduced by the British remain popular today. Begalis prefer soccer, Punjabis like hockey, and residents of Bombay prefer cricket. In the mountains, people enjoy climbing, hiking, and skiing. Those on the coast like swimming, fishing, and boat racing. Polo is played in northwest India and in the Himalayan regions.

Indians also like to play traditional indoor games such as parcheesi and chess, which originated in India. Another game originally from India, Snooker, a variant of billiards, was invented in 1875 in Jubbulpore, India.

Going to the movies is a popular form of entertainment, and television is available not only in the cities but in many of the villages. A traveling circus may come to town.

Children play many of the same games that are popular in the United States, such as jump rope, hopscotch, and swinging in a swing. They also play a game of five stones by tossing them in the air and catching them in a variety of ways. Two outdoor games, something like tag but requiring breath control, are *kabaddi* and *kho-kho*. Yoga classes are also popular to discipline the mind and body.

Good facilities are available for modern sports such as soccer, field hockey, basketball, volleyball, and cricket. Clubs offer tennis, badminton, squash, golf, and billiards. The national cricket matches are particularly popular.

Customs and Traditions

Many holidays and festivals are celebrated each year in India. Among the spring festivals are *Basant, Mahavir Jayanti,*

Holi, Pooram, and *Baisakhi.* For Basant, it is customary for people to wear something yellow. Kite flying competitions are often held at this time.

The birthday of Vardhamana Mahavira, who started the Jain religion, is celebrated during *Mahavir Jayanti.* Jains come from all over to visit the shrine at Gimar.

Sikhs celebrate the beginning of their new year on April 13, toward the end of spring when winter crops are fully grown. The religious festival of *Baisankhi* is celebrated with temple prayers. Young people may go through a ceremony to join the Khalsa, or "pure ones." Later there may be a special meal followed by dancing.

Another important spring festival held in March or early April is Holi. It is a Hindu festival that marks the end of winter. Holi often begins with a huge bonfire. In villages today, some Indian mothers carry their young children in a circle around a blazing bonfire during Holi to receive God's blessings and protection for the child.

During the week of Holi celebration, some play practical jokes, especially spraying each other with water mixed with colored paints or powder, a custom that grew out of stories about tricks played by the Krishna, one of the forms taken by the god Vishnu, when he visits Earth.

At the same time as Hindus celebrate Holi, many Sikhs hold the spring festival of *Hola Mohalla.* This celebration includes sports competitions, horse riding, and mock battles.

Indians celebrate the date of independence from Great Britain on August 15 and also celebrate Republic Day, the anniversary when the Indians first declared their independence, on January 26. During the Republic Day parade, elephants with brilliantly painted trunks and legs march in a parade in the center of New Delhi.

During the holiday of *Dussehra,* which comes in autumn, people put up statues of a demon called Ravana. Firecrackers are placed inside the statues, and at the end of the festival, they are set on fire.

Divali (or *Diwali*) is celebrated by both Hindus and Sikhs during the new moon in late October/early November. Small lamps are put in doorways and windows. Candles are floated in the river. This five-day festival of lights is dedicated to Lakshmi, the Hindu goddess of wealth and beauty.

Indians prepare for the ceremony by cleaning and painting their homes in hopes that Lakshmi will visit bringing wealth and good fortune. Hindus go to their temples and then come home to eat special meals. They visit family and friends and bring gifts of sweets.

Dassehra and *Durga Puja* are held over ten days between the first new moon and full moon after the autumn equinox. Both festivals celebrate the *Ramayana.* Often a play, *Ram Lila,* is presented and may be spread over ten evenings.

While some Indians are celebrating *Divali,* people of Bengal hold a festival in honor of Kali, goddess of strength and death. Homes are strung with lights and shrines are built along the streets. Worshippers walk the streets, greet friends, and stop at the shrines to offer gifts to Kali. Foods are sold by street vendors, and at night fireworks are shot off. Then the images of Kali are taken to the river and set afloat.

In the state of Kerala, on the southern tip of India, at the end of the rainy season a harvest festival is held called *Onam.* People clean their floors while children collect flowers that are woven into colorful mats. The children are given new clothes and the family goes to the temple to give thanks. Afterwards there is feasting and boat races are held along the shores of the lagoons.

Brothers and sisters celebrate a special day called *Raksha Bandhan.* Sisters tie a bracelet called a *rakhi* around their brothers' wrists. A sister also puts a red dot on her brother's forehead and gives him treats. This is supposed to protect him during the year. In return, the brother promises to care for his sister, and he gives her a present.

Some Indian holidays are to thank the animals for their help. On one special day, the camels visit the little town of Pushkar in Rajasthan. During *Pushkar Mela* there are camel races, camel beauty contests, singing, and dancing. For *Pooram,* elephants wear gold head-ornaments in a parade. The men riding the elephants carry bright umbrellas and peacock feathers. *Naag Pachami* is the Festival of the Snakes. People give milk and flowers to the snakes that live in the temples.

In Tamil Nadu in southern India, a festival called *Pongal* (or *Ponggal*) honors the cows. It is held in January. People give thanks for the rain and for their rice crop. They use colored chalk and rice flour to decorate their front steps with Rangoli designs. On the third day of Pongal, the cows are bathed, their horns painted, and they are decorated with garlands of flowers.

Many parts of the world hold spring flower festivals. An especially colorful flower festival is held in Bangalore.

Suggested Activities

Writing

1. Gandhi was a champion of human rights. Students may want to write to an organization dedicated to helping people, ask for literature and information, and decide on a fund-raising project to support the activities of one of these groups. There may be an appropriate local organization, or students might write to American Friends Service Committee, 1501 Cherry Street, Philadelphia, PA 19102, or Save the Children, Public Affairs Office, 54 Wilton Road, Westport, CT 06880 or to CARE, 660 First Avenue, New York, NY 10016.

Reading

2. Students might enjoy reading and discussing together fiction that is set in India. The media specialist could help locate appropriate books. Two possibilities are *Tusk and Stone* by Malcolm J. Bosse (Front Street, 1995) and *Daughter of the Mountains* by Louise Rankin (Puffin Books, 1993).

Vocabulary

3. Devote a classroom bulletin board to special vocabulary students encounter in their research on India. Each special word and its definition could be printed on a 3 x 5-inch card and added to the bulletin board as part of the on-going study.

For example, the following words from studying the Taj Mahal might be added: crypt, cupola, finial, kiosk, mausoleum, minaret, mosque, niche, octagonal, pavilion, plinth, Raja, and symmetry.

Math

4. Invite a pair of students to read and study *The Rajah's Rice: A Mathematical Folktale from India* by David Barry (W. H. Freeman, 1994). Ask the students to share the book with the class and explain the mathematical concepts in the book. If it is appropriate, these students might arrange to share the folktale with an elementary school class of students.

Social Studies

5. Mother Teresa lived in Calcutta, India, and won a Nobel Prize for her work with the poor. Students might want to study about her life and then make an oral report to the class sharing what they learned. Possible sources of information include: *The Life and Times of Mother Theresa* (Chelsea House, 1998) by Tanya Rice; *Mother Teresa: Saint of the Poor* (Raintree Steck-Vaughn, 1998) by Nina Morgan; *Mother Teresa: Helping the Poor* (Millbrook Press, 1991) by William Jay Jacobs; and *The Young Life of Mother Teresa of Calcutta* (Young Sparrow Press, 1966) by Claire Jordan Mohan. An interesting Website for additional information is www.goodnewsmag.com/oct97/insider.htm.

Geography

6. At one time, India was a much larger country than it is today. As part of the arrangement to secure its independence from Great Britain, Muslims were given two parts of India, West and East Pakistan. Later, east Pakistan became Bangladesh. Another neighbor, Burma, changed its name. Invite a small group of students to make and label two maps to hang on a classroom bulletin board. One should show "old India" while the other shows India and its neighbors today.

Music

7. A music educator might visit the class and share tapes or CDs of Indian music. "North Indian Classical Music" (RDR-5101/2/314 from Multicultural Media in Barre, Vermont) is a set of 4 CDs that give an overview of Hindustani music. It includes performances on the raga form on string, wind, and percussive instruments, as well as vocal music.

Art

8. There is an area near Calcutta, India, on the edge of the Ganges delta, which is called the Sundarbans. This area is very rich in wildlife, including Royal Bengal tigers, crocodiles, monkeys, deer, monitor lizards, and wild boars. There are more than 300 species of birds, including the mynah and the fishing eagle. Ask a group of students who are interested in wildlife art to find photographs and sketches of birds and animals from this area and to draw them. Post the drawings on a classroom bulletin board.

Drama/Movement

9. Students might enjoy preparing and presenting a puppet show to younger elementary grade students based on the famous *Just So Stories* of Rudyard Kipling, who lived in India for many years.

Dress

10. Invite a pair of interested students to research traditional Indian clothing, photocopy pictures with permission, and make a presentation to the class. Included should be the dress of men worn at court, which includes *jama* (long gowns) made from cotton and tied at the right if they were Muslim and at the left if they were Hindu. Under this was worn *paijama* (loose fitting trousers that tapered at the ankles). Around the waist would be a *patka* (sash).

    Women at court would wear a tight fitting *choli* (bodice) of transparent material, and *paijama*. Over this they would wear a *pesvaj* (coat), a *patka* (sash), and an *odhni* (scarf) around their shoulders. The traditional dress of women in India is the *sari*.

Cooking

11. Burfi is a treat, a little like peanut brittle, which is served during *Divali*. It is easy to make.

Burfi

1 pound raw cashews
1 cup sweetened condensed milk
Butter for greasing pan
1 teaspoon flour

Cook the cashews in a frying pan over low heat, being careful not to burn them. Pour the nuts onto a pastry board and crush the roasted cashews with a rolling pin.

In a saucepan mix together one-half of the crushed cashews with the condensed milk and flour. Cook and stir the mixture over low heat until it is almost solid.

Grease a glass baking dish with butter. Press the cashew mixture into the greased dish. Pour the remaining cashews over the top and press them into the mixture. Let the candy cool and then cut it into small squares.

Culminating Activity

12. Invite students to choose a famous person or building from any time in India's history and write a brief report including a picture or photocopy (with permission) of the topic of the paper.

    Each picture should be 8 1/2 x 11 inches in size and the report should be printed on one side of the paper only.

    Students could give their report orally and then add it to a class book, *Faces and Places of India*, which could be bound and used for future reference.

    Among possible topics are: Akbar the Great, Guru Nanak, Mahatma Gandhi, Jawaharlal Nehru, Indira Gandhi, Rajiv Gandhi, Lord Mountbatten, Anita Desai, R. K. Narayan, Sir Alexander Cunningham, the Samnath Pur temple in Mysore, the caves of Ajanta, the Mamallapuram temple in Tamil Nadu, the Jama Masjid in Old Delhi, the Taj Mahal in Agra, the Bahai Temple, the Golden Temple of Amritsar, the Mysore Palace, and the Red Fort of Old Delhi.

Suggested Reading

Birch, Beverley (adapting the book of Michael Nicholson). *Mahatma Gandhi*. Milwaukee, Wisc.: Gareth Stevens, 1990.

Croft, Jennifer. *Ladakhi, Indigenous Peoples of the World*. Danbury, Conn.: Grolier Educational, 1995.

Cumming, David. *Countries of the World, India*. Hove, England: Wayland Publishers, 1988.

———. *Country Insight, India*. Austin, Tex.: Raintree Steck-Vaughn, 1998.

———. *The Ganges Delta and Its People*. Hove, England: Wayland Publishers, 1994.

———. *India*. Hove, England: Wayland Publishers, 1995.

Dhanjal, Beryl. *Armitsar, Holy Cities*. London, England: Evans Brothers, 1994.

Ganeri, Anita. *Exploration Into India*. London, England: Belitha Press, 1994.

Husain, Shahrukh A. *Focus on India*. London, England: Evans Brothers, 1986.

Johnson, Anne. *Naga, Indigenous Peoples of the World*. Danbury, Conn.: Grolier Educational, 1995.

Fisher, Leonard Everett. *Gandhi*. New York: Atheneum, 1995.

Hardy, Aruna. *Ravi of India*. London, England: Lutterworth Press, 1980.

Haviland, Virginia. *Favorite Fairy Tales Told in India*. Boston, Mass.: Little, Brown, 1973.

Kadodwala, Dilip. *A World of Holidays, Holi*. Austin, Tex.: Raintree Steck-Vaughn, 1997.

Kadodwala, Dilip and Sharon Chhapi. *My Hindu Life*. Hove, England: Wayland Publishers, 1996.

Kagda, Falaq. *Festivals of the World, India*. Milwaukee, Wisc.: Gareth Stevens, 1997.

Kanitkar, V. P. (Hemant). *Hinduism*. New York: Bookwright Press, 1986.

Kaur-Singh, Kanwaljit. *My Sikh Life*. Hove, England: Wayland Publishers, 1997.

———. *Sikhism*. Hove, England: Wayland Publishers, 1995.

Moorcroft, Christine. *The Taj Mahal*. Hove, England: Wayland Publishers, 1997.

Nottridge, Rhoda. *Spring, Let's Celebrate World Festivals*. Hove, England: Wayland Publishers, 1994.

Price, Christine. *The Valiant Chattee-Maker*. New York: Frederick Warne, 1965.

Rosen, Mike. *Autumn Festivals*. New York: Bookwright Press, 1990.

Ruth, Amy. *Mother Teresa*. Minneapolis, Minn.: Lerner Publications, 1999.

Schmidt, Jeremy. *In the Village of the Elephants*. New York: Walker, 1994.

Spellman, John W. *The Beautiful Blue Jay and Other Tales of India*. Boston, Mass.: Little, Brown, 1967.

Srinivasan, Tadhika. *India*. New York: Marshall Cavendish, 1990.

Tythacott, Louise. *Traditions Around the World, Dance*. New York: Thomson Learning, 1995.

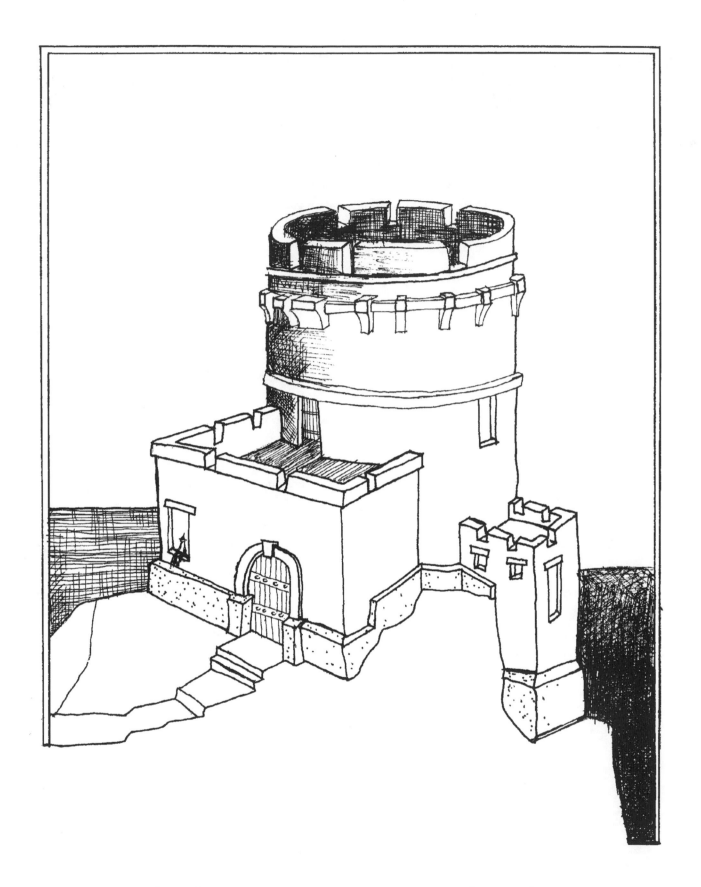

Then there came a tap-tap-tapping at the window.
The lazy girl ran to open it, and a wee woman dressed all in green climbed in.

Ireland

A Legend from Ireland

A popular Irish legend is "The Widow's Lazy Daughter." One version of this story can be found in *Favorite Fairy Tales Told in Ireland* by Virginia Haviland and another in *Hibernian Nights* by Seumas MacManus.

The Widow's Lazy Daughter

There once lived in the county of Donegal a poor, hard-working widow. She had a beautiful but lazy daughter who spent her time dreaming of living in a castle with a prince and being attended by servants. She would stroke the cat by the fire as she dreamed, and could not even be relied upon to stay awake long enough to stir and keep the stew from burning.

The widow was at her wit's end trying to get her lazy daughter to do any work in the house or the yard. One day, when the girl had again fallen asleep and burned what little food they had, the exasperated widow began to beat her daughter with a stick and the girl ran outside shrieking.

The king's son, who was riding by, stopped to investigate. "'Tis shameful to be beating this young lass," he said. "And I'll be asking you to explain it to me."

Not wishing to shame her lazy daughter before a stranger, the widow said, "Oh, my good lord, 'tis embarrassed I am that you should find us like this. But I don't know what to do with the lass. She works from morning to night, spinning, weaving and sewing. She refuses to rest, and I am entirely beside myself. I am forced to beat her to make her stop working."

'Tis what I've been searching for," the young man said. "I've been looking for more than a year for just such a lass to be my bride. I have brought several home to my mother, the queen, but when she examines them, she finds none of them can work. Your daughter is the answer to our prayers."

So saying, the prince helped the young woman onto his horse and tossed a bag of gold to the widow. "This will help to repay you for the loss of such a hard-working daughter."

The widow was delighted to see her daughter go off with the king's son, although she suspected that she would soon be sent home again.

The son took the widow's daughter to meet the queen. "Mother, this lass is just what we have been looking for. She's not only beautiful, but she's the hardest working girl in all of Ireland. She will be the perfect wife."

"Really?" the queen said. "And what work can she do?"

"Spin, weave, and sew," the prince said.

"Well, we shall see," said the queen. "Let her rest tonight, and tomorrow we will find out if she can spin."

In the morning, right after breakfast, the queen led the lazy girl into a small room with a spinning wheel and a stool. Stacks of carded flax were stacked next to the wall.

"You're to spin that flax into fine linen thread," said the queen. "At the end of the day, I'll see how you've done."

After the queen left, locking her in the room, the lazy girl wept bitterly. She had come to love the handsome prince of her dreams who praised her so highly to his mother, and now she would lose him because she didn't know how to spin.

There came a tap-tap-tapping at the window. The lazy girl ran to open it, and a wee woman dressed all in green climbed in. "Why are you crying so, lass?" asked the woman.

The lazy girl told the woman her plight.

"Ah," said the wee woman. "I'll help you. I'll spin that flax into linen for you if you'll make me a promise and keep it."

"I will," said the lazy girl, not even asking what the promise might be.

The wee woman pulled out her tiny spinning wheel and set to work. As the wheel whirled, the wee woman sang a strange song.

"I'll spin and spin all the day,

Never ever stopping to rest,

If on the prince's wedding day,

I can be an honored guest."

When all the flax was spun into linen, the wee woman said, "Now, don't you be forgetting your promise." And she left through the window.

When the queen unlocked the door, she looked at the linen in surprise and pleasure. "Well, well, well," she said. "Tomorrow we'll see if you can weave."

That night, the lazy girl sat at the table with the queen and the prince. The prince thought the girl was so lovely, it didn't matter if she could spin and weave. But he knew that his mother would never be happy with a lazy daughter-in-law.

Next morning, the queen again locked the lazy girl into a small room. This time there was a loom and a shuttle. "If this room is not filled with fine cloth by the end of the day," said the queen, "you'll not be marrying my son." She went out and locked the door.

Again the lazy girl began to cry, for she didn't know how to weave, either. There was a tap-tap-tapping at the window and the girl ran to open in. A second strange wee woman dressed all in green climbed in.

"Why are you crying, lass?" she asked.

The lazy girl told her story.

"I'll help you, if you'll make me a promise and keep it."

"I will," promised the lazy girl.

The wee woman set to work using her own tiny shuttle. And as she worked, she sang this song

"I'll weave and weave all the day,

Never ever stopping to rest,

If on the prince's wedding day,

I can be an honored guest."

When the room was filled with beautiful cloth, the wee woman said, "Now don't you be forgetting your promise." Then she left through the window.

When the queen returned, her eyes grew large, and she smiled as she saw the room filled with beautiful cloth. "Well, well, well," she said. "Tomorrow we'll see if you can sew."

The next morning the queen took the lazy girl to a small room and gave her a golden thimble and needle. "If you can sew this cloth into shirts for the prince, you may marry him. If not, it's back to your mother you'll be going," said the queen. She locked the door and left.

The lazy girl began to cry. There came a tap-tap-tapping at the window and she ran to open it. A third wee woman dressed all in green climbed in.

"And why are you crying so?" asked the wee woman.

The lazy girl told her story.

"I'll be sewing shirts for you," said the wee woman, "if you'll make me a promise and keep it."

"I will," promised the lazy girl.

The wee woman went to work, her needle moving as fast as flashes of lightning. And as she worked, she sang:

"I'll sew and sew all the day,

Never ever stopping to rest,

If on the prince's wedding day,

I can be an honored guest."

By the end of the day, there were dozens of beautiful shirts in the room. The wee woman slipped out the window saying, "Now don't you be forgetting your promise."

Shortly after, the queen came. She smiled in delight when she saw all the shirts. "You must be the hardest worker in all of Ireland," she said. "Tomorrow we will plan the wedding feast for you and my son."

The lazy girl was dressed in beautiful clothes for her wedding day, and all the powerful and rich in Ireland came to sit around the feast table to celebrate the wedding of the prince and his hard-working lass. Three chairs stood empty.

"Let the feasting begin," cried the queen.

But just then, the door to the great hall opened and in came a wee woman dressed all in green.

"Who invited you?" asked the queen.

"I am a guest, bidden by the bride," replied the wee woman, and as she walked toward an empty seat, everyone noticed her enormous foot.

The lazy girl nodded in greeting.

"And may I ask, how you come by that huge foot?" asked the queen.

"I have been spinning for years and years," said the wee woman, "and pressing my foot to the treadle has made it grow."

"If that's what comes of spinning," whispered the prince to his mother, "my beautiful bride shall never spin again."

As the first woman sat down, there came another knocking at the door. A second wee woman entered, dressed in all in green. "I am a guest of the bride," she announced, and as she walked toward an empty chair, everyone noticed that her arms were so long, her fingers touched the floor.

The lazy girl nodded in greeting.

"And may I ask how you came by those long arms?" asked the queen.

"I've been weaving for years and years, throwing the shuttle back and forth, and that has made by arms grow long."

"If that's what comes of weaving," whispered the prince to his mother, "my beautiful bride shall never weave again."

There came a third knocking at the door. In came another wee woman dressed all in green. "I am a guest of the bride," she announced, and as she walked to the last empty chair, everyone noticed what a long red nose she had.

The lazy girl nodded in greeting.

"And may I ask how you came by that long red nose? asked the queen.

"I've been sewing for years and years, stooping my head over the shirts until every drop of blood has run into my nose."

"If that's what comes of sewing," whispered the Prince to his mother, "my beautiful bride shall never sew again."

And so the prince married the lazy girl, and they lived happily ever after. And the wise queen was heard to remark, "It is better to have a princess who is blessed by the fairy people than one who can spin, weave, and sew."

Background Information

The Republic of Ireland covers the southern and central portion, or about 83 percent of the island of Ireland. The remainder of the island, Northern Ireland, is part of the United Kingdom of Great Britain and Northern Ireland.

Ireland is part of northwest Europe, bounded on the south, west, and northwest by the Atlantic Ocean. To the east is the Irish Sea, which separates it from Great Britain, only 100 miles away.

There are many small islands off the coast, including Achill Island, Clare Island, Valentia Island, Dursey Island, and the Aran Islands.

Ireland has a mild temperature averaging about 60°F in the summer and 40°F in winter. It seldom snows except in the mountains. There is, however, a lot of rain. Mountains receive about 60 inches of rain a year, while the Central Plain receives an average of 36 inches per year.

The Republic of Ireland is small, about the size of the state of Maine. It occupies 27,137 square miles. From north to south it measures a maximum distance of 273 miles, and 186 miles from east to west. Its population is 3,555,500.

There are three principal types of land areas on the island: seacoasts, a central plain, and mountain ranges.

Not too far inland from the seacoast are several mountain ranges. In the east are the Wicklow Mountains. In the west and the southwest are the Mountains of Donegal, the Mountains of Mayo, the Mountains of Connemara, and the Mountains of Kerry. The Mountains of Kerry contain the highest peak in Ireland, Carrauntoohill's Peak, at 3,414 feet above sea level.

The central plain contains green meadows and rich farmlands. Beef cattle graze here. Dairy cattle, pigs, sheep, and horses are also raised. Only about 10 percent of the farmland is used for growing crops such as barley, wheat, sugar beets, and potatoes. Irish farmers produce enough meat, milk, and other foods to supply the inhabitants and they export some, too.

Ireland lacks extensive mineral deposits. There is some poor quality coal, but peat from the heaths and bogs has been widely used as fuel. Peat comes from peat moss, made up of undecayed or partially decomposed plant matter at or near the surface of bogs.

There are several important rivers in Ireland. The Republic of Ireland's largest city, Dublin, is located on the River Liffey. Cork, the second largest city, is on the River Lee. The longest and most famous river in Ireland is the River Shannon, which begins in the north and winds for 240 miles before emptying into the Atlantic Ocean in the southwest.

Dublin is an important manufacturing city. Among its products are clothing, whiskey and stout, furniture, machines, chemicals, paper, and metals. Many products are shipped out of the port. Since the Republic of Ireland joined the European Economic Community in 1973, industrialists may export products duty-free to member countries. The Irish Republic has one of the fastest growing industrial sectors in Europe.

Other important cities include Cork, Limerick, Killarney, Waterford, and Galway. Cork is located in the far southern part of the country near the Atlantic Ocean. It is known for its beautiful churches. Major industries in Cork are food products, car manufacturing, and beer production. The Blarney Stone, a famous Irish landmark, is just five miles from Cork. Legend has it that anyone who kisses the stone will have the gift of persuasive talk.

Limerick is located in the southwest at the mouth of the River Shannon. It is the third largest city after Dublin and Cork. Food and clothing are among the major products that move from this port city out into the Atlantic Ocean.

Killarney, located in the southwest, is one of the leading tourist spots in the Republic of Ireland. It has fewer than 10,000 people but is famous for its scenic beauty, including lakes, mountains, and woods.

Waterford, with 30,000 people, is located in the southeast. It is a fishing center and has a major port. People all over the world collect and are proud of the high quality Waterford crystal that is made in this city.

Galway was founded in the 1200s and is in the western part of the country near Galway Bay. Many of the old Irish customs and the use of the Gaelic language are common here. Just across the Bay are the Aran Islands. Cut off from the rest of the country, people on the Aran Islands fish and farm much as they did centuries ago. Women on the Aran Islands are well known for the weaving of wool and making of sweaters.

History

Around 10,000 years ago, when the Ice Age ended, Ireland got its first inhabitants. These Stone Age people probably came from southwestern Scotland. Thousands of stone temples, sanctuaries, freestanding dolmens, and stone circles remain.

About 7,000 B.C., people who were hunters and gatherers moved into Ireland from Britain and Europe. The Bronze Age began in Ireland about 4,000 years ago. There remain examples of craftsmanship in armor, weapons, and ornaments. Around 400 B.C., Celt warriors came to Ireland from France. The coming of the Celts marked the beginning of the Iron Age in Ireland.

At first the Celts divided Ireland into a number of kingdoms. Then in the third century A.D. most of Ireland was united under a single Celtic high king.

Celtic culture and laws spread throughout the island and so did their language, called Gaelic. One form of their language, Irish Gaelic, is still spoken in Ireland. The Celts were known as great storytellers and among their many gods was Ogma, the god of storytelling.

St. Patrick was born in Great Britain, captured and raised as a slave in northern Ireland, and studied to become a priest in France. About 432, Pope Celestine I sent Patrick to Ireland to teach the people about Christianity. He is said to have founded 300 churches in Ireland.

In 795, the Vikings from Norway, Denmark, and Sweden invaded Ireland and some settled there. Some who stayed built forts that gradually grew into cities. Vikings founded Dublin, Limerick, Cork, and Waterford. By the year 1000, the Vikings controlled a large portion of Ireland.

In 1002, Brian Boru, a Christian, became High King of Ireland. He built forts and formed an army. In 1014, Brian Boru led his army into battle and defeated the Vikings. Following the defeat, some Vikings returned home while others stayed, married Christians, and became part of the people of Ireland. Ireland was then left alone for about 150 years.

In 1066 the Normans (Vikings who had settled in France) attacked and conquered England, and within a few years, the Normans from Great Britain attacked Ireland. In 1171, Henry II, the Norman king of England, went to Ireland

and declared himself King of Ireland. There then followed seven centuries of British rule.

Henry VIII had himself declared King of Ireland in 1541 and his daughter, Mary I, began evicting Irish from their land and putting in their place English settlers or loyal Irish. Elizabeth I, who became queen in 1558, was hated by the Irish for outlawing Catholic religious services in Ireland. James I, who followed her, placed Scottish and English Protestants in the northern part of Ireland. By 1650, four-fifths of Ireland had English landlords.

Throughout the 1700s, Irish Catholics were treated poorly. There were many rebellions against the English rule, but they all failed. Many emigrants chose to leave Ireland. One group of emigrants had no choice. Between 1788 and 1868, over 50,000 Irish were sent to Australia as prisoners.

In the 1840s hunger became a major problem in Ireland. When the potato crop was destroyed by disease, many people had nothing to eat. A million people in Ireland died of starvation or disease. Another million boarded ships and left, many for the United States and Canada. Others went to England. By 1841, over 400,000 Irish people were living in British cities.

A large number of those who sailed for the United States and Canada died on the journey over. They traveled in crowded ships and had little food. Many paid for their passage with money sent by a relative who had left earlier and had found work in the new country.

Irish women often worked as domestics, waitresses, or in textile mills. In cities such as New York, Boston, and Chicago, the Irish gradually came to dominate police and fire departments. With the gold rush in the 1850s, Irish from the east moved west. Some worked at building railroads. Others were miners.

In 1916 during the Easter Rebellion, the Irish declared themselves independent. Again the rebellion failed. But in 1920, the British Parliament divided Ireland into two separate, self-governing parts, both of which were still part of Great Britain. The north accepted this agreement and became part of the United Kingdom of Great Britain and Northern Ireland. The south refused to accept it, and in 1921 became the Irish Free State. After more quarrels and battles, in 1949 the Irish Free State declared itself independent and became the Republic of Ireland.

In Northern Ireland, Protestants and Catholics continued to fight. In 1969 after widespread rioting, England sent troops. The troops remain until the present time.

Government

The Sinn Fein Society formed the Irish House of Deputies and declared the Independent Republic of Ireland in 1919. The nation's first constitution went into effect in 1922. In 1937, a new constitution and a number of amendments were approved.

The Republic of Ireland left the British Commonwealth in 1948. It is now a parliamentary democracy led by a prime minister and a Parliament consisting of two houses of lawmakers.

The House of Deputies makes the laws for the Republic, and the people elect its 166 members for five-year terms. Citizens who are least eighteen years old may vote.

The Senate can present bills to the House of Deputies but cannot pass laws. The 60 members of the Senate are appointed by the prime minister and are representatives from education, agriculture, labor, industry, and public administration.

The president is elected every seven years and can serve for no more than two terms. The president appoints the prime minister and other officials, and is commander of the country's armed forces.

The prime minister is the most important government official. The prime minister is nominated by the House of Deputies and is appointed by the president to serve for a maximum five-year term. The prime minister selects from the parliament the heads of various government departments, who have duties similar to those of the cabinet of the president of the United States.

Local government in the Republic of Ireland is divided into twenty-seven county councils. Councils, elected by the people, along with county managers, govern the counties. They are responsible for planning and taxing but not for education or police functions.

Dublin, the capital of Ireland, is cut in half by the River Liffey. It has about 550,000 people. It is here that the lawmakers meet in Leinster House.

The Belfast Accord was passed in 1998. Under its terms, the forum for ministers from the Irish Republic to pursue joint policy making with the Northern Ireland Executive is a North-South Ministerial Council. This Council would meet on mutually agreed areas of common interest such as agriculture, tourism, environmental protection, welfare fraud control, and transportation.

The same accord states that lawmakers from the British and Irish parliaments, administrations for Scotland and Wales, the new Northern Ireland Assembly, and representatives of Britain's Isle of Man and Channel Island will meet twice yearly to work out common policies and actions.

Religion

The Republic of Ireland is about 97 percent Catholic. The few Protestants are mostly Anglicans, Episcopalians, Methodists, and Presbyterians.

One of the most important religious figures of Ireland is Saint Patrick. He introduced Christianity to Ireland in the fifth century A.D. The period from about A.D. 476 to 1000 is often called the Dark Ages. During this period, education declined throughout Europe. But Irish monks kept alive the knowledge of past cultures.

Today, almost every city or town in the Republic of Ireland has at least one well-attended Catholic Church.

Many Irish make pilgrimages to holy places during their vacations. Each year up to eighty thousand people walk to the top of Croagh Patrick in County Mayo. This is where it is thought, that in 441, Saint Patrick spent the forty days of Lent praying and fasting.

Education

Education is free, and children between the ages of six and fifteen attend school. Many children attend state-funded schools in their small towns. Others may travel a short distance to a larger town to attend a Catholic School. These students attend separate boys' and girls' schools and usually wear uniforms.

During their Primary Education, students learn reading, writing, arithmetic, and both the Irish (Gaelic) and English languages. They also study music, arts, and crafts.

Second Level education is similar to our high school years. Some students pursue a general course of study. Others attend special vocational schools to learn more about farming or skills for factory work.

After their Second Level education, some students go on to college or university. Trinity College (also called the University of Dublin) was founded in 1591. Located in Dublin, it has the country's largest book collection. It also is the repository of Brian Boru's harp, which is the national symbol of the Republic of Ireland.

The National University of Ireland has colleges in Dublin, Cork, and Galway. The Republic of Ireland also has colleges of education for teacher training, and The Royal College of Surgeons to provide training for doctors. There are also colleges that train farmers, fishermen, musicians, and lawmakers. Artists may attend the National College of Art and Design.

Immigrants

A disease infected the potatoes in Ireland from 1845 to 1847. This potato famine caused over a million Irish to starve to death. About 1.6 million Irish left the country during this famine and immigrated to England, Canada, Australia, or the United States.

In the United States, the Irish took on many occupations. Young women worked as domestic servants. The men worked in coal mines, gold mines, and copper mines. Many were involved in building railroads. In their early days in the United States, they struggled for their rights, and experienced prejudice toward Catholics. They often lived crowded together in tenements. But gradually many moved up into positions of wealth and power.

From 1981 to 1990, 32,800 Irish immigrated to the United States. During 1991 to 1995, another 53,200 came.

It is estimated that about 40 million people in the United States have Irish ancestors. This makes Ireland a popular place for tourists who seek out their families' villages and visit important historical and religious sites.

Language

The Celts brought the Gaelic language to Ireland, but when the English took control of the island, Gaelic was outlawed. In

1893, a Gaelic League was founded to restore Ireland's language. Today about one-fourth of the people in the Republic of Ireland know enough Gaelic to use it in conversation. About 50,000 people use it as their main language.

Most place names in Ireland are spelled in both Gaelic (Irish) and English. Children are taught Gaelic in school but most of the time they speak English.

The Arts and Sciences

Among the great writers who have come from Ireland are Jonathan Swift, George Bernard Show, John Millington Synge, William Butler Yeats, James Joyce, and Oscar Wilde, all of whom were born in or near Dublin. Among famous writers who were the children or grandchildren of Irish immigrants to the United States was the famous playwright Eugene O'Neil.

Cork has also produced famous writers, including Frank O'Connor, Sean O'Faolain, and Francis Sylvester Mahony. Other famous writers include Elizabeth Bowen, Oliver Goldsmith, Samuel Beckett, Liam O'Flaherty, Lady Augusta Gregory, and Brendan Behan.

There are many Irish poets who live and work today in the United States. Among these are Gerard Donovan and Eamonn Wall. In their poems, they speak of their immigrant status. Perhaps the most prominent Irish poet today is Eavan Boland, who lives in a suburb of Dublin. Her best-known book is *Object Lessons: The Life of the Woman and the Poet in Our Time.*

Among well known Irish painters are Jack Yeats, Paul Henry, George Russell, James Humbert Craig, W. J. Leech, Patrick Tuohy, Sean Keating, Terence P. Flanagan, John Keating, Gerard Dillon, and portrait painters John Butler Yeats and Estella Solomons. James Hoban, an Irish architect, designed the White House in the United States.

Famous early Irish composers, born in Dublin, were Michael Balfe and John Field. Ireland's musical heritage includes folk dances such as the Irish Jig and folk songs, which are often sung to the accompaniment of the harp, flute, or fiddle. Many Irish cities have opera houses and concert halls. John McCormack was a world famous opera star in the early 1900s.

Robert Boyle, who studied the expansion and compression of gases, is among the famous Irish scientists. And the renowned astronomer, William Rown Hamilton, was born in Dublin. John Philip Holland was an Irish experimenter credited with inventing the submarine. Ernest Walton, a scientist who won the Nobel Prize in physics in 1951, was born in Waterford.

The best known of the Irish philosophers was George Berkeley, who was born in Kilkenny.

Food

When people think of food in connection with Ireland, they may first think of the Irish potato, because of all the countries in northern Europe, it was in Ireland that the potato became most important. Some say the potato made its way to Ireland with Sir Walter Raleigh, the English explorer. Others say that the Irish took potatoes from the holds of ships from the Spanish Armada that were destroyed by storms off the Irish coast. However they got there, potatoes were well established in Ireland by the mid-1600s.

After its arrival, the potato made a tremendous difference in Ireland. A one-acre plot of land could supply enough potatoes to feed a family of five for a year. It is estimated that by the end of the 1700s, the average Irish person ate 8 pounds of potatoes a day.

One of the foods that is traditionally served on St. Patrick's Day is Irish Soda Bread.

Irish Soda Bread

4 cups flour
1 tablespoon double-acting baking powder
1 teaspoon salt
$3/4$ teaspoon baking soda
1 cup raisins, rinsed and patted dry
1 tablespoon caraway seeds
2 cups buttermilk

Preheat the oven to 350°F. Into a large bowl, sift together the flour, baking powder, salt, and baking soda. Stir in the raisins and caraway seeds. Add the buttermilk and stir the mixture until it forms a dough.

Turn the dough out onto a well-floured surface and knead it for one minute. Halve the dough, and with floured hands shape each half into a round loaf and transfer the loaves to a lightly greased baking sheet.

Cut an "X" a quarter of an inch deep across the tops of the loaves with a sharp knife. Bake the two loaves in the middle of the oven for 45 to 55 minutes, or until a tester comes out clean. Transfer the loaves to racks and let them cool.

Potato soup remains popular in Ireland today. It is made with onions, carrots, and potatoes. Another typical food is Irish stew, which usually contains mutton, onions, potatoes, parsley, and thyme. A traditional dish is called bacon and cabbage. Corned beef and cabbage is the American version of this dish. *Barm brack* is a fruit-filled, syrup-topped cake that is traditionally made at Halloween.

An unusual food is Carrageen moss jelly, which is made with *Carrageen,* an edible seaweed that often washes up on the eastern shore of Ireland in April and May. Dublin *coddle* is a stew made with bacon, sausages, onions, and potatoes.

Recreation

One of the games children play is hurling. For this game, which is somewhat like field hockey, each side has 15 players. Players use sticks that look like short paddles and they try to hit a small leather ball through their opponents' goalposts.

Hurling matches are held between county teams. The All-Ireland Hurling Championship is held each year in September in Dublin before crowds of up to 80,000 people. Women play a game similar to hurling called camogie.

Gaelic football, which is very popular, contains elements of rugby and soccer. Another popular ancient Irish sport is road bowling. Bowlers use metal balls and see who can use the least number of throws to complete a two- or three-mile race.

Horseracing is a favorite pastime and there are more than two dozen race tracks in the country. Greyhound dog racing is also popular.

Other sports, similar to those found in the United States, includ boating, golfing, swimming, fishing, horseback riding, bicycling, jogging, and boxing.

Customs and Traditions

An Irish custom from long ago was to welcome spring with great bonfires. Tradition has it that Saint Patrick celebrated one such spring at the Hill of Slane. Gradually the bonfires gave way to huge Paschal candles. On Holy Saturday fires were put out and then people gathered in churches to see the great Pashcal candle lit. They brought candles and lit them in the Paschal candle and took them home to re-kindle their fires and lamps.

Many countries hold special celebrations around the first of November, when spirits of the dead are thought to walk the Earth. On Halloween, Irish people hollowed out turnips and set candles in them to turn away demons who were afraid of the light. When the Irish came to America, they began using pumpkins for lanterns rather than turnips. The Halloween jack-o'-lantern has become very popular in the United States.

The Irish also brought with them stories of Jack-o'-lantern, who made a pact with the Devil. Jack was to have seven years of fun before the Devil came to claim him. When the Devil did come, Jack played a trick on the Devil. Unable to get into heaven or hell, Jack supposedly roams the earth, playing tricks on people.

Among many traditions from Ireland celebrated in the United States is St. Patrick's Day. It is said that everyone is Irish on this special day. In many places there are parades, dancing of jigs, the wearing of green, and eating special Irish foods such as Irish stew and soda bread.

Suggested Activities

Writing

1. One way to learn about life and activities in another country is to have a pen pal. This takes some money to pay for postage to a foreign country and some patience to write and wait for a reply. Yet receiving the mail from friends in other lands is exciting, and the letters can be shared with classmates. For a pen pal, you can write to Worldwide Pen Friends, P. O. Box 39097, Downey, CA 90241. Be sure to state your age, name, and address, and the country you want your pen pal to be from.

Reading

2. Ireland is famous for its limericks. Some students may enjoy reading a collection of humorous limericks, choosing a favorite, and reading it to the class. (Perhaps a few will want to write original limericks to read.) Two resources are *Talkaty Talker: Limericks* by Molly Manley and *Lots of Limericks*, selected by Myra Cohn Livingston.

Vocabulary

3. An ancient language of Ireland is Gaelic. Students who are reading books about Ireland may come upon words and phrases in Gaelic that interest them. Post a "Gaelic" chart on a bulletin board and encourage students to add to it. Here are some expressions to get you started: *sean-athair*—grandmother, *eaglais*—church, *clog*—clock, *Eanar*—January, *Luan*—Monday, *Deich*—ten, *buachail*—boy, and *cistin*—kitchen.

Math

4. Many Irish names begin with Mac, Mc, or O'. What percentage of the names included in your town or city's phone book begin in one of these three ways? How can you estimate the number of names in the phone book?

Social Studies

5. Add an Irish News section to a class bulletin board. Encourage students to bring in articles about the Republic of Ireland that they find in current newspapers and magazines.

Geography

6. Ireland is divided into four provinces: Ulster, Connaught, Leinster, and Munster. Ask a small group of students to make a map of Ireland, divide it into four provinces, and list the major cities in each province. Ask the students to list one famous historical spot in each province and tell why it is famous.

Music

7. Irish folk songs often feature the harp, flute, or fiddle. With the help of a music educator, locate a record or CD of Irish folk songs and play it for the class.

Art

8. Bruce Arnold's book, *Irish Art*, would be a good resource to share. With the help of an art educator, discuss some of the paintings in this book with the students.

Drama/Movement

9. Ask a group of students, working with an adult volunteer, to read one of George Bernard Shaw's plays and choose a short scene to present to the class.

Dress

10. Many of the Irish girls who came to the United States during the mid-1800s became domestic servants. Servants at this time dressed in a formal way. Ask a group of students to find (and with permission to photocopy) pictures of Irish servants dressed in their uniforms. Share these with the class.

Cooking

11. *Yellow Man* is an Irish candy treat that would be fun to make and share.

Yellow Man

1 tablespoon butter

1 cup brown sugar

4 cups corn syrup

2 tablespoons distilled white vinegar

1 teaspoon baking powder

Melt 1 heaping tablespoon of butter in a saucepan and use it to coat the inside of the pan. Add 1 cup brown sugar, 4 cups corn syrup, and 2 tablespoons of distilled white vinegar into the saucepan.

Stir over low heat until the sugar and syrup have melted. Bring the mixture to a boil and simmer without stirring.

Test the mixture by dropping a little of it in a glass of cold water to see if it sets.

Add 1 teaspoon baking power to the mixture—it will foam. Stir again and then pour it into a greased pan. After it has set, cut into small squares to serve.

Culminating Activity

12. Encourage students to do further research on the Irish who immigrated to work in the factories of England, the farms of Canada, the rich homes of the east coast of the United States or the railroad and mining camps of the western United States, or who came as prisoners to Australia. Ask each student to compose a letter to mail "home to Ireland" telling their relatives what it is like in the new world. Allow time for each student to read his or her letter aloud, and then post all of these letters on a bulletin board captioned "Letters from Irish Immigrants."

Suggested Reading

Arnold, Bruce. *Irish Art.* New York: Thames & Hudson, 1989.

Bateman, Teresa. *The Ring of Truth.* New York: Holiday House, 1997.

Climo, Shirley. *The Irish Cinderlad.* New York: HarperCollins, 1996.

Coffey, Michael, ed. *The Irish in America.* New York: Hyperion, 1997.

de Paola, Tomie. *Jamie O'Rourke and the Big Potato.* New York: G. P. Putnam's Sons, 1992.

Dunlop, Eileen. *Tales of St. Patrick.* New York: Holiday House, 1996.

Fradin, Dennis B. *The Republic of Ireland.* Chicago, Ill.: Childrens Press, 1984.

Haviland, Virginia. *Favorite Fairy Tales Told in Ireland.* Boston, Mass.: Little, Brown, 1961.

Holland, Gini. *Ireland Is My Home.* (Adapted from *Children of the World: Ireland*). Milwaukee, Wisc.: Gareth Stevens, 1993.

Johnson, Sylvia A. *Tomatoes, Potatoes, Corn, and Beans, How the Foods of the Americas Changed Eating Around the World.* New York: Atheneum, 1997.

MacManus, Seumas. *Hibernian Nights.* New York: Macmillan, 1963.

Murphy, Dervla. *Ireland.* Salem, N.H.: Salem House, 1985.

O'Brien, Maire and Conor Cruise O'Brien. *A Concise History of Ireland.* New York: Thames & Hudson, 1985.

Prior, Katherine. *The History of Emigration from Ireland.* Danbury, Conn.: Franklin Watts, 1996.

Stewart, Jillian, Editor. *Irish Cooking.* New York: Crescent Books, 1991.

Tourtellot, Jonathan B., ed. *Discovering Britain & Ireland.* Washington, D.C.: National Geographic Society, 1985.

The count found the laundry bag waiting by the front door.
He flung it on the horse and started off.

Italy
A Legend from Italy

There are many versions of this story in which the Devil is tricked by a washerwoman's daughter.
One of these, *Silver Nose*, is found in *Italian Folktales*, selected and retold by Italo Calvino. Another
is *Count Silvernose: A Story from Italy*, retold by Eric A. Kimmel with illustrations by Omar Rayyan.

Tricking Count Silver Nose

In northern Italy there lived a widowed washerwoman and her three daughters. The youngest daughter and the middle daughter were especially beautiful. The oldest daughter, Assunta, was plain, but she was clever and strong.

One day while the washerwoman was out in the yard scrubbing, and the youngest daughter was hanging up clothes on the line, a dashing gentleman came riding up on a black horse.

"I am told you have three daughters who know how to wash, sweep, and clean. I would like to take one of them to my castle to work for me," the gentleman said.

The old washerwoman would have been glad to send one of her daughters except for the fact that the gentleman wore a silver nose. She guessed he had been injured in a duel, and she worried that a quick-tempered man might harm her daughter. While the old woman hesitated, the youngest daughter came running up dazzled by the gentleman's fine cloak and beautiful horse.

"I'll gladly come with you," she said. And she lightly leaped onto the horse behind the gentleman.

He galloped off with the youngest daughter before the old woman could stop them.

A week passed, and the gentleman came riding up again on his magnificent steed.

"How is my youngest daughter?" the old woman asked.

"That's what I've come to see you about," said the gentleman. "I find there is too much work for one servant at my castle. I wish to take another of your daughters to my castle to work for me."

The middle daughter, who had been hanging up clothes, came running up. "I'll gladly come with you," she cried. And she lightly leaped onto the horse. They quickly rode away.

Exactly one week later, the gentleman came riding up again.

"How are my daughters?" the old washerwoman asked.

"That's why I have come," said the gentleman. "Even two servants are not enough to do the work in my castle. I have come to take your third daughter to help them."

The oldest daughter was suspicious of the gentleman but she wanted to find out if her sisters were safe, so she said, "I'll gladly come with you."

She climbed up behind the gentleman, and they rode away.

After a long ride, the gentleman pointed to a building and said, "I am a count and there is my castle."

When they reached it, the gentleman led the oldest daughter, Assunta, inside.

To Assunta's amazement, the castle appeared empty. There was no sign of her sisters or of anyone else. "Where are my sisters?" she asked. The count did not answer.

"I will show you to your room," the count said. He led Assunta up a winding staircase to the second floor. "There are thirteen rooms on this floor," the count said. He pulled from his pocket a set of iron keys.

Opening the first door, he said, "You will sleep here." Assunta looked inside and saw a small room with a bed.

The count led her down the hall, opening one door after another. In each, there was a pile of washing on the floor.

When he reached the thirteenth room, the count said, "Under no circumstances are you to unlock this door. It is forbidden for you to enter. Do you understand?"

"Yes," Assunta replied.

The count then gave her all thirteen keys. "You are to begin work tomorrow morning," he said. "I will be away all day, but when I come back, I will check on you."

"I'll start early in the morning," Assunta promised.

The count left, and Assunta went quietly into her room where she waited until it was dark and the castle was quiet. Then she crept quietly down the hall to the thirteenth door. Taking the key she unlocked it.

In the center of the room was a fiery pit with flames leaping into the air. Assunta peered into it. At the bottom she could see her two sisters being tormented by goblins. Her sisters called up to her, "Help us, Assunta!"

Quickly Assunta went next door and tied dirty sheets together until she had made a long rope. Then she went back to the thirteenth room. She tied one end of the sheet to the iron pull on the heavy door. Then, hand over hand, she lowered herself into the pit. In her mouth, she held a washing paddle.

As soon as she reached the bottom, she beat at the goblins with the paddle. "Quick," she called to her sisters. "One of you hold onto my neck and the other my waist." They did as she commanded, and Assunta climbed back up the rope carrying her sisters to safety.

She took them back to her room, where they explained that the count was really the Devil. They, too, had been brought to the castle and told not to open the thirteenth room, but they had opened it. When the count came home from a trip, he could smell sulfur and smoke in their hair. Knowing they had disobeyed him, the count cast them into the fiery pit.

"When the count is here, you must stay in this room and hide under the bed," Assunta said. "I'll think of a way to get you safely home. Now I must wash my hair so that the count will not guess I've been in the thirteenth room."

As soon as the count rode away the next morning, the three sisters set to work. They did load after load of washing, hanging out the clothes to dry.

That afternoon, when she heard the count's horse on the courtyard, Assunta sent her sisters to hide.

The count looked at the pile of clean clothes. Then he came over to Assunta and smelled her hair for smoke. When he could smell nothing unusual, he said, "Good. Perhaps I have finally found a hard working, faithful servant."

"I have a request," Assunta said. "You have many ruffled shirts. Properly treated they will be handsome indeed. My mother can iron these much better than I. Tomorrow morning I want you to take a load of clean shirts to her. You must leave early, go quickly, and not stop along the way. I will be watching you."

"If you come along to watch me, how will you get your work done?" asked the count.

"I will not go with you. But I have special powers, and I will see if you stop. If you waste time, arriving at her cottage at night and frightening her, I will know it. And I will no longer do your washing."

Early the next morning, Assunta put a few clean shirts in the bottom of a laundry bag. Then her youngest sister climbed in. Assunta packed a few more shirts on top and then tied the bag.

When the count tossed the laundry bag across the back of his horse, he complained, "This is terribly heavy."

"It's not my fault you have so many clothes," retorted Assunta.

The count rode off. Halfway to the washerwoman's home, the count stopped. "This laundry bag is too heavy," he said. "I am going to look inside."

He lifted the bag to the ground, and at that moment, Assunta's sister did as she had been directed. She cried out loudly, "I can see you."

The count quickly flung the bag back on the horse. "If Assunta really can see me wasting time, and if I arrive late at her mother's house, she will be annoyed. And I may lose a good washerwoman," he muttered.

At the washerwoman's house, the count dropped off the bag. "I will have your shirts ready in three days," the washerwoman said. The count hurried away. As soon as he left, the washerwoman opened the bag and rejoiced to find her youngest daughter.

Back at the castle, the count sniffed Assunta's hair. It did not smell of smoke, and she and her sister had completed more of the washing. The count rejoiced in the excellent servant he had found.

The next day, Assunta repeated her request to the count to take clean shirts to her mother for ironing. This time, the middle daughter was in the laundry bag with a few shirts at the bottom and the top of the bag. Once again the count stopped and was going to peek inside the bag, but, following Assunta's directions, the middle daughter cried, "I can see you." The count flung the bag back on the horse and hurried on his way.

The count deposited his heavy load with the washerwoman and rode away. The washerwoman was delighted to have two of her daughters back home with her.

The count rode back to the castle. He checked Assunta's hair for smoke but found none. Assunta had done the laundry from another three rooms.

Again Assunta made her request that the count take more shirts to the washerwoman for ironing. "I will leave the bag by the front door," Assunta said, "for I am very tired from my hard work and do not want to awaken so early tomorrow morning."

The count found the laundry bag waiting by the front door. He flung it on the horse and started off. Halfway there, he again felt curious about the heavy laundry bag. He dropped the bag to the ground to open and peek in it, but as soon as the bag touched the ground, Assunta shouted, "I can see you."

The count picked up the bag and went to the washerwoman. As he rode up, Assunta's sisters hid in the house. "Your shirts will be ready in three days," promised the washerwoman.

The count rode off, and the washerwoman and her daughters opened the bag and found Assunta. They kissed and hugged one another and gave thanks. Then they hung a cross on their door, and the Devil, in the form of Count Silver Nose, never bothered them again.

When the three sisters married local boys, the old washerwoman gave each a handsome set of ruffled shirts.

Background Information

The Italian Republic forms the southern boundary of Europe. It is a long narrow peninsula that juts out into the water with a coastline of about 4,700 miles. Its position in the midst of five seas has made it important throughout history. The Adriatic Sea is to the east, the Ionian Sea and Mediterranean Sea are to the south, the Tyrrheneian Sea is to the west, and the Ligurian Sea is to the northwest.

Italy covers 116,341 square miles. From northwest to southeast, Italy is a little more than 670 miles. The widest spot in the north measures about 350 miles. Its neighbors are France to the west, Switzerland and Austria to the north, and Slovenia to the east. Italy stretches toward the northern coast of Africa, only 90 miles away.

To many people, the shape of the country resembles a high-heeled boot with the island of Sicily just beyond its toe. Also belonging to Italy are two islands to the west, Sardinia and Elba. The current population of the country is 57,534,088. Its capital city is Rome, known as "the eternal city."

In addition to the Italian Republic, on this peninsula there is the independent republic of San Marino, which is one of the oldest states in Europe and which covers 25 square miles. The Vatican City is also a separate state, about 109 acres in size, with its own flag, currency, and stamps. The Pope lives in The Vatican City.

Italy is divided into twenty regions and ninety-four provinces. The Alps stretch out along the north, and flowing from them to the east is the Po River. The eastern Italian Alps are called the Dolomite Mountains. The Apennine Mountains run down the middle of the country.

Just south of the Alps is an area called the Northern Plain or the Po Plain. Milan, the capital of Lombardy province and Italy's second largest city, is located here. It is known as the fashion capital of Italy.

The Northern Plain is a rich farming area, sometimes called the country's breadbasket. Primary crops are grapes, olives, citrus fruits, peaches, apricots, plums, tomatoes, vegetables, wheat, rice, and corn. Other crops include potatoes, onions, beans, sugar beets, tobacco, artichokes, garlic, and cauliflower.

Italy is the world's second largest producer of wines and the sixth largest producer of wool and cheese. Perhaps most famous is Parmesan cheese, which comes from Parma, but many other cheeses are also made, including mozzarella. Although Italy raises beef, pork, and lamb, it imports most of its meat.

Other agricultural areas of Italy besides the Northern Plain are the southern section, described as the "heel" of the boot, and a few small areas along the coast. The rest of the country is covered in rugged mountains and is very rocky.

Northern Italy has cold and wet winters, but its summers are hot and dry. Its climate resembles that of the European continent. Southern Italy has a Mediterranean climate with mild winters, sunny springs, and hot and dry summers. The Alps remain covered in snow in winter and summer.

In the summer, many Italian cities are uncomfortably hot. A scorching wind, the Scirocco, blows through Italy. This wind comes across the Mediterranean Sea from the Sahara Desert in North Africa. Many Italians take their vacations at this time, traveling to the mountains or to be near the sea.

Vesuvius, near Naples, erupted in A.D. 79 and destroyed Pompeii and Herculaneum. Italy still has active volcanoes. The highest volcano in Europe is Mount Etna in Sicily at 10,902 feet. The Lipari islands include the volcano on Stromboli.

Italy also has many industries. It is the fourth biggest steel producer in Europe. This steel is important to Italy's car industry. Italy is famous for several makes of car, including Fiat, Alfa Romero, Lancia, Lamborghini, and Ferrari. The two biggest industrial centers in Italy are Milan and Turin.

Italy has some natural resources, including iron ore, lead, zinc, aluminum, mercury, coal, and oil. Methane gas is an important source of energy and there are deposits in the Po Valley, in the province of Ravenna, and beneath the Adriatic Sea. Hydroelectric power is another major energy source. Italy is rich in marble, the most famous of which is found in the Carrara quarries in Tuscany. But Italy must import a considerable amount of raw materials, including its timber.

Italy's capital city, Rome, with 2.69 million people, has far more sights than can be discussed here. There are fountains, temples, basilicas, the Forum, and the Senate to name just a few. Perhaps the most famous sight in Rome is the Coliseum, or the Flavian Amphitheater. It has stood for nearly two thousand years through earthquakes, fires, and wars.

The Colosseum held three stories of seats for spectators. The seats just above the area were on a terrace called the *podum* where the nobles sat. Ordinary people sat above them. The central arena is 86 x 54 meters.

The men who fought in the arena were called gladiators. These men fought other men, usually prisoners or captives. Sometimes, however, Christians were thrown to wild beasts. Animals were kept in underground cages until needed.

Among the famous fountains in the city of Rome are the Fontana delle Tartarughe, designed in the sixteenth century, and featuring dolphin and tortoises, and the Fontana di Trevi, where people throw coins hoping to guarantee a return trip to Rome one day.

The Square and Basilica of St. Peter are enormous. In the first chapel to the right of the entrance to St. Peter's is the *Pieta*, a famous marble sculpture by Michelangelo made in the early sixteenth century.

There are many other important Italian cities. Venice, where canals take the place of streets, is built primarily on some 120 tiny islands on the Adriatic coast; flowing through the city of Florence is the Arno River; Milan is a bustling industrial city; Naples, the third largest city in Italy, still contains castles of feudal lords; and Palermo is Sicily's capital.

History

Primitive people roamed in Italy nearly 300,000 years ago. With the arrival of the Etruscans and the Greeks, Italy became more than a country of scattered primitive villages. Although no one is certain where they came from, the Etruscans arrived in the ninth century B.C. Between 700 and 500 B.C., the Etruscans ruled from Tuscany north to the Po Valley and south to Naples. In the eighth century B.C., there were Greek outposts in Sicily and in the south of Italy.

For 900 years, Romans ruled Italy. The Romans had enormous influence on the languages and legal systems of Western countries. The Roman emperor Constantine moved his capital to Constantinople in A.D. 330, and barbarians overran the Western Roman Empire. Rival rulers fought over Italian territory. Julius Caesar ended what was the Republic and became dictator. Then Augustus, the son of Julius Caesar, established the Roman Empire in 30 B.C.

Charlemagne had himself crowned emperor in Rome in A.D. 800, but his Holy Roman Empire fell apart after his death. By the twelfth century, independent communes in Italy became the city-states of Venice, Genoa, Florence, and Milan. It was not until 1861 that the kingdom of Italy was formed. In 1870 Rome was made the capital of a unified Italy.

In 1922, Benito Mussolini took power in Italy and set up a fascistic government. He joined with Adolph Hitler of Germany and fought against the United Kingdom, France, the Soviet Union, and the United States during World War II.

Government

When a unified Italy came into existence in 1861, its government was a constitutional monarchy. It was not until June 18, 1946, that the people voted to make Italy a parliamentary republic made up of an executive, legislative, and judicial branch. This design and division of power is similar to that of the United States.

The parliament has two chambers—the Senate and the Chamber of Deputies. The Senate has 315 elected members and 7 members nominated by the president in office. Senators serve for six-year terms. The Chamber has 630 deputies, representing 32 electoral constituencies, elected for five-year terms.

Senators and Deputies have equal powers, and both these bodies must approve laws. These representatives elect the president of Italy, who is the ceremonial head of state and serves for seven years.

Besides the president, the executive branch includes a cabinet, called the Council of Ministers. This Council is headed by the prime minister, who is appointed by the president.

The judicial branch of government is divided into the civil and criminal courts and the administrative courts. Judges dominate Italian trials. They question witnesses, investigate facts, and pass judgment. Juries are used in important cases and are made up of judges, not the general public. This system is based on ancient Roman law. Roman law also influenced the men involved in the writing of the American Constitution.

The different regions and communes in Italy are run by councils that govern a specific area. They deal with planning, public works, health, education, and public transport.

Unlike the United States, where the vast majority of citizens belong to one of two major political parties, Italy has a history of many major political parties with very diverse opinions.

Italian currency is called the lira and is written as LIT. Coins are made in the amounts of 50, 100, 200, and 500 lire. Notes are issued in the amounts of 1,000, 2,000, 5,000, 10,000, 50,000, and 100,000 lire.

Religion

Italy is primarily a Roman Catholic country. It is estimated that less than 2 percent of the population is Protestant, Jewish, or Greek Orthodox. Sometime between the ages of seven and ten, Catholic boys and girls make their first Holy Communion. They are usually confirmed between the ages of nine and fourteen.

The world headquarters for Catholicism, The Holy See, is located at Vatican City in the center of Rome. This is the office of the Pope, who leads the world's more than 540 million Catholics.

Education

Education is compulsory in Italy for children between the ages of six and fourteen, although some children may start nursery school when they are three years old. Catholic schools are not numerous in Italy. About 90 percent of all elementary children attend public schools, where priests teach religion.

The children attend primary school *(la scuola elementare)* until they are eleven. Like students in the United States, they learn reading, writing, and math.

Some children in school have a schedule similar to that of school children in the United States. They attend school five days a week, mornings and afternoons. Other Italian school children follow a different schedule. They attend school six mornings a week but only on some afternoons.

After primary school, children take written and oral tests before moving on to attend junior secondary school *(la scuola media inferiore)* for three years until they are fourteen.

Then children make choices about their future studies. Some attend a *liceo commerciale* and train for business. A *liceo scientific* trains technicians and engineering students. And a *liceo classico* is a traditional college preparatory course. A graduate of any *liceo* may go on to college. Still others choose to begin teacher training.

After five years, when they are nineteen, students take a demanding national exam, called the *maturita*, in order to get into college. Italy has 59 universities in 36 cities. The University of Bologna, begun in the eleventh century, is the oldest university in Europe.

Immigrants

Between 1850 and 1880 about 120,000 Italians left Italy each year for Europe, the United States, and South America. Between 1887 and 1900, half a million people left Italy each year. An estimated 26 million people emigrated from Italy between 1876 and 1976.

This was not a simple migration, however, because many who left returned. From 1905 to 1976, 8.5 million emigrants returned to Italy. Overall, about 40 percent of the Italians who went to the United States returned to Italy.

By 1910, more than 6 million Italians had settled in the United States. Many moved to neighborhoods where other Italians settled. Some cities have large Italian sections where restaurants, food stores, and shops offer goods that especially appeal to Italians. In 1920, more than half of all emigrants from Italy came to the United States. As late as the 1970s about 22,000 Italians a year still were coming to live permanently in the United States.

Many of the early immigrants were unskilled laborers and came to work in mines and the lumber and steel industries. The vast majority of workers on the Erie Canal were Italians. Italian women often worked sewing machines in clothing factories.

Many of the Italian immigrants moved from farming areas to a city life and took menial, low-paying jobs. Some were barbers, masons, waiters, shoemakers, and shopkeepers. In New York and New Orleans, many were fruit vendors.

In California, some Italians had success as farmers. Giuseppe Di Georgia became the largest fruit-grower in the United States by 1922. Another Italian in 1916 formed the Del Monte brand canned fruit and vegetable company, which was the largest seller of canned produce in the United States.

A. P. Giannini, also a California Italian, founded the Bank of Italy. By the middle 1920s the Bank of Italy had many branches and eventually became the Bank of America, the largest bank in the world.

Although the number of emigrants has sharply declined in recent years, approximately 250,000 Italians continue to visit the United States each year.

Language

Italian is the official language of Italy. It is based on the Florentine dialect. Italian has more Latin words than the other Romance languages such as Spanish and French, and its grammatical system is similar to that used in Latin. Latin remains the language of the Vatican city in Rome.

Each of the twenty regions has its own dialect, and sometimes people from one region are unable to understand people from another region. Dialect may be sprinkled with Spanish, Portuguese, French, or German words. With radio and television common now, standard Italian is becoming more common. Although many Italians speak in a dialect at home, they are likely to speak in standard Italian outside the home.

Other languages are also spoken, particularly around the borders, where German and French are common. People in Sicily speak Sicilian and the Sardinians speak a dialect called Sardo.

There is a strong Italian influence on the language spoken in the United States. Many words relating to music come from the Italian, such as libretto, maestro, piano, and tempo. Military terms such as corporal, colonel, and general also come from the Italian. Many words such as ghetto and fiasco are spelled exactly the same in Italian and English.

The Arts and Sciences

Italians are renowned for masterpieces in architecture, painting, music, literature, and film. One of the first figures to emerge during the Renaissance was Leon Battista Alberti, famed as an architectural designer. The Baroque period was heavily influenced by the architecture and sculptures of Giovanni Lorenzo Bernini and by Francesco Castelli Borromini.

In the area of art, one of the earliest of the great masters was Giotto (di Bondone) from Tuscany, who introduced fresco cycles during the Italian Gothic period. These told the story of a saint or prophet. The most famous is the St. Francis cycle at Basilica di St. Francesco in Assisi.

Among all the great names of the Renaissance, two stand out. Michelangelo Buonarroti is best known for the Sistine Chapel in Rome and for his carved sculptures of *David, Moses,* and the St. Peter's *Pieta.* Leonardo da Vinci is famous for his paintings, *The Last Supper* and the *Mona Lisa,* as well as for many designs and inventions.

A few of the other famous Italian artists include Sandro Botticelli, Fra Filippo Lippi, Titian (Tiziano Vecellio), Raphael (Raffaello Sanzio), Donatello (Donato de Betto di Bardi), Benvenuto Cellini, Piero di Cosimo, and Jacopo Robusti Tintoretto. Currently 50 million visitors a year, many of them art lovers, visit Italy's famous public piazzas, churches, and museums.

Italy is equally famous for its contributions to music. Among Italy's famous composers is Antonio Vivaldi, who composed *The Four Seasons.* Italians composed some of the most famous operas in the world. Gioacchino Rossini is known for such operas as *The Barber of Seville* and *William Tell.* Giuseppe Verdi composed *Il Trovatore, Rigoletto, Aida, Otello,* and *Falstaff.* The works of Giacomo Puccini include *La Boheme, Tosca, Madame Butterfly,* and *Turandot.* Famous singers from Italy include Enrico Caruso and Luciano Pavarotti.

Italian craftsmen are well known for their exceptional violins. Among these craftsmen were the families of Amati, Guarneri, and Stradivari. Niccolo Paganini was the leading violinist of his generation.

One of the great early figures in literature is Dante Alighieri, who wrote *The Divine Comedy.* Other famous names among great medieval writers were Francesco Petrarch, Giovanni Boccaccio, and Machiavelli. Carlo Goldoni is generally regarded as the founder of modern Italian comedy.

Many famous filmmakers with whom American audiences will be familiar are Roberto Rossellini, Federico Fellini, Franco Zeffirelli, and Bernardo Bertolucci.

One of the great Italian scientists was Galileo. Galileo was a mathematician and invented the telescope. He was the first to suggest that the earth was round, and that it was but one of several planets orbiting the sun.

Food

A typical Italian family has a simple breakfast of a roll with milk for children and with coffee for adults. The main meal is usually served at noon. There will probably be a pasta dish, then fish or meat with vegetables, and fruit for dessert. It is likely that wine will be served with dinner and with the evening meal.

Because Italy was not a unified country until rather recently, foods and recipes come from different regions. Each is known for special dishes, techniques, and unusual flavorings. Some recipes require locally grown greens and herbs.

Italy is perhaps most famous for its pasta. More than 500 varieties are eaten there today. These varieties include spaghetti, tagliatelle, ravioli, vermicelli, tortellini, farfalle, ruote, and penne. Pasta is often served with a sauce but may be served with butter or olive oil, garlic, and herbs.

Where lots of fruit is grown, such as high above Lake Como, in a mountainous area dotted with many apple orchards, you find many recipes using apples. This recipe serves 6.

Paradel (Apple Bread Pudding)

5 large slices of stale country-style bread

³/₄ cup milk

5 Golden or Red Delicious apples, peeled and cored

¹/₄ cup sugar

Grated zest of 1 lemon

¹/₃ cup (12) walnuts that have been toasted for ten minutes in 350°F oven and then chopped

1 egg, room temperature

1 teaspoon vanilla extract

1 tablespoon unsalted butter

About 30 minutes before cooking, break up the bread in your hands and put it in a large bowl. Pour the milk over the slices and leave them to soften.

Preheat the oven to 350°F. Butter a deep 9 ¹/₂-inch baking dish, such as a soufflé dish.

Cut the apples into thin slices and add them to the bread in the bowl. Mix in the sugar, lemon zest, and walnuts. Beat the egg and vanilla together in a small bowl and stir them into the apple and bread mixture.

Spread the mixture into the prepared baking dish. Scatter flakes of butter over the top. Bake for 1 hour to 1 hour and 15 minutes until the apple slices are tender and the top is lightly golden and crunchy.

Because most of Italy is surrounded by water, fish is an important part of the Italian diet. Sardines even get their name from Sardinia, which is famous for its fish soup.

In Italy, the word gelato is applied to desserts such as sherbet and ice cream. A gelateria serves many kinds of ice cream using fresh ingredients such as fruit, freshly brewed coffee, along with cream, sugar, and egg yolks. Some of these ice creams have chopped candied fruits and nuts. There are also many coffee bars where cappuccino, espresso, and cafe latte are served.

Recreation

As is the case throughout most of Europe, soccer is the most popular sport in Italy. Children start playing at an early age. There are sixteen first-division soccer teams in Italy that play for the national title. The winners play other European teams. At Olympic Stadium in Rome, a soccer match may draw 100,000 fans.

Although they learned soccer from the British, Italians learned their baseball and basketball from Americans. Both are popular sports and are often coached by Americans.

Italians are fond of many of the same sports found in the United States, such as skiing and tobogganing. Rugby and golf are also very popular. Many visitors to the lakes south of the Alps are windsurfers. Bicycling and car racing are other favorite pastimes. Many car-racing fans watch the Grand Prix at Monza.

Customs and Traditions

Ten national holidays are celebrated in Italy: New Year's Day on January 1; Easter Monday in April; Liberation Day on April 25; Labor Day on May 1; Republic Day on June 2; the Assumption of the Virgin on August 15; All Saints' Day on November 1; the Immaculate Conception, December 8; Christmas on December 25; and St. Stephen's Day on December 26.

Just as in the United States, on a national holiday banks and government buildings close. Many towns also hold a local "feast day" in honor of each town's patron saint. Often a figure of the saint it carried through the streets.

The ten days before Ash Wednesday is *Carnavale* or Carnival. The carnival in Venice is particularly famous. People dress up in fancy clothes, and many masked balls are held. There is a procession of gondolas along the Grand Canal. The Pope's traditional blessing is held in the Vatican on Easter Sunday.

On Easter Sunday in Florence, the *Scoppio del Carro* takes place. A cart containing fireworks is brought to the front of the cathedral. This holiday celebrates a time when knights returned to Florence after the First Crusade.

The *Palio* is held in Siena each year. This is a horse race, which is held on July 2 and August 15. Some people dress up in fifteenth century costumes. There are bareback horse riders.

Christmas celebrations include Midnight Mass on Christmas Eve and the exchanging of presents on Christmas Day as well as on January 6 or Epiphany. A favorite dish on Christmas Eve often features eel. Stuffed turkey or capon are often served on Christmas Day.

Most Christmas trees in Italy will have a nativity scene placed beneath them. The cradle is kept empty until December 25 when the figure of a baby is placed in it to complete the scene.

Tombolo, a game played in many families during the Christmas season, is similar to bingo. Each player has a card with twenty numbered squares on it. A caller picks numbers from a bag and calls the numbers aloud. Using markers, the players cover the called numbers on their cards. The player who is first to cover all squares calls out "Tombolo" and is the winner.

One of Italy's interesting events is Marostica's living chess game. In even-numbered years in September, the main piazza becomes a life-sized chessboard with citizens dressing up to represent the pieces in the game. This recalls a game played in 1454 in which two noblemen, instead of dueling, played chess to determine who won the hand of a young girl.

Suggested Activities

Writing

1. St. Francis of Assisi appears in many books, and visitors to Italy often visit his tomb. In the late 1990s, earthquakes destroyed some of this area. Invite a pair of students, with the help of a media specialist, to locate and read accounts of this series of earthquakes. These students should write a report in which they share with the class information about the damage that was done to this historical spot.

Reading

2. Students who are interested in the history of early peoples in Italy might want to read that part of William Shakespeare's play, *Julius Caesar,* that describes how the friends of Caesar murdered him. A discussion might follow about the possible motives of those involved in the plot.

Vocabulary

3. Create an Italian word/phrase bulletin board. Put a word or phrase in Italian on the bulletin board and cut from magazines a picture to define the word or phrase. Here are some to get you started: *il pane*—bread, *il latte*—milk, *il formaggio*—cheese, *le uova*—eggs, *le frutta*—fruit, *le verdure*—vegetables, *il pollo*—chicken, *il pesce*—fish, *il gelato*—ice cream, *la farmacia*—drugstore, *la macchina*—car, *la musica*—music, and *il libro*—book.

Math

4. The Vatican City is a separate state of about 109 acres. Ask students to convert 109 acres into another measurement. For example, how many square yards would this be?

Social Studies

5. Although Napoleon did not unite Italy, he created the Kingdom of Italy in the northeast with himself as king. Naples was a separate kingdom under Napoleon's brother's rule. Invite a small group of students to study this period of Italian history and using a panel format, have them share orally what they learn with the class.

Geography

6. With the help of a media specialist, find some books that describe the trip that Hannibal and his elephants took across the Alps to invade Rome in 218 B.C. Ask the students to trace his route on a map and describe his journey to the class.

Music

7. The national anthem of Italy is *Fratelli d'Italia*, composed in 1847 by Goffredo Mameli. It did not become the national anthem until 1946. With the help of a music educator, ask a student to find a recording of this anthem and bring it to class for students to hear.

Art

8. A visitor to Italy sees many coats-of-arms. Some of these originated in the Crusades, when they appeared on flags and banners. Bears, eels, doves, and dolphin are frequently pictured. Ask a pair of students to research Italian coats-of-arms, choose one, draw it, and share it with the class, explaining the various symbols used.

Drama/Movement

9. Savonarola provided leadership to the people of Florence at the end of the fifteenth century. He tried to make people better by burning "vanities" such as playing cards, false hair, worldly books, etc. He was tried and hanged in 1498. A group of students might want to study this period of history and hold a mock trial in which they take the part of judges. When they are prepared, ask the group to perform before the class. Some will cite Savonarola's good works and others will condemn him for his severe attitudes.

Dress

10. There have been many famous Italian dress designers, past and present. Ask an interested group of students to research some of these designers and report to the class orally, showing pictures where possible, explaining what they have learned. Possible names for research are Georgio Armani, Valentino, and Giovanni Versace.

Cooking

11. The most basic recipe in Italy is for pasta. Invite students to try this dish at home.

Pasta

1 cup flour
1 egg
water
oil
butter and Parmesan cheese to taste

Place 1 cup of flour in a small bowl. Crack an egg into a cup. Use a half eggshell to measure a half-eggshell of water and a half-eggshell of oil to add to the egg. Mix together. Then add to the flour. Knead. Roll out the dough on a well-floured board. Roll the dough thin. Fold both ends of the dough to the middle. Slice through to make noodles about $1/4$ inch wide. Unfold the noodles and boil them for 2 minutes in salted water. Serve warm with butter and sprinkled Parmesan cheese.

Culminating Activity

12. Students might enjoy preparing an historical pageant of Italy to share with another class or with family and friends. From a list of famous names in Italian history, each student will choose to present a character in the pageant. Simple costumes might be used.

Students would prepare notes on 4 x 6-inch file cards to which they can refer when making their presentations. Each character should give his/her name, dates in history, and the events for which that character is remembered. Among many possibilities for characters are: Julius Caesar, St. Francis of Assisi, Dante, Petrarch, Columbus, Savonarola, Botticelli, Michelangelo, Leonardo da Vinci, Napoleon, Mazzini, Garibaldi, Cavour, King Victor Emmanuel II, and Grazia Deledda.

Suggested Reading

Allen, Derek. *Italy*. Austin, Tex.: Raintree Steck-Vaughn, 1996.

Borlenghi, Patricia and Rachel Wright. *Italy.* New York: Franklin Watts, 1993.

Chrisp, Peter. *The Colosseum.* East Sussex, England: Wayland, 1997.

Field, Carol. *In Nonna's Kitchen: Recipes and Traditions from Italy's Grandmothers.* New York: HarperCollins, 1997.

Galvino, Italo. *Italian Folktales,* selected and retold by Italo Calvino. New York: Harcourt Brace Jovanovich, 1980.

Harris, Nathaniel. *A History of Italy through Art.* East Sussex, England: Wayland, 1995.

Hauser, Ernest O. *Italy: A Cultural Guide.* New York: Atheneum, 1981.

Jarman, T. L. *A Picture History of Italy.* New York: Franklin Watts, 1961.

Kimmel, Eric A. *Count Silvernose: A Story from Italy.* New York: Holiday House, 1996.

Milande, Veronique. *Michelangeo and His Times.* New York: Henry Holt, 1995.

Powell, Jillian. *Italy.* New York: Bookwright Press, 1992.

Sherwood, Rhoda Irene, ed. *Italy: Children of the World.* Milwaukee, Wisc.: Gareth Stevens, 1989.

Stein, R. Conrad. *Italy: Enchantment of the World.* Chicago, Ill.: Childrens Press, 1984.

Unger-Hamilyon, Clive and Irma Kurtz. *The Children's Guide to Rome.* London, England: Blackie & Son, 1984.

Winter, Jane Koben. *Italy: Cultures of the World.* New York: Marshall Cavendish, 1995.

When he sneezed, Inchling flew out. The Oni turned and ran, dropping his magical wooden hammer in his haste.

Japan
A Legend from Japan

There are many versions of this folktale, including one by Hoshiko Uchida, "Isun Boshi, The One-Inch Lad," which is included in *The Dancing Kettle and Other Japanese Folk Tales*. Another, "Little One-Inch," appears in *Japanese Children's Favorite Stories*, edited by Florence Sakade. Others include *Little Fingerling* by Monica Hughes and *Little Inchkin* by Fiona French.

The Inchling

Once long ago on the outskirts of Naniwa, a small village in Japan, there lived an old man and an old woman. The two were very happy except for one thing. They had no children who would grow up to care for them and brighten their old age.

One afternoon they visited the temple and they prayed for a son. As they left the temple and walked home, they heard cries coming from a clump of grass. When they went to investigate, they found a tiny baby boy wrapped in a red blanket. The child was no bigger than the old man's thumb.

"It is a son in answer to our prayers," the old woman said.

The old man and the old woman were delighted. They took the boy to their humble home and named him Issun Boshi, the Inchling. They raised the boy with loving care. He did not grow larger as other children did, but he proved himself to be both brave and wise. He helped his parents in every way that he could.

When the boy was fifteen, he bowed before his parents. "Honored Mother and Honored Father," he said. "I am a man now and I have seen little of the world. I must go out and make my own way. I beg you to allow me to visit the city of Kyoto."

"But why do you wish to go, my son?" his mother asked. "In the city you might be stepped on and killed."

"I must go and make a name for myself so that you will be proud of me," the boy said.

"We are already proud of you and always will be," said his father. "But I know that the time has come for you to go out into the world. You may leave tomorrow."

That night his father made a sword for the boy from a sharp sewing needle and a scabbard of straw. His mother made the boy a handsome new kimono that looked like a tiny jewel in the palm of her hand.

The next morning, Inchling put on his new kimono and strapped his scabbard to his side. He bowed low and bid his parents goodbye. His father gave him a lacquered red rice bowl and a pair of chopsticks. "These will serve as a boat and oars when you reach the river," explained his father.

Holding the bowl over his head to keep off the sun and carrying the chopstick and a square cloth containing rice balls and salted plums under one arm, the boy set off. When he reached the Yodo River, he climbed into his boat.

It took several days and nights before Inchling reached Kyoto. Then he carefully made his way to the very middle of the city. Pausing in front of a grand home, Inchling stared in wonder. He asked a passerby the name of the lord who lived there. Inchling waited on the front step until the lord, dressed in rich robes, came out.

"Oh, lord, I wish to serve you," Inchling called up to the man.

"Who is speaking?" asked the lord. He looked about but could see no one.

"It is Inchling who speaks," cried the boy. "I am down here by your feet. I have traveled a great distance to become your follower."

The great lord looked down and was astonished to see the tiny boy. "Well, well," the great lord said. "You are tiny, but you have a mighty voice." The great lord picked up Inchling and brought him inside where the boy became a respected member of the household.

Everyone grew fond of Inchling, especially the lord's daughter, Haru Hime, Princess of Spring. Inchling became her personal servant.

One day the Princess and her attendants went out to make a pilgrimage to the shrine of Ise. Inchling rode on the princess's shoulder.

After they left the shrine, a huge red monster appeared. This Oni had fearsome teeth and a horn on top of its head. It frightened away all the attendants and looked so fierce that the Princess fainted.

"How dare you frighten the Princess," shouted Inchling. And he drew his sword and began to attack. He climbed up the kimono of the Oni and jabbed him fiercely about the face. The Oni picked up Inchling and said, "You are so small that I'll eat you in one bite." So saying, the monster swallowed Inchling.

Inchling brandished his sword and repeatedly stabbed the Oni's stomach. The pain was so great that the Oni began to scream and dance about. Inchling made his way back up to the Oni's mouth. He stabbed the Oni's tongue and tickled his nose, making the Oni sneeze. When he sneezed, Inchling flew out. The Oni turned and ran, dropping his magical wooden hammer in his haste.

The Princess awoke. She found that all her attendants had fled except for the brave Inchling. "And look what the Oni has left behind," she said. "It is a magic mallet, Uchide-no-kozuchi. With it, you may wish for whatever you like, Inchling."

"All that I ever want is to serve you and your father," Inchling replied. "And perhaps to be a little taller."

The mallet was too heavy for Inchling to lift, but the Princess raised it and struck the ground.

The earth shook and the wind blew. The Princess and Inchling covered their eyes. When they opened them again, Inchling stood before the Princess a tall and handsome warrior.

They went home and the wealthy lord gave permission for Inchling to marry his daughter since he had saved her life.

The Princess and Inchling were wed and were given a beautiful home of their own. They journeyed to Inchling's village, where the old man and the old woman stood amazed as they gazed at their tall and handsome son.

The brave son took his mother and father home with him, where they lived together in happiness all the days of their lives.

Background Information

Off the east coast of Asia are more than 3,000 Japanese islands, stretched in a long narrow chain. The four main islands are Hokkaido, Honshu, Shikoku, and Kyushu. These islands are bounded on the east by the Pacific Ocean and on the west by the Sea of Japan and the East China Sea, on the south by the Philippine Sea, and on the north by La Perouse Strait. The area covers 145,850 square miles.

The island of Kyushu is in the far, southwestern part of Japan. The land in the southern part of this island is a plateau made of volcanic ash and lava. In the center of the island are steep, forested mountains. The northern part is covered in low hills and wide plains. The northern cities today are manufacturing centers.

East of Kyushu is the island of Shikoku. It has a rocky coast with many fishing villages. Inland are ridges and valleys. Tosa Bay is on the southern coast and is bordered by a narrow plain. The northern coastal area is covered in rice fields. There are also industrial cities located in the north.

Going northward you reach Honshu, which is Japan's largest and most important island. There are farms, towns, and cities in the lowlands along the coast. Inland it is more rugged and there are forests on the steeper slopes. Going eastward across Honshu are the highest mountains in Japan, including Mount Fuji. Northeast of Mount Fuji is the Kanto Plain. This large lowland contains rice fields and industrial cities. Farther north is the Sendai Plain. North of Honshu is Japan's second largest island, Hokkaido.

There are plains along the southern and eastern coasts of the island. Forested mountains cover much of the rest of the island. Hokkaido has fewer cities and larger farms than most of the other islands. This island has long and cold winters.

The population of Japan is 125,716,637, with an annual growth of .3 percent. More than 80 percent of Japan is covered in almost uninhabitable mountains, so population centers are dense.

The largest lowland plain is on Honshu's southeast coast, around the capital city of Tokyo. More than 11 million people live in the Tokyo metropolitan area. Nearby in Yokohama, about 3 million people live. Southwest of Tokyo, about 12 million people live on the plain around Osaka.

The area between Tokyo and Osaka contains one-third of Japan's total population.

Japan's climate is temperate, much like the climate on the east coast of the United States. The surrounding oceans bring humidity and rain, but most of Japan is dry in late autumn and winter. An exception is the west coast of Honshu, which gets up to 72 inches of snow.

Because numerous faults run beneath the islands, Japan has frequent earthquakes. In late summer and early fall, typhoons often strike parts of the country.

Waterpower is abundant and is used to produce electric power. Japan's leading mineral resource is coal, but it is poor quality. Most of the coal that is mined is used as fuel in thermal power plants. This coal comes from the islands of Kyushu and Hokkaido.

Japan has only small amounts of oil and so must import most of its oil from Saudi Arabia and Iran. Japan mines only a small amount of the iron ore needed by its factories. Japan buys iron ore from Australia, India, and other countries. Limestone and sulfur are plentiful, but Japan imports most of its tin, bauxite, copper, lead, and zinc.

Japan has large forests but cannot meet its need for wood. It imports two-thirds of the wood that it needs from the United States, Malaysia, Indonesia, and Russia. It also imports wood pulp from Canada and the United States.

Japan is one of the world's leading fishing nations, with modern fishing vessels in the home waters of Japan and in distant fishing grounds. Today, almost all of the cultured pearls in the world come from Japan.

Mount Fujiyama is Japan's highest mountain. It is on the island of Honshu about 62 miles southwest of Tokyo. It is the site of three volcanoes. Mount Fuji is 12,388 feet high, and its crater measures 1,640 feet in diameter.

History

Human skeletons found in Japan have been dated from 8,000 B.C. The earliest inhabitants were probably a group of people called *Ainu*. These Stone Age people had wavy hair and light complexions and a unique language. They lived chiefly by hunting and fishing. Today about 20,000 of this distinct cultural group still survive on the northern island of Hokkaido.

It is believed that during the second and first centuries B.C., other early inhabitants came from northeastern Asia. Some probably came from the Korean peninsula. Others may have come from the South Pacific. Since A.D. 400, there have been no migrations to Japan.

The largest ethnic minority in Japan is Korean. There are 700,000 Koreans in Japan, with roots going back to World War II when Koreans were brought to Japan to replace Japanese workers who were in the armed services.

Japan's first emperors reigned sometime after A.D. 300. The Japanese borrowed heavily from China. They adopted the Chinese writing system sometime in the fifth century. Buddhism was introduced into Japan in 552. Many Japanese went to China to study.

Japan's leaders tried to create a strong central government with power in the hands of the emperor. But in actuality, beginning in the mid-800s, emperors were primarily figureheads. Landowning noblemen held real power.

Provincial leaders set up bands of warriors for protection. Heads of these bands called themselves *shoguns,* or chief commanders. This system was similar to the lords and knights of feudal Europe. *Samurai* warriors served their overlords. For about 700 years, shoguns and their samurai ruled Japan.

In the middle of the 1500s, trade developed with Portugal, Holland, Spain, and England. Jesuit missionaries came, and by the early 1600s had converted 300,000 Japanese to Christianity.

Beginning in 1600, the Shoguns from the House of Tokugawa used Edo (later Tokyo) as their capital, and began a 250-year period of peace and isolation. A council, or *Bakufu,* assisted the Shogun. In 1853, Commander Matthew Perry sailed into Edo Bay with a letter from the President of the United States demanding that Japan open its ports to American ships and trade.

In 1863, there was a samurai rebellion against the Shogun and a collapse of the Shogun-Bakufu system. This period was known as the *Meiji Restoration.* The name *Meiji* means "enlightened rule." The young emperor, Mutsuhito, was mainly a symbol, but during this period, the feudal system was abolished and Japan became industrialized. The judicial process and laws were reformed, an educational system was put in place, and a Bank of Japan was established in 1877.

The Japanese fought a war with China in 1894–1895 and acquired the island of Formosa (Taiwan). Then in 1904, Japan fought Russia and won a number of victories, gaining rights in Manchuria and Korea. In World War I, Japan fought with the Allies and after victory acquired almost all of Germany's island empire in the Pacific. Japan annexed Manchuria in 1931 and entered a full-scale war with China in 1937.

Japan fought against the Allies in World War II and bombed Pearl Harbor, Hawaii, on December 7, 1941. Japan surrendered on September 2, 1945, after the atomic bombing of the cities of Hiroshima and Nagasaki. As a result of its defeat, Japan lost its military conquests and its armed forces were disbanded.

In the years that followed the war, an amazing economic recovery took place in Japan. Japanese products became very common in the United States. This includes Japanese automobiles, cameras, radios, and all kinds of electronic equipment such as televisions, video recorders, and video games.

Government

Under Emperor Mutsuhito (1867–1912), Japan developed an emperor system of government. The emperor had nominal power. The newly formed government was based on Western principles with ministries, a cabinet, a privy council, civil service, and local government. There was a House of Representatives and a House of Peers.

After World War II, General Douglas MacArthur, commander of the occupation forces in Japan, gave the people of Japan a democratic constitution. The new constitution stripped all power from the emperor, who became only a "symbol" of the state. Most duties of the emperor today are merely ceremonial.

The new constitution abolished the House of Peers. Power was placed in the hands of the National Diet, or parliament. One important provision of this 1947 constitution is that there shall be no discrimination in political, economic, or social relations based on sex. The 1947 constitution also gave rights to citizens, including the right of all Japanese to vote if they are twenty years of age or older and the right to bargain through unions and to receive an education.

The Diet consists of an upper House, called the House of Councillors, and a lower House, called the House of Representatives. The House of Councillors has 252 members. Councillors are elected to serve for six years, with half the seats up for election every three years. The 511 members of the House of Representatives are elected for four-year terms.

The House of Representatives elects one of its members to serve as prime minister. The one chosen is usually the leader of the political party with the most members in the Diet. The prime minister selects members of the cabinet. The majority of the cabinet must be chosen from among the members of the Diet.

The prime minister and the cabinet serve as long as they have the support of a majority of the House of Representatives. If they lose this support, they must resign or must dismiss the House of Representatives and call a national election within forty days.

Government leaders, including the prime minister and cabinet members, are active in working with the various political parties over legislation that is going to be presented to the Diet. As a result, almost two-thirds of all bills adopted by the Diet are passed unanimously.

The highest court in Japan is the Supreme Court, made up of 1 chief justice and 14 associate justices. This court, much like the Supreme Court of the United States, decides if laws are in agreement with the constitution.

Japan also has a number of lower courts. Judges are appointed by the cabinet from a list of candidates approved by the Supreme Court. Minor crimes are tried in summary courts while more serious crimes go to district courts.

Japan is divided into forty-seven districts called prefectures. People who live within a district elect a governor and a lawmaking assembly. Cities and towns also have an assembly, whose members are elected by the local citizens.

Japan became an independent nation on April 28, 1952, when a peace treaty signed in 1951 went into effect. Since that time, moderate conservative governments have ruled Japan.

Religion

Japan's oldest religion is *Shinto*. It is a religion founded on nature myths and rituals. In modern Japan, Shinto survives mainly in special ceremonies and annual shrine festivals, where traditional clothes are worn.

Most contemporary Japanese are Buddhists. Buddhism was brought to Japan from China and Korea in the sixth century. Many people consider themselves both Shintoists and Buddhists. One form of Buddhism in Japan is Zen Buddhism. Since World War II, another form of Buddhism, *Soka Gakkai*, has grown in strength.

About 1.5 million Japanese are Christians. Of these, about 60 percent are Protestants and 40 percent are Catholics. Christianity was brought to Japan in 1549. For a time, the Christian religion was banned in Japan, but the ban was lifted, and Christianity grew.

Education

Children attend six-year elementary schools and a three-year junior high school. About 94 percent of the children go on to a three-year high school, and 40 percent of the senior high graduates go on to higher education.

The school year in Japan begins on the first of April. The year is divided into three terms: April to July, September to December, and January to March. School usually begins with a morning ceremony called *chorei*. Announcements are made at this time and students sing a few songs.

In elementary school, students study reading, calligraphy, arithmetic, social studies, science, physical education, art, music, and the Japanese language.

In junior high school, students continue their study of Japanese language, science, mathematics, social studies, music, and art. Most students also learn to read and write some English during these years. Students may also take classes in workshop, agriculture, or homemaking.

In Japanese, each word has its own special mark. Children learn three forms of writing: *hiragana, katakana,* and *kanji*. Kanji characters were developed from ideograms brought to Japan from China. Much of the time in school is spent learning to write these Japanese symbols.

After the age of fifteen, children in Japan are not required to attend school, but approximately 85 percent of them do. In high school, students take Japanese language, social studies, mathematics, science, a foreign language, health, and physical education. Those bound for college take advanced courses. Those not planning on college may choose courses that will train them for careers in manufacturing, business, farming, and nursing.

Literacy in Japan is almost 100 percent. Beginning in first grade, children are given homework. The school day in Japan is longer than that in the United States, and children attend school five and one-half days a week. The extra half-day classes are held on Saturdays twice a month.

Scores on examinations determine entrance to a public university. These are given in February or March of each year.

Approximately 2 million students attend Japanese colleges and universities. They may specialize in such topics as law, medicine, education, engineering, or literature. There are over 400 universities in Japan, of which the highest ranked is Tokyo University. There are also several hundred junior colleges and technical colleges.

Immigrants

Between 1638 and 1868, emigration from Japan was forbidden by the shoguns. Japanese laws prevented people from other countries from entering Japan. In 1854, Japan and the United States signed formal treaties opening up Japanese ports to foreigners for trade. The Japanese government allowed the first group of Japanese to leave Japan and settle in a colony in California.

By the late 1800s, many Japanese men were coming to the United States. Some were students who planned to study in the United States and then return to Japan. Some hoped to get their own land. Others were fleeing high taxes. As of 1900, more than half of all Japanese living abroad lived either in mainland United States or in Hawaii.

Hawaii was a major destination of Japanese emigrants in the 1880s. Many came to work in the sugar industry. From 1885 to 1894, 28,000 Japanese immigrated to Hawaii. In 1899, Hawaiian plantation owners imported 26,000 contract workers from Japan.

Around 1900, there were 85,000 Japanese in the United States and two-thirds of these were in Hawaii. By 1920, there were more than 220,000 Japanese, with half living on the mainland of the United States.

Many of the early immigrants to the United States were successful farmers. Some of these eventually saved enough money to buy their own farms. By 1940, half of the produce on the west coast was sold by Japanese wholesalers.

Other Japanese worked in fisheries and canneries. Many came to Terminal Island near Los Angeles. Others fished off the coasts of California, Oregon, Washington, and Alaska.

Japanese in smaller numbers worked at other jobs. Some mined for gold and silver in Utah or for coal in Colorado. Some worked in lumber mills or helped to build railroads.

Between 1900 and 1920, 20,000 Japanese women came to the United States, mostly to become brides to the Japanese men who were already here. Then the Japanese government refused to let any more women come.

The Japanese living in California right after the beginning of World War II were considered a threat. Some thought they would aid our enemies if Japan attacked the United States. These people were sent to camps in California and in places such as Colorado, Montana, and South Dakota. They were kept in these camps until the war was over. The Japanese in Canada were also sent to internment camps.

After World War II, in 1952, Japanese were allowed to become citizens of the United States. The large amount of fairly recent immigration is the result of the elimination of national origin quotas in 1965.

By the middle of the twentieth century, more than 90 percent of all Japanese living in the Western Hemisphere were in Brazil or the United States. By 1970, there were nearly a half million Japanese in the United States.

Asian Americans are the fastest growing group in the United States today. And Japanese make up a sizable portion of that group. Between 1820 and 1996, 498,333 Japanese immigrated to the United States. It is expected that there will be 10 million Asians in the United States by the year 2000.

Language

Japanese language, even in ancient times, was easy to write phonetically. It had forty-seven syllables. Two systems of syllable writing, both called *kana,* were developed in the ninth century. This system was used for informal purposes and popular literature. Scholars, however, wrote using the complicated Chinese characters.

There are several different forms of spoken Japanese. Three of these forms, or styles, are referred to as the plain, the polite, and the honorific. The speaker chooses the form that is appropriate for the situation and for the people involved. For written language, the Japanese in the fourth century A.D. borrowed the Chinese system of writing. They used Chinese picture words, called *kanji,* to write their own Japanese language.

Japanese continued to use kanji but they also use *kana.* Kana stand for different sounds and are put together to form words. Both kana and kanji are commonly written in columns, from top to bottom on a page, beginning on the right and moving left.

Japanese is considered a difficult language to learn because one needs to remember a large number of kanji, approximately 1,800, just to read the newspaper.

The Arts and Sciences

The earliest culture known in Japan is called *Jomon.* These people, who lived 4,000 years ago, made small figurines and twisted rope decorations on clay pots.

About 1,700 years ago, Japanese emperors were buried in stone chambers covered with mounds of earth. *Haniwa* were set around the mounds to keep the earth from washing away. The haniwa, which were baked in a hot oven, were cylinders with figures modeled on top. Many haniwa were modeled in human and animal forms.

Japanese artists often paint mountains, mists, valleys and rivers. Landscapes are not realistic but have a dreamlike quality. Many Japanese paintings were made on scrolls. After Portuguese travelers reached Japan, Japanese artists were fascinated by their appearance and by their ships. Many of these were depicted in screen paintings. Scrolls were also used to show lives of priests and monks, historical events, and everyday life.

In more recent years, Japanese painters such as Harunobu, Utamaro, and Hiroshige show scenes of ordinary people such as a mother bathing a child or a couple walking in the snow. These artists made wood-block prints. One of the most famous prints, by Hokusai (1760–1849), which belongs to the Metropolitan Museum of Art, shows a gigantic wave with Mount Fuji in the background. Near the end of World War II, the United States dropped atomic bombs on the Japanese cities of Hiroshima and Nagasaki. The devastation of these two events is depicted in the Hiroshima Murals painted by Iri Maruki and Toshi Maruki.

About the year 1000, women began writing about courts in diaries and novels. The first known novel in Japan was *The Tale of Genji,* written by Lady Murasaki, a lady-in-waiting to the Empress.

Natsume Soseki (1867–1916) is acknowledged as the greatest Japanese novelist of the Meiji period. One of his most popular novels, published in 1906, was *Botchan.*

More modern Japanese novelists include: Yukio Mishima, Junichiro Tanizaki, and Yasunari Kawabata. Kawabata was the first Japanese to receive the Nobel Prize for literature.

Millions of Japanese express themselves by writing poetry. Poetry magazines and study groups are popular and there is a national poetry contest. Even the emperor contributes a poem. Haiku, a form of Japanese poetry, is very popular. Some newspapers even carry daily Haiku columns.

Noh drama is popular in Japan. It originated in the 1500s and is highly stylized. The chanting of a chorus is an important part of a Noh play. Noh combines music, dance, and poetry. The players wear masks that express emotion.

Kabuki drama, which is colorful and melodramatic, developed in the late 1600s. It involves elaborate sets and costumes, and the action is often violent. There are dance interludes, and the actors group themselves in symmetrical compositions. Frozen poses are often assumed by actors to emphasize an important point in the plot.

The musicians who provide background music for Kabuki drama play instruments such as flutes, drums, gongs, and the samisen. A samisen has three strings and is shaped something like a banjo. Bunraku also originated in the late 1600s and involves the use of almost life-sized puppets. This is adult theatre with wide-ranging themes. Three operators control each puppet. Storytellers and samisen accompanists join the puppeteers.

The Japanese have interesting instruments, many of which originated in China. *Shakuhachi* are instruments played like flutes. They are made from long bamboo poles and have finger holes. A Japanese *koto,* which is played like a guitar, has 13 silk strings. *Taiko* is an ancient form of drumming using drums and percussion instruments that come in many shapes and sizes.

The folding fan or *sensu* was invented in Japan in the seventh century. Sensu were carried at court and emperors often gave them as gifts. The sensu were decorated with designs, crests, paintings, and even poems.

The ancient gardens around Kyoto are creations of Oriental art. They produce aesthetic pleasure and promote a meditative calm. Contemplation of man's place in the universe is a part of Zen, a Buddhist sect. Zen gardens use stark designs.

Japanese also show their love of nature and a contemplative side in their home gardens. They may landscape a tiny garden to create in miniature mountains, forests, and water. Both men and women also practice flower arranging *(ikebana).*

Ikebana has become popular in the United States and so has Japanese bonsai, the art of growing miniature trees in containers.

The tea ceremony is a traditional art that involves a formal way of serving tea that emphasizes the beauty of the pottery and the grace of the server.

Shodo, also known as calligraphy, is a traditional Japanese art form. Excellent writing is associated with people who have superior inner character. One part of shodo is making your own *sumi,* or ink, by rubbing an ink stick on a stone that has a small pool of water at one end.

There are more than four hundred schools of dance in Japan. In the eighteenth century, there were four famous choreographers: Fujima, Hanayagi, Wakayagi, and Nishikawa. Senzo Nishikawa started the Nishikawa school and it is one of the more popular forms. Dancers wear a cotton robe called a *yukata.* The dancer often holds a fan or paper umbrella.

Japan is a land of song, from old folk songs *(minyo)* to the latest in electronic music. In the 1970s, Japan gave the world *karaoke,* which involves an ordinary person singing along in accompaniment to prerecorded music.

Films made in Japan are ranked among the best in the world and many are distributed to western countries. Some of the most popular, *Rashomon, To Live,* and *Seven Samurai,* were directed by Akira Kurosawa.

Food

The cooking throughout the major islands of Japan emphasizes fresh and natural food. Hokkaido produces high quality dairy products. Many dishes from this island feature Hokkaido salmon. Because of their cold winters, these islanders also enjoy hearty stews and one-pot dishes.

On the main island of Honshu there are many fine international restaurants in Tokyo, Osaka, and Kyoto. Some of these feature a nouvelle Franco-Japanese cuisine.

The island of Kyushu has a style of cooking known as *agemono,* or deep-frying. Pork is very popular. Korean foods, including spicy meat dishes, are popular in the Kyushu area.

With adult help, students may enjoy a dumpling-making party.

Pork and Cabbage Dumplings
Dipping Sauce

1/2 cup soy sauce

1 tablespoon water

2 teaspoons sugar

2 tablespoons rice vinegar

1 minced green onion

1 minced garlic clove

1/2 teaspoon sesame oil

1 teaspoon dry roasted sesame seeds

To prepare the dipping sauce, combine in a small bowl the soy sauce, water, sugar, rice vinegar, minced green onion, minced garlic clove, sesame oil, and dry roasted sesame seeds. Let the sauce stand at room temperature for about 30 minutes. (Makes 3/4 cup.)

Pork & Cabbage Filling

1 cup minced green cabbage

1 teaspoon salt

1 pound ground pork

3 tablespoons soy sauce

1 minced garlic clove

1 teaspoon minced fresh gingerroot

1 minced green onion

1 teaspoon cornstarch

$^1/_4$ teaspoon sesame oil

2 dashes of ground black pepper

$^1/_2$ teaspoon sugar

1 10-ounce package of round gyoza skins
  (about 54 skins)

Cornstarch mixture

In a small bowl, blend 1 tablespoon cornstarch
  and 1 tablespoon water.

Place the minced green cabbage in a small bowl. Sprinkle with salt. Let stand for 1 hour. Rinse cabbage in a strainer and drain well.

In a bowl, combine cabbage with ground pork, soy sauce, minced garlic clove, minced fresh gingerroot, minced green onions, cornstarch, sesame oil, black pepper, and sugar. The mixture will be moist and soft and should be used immediately.

Place one teaspoon of the pork and cabbage filling in the center of each gyoza skin. Fold skins in half, forming semicircles. Seal the edges with the cornstarch mixture.

Place the dumpling on a tray, press bottoms to flatten slightly. Cover with plastic wrap to prevent drying.

In a large skillet, heat 2 tablespoons of oil over medium-high heat. Place half the dumplings in the hot oil and fry for 2 to 3 minutes until golden brown. Add one quarter cup chicken stock to the dumplings. Cover skillet with a tight-fitting lid and steam the dumplings for 2 to 3 minutes. Remove cover and cook until any remaining liquid has evaporated. Fry dumplings a few seconds longer to crisp bottoms. Wipe skillet clean and repeat with the remaining half of the dumplings. Serve with dipping sauce.

Chopsticks are simple eating utensils that have been used for more than 1,000 years in Japan, where they are known as *hashi*. They usually measure about eight inches long except for longer ones used for cooking and serving. Hashi are made out of wood, bone, ivory, gold, and silver.

Rice is the main food in the Japanese diet. Fish is also popular and is eaten raw, fried, broiled, or sun-dried. Vegetables are often cooked in oil for only a minute or two over a very hot fire.

At weddings and tea ceremonies, sweets are often served. These are made from sugar and rice flour and are known as *higashi*. They are molded into shapes such as chrysanthemums and leaves.

Recreation

Almost all of the sports popular in the United States are common in Japan, including baseball, which the Japanese call *basuboru*. Many Japanese professional teams have English names such as Giants and Dragons. There are two professional baseball leagues in Japan, and they hold a Japanese World Series.

Japan has over 1,700 golf courses and it is estimated that over 18 million Japanese are golfers.

The most popular native sport in Japan is sumo wrestling. This sport is probably 2,000 years old and may be associated with Shinto religious rites. The wrestlers wear only loincloths while the referees wear robes similar to those worn by priests. Sumo wrestlers, who may weigh over 300 pounds, are big and strong.

Martial arts are very popular in Japan and many of these have been exported to the United States, where experts teach children and adults. In Japan, students often take lessons on Saturday mornings. In *kendo*, which is like fencing, people dress in skirtlike trousers and wear chest protectors, hip protectors, and a jacket. They also wear a facemask and gloves. They practice hitting with wooden *shinai* (bamboo poles) in specific strokes.

Judo is another traditional martial art. Judo trains the mind as well as the body. Jigoro Kano founded the first judo school in 1882. Students practice throwing one another down on mats.

Customs and Traditions

At one time, parents, who used a go-between, arranged marriages in Japan. Today, many Japanese still follow their parents' guidance in selecting a marriage partner. Japanese couples are usually married in a Shinto ceremony. The bride wears a kimono with a white headdress.

In Japan, the New Year's celebration is called *Shogatsu*. This festival is probably the most important celebration held in Japan. On this night, the family stays up late to welcome the first hours of the New Year. Everyone dresses in kimonos and visits a shrine. Fortunes printed on paper ribbons are given away outside the shrine. After the children read their fortunes, they tie them to a small tree.

An adult catches a spark with a rope from the torch in the shrine. The rope is used at home to light the stove and cook the first meal of the new year. The special spark is to keep sickness away. At midnight a gong is rung. The tolling means that the mistakes of the past are forgiven.

People call on family and friends, and during the visits, presents are exchanged. Offices and schools close. Many houses are decorated. Typical decorations include fern leaves, oranges, or lobsters that represent good luck or good wishes. Small pine trees may be placed near the doorway to symbolize long life.

Although the New Year's holiday officially ends on January 3, more events take place until the middle of the month. On January 6, Tokyo firemen have a tradition of performing acrobatic tricks on the tops of their ladders.

In the northern city of Sapporo, a Snow Festival is held every year on the second Thursday of February. The city's main square is used to house spectacular ice and snow sculptures.

The Doll Festival is held on March 3. Japanese girls dress in kimonos and display their special dolls. These dolls are not played with but are brought out just for the Doll Festival. The girls greet visitors at the door and serve guests rice cakes and candies shaped like fruits. Long ago, this day marked the beginning of spring. People rubbed themselves with paper dolls to be rid of the winter spirits. Then they threw the dolls in the river to be washed away.

The Boy's Festival is held on May 5. It begins with a special bath that is said to wash away any bad luck. Many Japanese homes will display banners shaped like carps that hang from bamboo poles on this day. The carp represents strength and bravery. The boys also display dolls of Japanese heroes and warriors.

On May 17 and 18, the march of the samurai takes place in Nikko. This ceremony commemorates an historical event. When the deceased shogun, Tokugawa Leyasu, was carried to his shrine, there was a procession of the samurai who served in his army.

The Bon Festival, or Feast of Lights, is held in mid-July. At this time of year, Japanese of the Buddhist faith honor their ancestors. Streets and houses glow with lanterns and small fires. It is believed that the spirits of those who have died will visit their relatives during these three days, guided by the lanterns and fires.

In mid-July many people come to Kyoto to celebrate the Gion Festival. Every year, one lucky boy is chosen to be the festival's pageboy. He wears the robe and hat of a priest. The festival is held in memory of an offering made by the emperor that warded off a terrible disease in the city of Kyoto.

Every year in August and September, Shinto priests take part in a fire-walking ceremony. By walking across coals, the priests prove that fire can be controlled.

The Seven-Five-Three Festival is held on November 15. Mothers and fathers bring their children to shrines to give thanks for their having reached the ages of three, five, or seven. They pray for the future health and happiness of these children.

Suggested Activities

Writing

1. There are numerous books on the Japanese poetic form called Haiku. Haiku are three-line poems, usually on a nature topic, which contain five syllables in the first line, seven in the second, and five in the last line.

> *Silver dragonfly*
> *Hovers near the berry bush*
> *Darts swiftly away.*

Share Haiku with students and encourage them to write their own.

Reading

2. Yasunari Kawabata was the first Japanese to receive the Nobel Prize for literature. Many of his books have been translated into English. Invite students to read either *Snow Country* or *A Thousand Cranes*. After students have read the book, let them hold a book discussion.

Vocabulary

3. Throughout the unit of study on Japan, the teacher might encourage students to add to a Japanese word/phrase wall.

   These words and phrases will be found in books and magazine articles that the students are reading about Japan. Here are a few to get you started: *kimono*—a traditional Japanese robe, *kodomo*—children, *obi*—a sash worn with a kimono, *sensi*—teacher, *sushi*—vinegared rice with raw fish, vegetables or omelet, *Tatami*—thick mat made of rice straw, and *Yen*—Japanese money.

Math

4. After reading about Japanese houses, a pair of students may wish to design one to scale and build a model to share with the class. The floors of Japanese houses are covered in thick tatami mats that are three by six feet in size. These mats determine the size of the rooms and the size of the house. Over the rough sub-floor are the tatami mats. Interior walls are sliding panels *(fusuma)*. Exterior wall panels *(shoji)* also slide away to reveal the garden.

Social Studies

5. A pair of students might want to research and prepare for the class a chart showing a list of the Japanese emperors and when they were in power. One place to seek out this information is at http://www.japan-guide.com/e/e2135/.html.

Geography

6. The rise of the Japanese to successful industrialization after World War II has been called a "miracle." Japan was not the only country to experience this rapid industrial growth. Those countries bordering the Western Pacific are called the Pacific Rim countries. Make a map of this area to display in the classroom. Among the Western Pacific Rim countries, students should show Japan, South Korea, Taiwan, Singapore, Hong Kong, Malaysia, and parts of China.

Music

7. Students might enjoy listening to the music of Osamii Kitajima, a Japanese artist who combines electronic sounds with ancient music. Your school music educator might assist in locating his CDs. Possible titles include *The Source* (Sony/USA), *Beyond the Circle* (Cyber Octave/USA), and *Sweet Chaos* (Mesa/Bluemoon/USA).

Art

8. In Japan, gift wrapping, *tsutsumi,* is very important. Making the box and lid or package, choosing the paper, adding the decorations are all part of the aesthetic.

   The art specialist might be involved in helping students, step by step, to create a gift box that they could use for a present to be given on a special occasion.

   Several books are available for reference, including *Gift Wrapping: Creative Ideas from Japan* by Kunio Ekiguchi.

Drama/Movement

9. Invite one group of students to investigate *Noh* drama and another to learn what they can about *Kabuki* theatre. Both groups should report to the class what they learn and photocopy (with permission) or bring in books with pictures to show scenes from Japanese drama.

Dress

10. Samurai warriors are known for their armor. But the underpinnings of their costume are also interesting. Invite a pair of students to find pictures of samurai warriors, and with permission, to photocopy and share these with the class. One source that shows the stages of dress of a samurai warrior is pages 65 to 73 in *Early Japan* by Jonathan Norton Leonard.

Cooking

11. A Japanese tea ceremony, *cha-no-yu*, would prove interesting to students. Check to see if a Japanese member of the community would be willing to visit a classroom and demonstrate and explain the tea ceremony. The guest might perform this tea ceremony for another special guest or for one of the students in the class while the other students watch.

    The rituals of the tea ceremony are complex and each movement has special meaning.

Culminating Activity

12. A culminating activity would be to hold a Spring Festival. Students could show parents reports and projects completed during their unit of study. The room might be decorated with origami paper flowers. A bulletin board may display original Haiku poetry. Snacks such as *onigiri* might be served. (A recipe may be found in Susan McKay's *Japan*.)

Suggested Reading

Bornoff, Nick. *Country Insights: Japan.* Austin, Tex.: Raintree Steck-Vaughn, 1997.

Dower, John W. and John Junkerman, eds. *The Hiroshima Murals: The Art of Iri Maruki and Toshi Maruki.* Tokyo, Japan: Kodansha, 1985.

Ekiguchi, Kunio. *Gift Wrapping: Creative Ideas from Japan.* New York: Kodansha, 1985.

French, Fiona. *Little Inchkin.* New York: Dial Books, 1994.

Glubok, Shirley. *The Art of Japan.* New York: Macmillan, 1970.

Heinrichs, Ann. *Japan.* Danbury, Conn.: Childrens Press, 1997.

Hughes, Monica. *Little Fingerling: A Japanese Folktale.* Nashville, Tenn.: Ideals Childrens Books, 1989.

Ishii, Momoko. *Issun Boshi, The Inchling.* New York: Walker, 1965.

Ishimoto, Kiyoko and Tatsuo. *The Japanese House . . . Its Interior and Exterior.* New York: Bonanza Books, 1963.

Kuklin, Susan. *Kodomo, Children of Japan.* New York: G. P. Putnam's Sons, 1995.

Lee, Joann Faung Jean. *Asian Americans.* New York: New Press, 1992.

Leonard, Jonathan Norton. *Early Japan.* New York: Time-Life Books, 1968.

McKay, Susan. *Festivals of the World: Japan.* Milwaukee, Wisc.: Gareth Stevens, 1997.

Meyer, Carolyn. *A Voice from Japan: An Outsider Looks In.* San Diego, Calif.: Harcourt Brace Jovanovich, 1988.

Midorikawa, Yoichi (photography) and Margoichi Kushida (text). *These Splendored Isles.* New York: Walker/Weatherhill, 1970.

Nardo, Don. *Modern Japan.* San Diego, Calif.: Lucent Books, 1995.

Pitts, Forrest R. *Japan.* Grand Rapids, Mich.: Fideler, 1981.

Ross, Stewart. *Causes and Consequences of the Rise of Japan and the Pacific Rim.* London, England: Evans Brothers, 1995.

Rutherford, Scott, Executive Editor. *Tokyo, Insight Guides.* New York: Houghton Mifflin, 1996.

Sakade, Florence. *Japanese Children's Favorite Stories.* Rutland, Vt.: Charles E. Tuttle, 1958.

Schemenauer, Elam. *Japan.* Plymouth, Minn.: The Child's World, 1998.

Slack, Susan Fuller. *Japanese Cooking.* Tucson, Ariz.: HP Books, 1985.

Time-Life Books Editors. *Japan.* Alexandria, Va.: Time-Life Books, 1985.

Uchida, Yoshiko. *The Dancing Kettle and Other Japanese Folk Tales.* New York: Harcourt, Brace & World, 1949.

Westridge Young Writers Workshop. *Kids Explore America's Japanese American Heritage.* Santa Fe, N.Mex.: John Muir, 1994.

Mexico

A Legend from Mexico

The story of a little cuckoo who braved a fire to save seeds for the next season has been told in several versions. One is found in the book, *Cuckoo*, by Lois Ehlert, and another is "The Cuckoo's Reward" in Genevieve Barlow's *Latin American Tales: From the Pampas to the Pyramids of Mexico*.

The Brave Cuckoo

One of the wisest gods to rule over the Yucatan in southern Mexico was Chaac, God of the Field and Crops. Late one afternoon Chaac called all the birds to meet with him. When the twittering, cooing, and hooting died down, he spoke.

"Early tomorrow morning, I need your help," Chaac told the birds. "Sometime tomorrow, the Fire God will burn the stubble from the old fields, and . . ."

Before Chaac could continue, there was a great disturbance. One bird had arrived late to the meeting. It was the beautifully plumed Cuckoo. She looked like a rainbow and she kept blinking her bright yellow eyes as she called out to each bird, "What are we to do? I didn't hear, and I've forgotten since last year."

Owl spoke up. "You cannot remember what to do, silly bird, because you did not even remember to come and help last year."

The cuckoo, feeling ashamed, fell silent.

Chaac continued, "Before the Fire God comes, I need each of you to gather your favorite seeds, as well as many seeds of corn, and pile them near the woods, so that when it is time, there will be seeds for planting to give us crops in the new year." Smiling at the cuckoo, Chaac said, "I am sure that you all will remember to help this year. Now rest, for tomorrow morning early you will have much to do."

All the birds nestled down for the night. Even Owl took a nap since he would be up early. But the cuckoo could not sleep. She was afraid she would fail to wake in time to help.

Suddenly, in the dark of night, the cuckoo saw flames flickering across the fields. The Fire God had decided to come under cover of darkness and trick them. He would burn all the seeds before the birds saved any for the new crop.

Where was Chaac? Busy somewhere else? There was no time to waste. The cuckoo flew straight to work.

It was more than an hour later that Owl woke to the smell of smoke. Quickly he hooted and awoke all the other birds. The birds and Chaac hurried to the fields, but it was too late. Fire covered the land.

As they perched at the edge of the forest and watched, the birds saw something gray flitting across the sky.

"It must be a heavenly bird," Chaac said, "for no ordinary bird would dare to fly through that fire and heat."

As they watched, the gray bird flew out of the smoke and landed in a small pool nearby where it cooled

"Before the Fire God comes, I need each of you to gather
your favorite seeds."

itself. The birds crowded about. "It's the cuckoo!" cried Owl. "Her lovely bright feathers have turned gray in the smoke, and her bright yellow eyes are all red."

"Do not worry," called the cuckoo. "I was able to save seeds for the new crop." She flew to a great heap of seeds and corn that she had piled near the edge of the pool.

"Dear, brave cuckoo," said Chaac, "you have saved enough seeds so that we will all have food. And you deserve a reward."

Owl spoke. "As a token of our gratitude, we birds promise that we will care for your children and your children's children forever and ever."

And that is how the cuckoo came to have gray feathers and flaming red eyes and why to this day she lays her eggs in the nests of other birds who will care for them.

Background Information

Mexico is in southern North America and covers an area of 756,066 square miles. It is bounded on the north by the United States, on the south by Guatemala and Belize, on the east by the Gulf of Mexico and the Caribbean Sea, and on the west by the Gulf of California and the Pacific Ocean.

Mexico has a population of 97,563,374. About 30 percent of the population is pure Indian. Of the remaining, the majority are *mestizo*, a combination of Indian and Spanish. Mexico's capital is Mexico City, which has a mean temperature of 57°F in January and 63°F in July. Approximately one-fifth of all Mexicans live within the city's metropolitan area.

Only about 9 percent of Mexico's land is under cultivation. The northern part of the Central Plateau that extends from the border of the United States to San Luis Potosi is too dry to farm without irrigation.

The southern part of the Central Plateau, which is higher and gets more rain, is more productive. This area extends from San Luis Potosi to Guadalajara on the west and south to Mexico City. This is the richest and most populous part of the country. It contains about half of Mexico's total population.

The most developed region is the Valley of Mexico where Mexico City is located. This valley is about 50 miles long and 40 miles wide with moderate rainfall and sunny weather year-round.

On the east, west, and south, the Central Plateau is bordered by mountain ranges. The eastern mountains are the Sierra Madre Oriental, and the western mountains are the Sierra Madre Occidental. South of Mexico City, these two ranges come together in a volcanic zone that still contains active volcanoes. In this area is Pico de Orizaba, which at 18,700 feet is the third highest mountain in North America.

Coastal plains on the east and west, desert on the northwest, and jungles to the south, rim the Central Plateau and mountains. In the eastern Gulf coastal plain, the busiest city is Veracruz, a major port city for products from the Central Plateau. The state of Veracruz also has substantial oil fields.

The western coastal plain is narrow. The Sonoran desert is in the northwestern corner, and in the extreme west, the Gulf of California separates the long finger-like Baja California from the mainland. Few people live in the mostly barren and mountainous Baja California.

In the southern section of the western coastal plain, the hot climate and high rainfall support the production of sugarcane, bananas, and coconuts. Fish are abundant here. In Tabasco state there is oil. The main city in this area is Villahermosa.

The Yucatan Peninsula is not well suited for farming, although a plant called henequen is grown here, and sisal fibers from this plant are basic to the economy. This area is famous for the Maya-Toltec ruins at Chichen Itza.

Quintana Roo is covered in tropical rain forests. Off the coast are the islands of Cozumel and Mujeres, favorite tourist attractions.

All of Mexico is either tropical or subtropical and would be universally hot were it not for its mountains. Where there is enough rainfall, heat-loving plants such as bananas, coffee, tobacco, sisal, and sugarcane are grown. At higher elevations, farmers grow maguey, wheat, beans, and corn. About a quarter of the population is engaged in agriculture.

In the distant past, Spaniards came to Mexico seeking gold and silver. But by far the most valuable mineral resource today is petroleum. Mexico is one of the world's major oil-producing countries. In addition to petroleum and natural gas, Mexico has considerable deposits of iron ore, coal, zinc, copper, and lead. Mexico continues to be one of the world's chief producers of silver, accounting for 20 percent of world silver production.

Tourism is an extremely important business. Tourists from the United States and from all over the world vacation at resorts and also buy folk art and handicrafts.

Major cities of Mexico include Mexico City, the oldest city in the Americas and one of the largest cities in the world, with a population of more than 20 million people in the greater metropolitan area. It is built on the Aztec ruins of Tenochtitlán. Earthquakes sometimes hit the city. The one in 1985 caused much damage and loss of life. The National Palace and many government buildings are in the old Spanish section of the city called Zocalo. Just outside the city limits is the campus of the University of Mexico.

Mexican people often say "La Republica" when referring to the country of Mexico and say "Mexico" when they refer to Mexico City. The city is filled with street vendors. There are also mimes, clowns, jugglers, and magicians crowding the busy streets.

Mexico City has many parks and squares. The most famous of these is Chapultepec, which is a 1,000-acre reserve. One million people may gather in this park on a Sunday where there is a zoo, a miniature railway, three boating lakes, and a botanical garden. The park also contains the National Museum of Anthropology.

Guadalajara is the second largest city in Mexico and is northwest of Mexico City. Its industries include producing leather goods, glass, pottery, and tequila.

Monterey is the third largest city and is located in northern Mexico. It is a center for steel and iron and has many textile plants, breweries, and flour mills.

The two leading port cities of Mexico are Tampico and Veracruz, both located on the Gulf Coast.

History

Mexico is the only nation in North America with a history that dates back earlier than Columbus. Scholars believe that Indians migrated from Asia across the Bering Straight thousands of years ago and spread southward into North and South America. In Mexico about 5,000 B.C., they began cultivating food plants.

Before 1,000 B.C., pottery, tools, and irrigation had come into wide use. One the ancient peoples of this time were the *Olmecs,* thought to be the first major civilization in Mexico. They knew how to process rubber and fibers, including cotton. Carvings from this era have been found in the states of Veracruz and Tabasco.

Between 650 B.C. and A.D. 150, the Valley of Mexico became thickly populated. The period A.D. 150 to 900 is known as Mexico's Golden Age. The most famous civilization of this period was Mayan and included splendid architecture, astronomy, hieroglyphic writing, an accurate calendar, and sculpture. Gradually temple cities were abandoned. Toltecs, warriors from the north, moved in around A.D. 900. One of their major deities was Quetzalcoatl, the Plumed Serpent. By A.D. 1000, the Toltecs had extended their power southward to the Mayan center in Yucatan. By 1500, there had been many wars, which weakened the Toltecs and tore the Yucatan society apart.

The last groups to arrive in the Mexican highlands were the Aztecs, who came to the spot that is now Mexico City in 1325. In an island on Lake Texcoco, the Aztecs built the great city of Tenochtitlán. They ruled an area as far north as San Luis Potosí and southward to Mayan territory.

In 1519, Hernan Cortez landed on the coast of Mexico with 11 ships and over 500 men. Thinking they may have represented a god, Quetzalcoatl, Montezuma sent them presents of gold and silver. Cortez went to Tenochtitlán and took the King hostage. When Cortez left to fight off an expedition he had heard was coming from Cuba, Pedro de Alvarado was left in command.

The Aztecs rebelled and killed Montezuma. When Cortez returned, most of his men were killed, but Cortez escaped. Smallpox struck and killed many of the Aztecs, including their new chief. Cortez recruited other Indians and put himself back in power. He named the country New Spain.

During the three centuries that followed, Spanish viceroys ruled Mexico. These Spaniards introduced the wheel, sugarcane, and domesticated animals such as the horse, ox, donkey, and mule. The Spanish settled about 100 towns in Mexico and expanded into what is now California.

After the successful American Revolution and French Revolution, some people in Mexico, such as Father Miguel Hidalgo, began discussing Mexican independence. There was a call for revolution on September 16, 1910. This turned out to be far from the "peaceful revolution" that had been hoped for. There were many battles. Father Hidalgo was beheaded.

Between 1821 and 1876 civil war was nearly continuous in Mexico. Forty different presidents were briefly in power. Santa Anna overturned the government in 1823, and declared Mexico a "republic."

Texas declared its independence from Mexico in 1836. In 1846 when the United States annexed Texas, war broke out and the United States invaded Mexico. The United States won easily. What had been the northern part of Mexico now belonged to the United States. Eventually it became the states of Texas, New Mexico, Arizona, California, Colorado, Nevada, Utah, and Wyoming. Spain had claimed this territory earlier, and when Mexico declared its independence under the leadership of Agustin De Iturbide in 1821, Iturbide had claimed the land from Spain.

Santa Anna was exiled, and Benito Juarez became president of Mexico in 1861. The country was bankrupt and owed money to France. So Napoleon III of France invaded and took over Mexico from 1862 to 1864. Even today, Mexican law is based on the French system. Napoleon gave the crown to Archduke Maximilian of Austria. When Napoleon withdrew his troops in 1867, Maximilian was executed, and Juarez took over again as president.

In 1876 Porfirio Diaz took power and ruled as a dictator for 30 years. The people were worse off than ever and started a revolution in 1910 that lasted until 1920. They established a Constitution in 1917 that is still in force.

Government

Mexico's government is a federal republic, combining elements of democracy with elements of a dictatorship. The 1917 constitution divided the government into three branches: executive, legislative, and judicial. It also established the state governments.

The president is elected to a term of six years by popular vote and cannot succeed himself. He appoints a cabinet and also appoints a successor from the same party to run in the next election. This successor must be Mexican-born of Mexican parents, male, at least thirty-five years old, and may not be a member of the clergy. Because congress has no veto power, the president of the country virtually rules single-handedly.

The 128-member Senate and the 500-member Chamber of Deputies are elected by popular vote. The voting age is eighteen, and women secured the right to vote in 1955. A Supreme Court heads the judicial branch, with justices appointed for life. These justices in turn appoint district and circuit court justices. There are 21 circuit courts and 68 district courts.

A second level of government is that of the states. Mexico is a federation of 31 states and one federal district. Each is administered by an elected governor and has its own government and local laws for education, police, and taxes. The governor is elected every six years.

Religion

More than 90 percent of the population of Mexico is Roman Catholic. But there is a strong influence in the church of Indian beliefs and customs. Saints of the Catholic Church are venerated in rites that resemble ancient Indian religious rites.

Saints are a central part of Mexican life. Towns have patron saints and the calendar contains feast days for the saints. On his feast day, a statue of the saint is carried through the town. There is a parade and there may be bands and fireworks.

December 12 is an important Catholic holiday. On the "Day of our Lady of Guadalupe," over 6 million Catholics travel to her shrine, La Villa, in Mexico City. This day celebrates the vision of a native Mexican who believed that

Mary appeared and spoke to him. There are flags, bands, parades, and fireworks for this holiday that lasts all day and into the night.

The Mexican constitution guarantees freedom of religion, so although most people are Catholic, there are small communities of Protestants and Jews. There is also a group of Mennonites from Europe who came to Mexico over 100 years ago seeking religious freedom.

Education

Before the Revolution of 1910, 80 percent of the Mexican people could not read or write. Illiteracy is now down to 13 percent and the rate is still falling. The shortage of schools in Mexico was addressed through prefabricated schools that villagers could erect under the guidance of a federal engineer. But there are many areas where improvement is needed. The average class has one teacher for forty-five students, and many of the students double up at desks and share textbooks.

Free and compulsory education came with the constitution in 1917. By law, children are supposed to attend school until they are fifteen years old. The National Commission for Free Distribution of Books supplies free textbooks to all elementary schools.

Some parents pay to have their children attend preschool. The primary school education *(primaria)* lasts six years. Most children begin their school day at 8:00 A.M. and stay until 2:00 P.M. They usually have a mid-morning snack and then a late lunch.

Although almost all very young children do go to school, it is estimated that attendance of older children is only about 44 percent. High school *(secundaria)* is another three years. Some students go to *preparatoria* (college preparatory school) next. This lasts for four more years.

One out of three Mexicans is under fifteen years old. Because it is hard to support large families, some young people quit school to help their parents. Other children are on their own at an early age. It is estimated that 1.5 million Mexican children live on city streets. Their "families" are gangs or other street youth. These children do not attend school.

Mexico has more than 300 professional schools, including universities, teacher-training colleges, and technical schools. The National Autonomous University of Mexico was founded in 1551 and is the oldest university in North America.

Immigrants

Many Mexicans who lived in upper Mexico in 1848 automatically became citizens of the United States when the United States took that territory after the Mexican War as part of the Treaty of Guadalupe Hidalgo. These people are sometimes referred to as "immigrants who never left home." Some learned to speak English, but many retained their Spanish language.

Because the United States and Mexico share a border, there is much easy traveling back and forth between the two countries. This has increased immigration as relatives living in the United States encourage friends and relatives to join them and to achieve a higher standard of living.

In 1942, needing more farm laborers because many U.S. citizens were in the armed services, the U.S. government began a *bracero* program. Mexican citizens were given free transportation into the United States and guaranteed minimum wages and support to harvest farm products. They often lived in substandard housing and were paid less than Mexican Americans.

The bracero program was suspended after World War II, but in 1951 it was reinstated until it was finally terminated at the end of 1964. Almost 5 million Mexicans entered the United States under this program, and with the help of their employers, some stayed and achieved resident status.

Each year thousands of Mexicans apply to legally immigrate to the United States, where they hope to find work and to have a better standard of living. According to the U.S. Immigration and Naturalization Service, during the period 1981–1989, 975,657 people legally entered the United States from Mexico.

Since only a small number of those who apply are accepted, many illegal immigrants slip across the border each year. For example, from October 1, 1989, to September 30, 1990, more than 1 million people were apprehended trying to cross the border from Mexico. Most of these were men.

Once inside the United States, they try to find jobs, and if they succeed, many send much of their pay back to Mexico to support their families.

Between 1981 and 1990, 1,653,300 Mexicans immigrated to the United States. During 1991 to 1995, another 1,487,800 came.

Language

Spanish is the national language of Mexico, although more than fifty Indian languages are still spoken. Among these Indian languages are Mayan, Mixtec, Otomi, Tarascan, Zapotec, and Nahuatl, the tongue of the Aztecs. About 1 million of the Indians know only their Indian language and speak no Spanish.

Many Spanish words and place names are common in the United States, especially in the Southwest and West. Cities such as Santa Rosa and San Antonio, mountains such as the Sierra Nevadas, and rivers such as the Rio Grande have names that are traced back to Spanish explorers and to Mexican American settlers.

Many words in English came from the native Nahuatl language. Words such as coyote, tomato, and chocolate have Aztec roots.

The Arts and Sciences

One of the special contributions of Mexican artists are magnificent murals. Hundreds of years ago, the Maya painted murals. Mural painting flourished right after the Revolution of 1910. Three of the major art figures are Diego Rivera, Jose Clemente Orozco, and David Alfaro Siqueiros. Later painters of note include Rufino Tamayo, Juan Soriano, and Jose Luis Cuevas.

Traditional Mexican music is played in villages throughout Mexico. Musicians play on xylophone-like instruments called marimbas. Nortenos music sounds like country-western music. There are usually three players, a guitarist, an accordion player, and a singer who may also play on a piece of wood with drumsticks.

Mariachi bands are groups of six to eight musicians. They may play at weddings and celebrations. They also often play in plazas, restaurants, and taverns. Often they wear uniforms that include wide-brimmed hats. A mariachi band typically has a singer, two violinists, two guitarists, two horn players, and a bass player.

Maria Grever is a popular songwriter. Distinguished leaders in Mexican folk music include composer Carlos Chavez and dancer Amalia Hernandez. Hernandez formed the Ballet Folklorico in 1952. Folklorico has three troupes of dancers; two tour the world while the third performs at the Palace of Fine Arts in Mexico City. Many of their ballets are based on stories of the early gods and emperors of Mexico.

There are eight major symphony orchestras in Mexico. Carlos Chavez is the most famous classical composer. In 1917, he wrote his first symphony at the age of eighteen. He worked as a conductor and teacher and is responsible for the creation of the National Opera of Mexico.

Delving into the philosophy of Mexican life and culture are writers Samuel Ramos and the late Octavio Paz. Greats in the field of literature include: Alfonso Reyes, Mariano Azuela, Agustin Yanez, Juan Jose Arreola, Juan Rulfo, Sergio Galindo, Gustavo Sainz, and Carlos Fuentes.

One of Mexico's earliest poets was Sister Juana Ines de la Cruz, a seventeenth-century nun. Four modern poets of note are Jose Gorostiza, Carlos Pellicer, Octavio Paz, and Xavier Villaurrutia. Two modern playwrights of distinction are Emilio Caballido and Sergio Magana. Nobel prize-winning author Gabriel Garcia Marquez also lives in Mexico.

Folk art has been popular in Mexico from the time of ancient civilizations. The silversmiths of Taxco are famous for their jewelry. The craftsworkers of Talavera are renowned for their terracotta pottery. Beautiful hand-blown glassware comes from Jalisco. Villages in the Oxacan Valley specialize in painting wooden carvings of people and animals.

Food

Mexican cooking dates back to the Indians, who had developed a varied diet before the Spanish conquerors arrived in the sixteenth century. Maize is the most important food, from which Mexicans make tortillas, which are flat, cornmeal pancakes. Among their vegetables are squash, sweet potatoes, peppers, beans, chile, and tomatoes. Fish and shellfish, particularly along the coast, are an important part of the diet as are a variety of tropical fruits in the warm coastal regions.

To the basic Indian foods were added the dishes that the Spaniards brought, which included such additions as beef, cheese, and onions.

Favorite Mexican food today includes tacos and enchiladas, consisting of meat, chicken, or cheese rolled in tortillas. Tamales are another popular dish. These are corn dumplings filled with meat and steamed in cornhusks. Another famous dish is mole, which blends turkey or chicken with spices, nuts, and a spice of bitter chocolate.

In modern Mexico, people continue to eat beans almost daily. *Frijoles de olla*, black beans or pinto beans that are cooked for hours in a big clay pot, are often served after the main course and before dessert. *Frijoles refritos*, or refried beans, have a mixed European and American ancestry. The American pinto beans are mashed and cooked with lard.

Even the brief mention above shows the influence of Mexico on the diet of many people in the United States. Not only are these Mexican dishes prepared in many homes in the United States, they are also available in restaurants and many fast food outlets.

For a quick appetizer, try the following.

Nachos Ole

1 ¹/₂ cups canned refried beans

Packaged corn tortilla chips

1 ¹/₂ cups shredded Monterey Jack cheese

1 ¹/₂ cups shredded Cheddar cheese

I large tomato

¹/₂ cup thinly sliced pickled jalapeno chilies

Heat the refried beans in a double boiler. Preheat the oven to 400°F. Blend the shredded Monterey Jack and Cheddar cheese in a small bowl. Chop the tomato. Spread 1 teaspoon of beans onto a tortilla chip. Arrange the chips close together in single layers on two large baking sheets. Sprinkle the chips with tomato, chilies, and the cheese mixture. Bake about 5 minutes until the cheese is bubbly and melted.

Recreation

Many of the games and sports played in Mexico are similar to those played in the United States, including swimming, fishing, and jogging. Young children play a game much like hopscotch called *el avian*.

Futbol, which is called soccer in the United States, is the most popular sport in Mexico. There are dozens of teams in the professional soccer league. Every four years, the most important soccer championship in the world, The World Cup Games, takes place. When a Mexican team is in the championship, everyone watches and listens on their television and radio sets. Big local games are held in Azteca Stadium in Mexico City and are attended by 100,000 people.

Beisball (baseball) is almost as popular as soccer. It was introduced into Mexico from the United States. Some players who start in Mexico later join major league ball clubs and play in the United States.

The Spaniards introduced *jai alai*, a handball-like game, into Mexico long ago from the Basque region. Two or four people can play it. Players catch a small, hard rubber ball in a wicker basket called a *cesta*. The cesta is strapped to the player's arm. The fast-moving game is played on a walled court called a *fronton*.

Men participate in a national sport called *charreria*, which is similar to an American rodeo. There are a series of events such as guiding a horse through difficult maneuvers, riding bucking broncos, bull riding, and lassoing.

Perhaps the most unusual spectator sport in Mexico is bullfighting, which was introduced into Mexico in the sixteenth century by the Spanish. Bullfighters are called matadors. There are over 220 bullrings in Mexico, the largest of which is the Plaza de Mexico Bullring, located in Mexico City. Bullfighting takes place from November to April.

Customs and Traditions

Children in Mexico celebrate the Day of Saint Anthony the Abbot on January 17. It honors the saint who loved children and animals. Young people wash and brush their pets and may even dress them in decorated hats or collars and parade them through the streets to the churchyard. The parish priest blesses the animals one by one.

Much like in the United States, Mexican children celebrate Easter with chocolate bunnies and decorated eggs. On the Saturday before Easter, it is popular to make a life-sized doll of Judas, who betrayed Jesus, and to hold a "Burning of Judas" celebration.

Just as we celebrate our Independence Day on the Fourth of July, Mexicans celebrate with a fiesta the date of Mexico's independence from Spain on September 16. There are elaborate fireworks.

On October 12 each year, many people celebrate the Day of the Race. It is a celebration of the mixture of peoples, races, and cultures that make up Mexico today: Native Mexicans; Mestizos who have mixed Native and Spanish ancestry; Mulattos who have a mixed Native and Black ancestry; and Criollos, the tiny part of the population of Europeans, Americans, and Canadians who live in Mexico. All celebrate together.

The Day of the Dead *(El Dia de Los Muertos)* is really a three-day fiesta beginning on October 31. Bakers bake the traditional *pan de muertos* and farmers harvest marigolds, the flowers of the dead. Part of the celebration is like a carnival, with children dressed up in ghoulish costumes begging for treats, and is very similar to our Halloween.

But this is also a time for families to reunite and remember those who have died. The first night, an offering of special foods is placed on a table with flowers and is made to the souls of the departed children. On the second night, a similar offering is made for souls of departed adults. Photographs of dead relatives are placed on the altar. For the next twenty-four hours, church bells toll continuously. Relatives come and there is feasting.

On November 2, All Souls Day, family members go to visit graves. They clear away weeds and bring flowers. They pray and sing by candlelight. The children dressed as ghosts and ghouls run through the streets holding out boxes or bowls for candy and coins.

In Mexico, Las Posadas is celebrated during the nine days before Christmas. Every night there is a fiesta. First there is a parade. The figure of Maria is carried in front of the parade for the first eight nights. She is followed by children dressed as angels. People carry colored lanterns. At the end of the parade, there is a party. Often a *piñata* is hung

filled with candy and little toys for the children. On Christmas Eve, the person who leads the parade carries the figure of the baby Jesus.

Most Mexican children do not receive presents on Christmas Day. Gift giving occurs on January 6, the day on which they celebrate the arrival of the Three Wise Men at the birthplace of Jesus. Many families eat a circular cake on this day called the Ring of the Wise Men. A little doll is included in the dough and is a surprise for the person who finds it.

Suggested Activities

Writing

1. *La Ruta Maya* (The Mayan Route) is the name of an ambitious project planned in the late 1990s by the governments of Mexico, Belize, Guatemala, El Salvador, and Honduras. The aim is to build a road connecting several large protected wildlife areas. Some logging companies appear to want to block the protection of this land and want to stop the project. Invite a group of students to investigate this topic and to write a short paper on what they learn. They should include a bibliography of sources of information.

Reading

2. Make available multiple copies of fiction books in which the story is set in Mexico. Allow students to choose a story, read it, and discuss it with others who chose that title. Here are some possibilities: Beatriz Eugenia De La Garza, *Pillars of Gold and Silver* (Piñata Books, 1997); P. J. Stray, *Secrets in the Mayan Ruins* (Silver Burdett Press, 1995); Marc Talbert, *Heart of a Jaguar* (Simon & Schuster, 1995); Jose Maria Merino, *Beyond the Ancient Cities* (Farrar, Straus & Giroux, 1994); and Charmayne McGee, *So Sings the Blue Deer* (Atheneum, 1994).

Vocabulary

3. During their study of Mexico, students may want to list and define as many Spanish words as they can find on 3 x 5-inch cards and post these on a bulletin board. Here are a few: *naranjas*—oranges, *manzanas*—apples,

cacahuates—peanuts, *calabaza*—pumpkin, *pan*—bread, *velas*—candles, *cempasuchil*—marigolds, and *flores*—flowers.

Math

4. Converting recipes gives excellent math practice. The following recipe will make 24 *Polvorones* (Mexican sugar cookies). A group of students can first determine how many cookies they wish to make for each student, and then convert the recipe into teaspoons and cups and convert Centigrade into Fahrenheit. Preheat oven to 150°C. Sift together 500 ml flour with 180 ml sugar and 2.5 ml cinnamon. Cream 250 ml butter with beater and gradually add the flour mixture. Divide the dough and shape it into 24 patties. Place on ungreased cookie sheet and bake for 25 minutes. Sprinkle extra sugar and cinnamon over the tops of the warm cookies if desired.

Social Studies

5. Invite a group of six students to work in pairs to learn more about Olmecs, Mayans, and Aztecs. Have them report what they learn orally to the class. The pairs might find the information for their reports on the Web. For information on Olmecs, see http://www.mexicana.com/english/community/29nf-olmec.shtmal. Leads to Aztec pages can be found at http://www.indians.org/welker/aztec.htm. And information on Mayans can be found at http://www.ref.rice.edu~jchance/mayainfo.html. A website with general information and history can be found *at The Illustrated Encyclopedia of Mesoamerica*, http://www.cultures.com/meso_resources/meso_ency-clopedia/meso_encyclopedia_home.html.

Geography

6. Mexico has had several earthquakes. One theory used to explain this is *plate tectonics*. Scientists believe that the earth's crust is made up of several different plates that are constantly moving. Mexico is located at a point where four plates meet. These are the North American plate, the Pacific plate, the Caribbean plate, and the Cocos plate. Invite a group of students to read more about plate tectonics and to share with the class what they learn.

Music

7. Linda Ronstadt is of Mexican and German ancestry and has won numerous awards as a singer. She began a serious study of the Mexican tradition in song in the 1980s. Her album of ballads, "Canciones de mi Padre," was widely acclaimed and would be an interesting one to share with students.

Art

8. With the help of the art educator or an adult volunteer, students may want to undertake painting a mural. Large roller sheets of butcher paper may be taped to a wall. A group of students may draw the scene for the mural, making a small detailed sketch. (It might be a market place in Mexico City or a rainforest jungle.) Then draw a grid over the sketch. Place a much larger grid over the blank butcher paper taped to the wall. Small groups of students can be responsible for transferring the part of the grid from the small sketch to the large grid on the wall. When the drawing is completed, it could be painted with tempera paint or finished with colored chalks.

Drama/Movement

9. The *jarabe tapatio* (Mexican Hat Dance) is the national dance of Mexico. The music educator or an adult volunteer might teach students to do the Mexican Hat dance. The simple version calls for the dancers to hop from heel to heel, to clap hands, and to promenade, much like a square dance, linking arms with other dancers as you meet them.

Dress

10. Most students will be familiar with the Mexican sombrero, but may not realize that there are several versions of this hat. Tall hats with turned up brims are common in the state of Morelos. The sombreros of the Huichol people have flat crowns, medium-sized brims, and are decorated with feathers. Farmers in the Yucatan wear braided palm-leaf sombreros. Invite students to find pictures of various sombreros and (with permission) to photocopy these and share them with the class.

Cooking

11. Any time is a good time for chips and dip. For a Mexican touch, make a guacamole dip.

Chips and Dip

3 avocados
2 chiles
1 small, white onion
1 branch of cilantro
1 tablespoon of olive oil
salt and lemon/lime juice for flavor

Peel 3 avocados and mash them with a wooden spoon. Finely mince two chiles, 1 small white onion, and 1 branch of cilantro and add these to the avocados. Stir in one tablespoon of olive oil. Season to taste with salt and freshly squeezed lemon or lime juice.

Culminating Activity

12. A piñata party would make a good culminating activity. The piñata could be made by blowing up a balloon and then covering it in papier mâché to form the base. When the papier mâché dries, deflate the balloon by cutting the end that is sticking out and pull the balloon from inside the papier mâché. Fill the base with pieces of wrapped candy, and then papier mâché over the opening. Then by adding strips, paper cones, and so on, the base could be shaped into an animal, ball, or star. Papier mâché pieces can be decorated with glued-on squares of crepe paper. Twist a square of crepe paper over a pencil eraser, dip it in glue, and then place the squares close together on the base. The piñata could be hung outside or in the gym while blindfolded students take turns trying to break it with a long stick. Once broken, the spilled candy can be shared by all.

Suggested Reading

Ancona, George. *Pablo Remembers: The Fiesta of the Day of the Dead.* New York: Lothrop, Lee & Shepard, 1993.

Barlow, Genevieve. *Latin American Tales: From the Pampas to the Pyramids of Mexico.* New York: Rand McNally, 1966.

De La Rosa, Angeles and C. Gandia de Fernandez. *Flavors of Mexico, Authentic Recipes from South of the Border.* San Francisco, Calif.: 101 Productions, 1978.

De Van Etten, Teresa Pijoan. *Spanish-American Folktales, The Practical Wisdom of Spanish-Americans in 28 Eloquent and Simple Stories.* Little Rock, Ark.: August House, 1990.

Ehlert, Lois. *Cuckoo: A Mexican Folktale.* San Diego, Calif.: Harcourt Brace, 1997.

Kalman, Bobbie. *Mexico, The Culture.* New York: Crabtree, 1993.

———. *Mexico, The Land.* New York: Crabtree, 1993.

———. *Mexico, The People.* New York: Crabtree, 1993.

Lannert, Paula. *Mexican Americans.* Vero Beach, Fla.: Rourke, 1991.

Lasky, Kathryn. *Days of the Dead.* New York: Hyperion, 1994.

McNeer, May. *The Mexican Story.* New York: Ariel Books, 1953.

Parker, Edward. *Mexico.* Austin, Tex.: Raintree Steck-Vaughn, 1998.

Perl, Lila. *Mexico, Crucible of the Americas.* New York: William Morrow, 1978.

Piggott, Juliet. *Mexican Folk Tales.* New York: Crane Russak, 1973.

Porter, Eliot and Ellen Auerbach. *Mexican Celebrations.* Albuquerque, N.Mex.: University of New Mexico Press, 1990.

Reilly, Mary Jo. *Cultures of the World, Mexico.* New York: Marshall Cavendish, 1991.

Stein, R. Conrad. *Mexico City.* Danbury, Conn.: Childrens Press, 1996.

Temko, Florence. *Traditional Crafts from Mexico and Central America.* Minneapolis, Minn.: Lerner Publications, 1996.

Wilkes, John. *Hernan Cortes, Conquistador in Mexico.* London, England: Cambridge University Press, 1974.

"Why, you're one of the slowest creatures on earth, and I wouldn't want any of my friends to find me in your poke-along company."

The Philippines
A Folktale from the Philippines

"The Carabao-Turtle Race" appears in *The Carabao-Turtle Race and Other Classic Philippine Animal Folk Tales* by Sylvia Mendez Ventura. It also appears in abbreviated form in *Filipino Popular Tales* by Denis S. Fansler under the title "An Unequal Match; or Why the Carabao's Hoof Is Split." Readers will not be surprised at the outcome because they will remember another famous race that took place between the tortoise and the hare.

The Race Over Seven Hills

Carabao (or water buffalo) was trotting along one summer morning feeling very out of sorts. He was hot and dusty and wanted very much to find a good water hole where he could cool off and wash the dust from his back.

Who should Carabao meet but Turtle. Turtle, a friendly little fellow, was delighted to see Carabao. He knew that Carabao was big and strong and thought he would be a valuable friend to have. Eager to make a good impression, Turtle walked up and said, "Good morning!" in his cheeriest voice.

"It's not so good," complained Carabao. "I feel hot and dusty. Could you tell me where to find the nearest pond so that I can cool off?"

"Certainly," said Turtle. "I know of a deep, cool pond, but it's some distance from here. I'll take you there."

"You don't have to take me there," said Carabao. "Just tell me where it is. I can find it."

"I don't mind showing you," insisted Turtle. "That way you won't get lost."

"I won't get lost, and I don't have the time to walk with a slowpoke like you. Why, it might take you a week to get there. Just tell me where it is."

Now this hurt Turtle's feelings. "I had thought we might be friends," Turtle said, holding back tears, "and that we could talk and walk together."

"Nonsense," laughed Carabao. "You'd be better off making a friend of someone like Snail. I'm a fast runner, you know."

"Are you saying that I'm as slow as Snail?" asked the Turtle.

"Yes, you are," said Carabao. "I suppose it comes of being so foolish as to carry your house on your back. Why, you're one of the slowest creatures on earth, and I wouldn't want any of my friends to find me in your poke-along company."

"I can run faster than you any day," Turtle blurted out. As soon as the words left his mouth, he regretted them for indeed Turtle knew he was not the fastest of runners.

"Don't be ridiculous," said Carabao.

"Race with me," said Turtle.

"It would be a waste of time," said Carabao.

"Very well," said Turtle. "Then I shall go everywhere and tell everyone I meet that you are a coward who is afraid to race with me."

Carabao looked at the determined little turtle. "Very well," he said. "I'll race you."

"Will you race me over three hills?" asked Turtle, for an idea was forming in his head.

"I'll race you over seven hills and beat you," bragged Carabao. "But we'll race in three days. It will take me that long to invite all my friends to come and watch."

"Very well," agreed Turtle. He was glad to have three days for he, too, had to gather his friends if he was to carry out his plan.

Carabao went off and invited all his friends to the race. Turtle met with seven other turtles and explained his plan to them. He said if they would help, he could win, and people would praise the turtle kingdom. They all agreed to the plan. Turtle sent each to one of the seven hills of the racecourse and told each turtle what he should say, and do.

The great race day finally arrived. All of Carabao's friends were there to cheer him on. Frog signaled the start of the race, and Carabao hurried off at a great pace leaving Turtle behind in the dust. After a bit, Carabao looked over his shoulder. Turtle was not even in sight.

Caraboa slowed down. He stopped to talk with friends and admire the flowers. He ambled up the first hill. At the top he was astonished to see Turtle. Turtle called out, "Here I am slowpoke. I've been waiting for you."

Carabao could scarcely believe his eyes. Quickly he charged forward and left Turtle behind in the dust. But when he got to the top of the second hill, Carabao found Turtle was already there.

Turtle called out, "Here I am, slow poke. I've been waiting for you."

Carabao trotted right past Turtle and this time he did not slow his pace. He came puffing up the third hill. To his amazement, not only was Turtle there waiting for him, he was passing time by swimming about in a small puddle.

The same thing happened at each hill. When Caraboa trotted to the top, there was Turtle. And it was Turtle, stepping across the finish line after the seventh hill, that Frog declared the winner.

Carabao's friends laughed and cheered Turtle. Hot, dusty, and tired, Carabao lost his temper and kicked Turtle Number Seven so hard that he flew high into the air. But, since turtles have hard shells, Turtle landed unhurt.

Carabao was not so lucky. He cried out in pain and looked down at his foot. His hoof had split in two. And from that day forward, all carabaos have split hooves.

Background Information

The Republic of the Philippines is an island country in Southeast Asia. It lies at the western rim of the Pacific Ocean and is north of the Equator. This archipelago covers a distance of 1,100 miles from north to south. It borders the South China Sea, the Philippine Sea, and the Celebes Sea. The total area of the Philippines is 115,860 square miles. Its population is 76,103,564. The people of the Philippines are called Filipinos.

The land is divided into 7,107 islands and islets, about one-third of which have names. Many are simply rocks or coral reefs. The water between the islands is not deep. Only 154 of the islands have land areas of over 5.5 square miles.

The two largest islands, Luzon and Mindanao, account for two-thirds of the total territory. Eleven of the islands comprise 96 percent of the total land area.

Luzon, to the north, is the largest island and is where the city of Manila is located. The longest rivers on Luzon are the Rio Grande de Cagavan, the Rio Grande de Pampango, and the Agno. Mindanao, to the south, is the second largest island, and is home to most of the nation's Muslims. Between these two islands are some medium-sized islands. These islands are located in the western Pacific Ocean about 500 miles southeast of China.

To the north of the Philippines lies the island of Taiwan, while to the south are Borneo and the islands of Indonesia. To the west, across the South China Sea, is the coast of Asia, and to the east is the Pacific Ocean.

Much of the Philippines is mountainous. The mountains run in the same direction as the island, north to south. The highest peak is Mount Apo, an active volcano on Mindanao, at 9,690 feet above sea level. Mount Pulong, on Luzon, is about 9,600 feet high.

The Philippines have thirty-one volcanoes, ten of which are active. This zone, with its mountains, is part of the "chain of fire" that runs along the borders of the Pacific Ocean.

In June 1991, Mount Pinatubo, about 50 miles from Manila, erupted although it had not been active for six hundred years. It did considerable damage to Clark Air Force Base, which belonged to the United States. In February 1993, Mayon Volcano in southeastern Luzon erupted, forcing thousands of people to flee.

Earthquakes also occur frequently in this area and are sometimes accompanied by tidal waves that have caused considerable destruction.

Forests cover half of the land. There are also mangrove swamps and coconut groves along the coasts. Bamboo, banana trees, and palms are plentiful.

The Philippines has a tropical climate, with wet and dry seasons. The average temperature is about 80°F except in the mountains, where it is cooler. The Northeast Monsoon blows between December and May, and the Southwest Monsoon blows between June and November.

Typhoons are common and are another source of rainfall. An average of about twenty typhoons (known locally as *bagyos*) hit the Philippines every year. These are strong tropical storms that blow in from the Pacific bringing high winds and heavy rains.

Because of high rainfall, the Philippines have a large number of lakes. The largest lake is Laguna de Bay southeast of Manila. It covers 350 square miles. Southeast of this lake is the well known Pagsanjan Falls.

The Philippines is rich in natural resources, including copper, gold, lead, nickel, iron, silver, zinc, chromite, cobalt, and manganese. Copper is mined mainly on the islands of Luzon and Mindanao. Copper and iron ore are exported to the United States and to Japan.

About 41 percent of Filipinos live in large towns or cities. A common sight in the city of Manila is Jeepneys, vehicles that are like enlarged jeeps used as taxis. They are decorated with chrome pieces, tassels, pictures, and streamers in all colors.

The oldest city in the Philippines, founded in 1565, is Cebu City. It is on the east coast of Cebu Island and is the second largest city in the Philippines. It is second only to Manila as a trading and education center.

Although most Filipinos are farmers, only about 15 percent of them own the land they farm. Most rent the land from wealthy landowners. There are few large plantations. An average farm is seven to ten acres in size, and many cash crops are grown on small farms only an acre in size. The *carabao*, or water buffalo, is a very important farm animal used to plow the rice fields.

Rice is the main crop on the northern island of Luzon. North of Mount Pulog are the Banaue rice terraces. These terraces, which are 6,000 feet up in the mountains, were built more than 2,000 years ago by the Ifugao tribe. They are still cultivated today. They look something like giant staircases and cover an area of 4,000 square miles.

Corn is grown in the central and southern parts of the country. Other major agricultural products that are exported are coconuts, sugarcane, and hemp.

At one time, Manila hemp, or *abaca,* was an important crop and perhaps the best known export from the Philippines. More recently it has been replaced on the world market by synthetic materials such as rayon and nylon. Among the most important exports today are pineapples and bananas. Another major export is timber. Philippine mahogany wood is very valuable.

The official capital of the Philippines is Quezon City, which is within the Manila area. Most people refer to Manila as the capital. Manila is the largest city in the Philippines and has about 8 million people and covers about 245 square miles. It is the islands' seat of government as well as the chief port and the commercial and cultural center of the Philippines. Around Manila are Caloocan, Quezon, Pasay, and thirteen other towns. About 10 million people live in this Metro Manila area.

Baguia, which is 155 miles north of Manila, serves as the nation's capital during the hot dry months of April and May. At 5,000 feet in the mountains, it is cool all year-round.

The old walled city of Manila was begun in 1571. Within the walls were many important buildings and old churches leveled during World War II. One church survived, Manila's San Agustin Church, built in 1599.

The oldest city in the islands is Cebu City, located on the island of Cebu. A cross stands there and encases fragments of the original cross believed to have been planted by Magellan and his crew. Cebu's San Agustin Church houses a hand-carved wooden image of the infant Jesus that is said to have been presented as a baptismal gift by Magellan to the wife of the Cebu chieftain in 1521.

Davao, on Mindanao, is the third largest city and is the major city in the south. It is the center of agricultural and mining industries. It is also famous for its tropical fruits.

Bacalod, located on Negros, is a major sugar center. Zamboanga, on Mindanao, is a growing industrial city.

The people in the Philippines today are very diverse. Although descended mainly from Malays, other racial groups have settled and left their influence, including the Chinese, Arabs, Indians, Spaniards, Americans, Japanese, and other Europeans.

In addition to those of mixed ancestry, there are still some who are descendants of ancestors who came long before the Spaniards. These are the Negritos, who live in the mountain jungles of Palawan, Panay, Negros, Leyte, Samar, and Luzon. And there are the Igorots, Philippine natives who live in the remote mountainous region of northern Luzon.

There are also the Muslims or Moros of Mindanao and the Sula Archipelago, who spend almost their entire lives afloat. Their religion, dress, and way of life is different from that of other Filipinos. They roam the coast in little houseboats or create stilt villages like the one in Zamboanga. These settlements are houses built on stilts above submerged coral reefs a mile or so from shore. At high tide boats provide the only link between the houses and the shore.

History

Ancestors of the Filipinos came from Asia. The earliest were probably hunters who followed game over land bridges that existed about 30,000 years ago, joining the Philippines to Asia.

Negritos, the ancestors of today's Filipinos, probably walked to the islands from Borneo and Sumatra.

Malay people then came from the south about 7,000 years ago. After land bridges sank into the sea, sailors continued to arrive by canoes from other islands in the South Pacific and from coastal areas in Southeast Asia. Among these were Indonesians and Malays. By A.D. 700, the Philippines also attracted traders from Japan and China. About 95 percent of the present Philippine population is Malay. About 1.5 percent are Chinese.

In the 1300s, parts of the Philippines were ruled by the Sumatra-based Madjapahit empire. Islam, which was sweeping across Indonesia during the 1400s, established a foothold on Mindanao. This faith united the people of the south.

In 1521, Ferdinand Magellan reached Cebu. Magellan was a Portuguese explorer in the service of the Spanish King. He claimed the islands for Spain and named them after the king, Philip II. Magellan was killed in a battle with Chief Lapulapu of Mactan Island just off the coast of Cebu.

Christian Spaniards began arriving in the Philippine Islands. A permanent settlement was made in 1565 in Cebu. From there, the Spanish spread northward. In 1571, Manila was captured, and the Spaniards built the walled city of Intramuros.

The Spanish Roman Catholic priests introduced Christianity, converting the people and building churches. By 1600, most of the Filipinos had accepted both Spanish rule and Catholicism, with the exception of the Muslims in the Sulu Archipelago and Mindanao. This Spanish rule lasted over 300 years.

Filipinos were forced to give up their land and work for their masters. These conditions eventually led to many revolts against Spanish rule, but these revolts were all easily put down.

The Spanish were only interested in trade and did little to develop the islands. This caused many Filipinos to hope for independence. Among them was Dr. Jose Rizal, the son of a sugar planter. He studied in Spain and then returned to the Philippines as a doctor. He wrote two books suggesting changes that were needed in the islands. Rizal was considered a traitor, and in 1896 the Spanish government executed him.

The death of Jose Rizal led to revolt throughout the islands. The leader of this revolt was General Emilio Aguinaldo. In 1898, when the Spanish-American War broke out over Cuba, a naval battle was fought in Manila Bay. The Filipinos fought with the Americans against the Spanish.

At the end of the war, Spain ceded the Philippine Islands to the United States, but the Philippines declared itself a republic on June 12, 1898. For three years, the Filipinos then fought the Americans. This fighting ended in 1901.

The United States sent teachers and Protestant missionaries to the Philippines. Education became free and compulsory and English became the language of instruction.

The United States began introducing self-government to the Filipinos. They formed a two-house legislature in 1916. The U. S. Congress established the self-ruling Philippine Commonwealth in 1934 and pledged to give the country independence in a decade.

After World War II broke out, the Japanese occupied the Philippine Islands between late 1941 and 1945. The Philippines finally became independent in 1946. Manual Roxas became the first president.

In 1972, President Ferdinand Marcos proclaimed martial law in the Philippines, and a Communist revolt posed problems. In 1983, an opposition leader, Benigno Aquino, was assassinated. After the downfall of Marcos, Aquino's widow, Corazon Aquino, became the seventh president of an independent Philippines.

Government

The government of the Philippines was modeled after that of the United States. The constitution of 1935 made the Philippines a democratic republic with an elected president and vice-president who could serve two terms of four years each.

But in 1972, President Ferdinand Marcos declared martial law because of violence and disorder in the country. Government troops fought against Communist guerillas. Marcos drew up a new constitution in 1973. He pushed through reforms on land ownership but remained in power as president for twenty years.

A year after Corazon Aquino became the new president in February 1986, a new constitution was approved. The new constitution limits the Philippine president to one six-year term. The government includes a president, a senate, and a house of representatives. It guarantees the right to form workers' unions, the right to a fair trial, and limits the role of the military in the government.

Democracy has struggled in the Philippines because the wealthy landowners influence their tenants by telling them how to vote, and only the wealthy can afford to run for office.

Religion

Christianity first came to the Philippines with Spanish rule. The Philippines is the only Christian nation in Asia. Today 85 percent of the population is Roman Catholic and another 10 percent is Protestant.

The Filipinos also established two denominations of their own, *Aglipayan,* or the Philippine Independent Church, established in 1902, and *Iglesia ni Kristo,* Church of Christ, founded in 1914.

The largest group of non-Christians in the Philippines is the Muslims, who form about 4 percent of the population. They practice Islam. There are also a small number of tribes who continue to practice the animist beliefs of their ancestors. They make offerings to numerous spirits, gods, and goddesses.

There is a sizable Chinese community on the island of Cebu, where they have built a Taoist temple and practice Taoism.

Education

About 88 percent of Filipinos read and write. The first six years of school is free and compulsory for all Filipino children. English and Pilipino are used to teach in the schools. A typical school day begins at 7:30 A.M. and ends at 3:50 P.M.

Students study reading, writing, and arithmetic. Like many schools in the United States, the day begins with students gathering to raise the flag and pledge allegiance to their country. Government schools are found in cities and towns and in almost all of the villages.

Although elementary education is compulsory, not all students attend all the time. If a boy is needed to help his father with fishing in the morning, he may not come to school until after lunch. If a girl stops school to work and help support her family, she may eventually return although she is older than other children in her grade.

After morning lessons in the elementary schools, there is a recess. When they return to class, students may study music and language. Then they have a half-hour lunch break. In the afternoon, students may study science and homemaking.

After this elementary education, about one-third of the children stop going to school in order to work on farms or to help support their families. The next four years of education is provided in private secondary schools, many of which are run by Catholic religious orders.

After secondary schools, those who can afford it may continue their education in colleges and universities. There are over 1,000 colleges and 63 universities in the Philippines. Among its famous universities are the University of the Philippines in Quezon City, the University of Santo Tomas in Manila, and the University of San Carlos in Cebu City.

The state-operated University of the Philippines is patterned after the U.S. land-grant college system. There are also private institutions and church-related schools.

Immigrants

More than 6 million Asians have immigrated to the United States since 1848. Many have come since the elimination of national origin quotas in 1965. Filipinos were first allowed to become citizens in the United States in 1946.

Many Filipinos immigrated to the United States after the Philippines became a U.S. possession. They could not become naturalized citizens, but their children born in the United States were full citizens. Some Filipinos came to the United States for college. Many of these became leaders in Philippine society on their return.

Hawaii began importing Filipino laborers in 1909, and by 1930 Filipinos were one of the largest ethnic groups in Hawaii. More than 125,000 Filipinos immigrated to Hawaii between 1909 and 1940. Many of these farm workers, called *Sakadas,* worked for three years and then returned home, but some remained in Hawaii and some came to the United States.

After 1923, many Filipinos came directly to the United States from the Philippines. Many of these were seasonal agricultural workers. Others became service workers in homes, restaurants, and hotels. Some went to work in Alaskan canneries.

Congress passed the Tydings-McDuffie Act in 1934, establishing the Philippines as a commonwealth and limiting immigration of Filipinos to fifty per year. Part of the reason for this action was the depression in the United States resulting in a scarcity of jobs. The Act meant that Filipinos who were in the U.S. and were not citizens were reclassified as "aliens."

Filipinos met with a great deal of discrimination in the United States but found some help through Catholic churches that acted as welfare agencies.

When Filipinos fought alongside Americans during World War II, American attitudes toward Filipinos changed drastically. And the new Immigration Act of 1965 made it much easier for Filipinos to enter the U.S.

In 1985, for example, over 37,000 Filipinos applied for permanent residency in the United States and over 2,300 applied for student permits. Some Filipinos immigrate to Canada, become Canadian citizens, and then come to the United States because of favorable quotas for Canadian citizens.

From 1981 to 1990, 495,300 Filipinos immigrated to the United States. During 1991 to 1995, another 292,500 came.

In the United States and Canada, the largest Filipino communities are in big cities such as New York, Los Angeles, Chicago, Toronto, Vancouver, and Montreal. Many of these newer immigrants are going into the sciences and medical professions.

In 1980, the six largest Asian Pacific American groups were, in this order: Chinese, Filipino, Japanese, Asian Indian, Korean, and Vietnamese. It is expected that by the year 2000 the order will have changed. The largest group will be Filipinos, followed by Chinese, Vietnamese, Koreans, Asian Indians, and Japanese.

By 1990, there were almost one and one-half million Filipino Americans in the United States population, including those in Hawaii.

Language

One hundred sixteen languages and dialects are spoken in the islands. A majority of Filipinos speak English in addition to their local dialects. English is one of the official languages and Pilipino, a language based on the Tagalog dialect of Luzon, is the other official language. Since radio and television are increasingly using Pilipino, it could eventually replace English. Other major languages include Visayan and Ilocano. A small number of old established families speak Spanish.

The Arts and Sciences

There are many tribal arts and crafts in the Philippines. The mountain tribes of northern Luzon became famous for their woodcarvings and later for carvings of Catholic saints. These are valuable to collectors today. They also make bowls and dishes for the home. Native groups produce beadwork, mats, and woven fabrics that are sold to tourists.

The music of the Philippines is a blend of Filipino and Western influences. Traditional *kundiman* sounds similar to German folk songs, while the *zarzuela* seems to be based on Italian opera. The National Folk Arts Center provides scholarships for those wishing to pursue studies in classical music.

The Popular Music Foundation of the Philippines supports composers who create original pieces in Pilipino. Among instruments used are Muslim gongs (*kulintang*), a two-stringed lute (the *hagalong*), a fiddle with human hair for strings, the jew's harp (the *dubing*), and the nose flute.

The dances of the Philippines draw upon Malay folk dances, traditional Muslim dances, and Spanish dances. The National Ballet Federation supports ballet, and modern dance is supported by the Cultural Center Modern Dance Group. Maniya Barredo, who was born in Manila, came to the United States to study ballet and became prima ballerina with the Atlanta Ballet. She also taught students back in the Philippines.

The most famous dance troupe in the country is the Bayanihan Dance Company, which performs throughout the world. The most famous of the Filipino dances is the bamboo dance.

Filipinos also take part in drama, particularly religious passion plays. Theatregoers can see many different kinds of plays, including Western, experimental, and street theatre. Some plays are presented in Tagalog.

The islands formed a huge market for Hollywood films, but now they are beginning to produce films in Pilipino featuring modern themes. The Philippines are now the fourth largest producer of movies in the world. A famous film festival is The Manila International Film Festival. The Experimental Cinema of the Philippines helps to fund film projects.

Early poems, songs, myths, and legends were handed down by word of mouth. There was a local script based on ancient Indian languages when the Spanish first arrived in the islands, but only a few scholars can read and write it now.

The first printed books were in Spanish, but today, Filipino literature is written in English and Pilipino. Carlos Bulosan was a Filipino American poet and writer. In his book, *America in the Heart,* he told about his life as an immigrant in the United States. One poet from the Philippines, Jose Garcia Villa, was named a National Artist in 1973. He sometimes teaches a poetry workshop at the New School in New York.

The Filipino Academy of Painting began in 1821. It concentrated on Spanish themes and techniques. At the Madrid Exposition in Spain in 1884, two Filipino painters, Juan Luna and Felix Resureccion Hidalgo, won prizes. More recently painters are expressing new ideas through their work. Displays are held at the Museum of Philippine Contemporary Art.

The best known sculptor from the Philippines was Guillermo Tolentino, who died in 1976. He created many bronze monuments commemorating events in Philippine history.

Food

The Philippine Islands are very western compared to much of Southeast Asia. A large number of Filipino dishes originated in Spain while others, such as steamed dumplings, fried noodles, spring rolls, and rice dishes, have a Chinese influence.

Rice is the staple food of the Philippines. It is served with a variety of dishes at almost every meal. Fish and other seafood is steamed or cooked lightly and served with sauces.

Fish caught in the sea and the rivers include tuna, mackerel, grouper, herring, mullet, flatfish, needlefish, sea bass, cuttlefish, prawn, and sardines.

A popular dish is *adobo,* consisting of chicken or pork simmered in oil and seasoned with vinegar, soy sauce, garlic, and spices.

In general, Filipino food is mildly seasoned, although in Bicol Province in the south of Luzon, chilies are used liberally. Common ingredients in many dishes are garlic, palm vinegar, green tamarind, coconut milk, soy sauce, and lime. Fried and barbecued meats and fish are popular. Cakes and pastries are very European in style although many have coconut as an ingredient.

As in most countries, Filipinos enjoy special Christmas treats. One specialty often served in the church courtyard after early morning mass is *puto bumbong,* a rice cake made with a bluish sticky rice steamed in a cylindrical bamboo mold. The cake is tapped out and served with a sprinkling of brown sugar and shredded coconut. Another rice cake is *bibingka,* made with rice, flour, eggs, and milk. It is baked and topped with cheese, grated coconut, and salted eggs. *Suman* is a mixture of sticky rice, coconut milk, and sugar wrapped in banana leaves and steamed.

A favorite food sometimes served on Christmas Eve and at other festival times is *rellenong manok,* boned stuffed chicken. The chicken is stuffed with pork, sausage, and pickles. Others enjoy *rellenong bangus,* or boned stuffed milkfish. Milkfish is native to most areas in the Philippines.

At many feasts and celebrations, Filipinos serve *Lechon,* a suckling pig roasted over a charcoal fire. A popular drink is *tuba* or coconut wine made from the sap of the coconut palm.

Many students will have tasted Chinese egg rolls and therefore might be interested in trying fried egg rolls from the Philippines.

Fried Egg Rolls (Lumpia)

1 tablespoon vegetable oil

1 small, finely chopped onion

3 large garlic cloves, crushed and then minced

1 pound lean, ground pork

1 1/2 cups, packed, shredded cabbage

1/4 pound bean sprouts

1 teaspoon salt

16 lumpia or egg roll wrappers

3 cups vegetable oil

Vinegar Dip

1/2 cup distilled white vinegar

1/4 cup water

2 large, minced garlic cloves

1/2 teaspoon salt

Combine all the ingredients for the dip and let stand while preparing the lumpia.

In a large skillet, heat 1 tablespoon oil over medium heat. Add onion and garlic and cook until tender but not browned. Add the pork. Stir to break up meat and cook until the meat is no longer pink. Add the cabbage and bean sprouts and cook until wilted. Stir in the salt. Cool thoroughly.

Place an egg roll wrapper with a point at the bottom on a cutting board. Place 1/4 cup filling on the wrapper, spreading the filling in a line just below the side points. Brush edges from side points to the top with water. Fold bottom point over the filling, side points to the center, and roll to the top.

Heat remaining 3 cups of oil in a wok to 360°F. Add the lumpia 4 at a time and fry 4 to 5 minutes until both sides are golden brown. Drain excess oil. Makes 16 lumpia that can be cut into thirds for snacks using the dipping sauce.

Recreation

Some games popular with Filipino children are integral parts of festivals. After the Santacruzan procession and feasting, for example, children play a variety of games. *Pabitin* involves a bamboo trellis with gifts such as coins, candy, and fruit. The trellis is lowered, and children leap up to grasp a gift, then the trellis is pulled up out of reach again.

Palo-sebo involves climbing up bamboo poles that lead to the tallest coconut tree. At the top of the tree, sweets and coins are tied for the children who climb that high.

Filipino children play *piko,* which is like hopscotch, and they enjoy walking on stilts. *Sipa* is played something like volleyball using a hollow wicker ball kicked over a net. Children play jump rope and baseball.

Basketball is a very popular sport played wherever a court can be set up. Every year Filipinos hold amateur and professional tournaments.

Cockfighting is popular with male adults, especially on Sundays and public holidays. Men bring their prize roosters to fight and bet on the outcome of the cockfight.

Jai alai is played in a long enclosed court with a granite wall at one end. A *cesta,* which is a crescent-shaped wicker basket, is laced to the player's right hand and is used to catch the hard rubber ball. This is also a popular spectator sport. It was introduced into the Philippines by Basques from Spain.

Other popular leisure time sports include swimming, volleyball, tennis, and horseracing.

Since World War II, Filipinos have become Asia's best chessplayers in international competitions. The world chess championships were held in Baguia City in 1978. Filipinos play chess in clubs, barbershops, and wherever they can set up a board. Two of their most famous players are Eugene Torre and Rosendo Balinas.

Customs and Traditions

During the third week in January, in the coastal village of Kalibo on the Philippine Islands, a three-day festival called Ati-Atihan is celebrated. The festival celebrates the sale of Panay island to ten Bornean chieftains back in the thirteenth century, and it also pays tribute to Kalibo's patron saint, Santo Nino.

The day begins with the beating of drums. People wear wildly colorful costumes and dance in the streets just as the Atis did. They sing songs that have been passed down for hundreds of years.

In Apalit in the Philippines, Saint Peter is the patron saint. They call him Apong Iro, which means Grandfather Iro. The Apalit River Festival in late June lasts three days. The major event is the four-mile river parade. Life-sized statues of Saint Peter and Saint Paul are made and carried through the streets of the town to the river where they are placed in pagodas mounted on barges. The pagodas are decorated with gold leaf and with paper flowers. The barges form a flotilla and sail down the river, past the village.

The Holy Week festival is held on the island of Marinduque and is known as the Moriones Festival. Many of the events take place in the capital city of Boac and the towns of Gasan and Mogpog. On Holy Wednesday, islanders dress as Roman centurions with Roman-style plumed helmets. On Good Friday, they re-enact the crucifixion of Christ. The story of the Roman centurion, Longinus, is dramatized on Sunday with its exciting, chase, capture, and execution.

Among the biggest festivals in the Philippines are those that take place in May, including Santacruzan. The Santacruzan is a thanksgiving for a bountiful harvest and a religious festival commemorating Queen Helena's search for the cross on which Jesus was crucified.

The festival begins with a procession, led by a brass band, followed by children of all ages dressed as kings and queens. Young girls offer garlands of flowers to the Virgin Mary and scatter flowers in the church. Then bigger girls take part in the procession. One girl is chosen to represent Queen Helena. She wears a white dress and holds a cross in her hands. Next to her is a little boy dressed as her son, Constantine. Behind them come followers carrying lighted candles and singing hymns and folksongs.

The *Carabao Festival* is also celebrated in mid-May in Pulilan and recognizes the farmer's faithful animal. The festival honors San Isidro Labrador, the patron saint and protector of farmers. Each family decorates a carabao and cart and goes to the church. The carabao are unhitched and forced to kneel in front of the church while a priest blesses the farm animals.

The Christmas celebration in the Philippines begins on December 16 with the first of nine pre-dawn masses and continues until January 6, Three Kings Day. The bamboo *parol* or star lantern is the symbol of Christmas in the Philippines. It represents the star of Bethlehem. Lantern competitions are held in many cities just before Christmas, with the most elaborate being the San Fernando Festival.

On December 16, well before dawn, the church bells toll and call the people to the first *Misa de Gallo,* Mass of the Rooster, since it is celebrated at 4:00 A.M. These masses, called *Simbang Gabi,* or Night Mass, culminate with the Christmas Eve midnight mass.

After each of the nine days of mass, outside in the church plaza there are foodstalls with tasty breakfast treats. Each evening there is caroling. Groups sing Filipino carols and English tunes, including "Jingle Bells."

Filipinos decorate their homes with purchased or homemade *parols* or lanterns, streamers, cards, candles, and wreaths. A few families will have expensive fresh pine trees from the forests of Baguio City, north of Manila, but most Christmas trees will be artificial. Public buildings and squares are decorated, too.

Churches contain a *belen,* or nativity scene, including shepherds, peasants, kings and angels, with the Holy Infant appearing at Midnight Mass on Christmas Eve. After midnight mass, the family feast of Noche Buena is held.

Some families exchange gifts with relatives on Christmas Eve while others wait until Christmas Day. On Christmas Day, the main entree is *lechon,* or roast, suckling pig. Dessert may be a creamy caramel custard known as *leche flan.*

New Year's Eve often includes a party with hats and noisemakers. In Manila, there will be extravagant fireworks displays launched from barges in the bay, and again there is feasting.

In addition to these festivals there are celebrations of Independence Day on the June 12, for Filipino-American Friendship Day on the July 4, and a recognition of Bataan Day to commemorate the fall of Bataan to the Japanese during World War II and the "Death March" of American and Filipino soldiers.

Suggested Activities

Writing

1. A group of students might wish to prepare written reports and gather pictures for a class bulletin board entitled "Animals of the Philippines." Included in their research could be wild pigs, civets, mongooses, carabao, tamarao, and tarsiers. On the Web, students will find a picture of a carabao at http://www.guam.net/special/pics/carabao-horns.JPG.html, and at http://www.interlog.com/~ctatro/philipp.htm they can find pictures of both a carabao and a tarsier.

Reading

2. Asian Americans faced hardship and discrimination when they moved to Hawaii, Canada, and the United States. Invite an interested group of students to read one or more of the following books and share what they learn in an oral report to the class: Roger Daniels, *Coming to America: A History of Immigration and Ethnicity in American Life* (Harper & Row, 1990); Harry H. L. Kitano and Roger Daniels, *Asian Americans: Emerging Minorities* (Prentice Hall, 1988); Antonio J. A. Pido, *The Philipinos in America* (Center for Migration Studies, 1986); Ronald Takaki, *Strangers from a Different Shore: A History of Asian Americans* (Little, Brown, 1989).

Vocabulary

3. A group of students doing research on Pilipino could create an interesting bulletin board by listing words and phrases in both Pilipino and English. They can gather these words from their reading and list them on 3 x 5-inch cards.

Here are a few to use as "starters:" *binibini*—Miss, *gigang*—Mrs., *ginoo*—Mr., *magandang umaga po*—good morning, *oo*—yes, *paki*—please, and *kamusta po kayo*—how are you.

Math

4. Here are some simple facts about Philippine immigration from Jodine Mayberry's book, *Filipinos.* Invite two students to prepare math problems for the class to solve using these facts. The students should also prepare an answer key.

Filipino-American Population, 1910–1960*

1910—406
1920—5,603
1930—45,308
1940—48,876
1950—61,645
1960—181,614

*Only 1960 figure includes Hawaii 69,070
Source: U. S Census

Social Studies

5. Although democracy was restored to the Philippines after martial law that was imposed by Ferdinand Marcos in 1972, there is still political unrest in the islands. Ask a group of interested students to study the current political situation and to share what they learn through a panel discussion.

   Research by this group should include information about the New People's Army, a Communist organization, as well as Muslim groups that oppose the government. In Mindanao and Palawan, Muslims have formed the Moro National Liberation Front and want to establish a separate state. Is the United States still giving financial aid to the Philippines?

Geography

6. To the east of Mindanao Island in the Philippines is the Mindanao Trench. At 34,218 feet, it is six times deeper than the Grand Canyon in the United States. The only known deeper spot on the ocean floor is the Mariana Trench, which lies off the island of Guam in the Pacific.

   Have an interested group of students study both the Mindanao and the Mariana Trenches and make an oral presentation to the class on what they learn, showing on a map where each is located. How do scientists go about estimating the depths of the ocean?

Music

7. If it is appropriate, the music specialist might gather some Philippine Christmas music and share this with the class. Possible songs include *Ang Pasko ay Sumapit* (Philippine carol), *O Naggasat Ketdin Dayto Nga Rabii* (Oh, How Blessed Is this Night), and *Dimtengen Kadatay* (Now He Is Here). The words and music to these songs can be found in *Christmas in the Philippines*, from World Book, 1990.

Art

8. Students may wish to make a typical Philippine Star lantern. Detailed directions for this art project are given on pages 65–69 of *Christmas in the Philippines*, from World Book, 1990. Materials include balsa wood, tissue paper, flexible wire, construction paper, foil, glue, tape, pencil, ruler, scissors, markers, glitter, and compass.

Drama/Movement

9. Try to locate someone in the community who will come to school to teach students *tinikling*, a bamboo pole dance. With a little instruction, students will be able to enjoy and perform this dance.

Dress

10. Ask a pair of students to research and find pictures to share with the class of the Filipino's national costume, the *barong tagalog*, which is a loose, embroidered shirt, worn over trousers, and the Filipina's national costume which is the *terno*, a long dress with puff sleeves.

Cooking

11. People in many countries make a practice of serving afternoon tea. Students might enjoy sampling Hot Ginger Tea *(Salabat)* from the Philippines. This recipe makes 4 to 6 servings.

Hot Ginger Tea (Salabat)
2 ounces gingerroot
6 cups water
$\frac{1}{2}$ cup packed light brown sugar

Thoroughly wash the gingerroot but do not peel it. Thinly slice the gingerroot until you have $1/2$ cup. Combine the gingerroot and water in a saucepan. Bring to a boil, and continue boiling gently, uncovered, for about 35 minutes. The liquid will be reduced to about 4 cups. Strain the liquid to remove the gingerroot and stir in the brown sugar until it is dissolved. Makes about 1 quart.

Culminating Activity

12. At the beginning of your unit of study on the Philippines, encourage each student to correspond with a pen pal in the Philippines. Students could write back and forth and save their letters. In advance, set aside an afternoon as Pen Pal Afternoon. Ask each student who heard from a pen pal to share during this time. The student could point out on a map where his or her pen pal lives and share highlights from letters. To get a pen pal, write to International Pen Friends, P. O. Box 65, Brooklyn, New York 11229.

Suggested Reading

Asian Cultural Centre for Unesco. *Festivals in Asia*. New York: Kodansha, 1975.

Editorial Department of World Book. *Christmas in the Philippines*. Chicago, Ill.: World Book, 1990.

Editors of Time Life Books. *South-East Asia*. London, England: Time-Life Books, 1987.

Fansler, Dean S. *Filipino Popular Tales*. New York: American Folk-lore Society, 1921.

Hansen, Barbara. *Barbara Hansen's Taste of Southeast Asia*. Tucson, Ariz.: HP Books, 1987.

Lepthien, Emilie U. *The Philippines*. Chicago, Ill.: Childrens Press, 1993.

Lye, Keith. *Philippines*. New York: Franklin Watts, 1985.

Mayberry, Jodine. *Filipinos*. New York: Franklin Watts, 1990.

Sherwood, Rhoda, MaryLee Knowlton, and Mark J. Sachner, eds. *Philippines*. Milwaukee, Wisc.: Gareth Stevens, 1987.

Ventura, Sylvia Mendez. *The Carabao-Turtle Race and Other Classic Philippine Animal Folk Tales*. Manila: the Philippines, Tahanan Books for Young Readers, 1993.

Viesti, Joe and Diane Hall. *Celebrate! in Southeast Asia*. New York: Lothrop, Lee & Shepard Books, 1996.

Wee, Jessie. *Philippines*. New York: Chelsea House, 1988.

Poland

A Tale from Poland

One version of this story, "The Jolly Tailor Who Became King," appears in *Favorite Fairy Tales Told in Poland,* retold by Virginia Haviland and illustrated by Felix Hoffman.

An earlier version of the story, "The Jolly Tailor," appears in *The Jolly Tailor and other Fairy Tales Translated from the Polish* by Lucia Merecka Borski and Kate B. Miller, illustrated by Kazimir Klepacki.

The Tailor Who Became King

In the town of Taidaraida lived a tailor name Joseph Nitechka. He was a happy man who wore a thin beard containing only one hundred and thirty-six hairs. On holidays, he would braid his beard and looked particularly handsome. Most tailors are thin, but Joseph was the thinnest of them all. He could pass through the eye of a needle, and thin noodles were the only food that could slip down his throat.

One day, a gypsy came to town, and while there, she cut her foot. The gypsy went to the tailor and he stitched up her foot so carefully that not a scar was visible. Before she left, the gypsy looked at the tailor's hand and read his future.

She said, "If you leave this town on Sunday and walk westward you will come to a place where you will be crowned as king."

The tailor just laughed. But that night he got to thinking. Perhaps what the gypsy said is true. So in the morning he started off, taking with him one hundred needles, a thimble, an iron, a pair of scissors, and a thousand miles of thread.

Uncertain which way was west, the tailor asked an elderly man. The man said, "West is where the sunsets," and he pointed the tailor in the right direction.

The tailor headed westward, but a wind came up, and since he was so thin, it blew him away. The tailor laughed in delight as he sailed on the wind. When the wind calmed down, it gently placed him on the ground. To his surprise, the tailor landed right in the arms of a scarecrow in the middle of a wheat field.

"What's this?" the scarecrow shouted.

"I'm so very sorry," the tailor apologized, as he scrambled out of the scarecrow's arms. "I got carried away by the wind. I'm Joseph Nitechka, the tailor."

The scarecrow was dressed quite elegantly in a blue jacket and trousers that were slightly torn, and wore a stovepipe hat on his head. He had sticks for feet and hands.

"I'm very pleased to meet you," the scarecrow said. "My name is Count Scarecrow. I stand here and frighten off the sparrows, though I would rather fight lions and tigers. Unfortunately, they seldom come to eat wheat. Where are you headed?"

He set to work and in no time at all had fixed Count Scarecrow's suit
so that it looked almost new.

"I'm going westward to a place where I shall be crowned king."

"Really?" said Count Scarecrow.

"Yes," said the tailor. "Would you like to come along?"

"I would, for I'm tired of standing here. But, could you possibly mend my clothes before we leave?"

"Of course," said Joseph. He set to work and in no time at all had fixed Count Scarecrow's suit so that it looked almost new.

As the two walked westward they had many adventures and became great friends. They often slept in wheatfields where the tailor tied himself to the scarecrow so that he wouldn't blow away during the night. If dogs attacked, Count Scarecrow would throw his foot at them, frightening them away. Then he would tie his foot back on again.

They continued on their journey until they reached the outskirts of Pacanow, a beautiful old town. They stopped and stared. Although it was sunny everywhere else, directly over the town rain poured down in buckets. A few townspeople ran out to meet them.

"Can you help us?" they shouted.

"What is happening here?" asked the tailor.

A Burgomaster spoke up. "Our king died a week ago, and since then, rain has poured down on us without stopping. It runs down our chimneys so that we cannot even light a fire."

"That's too bad," said the tailor.

"And the king's daughter keeps crying, and adds to the flood of water," said the Burgomaster.

"Oh, dear," said Count Scarecrow.

"Can you help us?" asked the Burgomaster. "The king's daughter has promised to marry the man who can stop the rain. He will become King!"

"Really?" asked the tailor. "Please take us to the princess, and we will see what we can do."

When Count Scarecrow and the tailor met the princess, the princess found the tailor to be very attentive and quite handsome. She repeated her promise that she would marry whoever stopped the rain and that her husband would become King.

The tailor thought hard about the problem for three days. Finally, he said to Count Scarecrow, "I believe the king was so great and mighty, that when he died and went to heaven, he made a huge hole in the sky. All I have to do is sew it up."

The tailor called the Burgomaster and told him to ask all the townspeople to bring their ladders to the town square. The ladders were tied together and leaned against the sky. Carrying with him an iron and a threaded needle, the tailor climbed up and up and up. Count Scarecrow stayed below and unwound the spool with a hundred miles of thread.

Just as he suspected, the tailor found a huge hole in the heavens. A torn patch of sky hung down, and through this hole, water poured on the town below. For two days, the tailor sewed. He sewed until his arms ached and his fingers were stiff. Finally, he pressed the sky with his iron and climbed back down the ladders fully exhausted.

Brilliant rays of sunshine poured down on Pacanow. The princess stopped crying and kissed the tailor affectionately. The Burgomaster brought a golden scepter and crown.

The people shouted, "Long live King Nitechka. Long live the king! May he marry the Princess and reign happily."

Count Scarecrow was named Great Warden of the kingdom and placed in charge of driving away sparrows from the royal head. The tailor and the princess were married immediately, and they lived happily in their kingdom where it never rained.

Background Information

The Republic of Poland is a relatively flat country in east central Europe with a population of 38,700,291. It is roughly rectangular in shape and occupies 120,728 square miles. Poland shares borders with Russia to the north; Lithuania, Belarus, and the Ukraine to the east; Slovakia and the Czech Republic to the south; and Germany to the west.

There are no natural boundaries to the east or west of Poland. To the south are the Sudetes at the border of the Czech Republic, and the Carpathian mountains at the Slovakian border. To the north of Poland is the Baltic Sea. Its coastline stretches for 326 miles.

Most of Poland is a great, rolling plain. More than 75 percent of the land is less than 650 feet above sea level. Woods cover about one-fourth of the country. There are also thousands of lakes.

Poland has cold, snowy winters and cool summers. Average temperatures range from 76°F in summer to 20°F in the mountains in winter. The record high is 100.4°F and the record low is minus 29°F. Rainfall averages 24 inches a year. The mountains may receive 31 to 47 inches, while the lowlands average about 18 inches of rain.

The main river, the Vistula, rises in the Carpathian Mountains, winds northward, and flows 680 miles before emptying into the Baltic Sea. The Vistula, and its tributaries, the Bug and the Pelica, drain about two-thirds of the country.

The Vistula River is used for transporting coal and lumber. Light boats can sail up the river as far as Krakow except when the river freezes in winter. Two other rivers, the Oder and Neisse, rise in the Sudetes and also empty in the Baltic.

About one-quarter of Poland's workers are engaged in some form of agriculture. Peasants sow by hand and use simple tools. Poland's largest crop is rye. Farmers also grow wheat, barley, oats, and sugar beets, but much of their grain and fodder is imported.

Polish farmers also grow fruit, including blueberries, strawberries, and black currants. They raise vegetables such as turnips, potatoes, cabbages, onions, and beetroot.

Poland has extensive coal deposits and some lead, zinc, natural gas, lignite, salt, copper, manganese, uranium, phosphates, and sulfur. Coal is Poland's major export. It ranks fourth as the largest coal supplier in the world. Most exports now go to European Community countries. Poland must import petroleum and iron ore.

When Communists were in power, industry was nationalized. After the Communist regime, price controls were abandoned and subsidies were slashed. There was inflation and unemployment. By 1994, the Polish economy began to show signs of recovery. More than half of the labor force is now employed in the private sector. Trade is developing with the West and particularly with Germany.

Foreign investments are coming into Polish businesses and industries. Firms such as Fiat and Coca-Cola are starting to invest. Computer firms such as IBM from the United States and TBT from Japan have opened branches in Poland.

Warsaw, the largest city in Poland, is located in the heart of the country. It is a center for trade and industry. It is also a cultural center with theaters, concert halls, museums, and libraries. It hosts many music festivals including the Chopin competition.

Warsaw was heavily bombed and was in ruins at the end of World War II. The Old Town was rebuilt. The reconstructed palaces and mansions now house various agencies and academies. A well known landmark is the Cathedral of Saint John, which dates to 1360. Casimir Palace, which is home to the University of Warsaw, was founded in 1818. South of the city is the Wilanow Palace. This was once the summer residence of Jan III Sobieski, a seventeenth century Polish king.

Cracow was the capital of Poland until 1609. It contains the royal castle of Wawel, built overlooking the Vistula River almost 1,000 years ago. Next to the castle is a cathedral that contains tombs of many of the country's kings and other famous men, including honored poets. Cracow is also the home of the Jagiellonian University, founded in 1364.

Cracow has a market square, The Rynek Glowny, which was once the largest square in Europe. In one corner of the square is the Church of Our Lady Mary. There are sidewalk cafes and flower sellers and booths selling folk art souvenirs.

One interesting spot in Poland is Bialowieze National Park, half of which is in Poland and the other half in Belarus. It has been a national park since 1919 and contains about 312,000 acres. In addition to being a primeval forest, the park provides a natural breeding place for wild bison. It is a major scientific center for forest conservation.

History

It is believed that Slavic tribes lived in Poland as early as 2000 to 1000 B.C. One of the largest tribes was the *Polanie*. Their name comes from a word that means "people who live in the fields."

In the tenth century, Prince Mieszko I married a Christian princess and converted to Christianity. That year, A.D. 966, is considered to be the date of the founding of Poland. At that time, several West Slavic tribes united to form small states. The Catholic Church sent missionaries to Poland.

After Mieszko died in A.D. 992, his son, Boleslaw the Brave, became prince of Poland. He made friends with the German emperor, Otto III. But after Otto died, Germany and Poland went to war. Boleslaw was eventually crowned king of Poland, and Poland became an independent nation.

After Boleslaw's death, Poland was divided into dukedoms and each nobleman kept a small army. Castles were built to defend its borders and Poland stretched from the Baltic to the Black Sea.

Poland was not united into one country again until the early 1300s. Ladislas the Short ruled for a time, and his son, Casimir the Great, ruled from 1333 until 1370. Because Casimir the Great had no children, it was decided that on his death, Casimir's nephew, King Louis of Hungary, would rule Poland. Then when Louis died, he had no sons, so his daughter, Jadwiga, was crowned "king" of Poland.

Jadwiga was convinced to marry Jagiello, grand duke of Lithuania. After it united with Lithuania in the fifteenth century, Poland became the largest country in Europe. Jagiellonian kings then ruled Poland for almost 200 years.

Russia, led by Tsar Ivan IV, invaded Poland. The Polish king Stefan Batory defeated the Russians in 1581.

Sweden occupied Poland from 1655 to 1660. There were other invasions by Russia, Prussia, and Austria.

King John III Sobieski was a fine military leader, but after his death in 1696, the Poles had no real self-government. Poland was erased from the map in the late eighteenth century by the so-called three partitions that divided the land once known as Poland between Russia, Prussia, and Austria.

For 123 years, from 1795 to 1918, Poland did not exist as a country, and it did not regain its independence until 1918 when the Treaty of Versailles established Poland as a fully independent republic.

The first president of this Second Polish Republic was Jozef Pilsudski. There were many economic problems and boundary disputes. In 1926, Pilsudski took over the country and ruled as a dictator until his death in 1935.

Nazi Germany attacked Poland in September 1939, beginning World War II. Sixteen days later, the Russian army attacked Poland from the east. The Polish army was defeated, and Poland was divided between Nazi Germany and Soviet Russia. More than one-fourth of the Polish people were killed or died as a result of this war.

Many Polish officers were captured, taken to the Katyn Forest in northeast Poland, and executed. Other captured Poles were sent to Russian prison camps in Siberia. Germans built many death camps on Polish soil, and in these, millions of Jews from all over Europe were shot or gassed to death. The Polish government has kept as memorials to these victims such places as Auschwitz and Treblinka.

After the war, the U.S.S.R. retained the eastern part of Poland, but Poland was given land in the west that formerly had belonged to Germany.

In the years following the war, Communists took over Poland. Under Communism, property was owned by the state. The government built factories and controlled the prices of manufactured goods and the amount of wages paid to workers.

Before World War II, more than half of the Polish people had been small farmers. But the new Communist system wanted to change this. The Communists combined small farms into large farms, took over the ownership of the land, and employed the farmers as part of the work force.

In 1956, there were workers' riots. Troops were brought in to control the workers. Top Soviet leaders flew into Warsaw and there was a showdown between the Russian leaders and the Polish party leader Wladyslaw Gomulka. Gomulka insisted that Poland had the right to be sovereign.

As a result of these actions, there were some liberal reforms. Some farms were given back to their owners. The Secret Police was abolished. But in a fairly short time, these reforms were wiped out again, and the country was in economic crisis.

There were more riots in 1970 and again in 1976. In 1978, the Polish archbishop of Cracow became Pope John Paul II. Poles then challenged their rulers, and in August 1980, Lech Walesa became head of a powerful trade union, Solidarity. Solidarity quickly grew to 10 million members and was the first free trade union in the Communist bloc.

In December 1981, after General Wojciech Jaruzelski had grown in power, he declared martial law and banned Solidarity. Many of the union leaders were arrested and charged with treason. Lech Walesa was imprisoned in the country in a hunting lodge.

Both U.S. President Ronald Reagan and Pope John Paul II supported Solidarity with funds. Printing presses, computers, and shortwave radios were smuggled into the country. These were used to help get out the message calling for resistance to Communist control.

Solidarity-led strikes paralyzed Poland in 1988. The government resigned, and Solidarity was legally reinstated. Legal rights were given to the Catholic Church, and the state media monopoly was lifted.

Solidarity made its way onto the ballot in June 1989 and won a huge victory. And in August of that year, the government elected its first non-Communist prime minister since 1948. The new prime minister, Tadeusz Mazowiecki, began moving Poland toward a market economy.

In 1990, Walesa won the presidency. In the years that followed, Poland faced high unemployment, high inflation, and its farms were on the verge of bankruptcy. Many political parties formed as major problems were faced. By 1995, Poland was once again on its way toward prosperity.

Government

The Republic of Poland adopted a Constitution on May 3, 1791, only four years after the United States Constitution. But soon after that, Poland was invaded and its constitution annulled.

Today Poland is a democratic republic working under the agreements developed in 1989 after Solidarity was victorious in the elections. Many aspects of this new democracy still remain to be worked out. A new constitution was drafted but the Sejm, or parliament, rejected proposals for constitutional amendments.

Parliament is made up of two houses. The Sejm has 460 deputies, each elected to a four-year term. The Senate has 100 members. The Senate has the power to veto Sejm decisions. The Sejm could only over-rule the Senate by a two-thirds majority vote.

The president is the head of state and may order parliamentary elections and dissolve the Sejm and Senate. The president is also supreme commander of the armed forces.

The prime minister is nominated by the president and is usually the leader of the political party with the most seats in the Sejm. The Cabinet is presided over by the prime minister.

The Sejm passes bills, adopts a budget, and appoints the 24-member executive council of ministers, or cabinet, which is headed by the prime minister. About twelve political parties currently hold seats in the Sejm. The Senate is the upper chamber of the National Assembly.

The judicial system in Poland is quite different from that of the United States. There is no jury system. Each case is heard by a judge and two "people's assessors." The people's assessors are ordinary people elected to this position by the local councils. The district court handles both civil and criminal cases. Serious cases are sent to county court. The supreme court, which meets in Warsaw, is the chief judicial body.

For the most part, lawyers in Poland are organized into collectives of about twenty lawyers working out of one office and sharing the income of fees fixed by the state. People needing assistance go to the collective office.

Local government is divided into forty-nine provinces *(voivodships)*, which include the three cities of Warsaw, Cracow, and Lodz. They have their own elected people's councils.

Religion

About 90 percent of Poles are Catholic, and attendance at mass is the highest in the world. About 90 percent of the children who are currently being born in Poland continue to be baptized in the Catholic Church.

The Catholic faith in Poland traces back to King Mieszko I, who was publicly baptized in A.D. 966. There are more than 14,000 churches and chapels throughout Poland. Many churches hold three or four services or masses. There are 2,500 convents and more than 500 monasteries. Many serious young students attend the Academy of Catholic Theology in Warsaw or the Catholic University of Lublin.

The holiest Catholic shrine in Poland is the impressive basilica of Jasna Gora, sometimes called the Shining Mountain. This chapel houses an image called The Black Madonna which, according to legend, was painted by St. Luke on a table top of dark cypress wood. Every August, thousands of pilgrims travel to Czestochowa to visit the chapel.

Education

There is virtually no illiteracy in Poland. Over 1 million children begin their education by attending 12,000 nursery schools. Education is compulsory and free for ages seven through fifteen.

High schools can be grammar, art, technical, agricultural, or professional. Students in specialized high schools study such subjects as German, English, biology, chemistry,

and mathematics. School usually begins at 8:00 A.M. and ends sometime between 2:30 P.M. and 4:00 P.M. Students are given a lot of homework.

Poland has about 100 institutions of higher learning including 11 universities. The Jagiellonian University in Cracow was founded in 1364.

Immigrants

Because of changing fortunes and boundaries, Poland finds itself with many minorities within its borders. When borders where changed in 1945, there were 700,000 Ukrainians living in Poland. Some moved to the Ukrainian Socialist Soviet Republic while others moved to western Poland to farm.

In the east of Poland are 170,000 Belorussians who live mostly in the Bialystok area. About 10,000 Lithuanians live in Poland near the border with Lithuania. The German minority in Poland lives mainly in the south and southwest.

During the sixteenth century, many Jews driven out of other parts of Europe were welcomed in Poland. They were encouraged to become shopkeepers and traders. By 1939, there were an estimated 3.5 million Jews in Poland, about 10 percent of the total population.

The Gorale are Polish highlanders who live in the southwest region of Poland known as the Podhale. Most live in small villages, raising sheep and goats and cultivating crops.

In the late nineteenth century, many Poles immigrated to Paris, London, and New York. They formed groups designed to help free Poland.

During World War II, when Germany over-ran Poland, 500,000 Jews from Warsaw and other nearby areas were incarcerated. Other camps were built, and millions of inmates were killed. Some were deported to slave-labor camps.

After World War II, the Soviet Union took over land that was formerly eastern Poland. Poland was given former German territory east of the Oder and Neisse rivers. This involved an enormous movement of people. About 7.5 million Poles moved from east to west while 6 million Germans left the country.

From 1981 to 1990, 97,400 Poles immigrated to the United States. During 1991 to 1995, another 114,300 came.

Language

Polish is a western Slavic language and uses the same alphabet as West European languages, with the exception of one letter and some accent marks. The earliest recorded use of Polish appears in twelfth-century church documents.

Not everyone in Poland speaks Polish as their home language. Some groups such as the Ukrainians and Belorussians are bilingual. There are also many dialects, known as Great Polish, Silesian, Little Polish, and Mazovian.

At different times during history, it was forbidden for the Polish language to be used in schools and offices. During the Communist regime, Russian was taught in all schools from grade five through grade twelve and the Russian language was compulsory in any degree course.

The Arts and Sciences

Poland is famous for various crafts. Many are specialties of particular regions. For example, the mountain folk of the Zakopane region paint on glass, while the village of Zalipie is famous for the flower paintings that decorate wooden houses and wagons. Koniakow is well known for its lacework, and Kielce for its black pottery. Special shops called *cepelia* have been set up to sell authentic crafts to visitors.

Poland has a strong literary tradition. Three Poles are Nobel laureates in literature. Henryk Sienkiewicz won the 1905 prize for his novels and is especially remembered for his religious novel, *Quo Vadis?* Wladyslaw S. Reymont won the prize in 1924 for his novel about the Polish people, *The Peasants.* And the poet Czeslaw Milosz received the prize in 1980. Milosz left Poland during the Communist regime and went to teach Polish literature at the University of California.

Many other well known writers were born in Poland but have been recognized for their writings in other languages. These include Joseph Conrad, Isaac Bashevis Singer, Jerzy Kosinski, Stanislaw Lem, and Tadeusz Konvicki. Uri Shulevitz, a children's author and illustrator, escaped from the Warsaw Ghetto when he was four years old.

Poles have also made a reputation for themselves in theatre and film. There are many large and small repertory theatres throughout the country. A Pole, Piotr Lebiedzinski, made one of the earliest movie cameras in 1893. Films by Andrzej Wajda, such as *Man of Marble* and *Man of Iron,* have won acclaim throughout the world. Roman Polanski lived in Nazi-occupied Poland. He went on to make movies such as *Repulsion* and *Rosemary's Baby.*

Foremost among Polish musicians is Frederic Chopin (1810–1849), who wrote waltzes, etudes, ballads, sonatas, and nocturnes, many of which were based on folk themes. One of the monuments to Chopin is in Lazienki Park in Warsaw. Witold Lutoslawski was a Polish composer born in 1913. He is remembered for his *Cello Concerto* and for *Variations on a Theme of Paganini.* Stanislaw Moniuszko wrote operas about Poland. Henryk Wieniawski made his reputation as a violinist and composer.

Performer Ignace Jan Paderewski was a world famous pianist, and Wanda Landowska was one of the world's finest harpsichordists. Arthur Rubinstein held an international reputation for excellence and was for many years the world's best-loved pianist. He is remembered for his recordings of Brahms, Schumann, and Chopin.

Today there are 17 conservatories of music and over 100 music schools in Poland. And Poles continue to enjoy folk dances such as the polonaise, mazurka, and krakowiak.

Perhaps the most famous of Polish painters is Jacek Malczewski (1854–1929). One of his works, *Sunday in a Mine,* depicts Poles who have been sent to Siberia. Other well-known artists include Jan Matejko and Jozef Simmler.

The most famous student at Jagiellonian University in Cracow was Nicolaus Copernicus (1473–1543), an astronomer who was the first to declare that the earth revolves around the sun.

In Warsaw there is a radium institute and hospital built to honor Marie Sklodowska Curie. This Polish girl who went to France and married Pierre Curie is the only person to have won the Nobel Prize in both physics and chemistry. She was one of the first scientists to investigate radioactivity and the first to recognize that radioactivity is the result of changes in the atoms of an element.

Food

Polish people enjoy their food and are adept at taking simple, inexpensive ingredients and turning them into delicious meals.

The Polish have adapted several Russian dishes, such as *borshch,* and made changes to suit their taste. Polish preserves, such as pickles, are regarded worldwide as outstanding.

Mainstays in the Polish diet are potatoes, cabbages, beets, mushrooms, dairy products, and pork. Favorite dishes include *bigos,* a mixture of sauerkraut and sausage, and *kielbasa,* smoked sausage. Beet soup, *barszca,* is popular, as is *kolduny,* a pastry with a meat filling. Poles also enjoy many delicious fish dishes such as carp, pike, crayfish, cod, and herring.

Poles enjoy eating beef and pork, and the most common meat dish is a fried pork cutlet served in a thick sauce. Polish ham and bacon are exported, as is their vodka, which is made from potatoes and grain.

Other national dishes are *golabki,* cabbage leaves stuffed with minced meat and rice; *bigos,* sauerkraut with spicy meat and mushrooms; *flaki,* tripe served boiled or fried with carrots and onions; and *golonka,* pig's leg with horseradish and pease pudding.

Soup is frequently served and is usually thick and hearty. In soups you might find sauerkraut, potatoes, peas, barley, mushrooms, vegetables, beetroot, or a mixture of all of these. There is also sour rye soup, oat soup, beer soup, and onion soup. In the summer, Poles sometimes serve a cold soup made of pureed strawberries, apple, cherries, blueberries, or raspberries thickened with sour cream. A soup may also contain sour cream dumpling and noodles.

Breads and cakes are very popular, especially rye bread. At home, Poles eat bread with butter or margarine and different kinds of jam. *Sernik,* a cheesecake, is popular, as is sponge cake. A wedding cake is often ring-shaped, and small cakes in the shape of animals are showered on the bridal couple. At baptisms, a cake may be four feet long because of the belief that the good luck of the child depends on the size of the cake. Special cakes called *kolacz* are served at funerals.

Because poppies are abundant in Poland, poppy seeds are used in many different dishes. This dish is traditionally served on Christmas Eve.

Noodles with Poppy Seed
(Kluski z makiem)

1 16-ounce package of shell macaroni, cooked
1 12½ ounce can Solo, poppy seed pastry filling*
4 tablespoons honey
1 cup half-and-half
½ cup golden raisins
1 tablespoon margarine
*This is a thick, sweet mixture made from poppy seeds and corn syrup.

Cook the noodles according to the directions on the package. Combine poppy seed filling, honey, and half-and-half in a mixing bowl and stir until smooth. Stir in raisins.

Melt butter in a double boiler. Add the poppy seed mixture and heat thoroughly. Pour the poppy seed mixture over hot, drained noodles and serve immediately. Serves 10 to 12.

Recreation

Many Poles and visitors make use of the Tatra mountains at Poland's southern boundary. Hikers and campers use the area in the summer, and skiers come in winter.

Swimming, including synchronized swimming, gymnastics, volleyball, basketball, tennis, ice-hockey, and soccer are popular activities. Canoeing is a major sport on the thousands of lakes in northern Poland. Running, including marathon races, is becoming more popular, as is motorcycle racing.

For adults, soccer is the most popular spectator sport. Some boys have soccer practice for an hour after school three times a week. On Saturdays, a street may be closed and goalposts put up for a soccer game.

Poland has three soccer leagues; two are national and the third is provincial. Some teams are sponsored by and named after factories. The season lasts from March to November. Poland won the silver medal in soccer at the 1992 Barcelona Olympic Games.

The Polish are fond of horses, and many Poles enjoy horseback riding. Poland has a long tradition of breeding Arabian horses.

Many people in Poland like to visit spas to rest and get back their energy. Spas are usually located at places where the water is particularly rich in minerals. The biggest spa in Poland is in Ciechocinek, near the center of the country.

Customs and Traditions

The Polish celebrate many harvest festivals. It is common for girls to carry a harvest wreath of corn. After their dance, the girls present the wreath to the farmer, who will start the next year's sowing with seed crumbled from the wreath. One of the biggest festivals held in the country is the Tatra Autumn Festival, which draws people from all over the world.

Another holiday celebrated in the autumn is All Hallows' Eve on October 31. Some people visit cemeteries, light candles, and place food on the graves of their ancestors to celebrate this occasion.

The Tatras are the home of the Gorale mountain people, who still speak their own language and maintain several customs. When a mountain man dies, he is dressed in his white suit and embroidered coat and vest. On top of his coffin is placed the object that was so important to him in life, his mountain axe, or *ciupaga.*

There are many festivities associated with Holy Week. Many Polish families make elaborate preparations for Easter by making beautifully decorated eggs called *pisanki.* The eggs are dipped in bright dyes and have different designs.

On Palm Sunday, many towns hold processions. The "palms" may be decorated with flowers, ribbons, and colored paper. Some communities celebrate Maundy Thursday by hanging a stuffed figure and then burning it or throwing it in the river for good luck. Some families choose to fast on Good Friday. On the Saturday before Easter, it is customary for families to take their bread, salt, sugar, and decorated eggs to be blessed in the church. Sometimes the village priest visits families and blesses the Easter table.

On Easter Sunday after the church service, families gather for the holiday meal. The blessed egg is cut and shared with family and guests. Then the meal continues with ham, sausages, salads, *babka* (the Polish national cake), and perhaps a sweet cake such as *mazurki,* which is filled with nuts, fruit, and honey. Cakes are often decorated with the Paschal Lamb. Polish people do not cook on Easter, so the food that is prepared earlier, called *hallow-fare,* must last the whole day.

On Easter Monday, people wear old clothing if they are going to participate in *smigus-dyngus,* which is a water-throwing game. Boys and girls try to drench each other with water.

Jewish people in Poland celebrate Chanukah, the eight-day holiday that begins on day 25 of the Hebrew Month of Kislev (November–December) celebrating the victory of a small band of fighters over a king's huge army in their struggle for religious freedom. It also celebrates the jar of pure oil that miraculously burned not for just one day but for eight days in the ancient Temple in Jerusalem. They enjoy foods prepared in oil, playing games of *dreidel* (a four-sided spinning top), and exchanging gifts.

Christmas time in Poland is called *Boze Narodzenie.* The celebration begins on Christmas Eve and continues until January 6. Just as many American Christian families create a Nativity scene to display in a window or place under a tree, so do young people in Poland. They assemble in a box a *szopka,* which is a small stable with figures of the baby Jesus, Mary, and Joseph along with donkeys, lambs, shepherds, and the Three Kings.

The Christmas Eve supper is called *Wilia.* The celebration begins as soon as the first star is seen. The family places straw under the table to represent the manger. In the center of the table, they place a bundle of hay. One empty place is left for a stranger to join them.

The Christmas Eve supper begins with a special ceremony. The oldest member of the family, or the head of the household, takes a small bite from a rice wafer and passes it to the next oldest until it reaches the youngest child. The ceremony is to grant the wishes of each family member for the coming year. The Christmas tree is lighted for the first time that evening and family members exchange gifts.

There are ten special days that are celebrated and that the Polish Catholics call High Days: Christmas, the Circumcision, the Epiphany, the Ascension, Corpus Christi, the Assumption, Saints Peter and Paul Day, All Saints' Day, the Immaculate Conception, and St. Joseph's Day.

Official public holidays in Poland are New Year's Day on January 1, Good Friday in March or April, Worker's Day on May 1, Constitution Day on May 3, Corpus Christi in May or June, All Saints Day on November 1, National Independence Day on November 11, and Christmas on December 25 and 26.

Families hold "birthday" celebrations on Name Days or the feast day of the saint after whom one is named. Mother's

Day is also an occasion for special recognition and is often celebrated with a play or special performance at school.

Suggested Activities

Writing

1. One of the exciting leaders in Poland was Lech Walesa. A small group of students might want to read from a variety of sources about this man, write a paper explaining his main contributions to Poland, and share it with the class. The paper should contain a bibliography of sources of information. One source might be *Lech Walesa* by Ann Angel and Mary Craig (Gareth Stevens, 1992.) The Web will provide more information, including the site at http://cgi.pathfinder.com/time/time100/leaders/profile/walesa.3.html.

Reading

2. A small group of students might form a book discussion group. A possible book for this unit of study is *The Silver Sword* by Ian Serraillier (S. G. Phillips, 1959).

    This book tells the story of a Polish family. The Balicki children are separated from their parents during World War II in Warsaw, but with hope and courage, they achieve the almost impossible.

Vocabulary

3. As students study the history of Poland, they will add a number of new words to their vocabulary. A bulletin board might be set aside for vocabulary building. As students come across words in their reading, they can write the word and its definition on a 3 x 5-inch card and add the cards to the bulletin board display. Here are some possibilities: Aryans, bloc, cold war, détente, holocaust, manifesto, Marxist, Nazi, partisan, regime, and Reich.

Math

4. Before World War II, 60 percent of the people of Poland worked on farms, and farm products were the most important part of the country's economy. After the war, Poland became industrialized and many people moved from the country to the city. Have a pair of students research and prepare a pie graph showing the percentage of people in Poland currently involved in different occupations. Post the graph in the classroom.

Social Studies

5. Lech Walesa won the Nobel Peace Prize in 1983. A group of students may want to research and find out more about this prize and report what they learn to the class. When and how did the prize originate? Who are some of the people throughout history who have won this prize?

Geography

6. Since Poland disappeared from maps of the world for over 100 years, it would be interesting if students could find (and with permission, photocopy) maps showing Poland in Europe today and a map showing Europe without Poland at the close of the eighteenth century. Both maps should be brought in and shared with the class.

Music

7. With the help of the school music educator, try to locate and play for students music from Poland's southeastern Tatra Mountains. One source is *Fire in the Mountains: Polish Mountain Fiddle Music, Volume 1—The Karol Stoch Band Classic Recording from 1928–1929*. This is available as a CD, Order # YAZ-7012 from Multicultural Media, RR3, Box 6655, Granger Road, Barre, Vermont 05641. You may also visit their Internet site at http://www.worldmusicstore.com.

Art

8. A white eagle is a part of Poland's national coat-of-arms. With the help of a media specialist, have two children research this coat-of-arms and draw it to share with the class. They should explain to the class the meaning of the various symbols.

Drama/Movement

9. There are many legends associated with Poland. For example, the mythical ruler Krak, who founded Krakow, killed the dragon of Wawel Hill that had terrorized the

people. With the help of a media specialist, have students locate and read a version of this legend and then rehearse acting it out for the class using simple props and costumes.

Dress

10. The Gorale of the Tatra mountains wear costumes at their religious festivals. Women wear lace-trimmed aprons over colorful skirts. They wear embroidered tops and black, gold-trimmed caps. The men wear white felt pants, sashes, and black-brimmed hats. With the help of a media specialist, invite a pair of students to find pictures of the Gorale people and to bring these to share with their class.

Cooking

11. With adult supervision and help, students might enjoy making poppy seed cookies to share with the class. These cookies are a favorite holiday treat in Poland. The following recipe yields 30 cookies.

Poppy Seed Cookies

1 cup poppy seeds
$1/2$ cup scalded milk, cooled to room temperature
$1/2$ cup butter
1 $1/2$ cups flour
$1/8$ teaspoon salt
$1/2$ teaspoon cinnamon
1 cup seedless raisins

Preheat the oven to 350°F. Grease a cookie sheet. Pour the cooled, scalded milk into a bowl. Add the poppy seeds and allow them to soak in the milk for 30 minutes.

In a large mixing bowl, mix the butter and sugar together until they are creamy. Continue to mix constantly while adding the flour, salt, cinnamon, raisins, and finally the milk with the poppy seeds. Mix until well blended.

Drop tablespoonfuls of dough onto cookie sheet, about 1 $1/2$ inches apart. Bake in the oven until lightly browned, about 20 minutes.

Culminating Activity

12. Members of the class might divide themselves into about four groups to study famous people born in Poland.

Possible candidates for study are: Marie Curie, Frederic Chopin, Joseph Conrad, Nicolaus Copernicus, Tadeusz Kosciuszko, Helena Modjeska, Ignace Jan Paderewski, and Pope John Paul II. Each group should study and learn as much as possible about the person they select and that person's contributions to the world. Then the group should decide how to present their information to the rest of the class. A day should be set aside to allow the study groups to make their presentations.

Suggested Reading

Angel, Ann and Mary Craig. *Lech Walesa: Champion of Freedom for Poland.* Milwaukee, Wisc.: Gareth Stevens, 1992.

Borski, Lucia Merecka and Kate B. Miller. *The Jolly Tailor and Other Fairy Tales Translated from the Polish.* New York: Longman's, Green, 1928.

Conner, Edwina. *Marie Curie.* New York: Bookwright Press, 1987.

Dobler, Lavinia. *Customs and Holidays Around the World.* New York: Fleet Press, 1962.

Donica, Ewa and Tim Sharman. *We Live in Poland.* New York: Bookwright Press, 1985.

Eisner, Heather, ed. *Bon Appetit Country Cooking.* Los Angeles, Calif.: Knapp Press, 1978.

Grady, Sean M. *The Importance of Marie Curie.* San Diego, Calif.: Lucent Books, 1992.

Greene, Carol. *Poland.* Chicago, Ill.: Childrens Press, 1983.

Haviland, Virginia. *Favorite Fairy Tales Told in Poland.* Boston, Mass.: Little, Brown, 1963.

Heale, Jay. *Poland.* New York: Marshall Cavendish, 1994.

Landau, Elaine. *The Warsaw Ghetto Uprising.* New York: New Discovery Books, 1992.

Lye, Keith and Henry Pluckrose. *Take a Trip to Poland.* New York: Franklin Watts, 1984.

Spiegelman, Judith. *UNICEF'S Festival Book.* New York: United States Committee for UNICEF, 1966.

Stewart, Gail B. *Poland, Places in the News.* New York: Crestwood House, 1990.

Worth, Richard. *Poland, The Threat to National Renewal.* New York: Franklin Watts, 1982.

Russia

A Legend from Russia

Among the versions of the Russian folk tale about Vasilissa and Baba Yaga is the one retold by Barbara Cohen in *Lovely Vassilisa,* with illustrations by Anatoly Ivanov. Another, "Fair Vasilissa and Baba Yaga," is retold by Charles Downing in *Russian Tales and Legends.* And in *Russian Folk Tales,* translated by Robert Chandler and illustrated by Ivan I. Bilibin, this story appears as "Vasilisa the Beautiful."

Vasilissa and Baba Yaga

A merchant and his wife had a beautiful little daughter named Vasilissa. When Vasilissa was only eight, her mother became ill, and the doctors could not cure her.

Her mother called Vasilissa to her. "It is time for me to give you a gift and my blessing," she said. Her mother handed Vasilissa a doll. "When you are in trouble, this doll will help you. Put some food in front of it and say, 'Eat, eat. Eat, my sweet.' After the doll has eaten, tell it your troubles, and it will help you."

Vasilissa took the little doll and put it in her pocket.

"God bless you, little one," her mother said. She kissed Vasilissa and then died.

Some months later the merchant married a widow with two daughters. The merchant thought his new wife would soon love and care for Vasilissa like her own children. But he was wrong. The stepmother did not like Vasilissa who was kind and beautiful and a marvelous spinner. Her own daughters were spiteful, plain, and clumsy. Vasilissa had to do all the work around the house.

When Vasilissa's father was away on business, her stepmother would be especially cruel to Vasilissa. When it got too difficult, Vasilissa would lock herself in the pantry, put her doll in front of her and say, "Eat, eat. Eat, my sweet." The doll would eat. Then Vasilissa would tell the doll her troubles, and the doll would say, "There, there, my dear. Do not fear."

The next day her stepmother and stepsisters would sleep late. When they awakened, they would find the house neat and tidy and Vasilissa sitting beneath a tree in the garden. They never suspected that the doll had done all the work.

When she was full grown, many young men came to court lovely Vasilissa and no one ever called on the stepsisters. This made Vasilissa's stepmother so angry that she decided to get rid of Vasilissa once and for all.

When her husband was away on a long trip, the stepmother closed up the house and moved with the three girls to a cottage in the forest. The stepmother knew that Baba Yaga, a terrible witch, lived in the forest and ate tender young people.

The first night at the cottage, the stepmother said, "I am going to bed. Before you sleep, you each have

The stepmother knew that Baba Yaga, a terrible witch, lived in the
forest and ate tender young people.

work to do. Eldest daughter, you must tat some lace. Youngest daughter, you must knit some stockings. Lazy Vasilissa, you must spin some yarn."

With that, she put out all the lamps and went to bed, leaving only a candle for light in a corner where the three girls were working. A few minutes later, the oldest daughter snuffed out the candle pretending it was an accident.

"We need light and must finish our tasks before we sleep or mother will be angry," she said. "My sister, go and get a special light from Baba Yaga, one that will not easily go out."

"No," said her sister. "Vasilissa must go, and she must not come back until Baba Yaga has given her a light."

The two sisters pushed Vasilissa out the door into the darkness.

Vasilissa pulled her doll out of her pocket and set it in front of her. She put a bit of bread in front of the doll and said, "Eat, eat. Eat, my sweet."

After the doll had eaten, Vasilissa cried, "Oh, little doll, I am afraid that Baba Yaga will eat me."

"There, there, my dear. Do not fear," the doll said.

Vasilissa set out through the forest. She walked for hours. Just as dawn was breaking, a horseman dressed in white riding a white steed galloped past. Vasilissa kept walking. As the sun rose high in the sky, a horseman dressed all in red and riding a red steed came galloping by. Vasilissa kept walking. As the shadows of evening began to envelop her, Vasilissa arrived at the hut of Baba Yaga. A fence made of skeletons surrounded the hut. Just then a third horseman, dressed in black and riding a black steed, galloped by.

At that moment, Baba Yaga came out of the forest. She sniffed the air. "I smell the meat of a Russian," she said.

Trembling with fear, Vasilissa bowed and said, "It is I, Grandma. I have come to ask for a special light."

Baba Yaga looked at her. Then she led the way into the hut. "We'll see what you can do to earn such a gift," she said. Baba Yaga sat at a table. "Bring me some food," she commanded.

Vasilissa went to the cupboard, which was filled with good things and quickly made a rich soup for Baba Yaga which she served with slices of bread.

Baba Yaga ate quickly, leaving one-half bowl of soup and a half a slice of bread for Vasilissa.

"I must leave early in the morning," Baba Yaga said. "You may spend the night and in the morning clean my house and yard and cook my food. Then go to the shed and take the sack of millet. Pick out all the grains that have turned black before I come home. You must do this just right or I will have you for my dinner."

Baba Yaga dropped off to sleep. Vasilissa set the doll in front of her and put a piece of her bread in front of the doll. "Eat, eat. Eat, my sweet," she said.

After the doll had eaten, Vasilissa said, "Oh, my dear doll, if you do not help me, Baba Yaga will eat me."

"There, there, my dear. Do not fear," said the doll.

The next morning, Vasilissa watched the witch leave. Her doll did all the work while she fixed a stew for supper.

When Baba Yaga arrived, she checked the millet, the yard, and the house. Then she said, "Servants! Grind my millet." Three pair of hands, one pair white, one pair red, and one pair black, came out of nowhere, snatched the millet, and carried it off to grind it fine. Baba Yaga ate her dinner.

Before she went to sleep, Baba Yaga said, "Tomorrow you must clean my house and yard and then go to the shed and dust each poppy seed you find there in the sack. Have a good meal waiting for me. If you do not do everything just right, I will have you for my dinner."

As soon as Baba Yaga was asleep, Vasilissa put a bit of bread in front of her doll and said, "Eat, eat. Eat, my sweet."

After the doll had eaten, Vasilissa said, "Oh, my darling doll. If you do not help me, Baba Yaga will eat me."

"There, there, my dear. Do not fear," said the doll.

The next day, Baba Yaga left early and the doll quickly set to work. All Vasilissa had to do was cook dinner.

When Baba Yaga got home, she inspected the house, the yard, and the poppy seeds. Then she cried, "Come, my servants, and squeeze the oil out of my poppy seeds." As before, three pairs of hands appeared and carried off the seeds.

Baba Yaga sat down to dinner.

As she ate, Vasilissa said, "I have a question, Grandmother."

"He who knows too much grows old too soon," Baba Yaga said.

But Vasilissa continued. "I saw a horseman on a white steed. Who is he?"

"Early Dawn," said Baba Yaga.

"And I saw a horseman all in red," Vasilissa went on. "Who is he?"

"Bright Day."

"I saw a third horseman all in black," Vasilissa said. "Who is he?"

"Black Night," said the witch. "They are my three faithful servants. Do you have any more questions?"

Vasilissa smiled. "He who knows too much grows old too soon," she said.

"Good girl," the witch said. "Now I have a question for you. How did you get all of your work done so quickly?"

"I had help from my mother's blessing," Vasilissa answered.

Baba Yaga looked startled. "You must go," she said. "You do not belong here."

Baba Yaga took a skull with glowing eyes from the fence and gave it to Vasilissa. "This light will show you the way home."

Carrying the skull for a light, Vasilissa walked through the woods until she reached her stepmother's house. She went inside.

Light from the skull's eye sockets shone on the stepmother and her two daughters. They screamed and ran, but the skull's light followed them. Soon they were burned to a small heap of ashes on the floor. Then the light in the skull went out.

Vasilissa buried the skull near the cottage and returned to her village. A kind old woman took her in. The months passed, and Vasilissa passed the time spinning wonderfully fine thread.

One night she fed her doll and said, "Eat, eat. Eat, my sweet." After the doll had eaten, Vasilissa said, "Show me how I can spin my thread into cloth."

"There, there, my dear. Do not fear," said the doll. "Get me reeds from the river bank and hair from the horse's mane. I will make you the kind of loom you need."

The next day, Vasilissa used the new loom to weave her thread into delicate cloth. She gave the cloth to the old woman who had taken her in.

"Here you are, grandmother," Vasilissa said. "You have been kind to me. Sell this at market and keep whatever money you get for it. It will be a small payment for your kindness."

Instead of going to market, the old woman took the cloth to the palace of the young Tsar and walked back and forth beneath his window until he noticed her.

"What are you doing there?" the Tsar called out. And he sent a servant to fetch her.

She bowed and handed him the piece of beautiful cloth.

The Tsar felt the cloth and said, "I must have this. What do you want for it?"

"It is beyond price," said the old woman. "It is a gift."

The Tsar gave the old woman presents and sent her home.

The Tsar gave the cloth to his tailors to make into shirts for him. They cut the cloth, but it was so fine they could not stitch it. So the Tsar sent for the old woman. "Only the one who made this cloth can stitch it," the Tsar said. "Take it home and make it into shirts for me."

The old woman took it home and told Vasilissa her story. Vasilissa set to work and made a dozen fine shirts from the cloth. The old woman took the shirts to the Tsar.

Then a servant came back and asked Vasilissa to come with him. "The Tsar wants to thank the person who has made him such a fine gift," the servant said.

At the palace, Vasilissa walked slowly to the throne room and bowed low before the Tsar.

The moment the Tsar saw her, he fell in love. They were married the very next day. The kind old woman came to live in the palace. When Vasilissa's father returned, he was overjoyed to learn what had happened, and he came to live in the palace, too.

Vasilissa was very happy. And she always carried her beloved doll in her pocket though she never again needed to call on its magic.

Background Information

The Union of Soviet Socialist Republics, or the USSR, existed from 1917 to 1991. The Soviet Union was made up of fifteen republics, and The Federation of Russia was the largest one of these. The others were: the Ukraine, Moldova, Belarus, Lithuania, Latvia, Estonia, Azerbaijan, Armenia, Georgia, Kazakhstan, Kyrgyzstan, Turkmenistan, Uzbekistan, and Tajikistan.

After the break-up of the USSR in 1991, the Russian Federation, became a separate country. Twelve of the original fifteen USSR republics (all except the three Baltic states of Estonia, Latvia, and Lithuania) keep in contact through an organization called the Commonwealth of Independent States (CIS) with headquarters in Minsk.

The Russian Federation, or Russia, as it is usually called, is the largest country in the world, with an area of 6,592,800 square miles. Russia consists of eighty-nine parts: 21 republics, 6 territories, 49 provinces, 10 autonomous areas, 1 autonomous Jewish region of Birobijan in the far southeast, and 2 cities with federal status (Moscow and St. Petersburg).

Russia lies in both Asia and Europe. The line dividing the two parts of Russia (European Russia and Asian Russia) follows the Ural Mountains and the Volga River.

There are 147,987,101 Russians and more than 10 million of these live in Moscow, the capital, which is the world's eleventh largest city. Russia's largest coastline is on the Arctic sea, which is impassable most of the year because of ice. An exception is the port of Murmansk, warmed by the North Atlantic Drift of the Gulf Stream, which is open year around. Along the Pacific Coast, the most important port is Vladivostok, but it is often unusable due to fog and ice. St. Petersburg, on the river Neva, is the port closest to population centers, but it is open only from May to October.

Russia is mainly lowland fringed with mountains. In the east is the Great Russian Lowland, which is separated from the West Siberian Plain by the Ural Mountains, the major north-south mountain range. The Caucasus Mountains run between the Black and Caspian Seas. They contain Mount Elbrus, the highest peak in Europe, at 18,511 feet high.

The Trans-Siberian Express train takes more than a week to cross Russia. The railway line, the longest in the world, is more than 5,750 miles long.

The Arctic north of Russia has long winters and extreme cold. The few people who live in Arctic Russia survive by herding reindeer, hunting, and fishing. Far northern Siberia has ice and snow for ten months of the year. The northeastern part of this region contains rich mineral deposits.

A coniferous forest region, the *taiga*, stretches across Russia covering about one-half of the nation's land. This area has about one-third of the world's forestlands, including spruce, pine, birch, and aspen. Further south is the steppe zone, with a milder climate and fertile soil.

Russia has many lakes and rivers. Ladoga, near St. Petersburg, is the biggest lake in Europe. Lake Baikal is the world's largest freshwater basin. Russia's rivers provide water links across the land and are also used for hydroelectric power. The most important rivers in European Russia are the Pechora, Dvina, Neva, Neman, Dnieper, Don, and Volga. The Volga is Europe's longest river. The major rivers in Asian Russia are the Amur, Yenisei, Lena, and the Ob-Irtysh system.

Russia has some of the world's richest reserves of minerals. There are huge fields of coal, oil, and natural gas. Much of Russia's oil and natural gas is exported to Western Europe and is used to pay for food imports. In the Ural mountains there are deposits of iron ore, copper, gold, and precious stones. Russia also has deposits of bauxite, nickel, lead, zinc,

magnesium, silver, and platinum and has vast forests and fishing grounds.

Cattle are raised in European Russia and in southwest Siberia. The southern steppes produce wheat, barley, and maize.

About 82 percent of the population of Russia consists of ethnic Russians. These people are sometimes called Great Russians. The remaining 18 percent include about forty different nationalities.

Russia has many important cities, but chief among these is Moscow. In the heart of Moscow is the Kremlin, a large triangle enclosed by a brick wall. The Kremlin began as a wooden fortress in 1156. There are cathedrals and palaces that have been converted to government buildings, a theatre, and a museum. Many of Russia's most valuable artistic and historical treasures are kept here. The tallest structure in the Kremlin is the Great Bell Tower. Outside the Kremlin is Red Square. At the south end of Red Square is St. Basil's Cathedral, built by Ivan the Terrible.

Another major Russian city is St. Petersburg, with approximately 5 million people. It was known as Leningrad from 1924 to 1991. It is the most westerly Russian city and is a rather young city that began in 1703.

Vladivostok is the biggest city on the Pacific coast of Russia. It is a port on the Sea of Japan and is a base for the Russian navy. About 600,000 people live in this city.

History

The first people to live in Russia were probably Stone Age hunters who moved from Asia toward the Baltic Sea. The southern steppes of Russia were home to the Scythians about 2,500 years ago.

By the eighth century A.D. Slavic tribes had founded trading towns on the European Russian plains.

Kievan Rus carried on trade with Byzantium, the Eastern Roman Empire with its capital in Constantinople. Prince Vladimir of Kiev was converted to Christianity in A.D. 988. Kievan Rus flourished for several centuries before being invaded by the Mongols, or Tatars.

Coming from Asia, the Tatars sacked Kiev in A.D. 1240 and pushed westward. They set up headquarters in Russia on the lower Volga River and ruled Russia for almost 250 years.

The Grand Duke Ivan III ascended the throne in 1462 and brought all the principalities under Moscow's rule, overcoming the Tatars. By then, the Turks had overrun Byzantium. Ivan married the niece of the last emperor and declared himself heir to the Byzantine Empire. He called himself Tsar, or emperor.

During the sixteenth-century A.D., Russia continued to expand. The new Tsar governed much as the Tatars had. Ivan IV came to the throne in 1533, and Boris Godunov seized the throne in 1598. There were invasions by Swedes and Poles and a peasant revolt.

In 1613, an assembly of noblemen and townspeople elected Michael Romanov as the Tsar. The Romanov family governed Russia for the next 300 years. Order was gradually restored and outlying areas were brought back under Moscow's control.

Tsar Peter I (Peter the Great) ruled from 1682 to 1725 and made Russia a major European power. He founded St. Petersburg and made it the capital. In 1762, after Tsar Peter III was murdered, his wife, Catherine the Great, reigned 1762–1796. Under her rule, Russia's borders extended

Napoleon invaded Russia in 1812. The country came together under the leadership of Alexander I. During the second half of the eighteenth century, Russian nobility lived well but the peasants who made up 94 percent of the population were very poor.

Serfdom was abolished after the country's defeat in the Crimean War in 1856. Alexander II became Tsar in 1855 and set the serfs free in 1861. Alexander II was assassinated in 1881 and was followed by Alexander III, who ruled until 1894. Nicholas II followed him and ruled until the Bolshevik Revolution of 1917.

Toward the end of World War I, the Tsarist government collapsed. Lenin returned from exile in Switzerland in 1917 and seized power. A new government was formed with Lenin as chairman of a cabinet called the Soviet of People's Commissars.

There was opposition to the Bolsheviks, and White Armies fought the Communist Red Army in a civil war that lasted nearly three years. The Bolsheviks won and implemented a new economic policy in 1921.

Providing enough food for the Russian people was hard both under the Tsars and under the new government. Although it is large, Russia has little fertile soil. In some places there is not enough rainfall or the growing season is too short for good farming.

The Union of Soviet Socialist Republics was established on December 30, 1922. It consisted of Russia and fourteen other republics: Armenia, Azerbaijan, Belarus, Estonia, Georgia, Kazakhstan, Kyrgyzstan, Latvia, Lithuania, Moldova, Tajikistan, Turkmenistan, Ukraine, and Uzbekistan.

Lenin died in 1924, and Joseph Stalin took control and launched an economic and social revolution in 1928. The emphasis was on developing industry. Peasants were forced to work on collective farms. Those who objected were purged. Hundreds of thousands of Russians were arrested and executed or sent to prison camps in Siberia.

In June 1941, Germany attacked Russia, and the Soviet Union was involved in World War II. This brought about an alliance with the Western powers, but after the war, the alliance broke down.

The Stalin era came to an end with his death in 1953. Nikita Khrushchev next led the country, and then was succeeded by Leonid Brezhnev in 1964. Khrushchev began to de-Stalinize Russia. Pictures and statues of Stalin were removed. During this time, Russians began to question the advantages of socialism compared to capitalism.

Although new laws made it possible for individuals to start their own enterprises, they often failed. Some foreign companies began investing, such as McDonald's, which introduced restaurants in Moscow in 1988, but shortages of goods and wage inflation continued.

Mikhail Gorbachev was chosen as General Secretary of the Communist Party in 1985 and began to push for reforms. He tried to loosen ideological controls and to restructure Russia's economics. But he appeared to be more popular abroad than he was at home. Then Boris Yeltsin became Russia's leader. He decided to step down and opened the country to new leadership in 2000.

In August 1991, the new Russian Parliament voted to dissolve the Soviet Union and to disband the Communist party. The Soviet Union was formally dissolved on December 25, 1991, and was replaced by the Russian Federation.

The Commonwealth of Independent States is an economic union formed in December 1991, in which each state or republic has its own government. In 1992, Boris Yeltsin began to introduce changes in Russia. About 10 percent of state farmland was turned over to private farmers, but a shortage of food and consumer goods continues.

Government

Russia is now a federation of eighty-nine regions and ethnic republics. In a treaty signed by local leaders and Boris Yeltsin in March 1992, the local governments received political and economic autonomy but pledged to remain a single state. Two republics, Checken-Ingushetia in the Caucasus and Tatarstan in Central Asia, did not sign the treaty. In a referendum held on December 12, 1993, the Russians voted to make Russia a democratic republic.

The main legislative body of the Russian Federation is a two-chamber Federal Assembly. A new constitution was approved in 1993, and Boris Yeltsin was elected president in that same year.

The president is head of state and commander of the armed forces and has similar duties to the president of the United States. The president can issue decrees on a number of subjects. The president's office is in the Kremlin.

The Federal Assembly (parliament) is made up of the Federation Council (the upper house), and the State Duma (the lower house). The Federation Council has 178 nominated members, 2 representatives from each of the eighty-nine parts of Russia. The members do not have a fixed term of office but continue as long as they are reelected as leaders in the regions. The State Duma has 450 members. Half are elected from the party lists, while the other half are elected by the regions. These two houses replace the former Supreme Soviet and are the highest representative and legislative body of the country.

In each of Russia's eighty-nine regions, there is a presidential representative. This allows the president to keep in touch with all sections of Russia. Each republic or region has its own court. The highest court, located in Moscow, is the Constitutional Court of the Federation.

Religion

Christianity was introduced in Russia in the tenth century. Following an East-West schism in 1054, Christianity was divided into the Orthodox and the Catholic denominations.

The Greek Orthodox Church and later the Russian Orthodox Church became firmly established in Russia.

The Bolsheviks disestablished the Orthodox Church. The Communist party considered religious belief to be unnecessary. During the Lenin era, many churches were destroyed, boarded up, or used for grain storage.

Since the late 1980s, the government has shown an increased tolerance for religious beliefs and actions. By 1992, 3,000 churches had been reopened.

The Russian Orthodox Church is headed by the Patriarch of all Russia and does not recognize the Pope, but this church is more similar to Catholicism than to Protestantism.

Catholicism has a small following in Russia, chiefly among Poles and Lithuanians. There are also a number of small Protestant groups that include Seventh Day Adventists and Jehovah's Witnesses. The Armenian Church, which is Christian and is a branch of the Gregorian Church, also has a small number of followers.

The Islamic religion has the second largest number of followers in Russia. Many of its adherents live in the Volga region. Also belonging to this group are people of the Northern Caucasus, including Tatars, Bashkirs, Chechens, Ingushes, and Dagestanis.

Buddhism is the third major world religion found in Russia. Most of these Buddhists live in Buryat, Kalmyk, and Tuva. They practice a form of Lamaism.

Education

Before the 1917 Bolshevik revolution, 75 percent of the Russian people could not read or write. After the revolution, schooling became available to everyone. Education became compulsory for children between seven and seventeen years of age.

Following the break-up of the Soviet Union and the establishment of the Russian Federation, education has been in some confusion. Money is scarce and the financing of schools is uncertain. But education is still compulsory and is provided by the state.

Schooling begins now at the preschool level when children are five years old. They learn to read, write, and count as well as play games. Students go to primary schools until they are ten, and then they go on to secondary schools. Most children attend school six days a week, from 8:30 A.M. to 2:30 P.M., Monday through Saturday, from September to May. Students study Russian, mathematics, geography, history, social studies, and a foreign language. English is the most popular foreign language.

There are three types of secondary schools. Most pupils attend general secondary schools. Gifted students are selected for special secondary schools, where they receive extra instruction in art, music, languages, or electronics. Vocational secondary schools concentrate on mathematics, chemistry, or physics.

Higher education, which begins at age eighteen and continues for five or six years, is state funded and is open to those who attain appropriate grades. In the 1900s, about 5 million students attended Russia's 519 higher education establishments and 2,600 technical colleges.

Immigrants

There are more than one hundred nationalities living in Russia, of which 80 percent are Russian. Other large groups include: Tatars, Ukrainians, Chuvashes, Bashkirs, Belorussions, Mordvinians, Chechens, Germans, Udmurts, Maris, Kazakhs, and Avars.

Russia also has populations of Gypsies and Jews. Many Russian Jews came to America in the 1880s. By 1914, one-third of all the Jews in Russia and eastern Europe immigrated, most to the United States. More recently, with the creation of an independent Jewish homeland, many Russian Jews immigrated to Israel.

From 1981 to 1991, 84,000 immigrants came to the United States from the Soviet Union. During 1991 to 1995, another 277,100 came.

Language

The Russians use the Cyrillic alphabet, which has thirty-one letters and two special signs. This alphabet, which is over 1,100 years old, is used to form all Russian words. It is believed that a Greek Christian, St. Cyril, first wrote down this script. Under Tsar Peter I, a civilian script, which was simpler, was introduced and is still used today.

Russian belongs to the Slavic group of languages. This group includes Polish and Czech. It is spoken by at least 25 million people.

People in Russia also speak languages that belong to other groups such as Turkic, Finno-Urgic, and Iranian. People in the Urals and Volga regions speak languages that are similar to Hungarian and Finnish.

The Arts and Sciences

Russia has a strong literary tradition. In the nineteenth century, Aleksandr Pushkin (1799–1837) emerged as a national poet. His most popular work is the novel-in-verse *Eugene Onegin*. Tchaikovsky made this into an opera.

In the early 1800s, Nikolai Gogol wrote important prose works such as *Dead Souls* and the play, *The Inspector General*.

The prose writers of the second half of the century who stand out are Turgenev, Dostoyevsky, Tolstoi, and Chekhov. One of Ivan Turgenev's greatest works was *Father and Sons*. The most famous novels of Fyodor Dostoyevsky are *Crime and Punishment, The Idiot,* and *The Brothers Karamazov,* all of which are psychological studies. Count Leo Tolstoi's two most famous works are *War and Peace* and *Anna Karenina*. And three of the best known plays of Chekhov are *Uncle Vanya, The Three Sisters,* and *The Cherry Orchard*.

Also during the nineteenth century, Russian music came into its own with the works of Mikhail Glinka, Nikolay Rimsky-Korsakov, Alexander Borodin, and Modest Mussorgsky. Arguably Russia's greatest composer is Peter Tchaikovsky, whose compositions became popular throughout the world.

In the twentieth century great Russian musicians include Alexander Skriabin, Sergei Rachmaninoff, and Igor Stravinsky.

After the death of Stalin, some writers published works through underground publishing houses. In 1957 Boris Pasternak's novel, *Doctor Zhivago,* appeared in the West and the following year won the Nobel Prize in Literature, but Pasternak was forced to decline the award.

In 1970, Aleksandr Solzhenitsyn was awarded the Nobel Prize in Literature, but he was denounced by the

Soviet press and was forced to emigrate. He did not return to Moscow until the summer of 1994.

Russians have also contributed to the ballet. Many cities have their own ballet companies. The most famous are the Bolshoi Theater in Moscow and the Maryinsky (formerly Kirov) in St. Petersburg.

A modern movement in ballet was started at the beginning of this century by Sergei Diaghilev. He founded the Ballets Russes, featuring the legendary dancers Vaslav Nijinsky and Anna Pavlova. Diaghilev's company performed Stravinsky's *The Firebird* in Paris in 1910.

Some of the oldest Russian paintings are called icons, which were religious pictures painted on wooden panels. It was customary for the painter to pray before beginning to paint.

During the eighteenth century, European portrait-style painting developed in Russia. Argunov and then Venetsianov painted the faces of peasant people. Alexander Ivanov took a quarter of a century to complete his canvas, "Christ Appears to the People."

In the early 1860s a group of artists led by Ivan Kramskoi formed a commune of free artists and explored realism. Most famous of the group was Vasily Perov.

Perhaps the most famous Russian artist of the twentieth century is Marc Chagall (1887–1985), who left Russia because of difficulties with the Communists and spent much of his time in exile in France.

Russia had a strong pre-Revolutionary tradition in science. Major figures include Dmitri Mendeleev in chemistry, Ivan Pavlov in physiology, and Konstantin Tsiolkovsky in the theory of rocket motion. In October 1957, the Soviet Union launched the world's first earth satellite, *Sputnik 1*. In 1961, they launched the first manned satellite carrying an astronaut.

Food

Although each region of Russia features special dishes, some traditional foods are eaten throughout the country. *Borsch* is a soup made from beetroots, cooked in stock, and served hot or chilled. Beef stroganoff is made with thin strips of steak, cooked with mushrooms, onions, black pepper, and sour cream. *Blinis* are little pancakes that are made from buckwheat flour.

Black bread and a cereal called *kasha* are both basic in the Russian diet. Russian meals often feature hearty soups and stews containing cabbage, potatoes, meat, and fish.

A great delicacy served in Russia is caviar. This is fish *roe*, or eggs. The most expensive caviar comes from Beluga sturgeon. Since Russia has many rivers and lakes, many freshwater fish are cooked and served.

Tea is often served from a *samovar*. Traditional samovars are heated by burning charcoal, but modern ones use electricity. A china teapot may be kept warm by placing it on top of the samovar.

Some Russians drink vodka, a strong, clear, alcoholic spirit. Originally it was made from wheat, but vodka is now made from other grains and potatoes. Another favorite drink is *kvas,* a weak, fermented drink made from black bread and honey.

Recently food stalls and cafes have started to appear along the streets and parks to sell "fast foods." They sell coffee and hot meat snacks such as *shashlik* or *kebab*.

Pirozhki, a meat-filled pastry, is a favorite meal. The following recipe makes 12 to 18 pirozhki.

Pirozhki
Filling
4 tablespoons sunflower oil

3 medium onions, peeled and chopped

1 1/2 pounds ground beef

1 teaspoon salt

1/8 teaspoon pepper

Dough
2 cups all-purpose flour

1/8 teaspoon salt

1 egg

1/2 to 3/4 cup skim milk

melted butter

In a large frying pan, heat 2 tablespoons oil over medium-high heat for 1 minute. Add onion and sauté until golden brown. Remove from pan and set aside.

Add remaining oil to pan and heat for 1 minute over medium-high heat before adding meat and cooking until brown. Break the meat into small pieces and drain off the fat. Put the drained meat in a bowl and add the onions, salt, and pepper. Blend and mash well with a fork.

In a medium bowl, mix flour, salt, and egg. Add the skim milk a little at a time, until dough is stiff. Knead the dough for 2–4 minutes on a floured board. Roll out dough to ¹/₈ inch thickness with a rolling pin. Use a glass or cookie cutter to cut out rounds of dough about 3 inches in diameter.

Preheat oven to 400°F.

Put 1 tablespoon filling on one-half of each dough circle. Moisten the edges of the dough. Fold the dough over the filling and press the edges together with your fingers and then with the tines of a fork. Be sure each is well-sealed.

Place the *pirozhki* on a greased cookie sheet and bake for 30 minutes, or until golden brown. Remove from the oven and brush with melted butter. Serve at room temperature.

To preserve food for the long winter, Russians use such methods as pickling and salting. Pickled cucumbers and mushrooms and salted herrings are favorites.

A guest is well fed at a Russian table. The meal will probably begin with bread and cold appetizers of meat, ham, fish, and vegetables. Then two soups will be served, *shchi*, a vegetable soup, and *Ukha*, a hot fish soup. The main course might be fish or meat, boiled or fried, and garnished with vegetables. A meat pie such as *kulebyaka* might be served. For dessert there will be coffee or tea and perhaps spice cake. Jams may be served so that guests may add a spoonful of jam to their tea instead of using sugar to sweeten the flavor.

Recreation

Gymnastics is a popular sport in Russia. Football (soccer) clubs such as the Moscow Dynamo have an enthusiastic following. In winter, Russians like to watch ice hockey matches.

One sport at which Russians excel is ice-skating. Many times Russian couples have won the Olympic gold medal for pairs figure skating. Lots of Russians go ice skating at local rinks.

Chess is very popular in Russia, where in the summer, people play chess in the open air. Russia has produced many grandmasters including Gary Kasparov and Anatoly Karpov. Stamp collecting is also popular and there are thousands of stamp clubs.

Russians also enjoy hiking, mountain climbing, river kayaking, and canoeing and summer boating on lakes.

Russian sports societies have major soccer, basketball, and ice-hockey teams with millions of fans. Baseball is also becoming popular. The first national baseball championships were held in 1989.

Customs and Traditions

During the 1920s and 1930s, the communist regime in Russia attempted to do away with old rites. Easter, Christmas, and New Year festivities were abolished. The various religious feasts were replaced with celebrations of the birthdays of revolutionary leaders and with anniversaries of various revolutions. Since the break-up of the Union of Soviet Socialist Republics, many of the old festivals are gradually coming back into favor.

Among political and patriotic holidays, Russians celebrate National Day on November 7, the anniversary of the 1917 Revolution. On March 8 each year, Russians celebrate Women's Day. Schools and offices are closed and many women receive flowers from their families. On May Day, May 1, a Day of International Solidarity of Working People (something like Labor Day) is celebrated. Victory Day is celebrated on May 9 and commemorates the end of World War II. Military parades are often held and fireworks are shot off.

Among traditional holidays is the celebration of New Years. At New Year, Grandfather Frost brings presents to the Russian children in a sleigh. Sometimes Snowgirl assists him. The Russian Orthodox Christians celebrate Christmas Day on January 7 because they follow a different calendar.

Shrovetide (called Butter Week in Russia) is a popular holiday that occurs the day before Ash Wednesday, the first day of Lent in the Christian calendar. People feast and sometimes burn a straw figure representing winter.

There are other spring festivals celebrated by Russia's different ethnic groups. *Sabantui* is celebrated by the Tatars and *Navruz* by other Muslim peoples to celebrate sowing spring crops and the coming of summer. The Buryats have a similar holiday, *Surkharban,* celebrated in the summer after crops have been sown.

Just as young children in the United States may believe in a tooth fairy, in Russia a child will throw his or her recently removed tooth under the bed, believing the tooth mouse will come during the night, take the tooth away, and bring the child a new one.

Suggested Activities

Writing

1. The bear is often used as a symbol for Russia. It is estimated that there are about 126,000 brown bears in Russia. Another of Russia's famous animals is the endangered Siberian tiger.

    Invite one group of students to write a paper about the Siberian brown bear, including its size, habitat, food, etc. Another group might write a paper about the Siberian tiger. Each paper should include a bibliography listing at least three sources of information. Among the sources might be the following two websites: http://worldkids.net/critters/mammals/tiger/.htm and http://www.tigerlink.com/siberia.html.

Reading

2. Many Jews fled Russia in the early 1900s. Students might form small book discussion groups and read and discuss a book that deals with this topic. Here are suggested titles: Kathryn Lasky's *Dreamers in the Golden Country: the Diary of Zipporah Feldman, a Jewish Immigrant Girl* (Scholastic, 1998) describes the first eighteen months in New York City of a Jewish emigrant family in 1903–1904. A young Jewish girl in Fara Lynn Krasnopolsky's *I Remember* (Clarion Books, 1995) recalls her life in pre-1917 Russia. In Maxine Schur's *The Circlemaker* (Dial Books, 1994) Mendel Cholinsky, a twelve-year-old, tries to escape to America to avoid service in the Tsar's army. Thirteen-year-old Fagel is excited about the United States but can't forget her family

left behind in Russia in Vicky Shiefman's *Good-bye to the Trees.* A young Jewish girl writes her cousin about her flight from Russia in 1919 in Karen Hesse's *Letters from Rifka* (H. Holt, 1992).

Vocabulary

3. A vocabulary bulletin board could be helpful during this unit of study about Russia. Students can be encouraged to write words they meet in their reading, including a short definition on 3 x 5-inch file cards and pin these on the bulletin board. Some of the following words would be of interest: taiga, steppe, Bolsheviks, proletariat, bourgeoisie, The Iron Curtain, *perestroika,* Cheka, cossack, Tsar, and *glasnost.*

Math

4. Russia is so large that it spans eleven time zones. Invite a pair of students to research time zones and to prepare a map of Russia dividing it into zones. This time zone map should indicate what time it is in each of the zones when it is midnight in Moscow. Post the time-zone map on a bulletin board to share with students.

Social Studies

5. One of the world's worst nuclear accidents took place in the Ukraine in 1986 at Chernobyl. Ask a small group of students to research this accident and to prepare a written report with bibliography to share with the class. The bibliography should contain at least three sources of information.

Geography

6. The population of cities varies from year to year. But the city of Moscow currently has more than 10 million people. Ask a pair of students to do some research. What are the dozen most populous cities in the world? Ask the students to share this information with the class and to point out the location on a world map of these populous cities.

Music

7. With help from the school's music educator, play for students and discuss a variety of the works composed

by Stravinsky to show the great range of his work. These might include short songs like *Four Russian Peasant Songs* or *Recollections of My Childhood*, along with part of one of his ballets such as *The Firebird*, and perhaps a humorous piece such as *Circus Polka*.

Art

8. With the help of the school's art educator, have a pair of students locate pictures of icons, famous Russian religious paintings. With permission, have the students photocopy examples of some of this work and bring them to share with the class.

Drama/Movement

9. From your library or video store check out a video of *Swan Lake* to show and share with the class. Several versions are available. One is *Ballet Favorites: Live Performances from Swan Lake, The Nutcracker, The Sleeping Beauty, Romeo & Juliet, Giselle, and Don Quixote*, National Video Corporation, 1988, 1 VHS cassette, 59 minutes, starring Mikhail Baryshnikov.

Dress

10. Encourage students as they are reading about Russia and the celebration of its traditional holidays to photocopy (with permission) the ethnic costumes that are worn and to share these with the class. Particularly interested students might enjoy looking through Auguste Racinet's *The Historical Encyclopedia of Costumes* (Facts on File, 1988).

Cooking

11. The following recipe is for a simple apple/pastry dish that is popular in Russia.

Pirog

    4 small apples
    3 eggs
    1 cup white sugar
    1 cup flour
    Dab of butter

Preheat the oven to 375°F. Lightly butter an 8-inch cake pan. Cut cored, unpeeled apples into small pieces. In a large bowl, mix the eggs, sugar, and flour. Place the chopped apples into the buttered pan. Pour the egg mixture over the apples. Bake for 35 to 40 minutes or until the top is golden brown. After it is cool, cut into slices.

Culminating Activity

12. Writing and illustrating a book of *Famous Russian People* could involve the entire class in research, writing, editing, and using computer skills. Each page of the book might focus on a different personality, and each student could select someone for inclusion. These could range from Yuri Gagarin, the first person to orbit the earth, to ballet dancer Mikhail Baryshnikov, to one of the Tsars, to Marx, Engels, and Lenin, to Raisa Gorbachev.

Suggested Reading

Arnold, Helen. *Russia*. Winchester, England: Zoe Books, 1995.

Baruth, Philip E., ed. *Holiday Cooking Around the World*. Minneapolis, Minn.: Lerner Publications, 1988.

Bauman, Amy, ed. *Mikhail Gorbachev*. Milwaukee, Wisc.: Gareth Stevens, 1992.

Bilibin, Ivan I., illustrator. Translated by Robert Chandler. *Russian Folk Tales*. Boulder, Colo.: Shanbhala Publications, 1980.

Clark, Mary Jane Behrends. *The Commonwealth of Independent States*. Brookfield, Conn.: Millbrook Press, 1995.

Cohen, Barbara. *Lovely Vassilisa*. New York: Atheneum, 1980.

Cumming, David. *Russia*. Hove, England: Wayland, 1994.

Davies, Kathy. *A First Guide to Russia*. Winchester, England: Zoe Books, 1995.

Downing, Charles. *Russian Tales and Legends*. Oxford, England: Oxford University Press, 1996.

Dunn, John M. *The Russian Revolution*. San Diego, Calif.: Lucent Books, 1994.

Haskins, Jim. *Count Your Way Through Russia*. Minneapolis, Minn.: Carolrhoda Books, 1987.

Holmes, Burton. *Moscow.* Philadelphia, Pa.: Chelsea House, 1998.

Kallen, Stuart A. *The Brezhnev Era, 1964–1982.* Edina, Minn.: Abdo & Daughters, 1992.

————. *Gorbachev/Yeltsin: The Fall of Communism.* Edina, Minn.: Abdo & Daughters, 1992.

————. *The Lenin Era, 1900–1924.* Edina, Minn.: Abdo & Daughters, 1992.

————. *The Stalin Era, 1925–1953.* Edina, Minn.: Abdo & Daughters, 1992.

Kendall, Russ. *Russian Girl: Life in an Old Russian Town.* New York: Scholastic, 1994.

Lorimer, Lawrence T., Editorial Director. *Lands and Peoples, Special Edition: Life After Communism.* New York: Grolier, 1993.

Lye, Keith. *Passport to Russia.* New York: Franklin Watts Books, 1996.

McLeish, Kenneth and Valerie. *Stravinsky.* London, England: Heinemann, 1978.

Nadel, Laurie. *The Kremlin Coup.* Brookfield, Conn.: Millbrook Press, 1992.

Perrin, Penelope. *Discovering Russia.* Winchester, England: Zoe Books, 1994.

Popescu, Julian. *Russia.* Philadelphia, Pa.: Chelsea House, 1999.

Resnick, Abraham. *The Union of Soviet Socialist Republics, A Survey from 1917 to 1991.* Chicago, Ill.: Childrens Press, 1992.

Sallnow, John and Tatyana Saiko. *Russia.* Austin, Tex.: Raintree Steck-Vaughn, 1997.

Schecter, Kate. *Boris Yeltsin.* New York: Chelsea House, 1994.

Torchinsky, Oleg. *Russia.* New York: Marshall Cavendish, 1995.

Wheeler, Jill C. *Raisa Gorbachev, Leading Lady.* Edina, Minn.: Abdo & Daughters, 1992.

Senegal
A Legend from Senegal

Birago Diop was born in Senegal in 1906, studied in France, and returned to Africa. Amadou Koumba was the storyteller in Mr. Diop's grandmother's house. Birago Diop wrote down some of the folktales he heard. He published these stories in French and they appeared as *Les Contes d'Amadou Koumba* in 1961. One of these stories was "Maman-Caiman." Rosa Guy met Mr. Diop when she was on a trip to Senegal and translated his story into English. John Steptoe illustrated her picture book, *Mother Crocodile*.

Mama Crocodile

Golo, the monkey, was wicked and went about spreading gossip to anyone who would listen. One day Golo was teasing Dia, Mama Crocodile, and she snapped at him. This made Golo very angry so he went about telling tales about her. He said that although Dia had a wonderful memory, she talked nonsense and he thought this creeping crocodile must be the craziest of all creatures that walk, fly, or swim.

Dia was far from crazy, but it was true that she had a wonderful memory, perhaps the best memory on earth. Dia swam in a busy river and sunned on its sandy banks. As she swam and sunned, she listened to the stories that the fish and the river birds told, and she listened to the tales of the women who washed their clothes in the river.

Often times donkeys and camels stopped by the river to rest and take a drink. Dia listened to their gossip, too. And the remarkable thing was that Dia remembered every story that she ever heard.

But while Dia swam and sunned and listened to stories, Golo, the monkey, went about telling everyone that Mama Crocodile was crazy. He told this to the rabbit, to the hyena, and to the parrot. What was worse, he even told Dia's children that Mama Crocodile was crazy.

Often Mama Crocodile would call her children and say, "Now listen to your Mama." Then she told them stories. She told them about hunters she had seen. She told them of warriors who had passed by the waters where their great-grandmother lived as they went on their way to capture slaves and hunt for gold.

The crocodile children would rather play than listen to stories of things that had happened so long ago. They yawned as they listened and remembered that Golo had told them Mama Crocodile was crazy.

When Mama Crocodile told her children that men had killed mighty elephants and used their tusks for jewelry, that men had killed the zebra and the panther, and used their skins to make coats and decorate their houses, and that men killed animals not to eat but just to hang their heads on walls for decorations, the little crocodiles would squirm with boredom.

Mama Crocodile said, "We must leave these waters at once.
It is too dangerous to stay."

"Why do you tell us these stories?" asked one of her children.

"Yes, why?" asked another. "We are not like those other animals. We are smarter and tougher."

"I tell you these stories," Mama Crocodile said, "so that you will learn from the experience of others to be wary of man."

Every day as the sun sank into the sea, Mama Crocodile called her children to her. "Come listen to your Mama," she said. And then she told her stories of long ago. She told of battles that men had fought near the river and how the waters had run red. She told how her great grandmama had to search the muddy bottom of the river for a trail to follow in order to leave that dangerous place and find other waters in which to live.

Mama Crocodile told of hundreds of men at war. So many were killed that Dia's grandmother also had to search the muddy bottom of the river for a trail to follow to leave that dangerous place, and how that trail had led to this spot where they all now lived.

The little crocodiles only half-listened. They dreamed and dozed. Ibis, the wisest of all birds, had also told the little crocodiles stories. And sometime, even while Mama Crocodile talked, the little crocodiles dreamed of places the Ibis had told them about, places where the sun god was born, and places where crocodiles were gods.

One morning, while Mama Crocodile was sunning herself, she saw a flock of crows passing high over the river. She listened carefully to the tale they told.

The yellow sun

The sun of early dawn,

Casts its gold across the river.

In the middle of the day, another flock of crows flew across the river and Mama Crocodile listened to them.

The bright sun

The sun of high noon

Casts its white glare across the river.

And then at twilight, other crows came. They flew low to the water and Mama Crocodile listened to them.

The red sun,

The sunset sun,

Casts waves of blood across the river.

Mama Crocodile called out to the crows. "What is happening?" she asked. "Why are you flying away?"

"War," the crows said. "Men from the West have declared war on men from the East."

Quickly, Dia called her children. "Come listen to your Mama," she said.

When the children came, Mama Crocodile said, "We must leave these waters at once. It is too dangerous to stay. The men from the West have declared war on men from the East."

"What does that matter to us?" one of the little crocodiles asked. "What do we care what the men do?"

"We don't want to leave," the little crocodiles insisted. And although they did not say it out loud, they remembered what Golo had told them. Mama Crocodile was crazy.

The young crocodiles closed their eyes and closed their ears. Mama Crocodile was very sad, but she swam deep to the bottom of the river and found the well-worn trail. And she left.

The little crocodiles shook their heads. "That's crazy talk," they said. And they stretched out on the bank.

Before long, the sound of shots rang out. Golo, the monkey, jumped high into the branches of the tree to hide. The Rabbit and all her relatives hopped quickly to the thicket to hide. The Hyena and all her children left for the distant plains. And the parrot flew high into the trees and hid her head beneath her wing. Only the young crocodiles remained.

They watched as the men from the West and the men from the East crossed and re-crossed the river, killing more and more men. Finally they heard the men from the West shout, "We have won."

By now the young crocodiles were tired of the constant battles and hoped that the men would leave. Then they heard one of the men from the West say, "Let us bring something back to our wives. What better gifts than skins of crocodiles so they can make themselves handsome purses."

The men from the West turned their rifles on the young crocodiles. Bullets rained down on them as the little crocodiles dived deep. They were frightened and knew that when they came up for air, they would surely be shot. But some of the crocodiles remembered the tales of Mama. They dove deeper and felt the well-worn trail that Dia had talked about.

The young crocodiles surfaced far from the hunters. Then they dove deep and followed the trail again, moving many miles from their old home. Here they found Mama Crocodile, who was over-joyed to see them.

"Come listen to your Mama," she called to them. And now the young ones did not close their ears. They had learned that though the talk of old ones may sound crazy, it is filled with wisdom.

Background Information

The Republic of Senegal is on the Atlantic coast of West Africa, bounded on the north by Mauritania, on the east by Mali, on the southeast by the Republic of Guinea, and on the south by Guinea-Bissau. Thrust into the country of Senegal for about 200 miles on both sides of the Gambia River, and completely surrounded by Senegal except for a very short coast line, is the country of Gambia, which has strong cultural and commercial ties to Britain.

Senegal is in that part of Africa below the Sahara Desert and is called the sub-Sahara. The northern and central areas of Senegal are dry and are home to baobab trees and acacia. There are swamps in the far southwest and tropical forests in the southeast.

In the northern section, which is semi-arid, rain falls only occasionally. In recent times, there have been severe droughts, forcing the nomadic people who live in this area to move farther and farther south. Some of these northern people are lighter-skinned Arabic-speaking people called Berbers. They wear long, loose robes to protect themselves from sun and sand. Many of these people are also Muslims, and Islamic law requires that their bodies be covered.

Farther south, the Senegalese people tend to have darker skin. Because of heat and humidity they wear a minimum of clothing.

Most of Senegal is rolling plains about 500 feet above sea level. The plains slope from the foothills toward the Atlantic and the Sahara. In the south is the Casamance River, around which there are swamps and woodlands. The oil palm, raffia palm, and mangroves grow in this area.

The Casamance area is home to the Diola, Mandinka, and Tukulor people. These people trade with their neighbors in Guinea-Bissau and have resisted both Islam and Christianity. Most still hold to their animistic religions. This is an excellent area for growing rice, millet, sorghum, maize, groundnuts, dates and other fruit, and cotton.

Since Senegal is mostly flat, the rivers are slow moving and collect a great deal of silt. When the rivers flood their banks in the rainy season, they leave behind fertile soil in which people can raise crops part of the year.

The longest river in the country is the Senegal River, which flows along the northern border between Senegal and Mauritania. It flows northwest, cutting through the Sahel Desert and emptying into the Atlantic Ocean. During the rainy season, this river is navigable all the way from Saint Louis on the Atlantic Ocean to Mali.

When the Senegal floods, it floods the whole valley. The Tukulor and Peul peoples, who live in the valley, build their homes on stilts or on high ground. When the rains stop, and the river water recedes, the people plant millet or peanuts in the rich silt left behind. They harvest their crops and live off them until the next rainy season.

Cutting across the center of Senegal is the Saloum River. The Casamance, Senegal, and Saloum Rivers all have ports for ocean-going ships. The Faleme River runs along the eastern border between Senegal and Mali. Most of the area around it is poor grassland.

Senegal is close to the equator so it is warm all year long. Although the temperature of Senegal remains fairly constant, there is a wet season (summer) and a dry season (winter). The wet season runs from June to October. During this time, the southern part of the country gets quite a bit of rainfall. The northern section of the country, however, receives less than 20 inches of rainfall a year. The coolest part of Senegal is in the foothills of the Fouta Djallon mountain range, most of which lies across the border in Guinea.

Most Senegalese live along the Atlantic Coast. Here there are ports supporting trade, there are business opportunities, there are fish to eat and sell, and there is a fertile soil around those spots where rivers empty into the sea. This coastal area also enjoys cool ocean breezes.

The coast from Saint-Louis to Dakar is called *La Grande Cote,* or "the long coast," while the coast from Dakar to the Sine-Soloum Rivers is called *La Petite Cote,* or "the short coast." Because *La Petite Cote* south of Dakar has such a pleasant climate, it has become an important resort area for tourists from Europe.

The population of Senegal is 9,403,546. It occupies 75,951 square miles. Approximately 1 percent of the population is not African. This 1 percent includes Europeans, Syrians, and Lebanese. These non-Africans live mainly in large cities and work in teaching, technical, and administrative positions.

The Wolof make up 36 percent of the population. Most of these people live between Saint Louis and Dakar. They are farmers who raise millet and peanuts. Although they are for the most part Muslims, they make offerings to various deities.

Closely related to the Wolof are the Lebu. These people are primarily fishermen and live in the Dakar area. Between Dakar and Gambia are the Serer people. The Serer are smaller in stature than the Wolof. The Serer are also peanut farmers, and they keep cattle, sheep, and goats.

In the Senegal River Valley, the Tukulor and Fulani live. The Tukulor are dark-skinned and are farmers. The Fulani are light-skinned and are nomadic herdsmen. The Fulani also live in the Casamance region, where they are settled rather than nomadic.

The Diola, who are related to the Serer, live south of Gambia and are also farmers. The Mandinka-Bambara live in the foothills of the southeast. They are farmers and primarily grow millet.

Most Senegalese are divided into distinct social classes. In the highest class are nobles and freeborn peasants. Below them are artisans and the minstrels who are musician storytellers attached to nobles. At the bottom of these classes are descendants of slaves. Usually marriage takes place only within the same social class. In parts of the country, some of these class distinctions are beginning to die out.

In much of the country, farmers work small plots of land. They live together in villages with communal granaries and ovens. Their houses are made of sun-dried bricks with thatched conelike roofs. Extended families may live together.

Except among the small number of Christians, polygamy is a common practice. A man may have more than one wife, but must be able to afford a separate household for each wife.

Senegal is primarily agricultural. It exports peanuts and peanut products. Peanuts are also grown for domestic consumption, as are millet, sweet potatoes, maize, rice, and vegetables. The government has promoted the planting of cotton and sugarcane.

Commercial fishing is an important industry. Fish now make up 30 percent of the country's exports. There is also a limited amount of manufacturing, including making textiles and chemicals, and food processing.

Calcium and aluminum phosphate are mined for export. Other small deposits of minerals include salt, natural gas, marble, iron ore, gold, and petroleum.

The capital of Senegal is Dakar. It is also the largest city in the country and is located on the Cape Verde or Cap Vert Peninsula, which is the westernmost point of the African continent. The way the land curves creates a sheltered harbor, and it is a major port. The Yoff International Airport located in Dakar is a principal stop for planes going from North America to southern Africa and for planes traveling from Europe to South America. It is also the center of a network of railroads that link Senegal with Mali.

Dakar is a combination of black African, Islamic, and French influences. It is the only Senegalese city with skyscrapers. Some residents eat French cuisine in restaurants while others eat a one-pot meal such as *cheboudienne*, African style. You can buy delicate pastries and eclairs or shop in an African marketplace. Some people who work in Dakar live on the island of Goree and commute by means of a 22-minute ferryboat ride.

Dakar has three major markets. The Sandanga Market is done in Sudanese style and looks something like an Arabic palace. The Kermel market carries everything from fresh fish to audiocassettes. The Tilene Market is in the *Medine*, or old town, and carries more exotic items such as charms and potions.

Saint Louis, in the far north of Senegal, was the country's capital until 1958 and is the third largest city in the country. Founded in 1659, it was named for the king of France.

Saint Louis is the hub of the country's fishing industry. There are many wrought-iron balconies and beautiful gardens, which remind some visitors of New Orleans.

Other major cities include Diourbel, Kaolack, Thies, Ziguinchor, Rufisque, and Tambacounda. Diourbel and Kaolack have been nicknamed "groundnut capitals." The peanut production here is vital to the Senegalese economy. There are many craftspeople in Diourbel who create bronze and wooden sculptures, embroidery, leather work, and gold and silver jewelry.

Near Kaolack are the megaliths of Sine-Ngayene. The stones' purpose has puzzled scholars as well as local ethnic groups. The stones, of varying sizes, are arranged in lines or circles. In all there are more than 150 stones spread out among ten small villages.

Ziguinchor is on the south bank of the Casamance River about 45 miles from the Atlantic coast. There are some small industries here, and it serves as the main marketplace of this fertile region.

Tambacounda has only about 20,000 inhabitants, but it is the largest city in the eastern portion of Senegal. It is at the foot of the Fouta Djallon Mountains. Many people stop here before visiting Senegal's largest national park, Niokolo Koba National Park.

Goree Island lies about 2 miles west of Dakar, the capital of Senegal. On its northeastern coast is a calm bay. Today the island is a vacation place with seaside cafes. Before Europeans discovered it, a few fishermen and goat herders lived there and called the island Ber.

The Portuguese explorer, Dinis Diaz, landed on Ber in 1444 and claimed it for the Portuguese crown. He named the island Palma. Over time, the Portuguese developed trading contacts on the mainland. They traded with the Africans of the Jolof Empire. The Europeans brought guns, gunpowder, liquor, fabrics and jewelry, which they exchanged for leather, animal skins, ivory, gold, musk, amber and eventually, slaves.

Africans were captured by other Africans and sold to Portuguese traders as early as 1433. Palma lay at the beginning of the shortest route from Africa to the West Indies. Ships would dock and use the island as a stopover and a place to resupply with food and water. A prized island, Palma changed hands among various European nations seventeen times over three centuries.

The Portuguese would bring slaves, Africans taken from the Mandjak, Mandinka, Fula, and Balante tribes, to Palma. From this point, they would continue to the Cape Verde Islands 385 miles to the west, where the Africans were forced to grow sugar and maize. Before 1600, many of these slaves were exported to Colombia, Mexico, the Canary Island, and Seville, Spain.

In 1588, the Dutch settled on Palma and built two forts there. They renamed the island *Goede Reede,* or good harbor, and it soon became known as Goree. In 1619, a Dutch ship, probably sailing from Goree Island, brought the first slaves to Jamestown, Virginia. From Goree, Europeans shipped slaves to the West Indies.

Battles were fought for control of Goree among the Dutch, Portuguese, French, and British. In 1677, the French drove off the Dutch and kept the island for the next two centuries, replacing the Dutch forts with their own.

In 1786, King Louis XVI of France appointed Chevalier Jean Stanislas de Boufflers governor of Senegal. The governor transferred his administration from Saint-Louis to Goree, and the island thrived as the capital of Senegal. Elegant houses were built and some of the slaves were sold to members of the privileged class. Among these wealthy people were *signares,* women of African and European blood, who married wealthy Europeans.

Although other slave centers grew up along the shoreline of what is today Ghana, Goree remained an active and important port from which slaves were delivered to the Americas. In this triangular trade, Europeans shipped manufactured goods to the African coast, which they traded for slaves. The slaves were taken to the West Indies and the Americas. And finally molasses and other West Indian products were taken to Europe.

The House of Slaves is now a museum on the island of Goree. It once held 400 slaves at a time in cells on the ground floor. A passageway leads to "The Door of No Return." Slaves walked out the door, down a pier, and onto crowded ships.

The French abolished house slavery and indentured servitude in 1848, the same year that Senegal became a colony of France. At that time, three-quarters of the population of the island were slaves.

History

Because there was no written language, much of the early history of Senegal has been lost, but archaeological evidence shows that people have been living in the Senegal area for 15,000 years.

In 500 B.C. Hanno the Great, a navigator from Tunis, traveled to West Africa and wrote about what he found. Others, including the Greek historian, Herodotus, wrote about the area.

Then in 140 B.C. a Greek named Polybius visited Senegal and wrote about it in detail. In A.D. 141 the Romans drew the first known map of the Senegal area.

Around the end of the third century, the Ghanaians expanded and began to dominate the Zenega in the north of Senegal and the Wolof and Serer people in the south. One king ruled the Ghana empire.

Tekur was an ancient Tukulor kingdom, which developed in the Senegal River Valley in the ninth century A.D. It was at the southern end of the Moor's Saharan caravan trade route. The Almoravids, a branch of Muslims, brought their armies into Senegal, and the Tukulor people adopted Islam in the eleventh century.

Tekur had to fight to resist being taken over by the empires of Ghana and Mali. At various times Tekur had Wolof and Fulani rulers. By the fifteenth century, the Wolof's large coastal empire broke up into various states.

The first Europeans to arrive on the Cape Verde peninsula in 1445 were Portuguese sailors who established trading posts along the Atlantic coast. Nuno Tristao sailed up the mouth of the Senegal River in 1443.

The Portuguese were followed by the French, who came in 1570, and were in turn followed by the English and Dutch. In the seventeenth and eighteenth centuries, the French concentrated on the slave trade.

From 1500 to 1810, millions of Africans were taken from Africa and sold to work on plantations in the Caribbean and in North and South America. The majority of the slaves were taken from the Gambia area.

During the 1600s, many Europeans began to settle in the area. The Dutch established a settlement in 1617 on Goree Island. The French built a trading station at Saint-Louis in 1621. The English chartered a trading company in 1661. But it was the French who came to dominate the Senegal region.

In the middle of the nineteenth century, the French moved inland. They had heard tales of gold deep in the interior. Although Senegal was administered as an overseas province of France, it remained predominantly Muslim in religion.

Slavery eventually became unpopular throughout the world. British citizens were prohibited from engaging in slavery in 1807, and they extended their law into the Gambia. France prohibited slavery in its territories in 1848. People born in the four coastal cities of Saint-Louis, Goree, Rufisque, and Dakar in Senegal were given full French citizenship.

During the late 1800s, European countries competed for control of overseas colonies. By 1895, the boundaries of Senegal were set as a part of French West Africa.

After World War II, Senegal sought its independence. It became self-governing in 1958 and joined in the Mali Federation in 1959. When that federation broke up in 1960, Senegal became an independent country. Leopold Sedar Senghor became president and held that office until his retirement in 1980.

From 1982 to 1989, Senegal and Gambia united in a confederation called Senegambia. They agreed to work together on matters of defense and economic development. There were border conflicts with the country of Mauritania, with rioting and fighting.

Government

A new constitution for independent Senegal was drawn up on August 25, 1960. Leopold Senghor was elected president and Mamadou Dia became prime minister.

Senegal is divided into ten political subdivisions or regions. These are: Dakar, Thies, Louga, Saint-Louis, Diourbel, Fatick, Kaolack, Tambacounda, Kolda, and Ziguinchor. The voters elect a total of 120 representatives to the National Assembly for five-year terms. Each region also elects its governor.

Senegal is a now a multiparty democracy. Its president is limited to two, seven-year terms and serves as head of state. The post of prime minister of Senegal was abolished in 1983 and then was restored again in 1991.

Religion

Between70 and 90 percent of the Senegalese people are Muslim. But not all Senegalese Muslims are very strict and many practice an Islam blended with animist religions.

The practice of Islam in Senegal is organized around different brotherhoods. The Qadiriya is the oldest brotherhood and emphasizes law and learning. The Tidianes brotherhood mostly involves an educated elite who live in cities. The Mourides brotherhood is made up largely of orphans, farmers, and former slaves. The Layenes is a small brotherhood living on the Cap Vert Peninsula.

About 5 percent of Senegalese are Christians, and most of these are Catholics. The Christians in Senegal tend to be concentrated along the Petite Cote, where the French influence is still strong. Still others hold animistic beliefs in various spirits.

In Dakar, five times a day Muslims prepare for prayer. They splash water on their faces, hands, arms, and feet. Men, wearing *boubous*, which are flowing ankle-length robes, go to mosques and kneel to pray. Congregational prayer is held on Friday afternoons at the Grand Mosque of Dakar.

Education

The law requires that children attend school for six years, but it is estimated that only about 50 percent of Senegalese children attend elementary school, and only 15 percent attend secondary school. Senegal has a literacy rate of only 28 percent.

Infant mortality is very high in Senegal and 40 percent of the children die before they reach the age of five. As a result, children are precious, and their families do not like to send them far for school. Some villages have schools, but in others, children must attend boarding schools.

The children who do go to elementary schools, secondary schools, and on to the university are usually those who are wealthy and live in cities. University Cheikh Anta Diop, founded in 1949, is located in Dakar and is the country's only institute of higher learning.

Immigrants

In other chapters in this book, immigrants were people who willingly (even though sometimes reluctantly) left their homelands to seek work, opportunity, and a better life in a new land. The people who left Senegal did not come willingly. They were shipped and sold as slaves.

The peoples of Senegal began trading with Europe after the arrival of the Portuguese in the mid-fifteenth century. Until the end of the sixteenth century, this region was the largest supplier of slaves to Europe. The Senegal region exported an average of 2,000 to 3,500 slaves a year until the end of the eighteenth century.

The island of Goree off of Senegal was a major disembarkation point for the slave trade. Europeans began to look for slaves to work the sugar plantations of the New World. The Middle Passage was the name given to the transport of slaves from the west coast of Africa to the Caribbean. It was the middle part of the voyage from Europe to Africa, Africa to the Caribbean, and the Caribbean back to Europe. Sometimes it was called the triangular trade.

Slaves who had been captured from various African tribes were marched to the coast and sold to European slave traders. Then they were imprisoned there until a ship came to transport them. Good records were not kept, so it is hard to estimate how many slaves left Senegal, but at least 60,000 slaves were shipped from the Island of Goree to the Americas. Many died en route.

The Middle Passage Monument Project of 1999 held special activities in New York during June and July 1999. Ceremonial events involved a symbolic water burial of a monument honoring those who lost their lives en route to slavery between the fifteenth and nineteenth centuries. Six replicas of the Middle Passage Monument are planned for placement on land in Africa, the Caribbean, Central America, Europe, North America, and South America.

Many present-day African Americans may not know from what African nation their ancestors originated. Those who can afford it often make a pilgrimage back to Goree Island.

Language

The official language of Senegal is French, but most people speak Wolof. The Wolof make up over 40 percent of the Senegalese people and the Wolof language is spoken by about 80 percent of the people.

Government radio stations broadcast from Senegal in French and in Wolof, Malinke, Serer, and Pular. An international radio station in Dakar does 85 percent of its programming in French and the rest in English and Portuguese. The main newspaper of Dakar, *Le Soleil,* is printed in French. Senegalese textbooks are in French.

The Arts and Sciences

Rather than a rich tradition of written literature, there is a strong oral tradition in Senegal. The *griot* is a combination storyteller, musician, historian, and minstrel. The *griot* tells stories of history, of past empires, of gold and kings and slaves, and of the Wolof warriors who are national heroes. He also tells myths about owls and ants and the forces of life and death.

The first president of Senegal was also a well known French language poet and author, Leopold Sedar Senghor. His writing reflects his love of Africa and its people. As a student in Paris in the 1930s, he helped found the negritude, which was a black literary movement. He was admitted to the Academie Francaise. Senghor sponsored the first World Festival of Negro Arts in Dakar in 1966.

After Senghor, the most famous writer from Senegal is Birago Diop. Diop writes poetry and also stories drawn from Senegalese myths and legends.

Two writers who have attained prominence include Mariama Ba and Aminata Sow Fall. Both women write about everyday life in Senegal and particularly about women's issues.

The city of Thies is a center for arts and crafts, particularly famous for the unique tapestries made there. These wool tapestries are woven in bright colors and depict scenes of life in Senegal.

Senegalese dance is expressive, with emphasis on group participation. The dances are usually accompanied by chanting and the use of musical instruments such as drums and wood xylophones, which in Senegal are called balaphones.

African culture had a dramatic effect on dance in North America. Slaves became known for their varied animal dances, including the buzzard lope, turkey trot, and pigeon wing. There were also water dances, where slaves put glasses of water on their heads and danced while trying not to spill a drop.

During the cakewalk commonly held in Virginia at harvest time, slaves would dance along a path with pails of water on their heads. The dancing couple that was most upright and spilled the least water won a prize, usually a cake.

Patting Juba included stamping, clapping, slapping, and patting of arms, chest, and thighs. European settlers imitated the slaves' dances. The Charleston, for example, was originally a round dance performed by dockworkers in Charleston, South Carolina.

Food

West Africa is the name given to a cluster of countries along the coast of Africa stretching from Senegal to Nigeria. The climate is similar throughout this area, and many foods share popularity throughout the region. Every country in West Africa, except Liberia, was at one time a British or French colony. These colonial powers left behind them an influence on the foods and cooking methods of West Africa.

While some people in West Africa have started to follow the Western tradition of eating three times a day, most West Africans eat only twice a day. One meal is at noon and the other is in the evening. If breakfast is eaten, it typically would be corn porridge, fruit, bread, and tea. Snacks, such as bread and plantains, are eaten frequently.

A West African meal is likely to be made up of a thick stew or soup and a starch. The stew or soup will contain vegetables and a little meat, poultry, or fish. The starch may be bread or rice or *fufu*.

Fufu is made by making a flour of millet, yams, or plantains and then boiling it to a paste. To make the coarse flour, the millet is pounded with pestles in a large wooden mortar. This same method is used to make flour from corn and guinea corn. The flour is often made into porridge and cakes. Roots such as cassava are also pressed and dried and then pounded to make fufu.

It is usual to place the main dish on individual plates while the starch is served from a communal plate. Diners break off a piece of bread, or scoop up some fufu with their fingers, and use it to scoop spicy food from their plates.

Peanuts arrived in Africa in the 1500s, brought by Portuguese merchants and seamen. Peanuts were welcome because they were easy to grow and contain a high percentage of protein. Many groups in modern West Africa have

special recipes for "groundnut" stew. The Bombara people in Mali and Senegal make a peanut stew called *mafe*, which includes chicken, okra, tomatoes, and sweet potatoes.

Groundnut (or peanut) sauce is also enjoyed throughout West Africa. Groundnut sauce is sometimes substituted for meat dishes and is often served over rice, potatoes, sweet potatoes, or plantains. With adult volunteers to assist, the following sauce would be simple for students to make and could be served over rice or potatoes.

Groundnut Sauce
2 tablespoons vegetable oil
1 medium onion, peeled and chopped
2 medium tomatoes, cut into small pieces
1 small eggplant, peeled and cut into small pieces
$^1/_2$ cup natural peanut butter
$^1/_4$ cup water

Heat the oil for 1 minute in a large frying pan. Add the onions and sauté until transparent. Then add the tomato pieces and cook for another 5 minutes. Add the pieces of eggplant and cook for 5 minutes more.

In a small bowl, combine peanut butter and $^1/_4$ cup water and stir to make a smooth paste. Add the paste to the tomato mixture and stir well.

Reduce the heat to medium-low and simmer, uncovered, for about 10 minutes until the eggplant is tender.

Serve over rice or potatoes. Serves 6.

Recreation

There are several sports stadiums in Dakar. The most popular sport in the city, or in small towns, is wrestling. Throughout Senegal, soccer is popular both for playing and for watching.

Customs and Traditions

Senegal recognizes four holidays: New Year's Day on January 1, Labor Day on May 1, National Day on April 4, and Christmas on December 25.

In addition, many Islamic holidays such as *Mauloud* and *Tabaski* are recognized. They may fail on different days each year as they are based on the Islamic lunar calendar.

Touba normally has a population of about 25,000, but it is a sacred city of an Islamic brotherhood. Once a year, about 250,000 pilgrims of the Mourides Islamic Brotherhood come to celebrate Magal, the birthday of Amadou Bamba, a great *marabout*, or religious leader. People begin to assemble several days before Magal, and celebrate all through the night. At these festivals, men often play instruments made from gourds.

Suggested Activities

Writing

1. Although there are many different peoples in Senegal, the dominant group is the Wolof. Ask a pair of students to do some research on the Wolof and to prepare a written report on what they learn, including a bibliography of their sources of information. Their report should be shared with the class.

Reading

2. Many different African peoples live in West Africa, including the Asante, Dogon, Edo, Ewe, Fanta, Fulani, Hausa, Igbo, Malinke, Mossi, Songhay, Soninke, Wolof, and Yoruba. With the help of a media specialist, have students read some of the available materials about these peoples and report orally to the class on what they learn. One such book, *Malinke*, by C. O. Nwanunobi, is part of the Heritage Library of African Peoples (Rosen Publishing Group, 1996).

Vocabulary

3. One group of people who live in Senegal are the Malinke. They have many proverbs. Students should collect these proverbs from their reading throughout the unit, write the proverbs and their meanings down, and share these on a classroom bulletin board. When several have been collected, the class might discuss what the proverbs mean. The following were taken from page 60 of *Malinke* by C. O. Nwanunobi.

Malinke Proverbs and Translations

kuno se lii, naanaa mee lii.

Your hair can be styled as you please; your future cannot.

maxafeno le se kinoo diyaa

The sauce makes the dish delicious.

kanijuo man kunan bari a dino ye kunan.

The spice plant is not pungent, but its shoots are.

suo se i bori, i se a lafaa busa la.

You can make a horse gallop faster with the help of a whip.

moxo mee i buloo bula saanaa to.

A person shouldn't put his hands in snake's poison.

Math

4. A ton is 2,000 pounds. A metric ton is 2204.6 pounds. Using this information, answer the following questions. How many tons are in a metric ton? A "poor" year of peanut production in Senegal yields 400,000 metric tons. How many tons is that? A good year for peanut production in Senegal yields 1,400,000 metric tons. How many tons is that? What is the difference in tons between a "poor" year and a "good" year?

Social Studies

5. Invite a small group of students to learn more about the Niokolo Koba National Park. Where is it located? When was it established? What kinds of animals and birds live in the park? When this group of students has finished its research, have them report what they learn orally to the class. One source of information would be http://www.cco.caltech.edu/~salmon/wh-senegal.html.

Geography

6. Invite a pair of students to make a map of Africa on which they highlight Senegal. Within the country of Senegal, the students should show where the various people (Wolof, Lebu, Serer, Tukulor, Fulani, Diola, and Mandinka-Bambara) live.

Music

7. With assistance from the school's music specialist, various types of recordings of Senegalese music might be

shared with the class. The following are all available from Multicultural Media, RR3, Box 6655, Granger Road, Barre, Vermont 05641. You can find these on the net at http://www.worldmusicstore.com.

Yande Codou Sene and Yousou N'Dour Gainde: Voices from the Heart of Africa, CD Order # WDR-29, features a female choir accompanied by some of Dakar's finest drummers and violinists.

Sonar Senghor and His Troupe: Lost Africa, CD Order # TCD-1044, includes 18 selections of the rhythm, songs, and dialects of West Africa.

Keur Moussa: Sacred Chants & African Rhythms from Senegal, CD Order # ST-337, includes choral music from the Keur Moussa monastery in remote Senegal.

Art

8. Mosques have an interesting style of architecture. Invite a pair of interested students to find pictures of mosques from West Africa, and with permission, to photocopy these and share them on a classroom bulletin board.

Drama/Movement

9. Many groups in West Africa use masks in processions and dances. Working with the music and art educators in your school, a group of students may make masks and costumes and wear these in a simple dance that they present to the class. Drums may accompany the dance.

Masks usually depict the heads of animals such as antelopes, chameleons, anteaters, birds, and horses. The masks are not usually worn over the face but on a basket that is worn like a hat. This makes the dancers appear to be much taller than they are. The masqueraders' bodies are hidden by costumes.

Dress

10. People in Senegal wear long robes and hats. Many of these pieces of clothing are brightly colored. Invite a small group of students to work with the media specialist in finding pictures of people in Senegal in typical clothing. With permission, have the students photocopy

the pages of these books and magazines and bring them to share with the class.

Cooking

11. To prepare the national dish of the Wolof people of Senegal, adults may help students in making Jollof Rice.

Jollof Rice

1 pound of chicken, cut into pieces
$^1/_2$ teaspoon salt
$^1/_4$ teaspoon black pepper
$^1/_4$ cup vegetable oil
1 medium onion, peeled and finely chopped
1 quart water
2 cups white rice
1 teaspoon cayenne pepper
$^1/_2$ teaspoon dried thyme
2 large tomatoes, peeled and sliced
1 cup corn
1 cup diced carrots

Season the chicken pieces with salt and black pepper. In a large frying pan, heat oil over medium-high heat for 5 minutes. Add the chicken pieces and brown on both sides. Place the chicken in a large kettle or dutch oven and set aside.

Place onions in the oil in the frying pan and sauté until the onions are transparent. Add the onions to the kettle. Set frying pan aside without discarding the oil.

Put rice and water into a saucepan and bring to a boil. Turn the heat down and simmer for 8 minutes until the rice is partly cooked. Pour the water and rice mixture into the large kettle or dutch oven with the chicken and onions. Add cayenne pepper, thyme, and tomato slices to the kettle and stir well. Put the kettle over low heat for 10 minutes. Add corn and carrots to the kettle, stir well, and cover.

Cook over low heat for about 40 minutes. Serves 8.

Culminating Activity

12. The class might divide itself into five groups, with each group choosing a period of Senegal's history. Possible

divisions might be 1443 to 1658, 1659 to 1818, 1819 to 1895, 1896 to 1963, and 1964 to the present. For each period of history, the students might list important people and events on large charts and illustrate one of these events. The set of charts might be displayed along one wall of the room to give highlights of Senegal's history.

Suggested Reading

Barboza, Steven. *Door of No Return: The Legend of Goree Island*. New York: Cobblehill Books, 1994.

Beaton, Margaret. *Senegal*. Danbury, Conn.: Childrens Press, 1997.

Diop, Birago. *Mother Crocodile*. Trans. Rosa Guy. New York: Delacorte Press, 1981.

Geller, Sheldon. *Senegal, An African Nation Between Islam and the West*. Boulder, Colo.: Westview Press, 1982.

Harris, Colin. *A Taste of West Africa*. New York: Thomson Learning, 1995.

Johnson, Sylvia A. *Tomatoes, Potatoes, Corn, and Beans: How the Foods of the Americas Changed Eating Around the World*. New York: Atheneum, 1997.

Lowerre, Susan. *Under the Neem Tree*. Sag Harbor, N.Y.: Permanent Press, 1991.

Lutz, William. *Senegal*. New York: Chelsea House, 1988.

Mayer, T. W. *The Caribbean and Its People*. New York: Thomson Learning, 1995.

Nabwire, Constance and Bertha Vining Montgomery. *Cooking the African Way*. Minneapolis, Minn.: Lerner Publications, 1988.

Nwanunobi, C.O. *Malinke*. New York: The Rosen Publishing, 1996.

Rogers, Mary M., ed. *Senegal in Pictures*. Minneapolis, Minn.: Lerner Publications, 1988.

"I can live on land," he said, "and I would be happy to bring back a rabbit to his majesty. But there is one problem. I do not know what a rabbit looks like."

South Korea

A Legend from Korea

One version of this story appears in a collection called *Korean Folk and Fairy Tales* by Suzanne Crowder Han under the title of "The Hare's Liver." "The Hare's Liver" also appears in *Korean Folk-tales,* retold by James Riordan. Illustrated by Yumi Heo and written by Joanne Croder Han, the picture-book version of this story is called *The Rabbit's Escape.*

The Loyal Turtle

Long ago, the Dragon King fell ill in his kingdom beneath the sea. He called his royal ministers and his royal physicians to him. The physicians tried to determine what was wrong and how to cure the king. They consulted together and then one spoke.

"Oh, King, there is only one cure for you. You must eat the raw liver of a rabbit."

The Dragon King was not pleased at the thought of eating raw liver, but he trusted his doctors. He commanded his ministers, "Send someone to fetch me a rabbit at once."

"But your highness," his chief minister said, bowing low, "there are no rabbits in the kingdom beneath the sea. To find one, your subject must go up on land. What creature can we send from our kingdom that can live on land?"

From the crowd of subjects who had gathered in concern over the Sea King's health, a turtle slowly crawled forward until he stood before the throne of the king. "I can live on land," he said, "and I would be happy to bring back a rabbit to his majesty. But there is one problem. I do not know what a rabbit looks like."

"Thank you, my loyal subject," the Dragon King said. "We can solve that problem for you." He sent for the royal artist who quickly drew a picture of a rabbit and gave it to the turtle.

The turtle studied the picture, then he tucked it inside his shell, and left on his quest to cure the king. The turtle swam and swam until he reached land. He climbed up on the sandy beach and began looking about. Hours passed, and although the turtle saw many wonderful creatures, he did not see what he was looking for. Then, in a patch of clover, he spied a rabbit.

Having been told that rabbits are curious creatures, the turtle decided to pull inside his shell and wait for the rabbit to come to him. It wasn't long before the rabbit came up and knocked on the turtle's shell.

"Mr. Turtle," the rabbit asked. "Why are you so far from home?"

"I've been traveling," the turtle explained. "But I must admit I am disappointed. Your kingdom here on earth is nowhere near so lovely as my home beneath the sea. Have you ever visited the kingdom of the Dragon King?"

"No," the rabbit admitted. "But I do hope to go there some day."

"Why not today?" asked the turtle. "I am going to the sea kingdom this afternoon. I'd be happy to give you a ride. It would be something to tell all your friends about."

"I only wish I could," said the rabbit. "But I have heard that land animals cannot safely enter the sea realm."

"You are right," said the turtle. "There are only a few safe ways to go, and one way is to ride on a turtle's back. Rest assured that I can take you there."

"Really?" The rabbit hesitated. Then he thought of how he could brag to his friends. The rabbit climbed on the turtle's shell, and the turtle was relieved that he had tricked the hare. Swiftly he started the long journey back to the undersea kingdom.

"It's so beautiful here," the rabbit said as he gazed about the watery world. "I can hardly wait to return to land and tell my friends of all this beauty."

"To see something truly beautiful," the turtle said, "you would need to visit the palace of the Dragon King. I'm sure I can arrange this for you."

The turtle continued to swim toward the palace while the rabbit thought how his friends on earth would envy him when he told them about the sights he had seen.

When they finally arrived at the palace, the turtle left the rabbit in a large entrance hall while he swam ahead to make arrangements. Very quickly a group of swordfish came to escort the rabbit to the king.

"Hurry," one of the swordfish said, prodding the rabbit, "the Dragon King is very eager to see you."

"Why would a mighty king be eager to see me?" asked the rabbit.

Without stopping to think, the swordfish replied, "Because the king is ill and needs your liver to be cured."

The rabbit suddenly understood why he had been brought here and what a dangerous position he was in.

When they reached the Dragon King, the rabbit bowed and said, "Your majesty, I am so pleased to meet you. And I would gladly sacrifice my life for you, but alas, my liver is not with me this afternoon."

"What!" shouted the Dragon King. "Not with you? Don't be ridiculous rabbit. I don't believe you."

"But you must believe me, your majesty. You see, my liver has special powers. It is so valuable that I only carry it with me at night. Had the turtle only told me that you needed it, I would surely have brought it with me today. But he did not mention your illness at all."

"No one can take his liver in and out," said the Dragon King.

"Ah, your majesty. That indeed is true for most animals. But look carefully at my mouth. The reason I am able to take my liver in and out is because my upper lip is split."

The Dragon King stared at the rabbit's mouth.

"Let the turtle take me back to land as quickly as possible, your majesty, and I will gladly get my liver," said the rabbit.

"Go!" roared the Dragon King. "And be quick about it."

The turtle came swimming up and the rabbit climbed on the turtle's back. As quickly as he could go, the turtle returned to the sandy beach.

The rabbit hopped off and ran a few feet. "Hah!" he exclaimed. "You tried to trick me, but I have tricked you instead. I am safely back on dry land, and I will never return with you." And so saying, the rabbit hopped off out of sight.

The turtle wept at the thought of his beloved Dragon King dying. He would return in disgrace.

But a great god suddenly appeared. "Do not despair," the god said to the turtle. "I have been watching you and I am most favorably impressed with your loyalty to the Dragon King. Here, take these ginseng roots to your king. When he eats them, he will be cured."

"Thank you," cried the turtle. He took the ginseng roots and watched as the god disappeared before his eyes. As quickly as he could go, the turtle took the roots to his king. The Dragon King ate the roots and was cured.

As a reward, the loyal turtle was made the chief minister of the court. And from that day forward, the ginseng root was used to cure all kinds of illness.

Background Information

The Republic of Korea, often called South Korea, occupies less than half of the Korean Peninsula. The Sea of Japan on the east, the Yellow Sea on the West, and the East China Sea on the south border this Peninsula. The Military Demarcation Line (MDL) separates South Korea from North Korea. Sometimes Koreans call their country Choson, which means The Land of the Morning Calm.

Off the jagged west and south coasts of Korea are about 3,000 small islands. The largest of these islands, Cheju, contains South Korea's highest peak, volcanic Mount Halla, at 6,396 feet. The east coast, which faces the Sea of Japan, is smoother.

Because South Korea is so mountainous, some people refer to Korea as "the Switzerland of Asia." The Taebaek mountain range, an extension of the Nangnim range in the north, extends from North Korea into South Korea. The Sobaek range is located in the middle of South Korea, running roughly north to south.

The major rivers are the Naktong in the southeast, the Han, which flows through the capital city of Seoul, and the Kum, which provides water for the western lowlands.

The climate in South Korea is temperate, but South Korea is subject to earthquakes and is hit by at least one typhoon each summer. These typhoons bring high winds and heavy rain. The average rainfall in South Korea is 49 inches a year, with most of the rain falling between June and October.

Prior to 1965, most of South Korea was rural. But since that time there has been heavy industrial development so that currently 65 percent of the population is urban. About one-third of South Koreans live in four cities: Seoul, Pusan, Taegu, and Inchon.

Seoul is South Korea's capital and its largest city. It is located near the west coast. Inchon is the port of access to Seoul. Seoul is a city of contrasts. Old palaces and Buddhist temples are right next to new high-rise offices and apartment buildings and modern hotels. Seoul has a large and modern subway system.

Some palaces from the Yi Dynasty have survived in Seoul. The Toksukung Palace houses the National Museum of Art. In another palace is the National Folklore Museum. Kyongbokung Palace is at the east wall of Seoul and is famous for its beautiful gardens and pavilions.

Pusan is the second largest city in South Korea. It is a major port and is located in the southeast. Pusan has many factories. From here, fish, farm products, and manufactured goods are exported. It is also popular as a summer resort. It has hot mineral springs and good public beaches.

Taegu is located in central South Korea and is a major industrial center. It is a distribution center of farm products from the southern region of the country. Taegu is known for its medicinal herbs and for being the center of the apple industry. Taegu also has several universities and colleges.

Kyongju is near Mount Chiri National Park. The United Nations Educational, Scientific, and Cultural Organization (UNESCO) named Kyongju one of the world's most important ancient cities. It was the capital of the kingdom of Silla from 57 B.C. to A.D. 935. The Kyongju valley contains temples, tombs, shrines, pagodas, monuments, statues, and ruins.

In recent years, South Korea has become an exporter of industrial products to North America, Europe, Asia, and Africa. South Korea produces industrial machinery, electronic equipment, cars, leather goods, paper and paper products, tires, and sewing machines.

The farming regions in South Korea are mostly on the western and southern coasts. These are owner-operated farms where rice, barley, vegetables, and legumes are the chief crops. Tobacco is also grown. For the most part, farmers use simple tools, such as animal-drawn ploughs.

South Korea also operates a fleet of trawlers and is a major fishing nation. Thousands of coastal fishing boats operate in the waters around South Korea. The catch includes pollack, squid, octopus, anchovies, crabs, and mackerel.

South Korea imports fuel and most industrial raw materials. Its major exports are textiles, clothing, electrical machinery, footwear, steel, automobiles, ships, and fish. High tech products such as computers are a growing industry.

History

Until they became separate nations in 1948, North and South Korea shared a common history going back 5,000 years. The ancient kingdom of Choson is thought to have existed in Korea about 2300 B.C. The Chinese established a colony, Lolang, in Korea in the second century B.C. but were driven out in the seventh century by the Koreans.

The clans that descended from the people of Ancient Choson formed three kingdoms: Koguryo, Paekche, and Silla. Eventually Silla took over the entire Korean Peninsula. From A.D. 668 to 935, the Silla dynasty ruled the united peninsula. It was at its peak during the eighth century A.D. During this period Buddhism became strong in Korea.

During the 900s, the unified kingdom of Silla broke up in the midst of rebellion, and the Koryo dynasty rose. The Kingdom of Koryo lasted until 1392 A.D. In 1231, the Mongols from China invaded, and there were also invasions by Japanese pirates.

A Korean general, Yi Sung-gy, came to power. The Yi dynasty that he established lasted from 1392 to 1910, and the nation's capital was moved from Kaesong to Seoul. The greatest ruler during this period was King Sejong. Korea was still threatened by both Japan and China. Fighting with the Japanese lasted from 1592 to 1598. China attacked again in 1627.

The Yi dynasty established a closed-door policy, trying to have as little as possible to do with the outside world. As a result of this policy, Korea was known as the "hermit kingdom." People traveled little beyond their borders.

After the Russo-Japanese war in 1904 and 1905, the Japanese moved in and annexed Korea in 1910, and they were not driven out until after the Japanese defeat in World War II in 1945. When they were in control, the Japanese tried to suppress Korean language and culture and make Korea more Japanese.

At the end of World War II, Russia occupied the northern half of Korea and the United States occupied the southern half of Korea. The Soviets refused to leave, and the Korean Peninsula was divided along the 38th parallel.

Americans controlled South Korea until 1948, when the Republic of South Korea was established. The Democratic People's Republic of Korea was established in the north just a month later.

In June 1950, troops from North Korea, supported by the Soviets, invaded South Korea. Some countries feared that the Russians intended to keep spreading Communism and that this step in Korea might be the beginning of another world war.

Help from the United Nations in the form of troops and supplies came to the aid of South Korea. General Douglas MacArthur was given permission to set up air and naval support operations around Korea. MacArthur ordered the bombing of North Korean troops.

Soon after, American and South Korean troops were joined by troops and supplies from fifteen other nations, under the command of General MacArthur. After the battle of Inchon, the North Korean invasion was repelled. Then the decision was made to cross into North Korea. The Communist Chinese Army crossed into the Korean Peninsula, and in October 1950 attacked and sent the Eighth Army into retreat.

At the village of Yudam, about 100,000 Chinese attacked the 24,000 marines who made up the X-Corps. The retreat south through the snowy mountains was very difficult.

President Truman fired General MacArthur on April 11, 1951. General Walker was killed near the frontline, and General Matthew Ridgway took command of the Eighth Army. He succeeded in pushing the North Koreans back to the 38th parallel and retook the capital of Seoul.

In the months that followed, both sides pushed the war back and forth. It seemed clear that neither side could win a victory, and so talks were started that led to an Armistice and cease-fire. A Peace Treaty was never signed.

Many soldiers and civilians were killed on both sides. The fighting finally ended in July 1953 and a Military Demarcation Line was established between North and South Korea.

North Korea, which is Communist, currently occupies about 55 percent of the Korean Peninsula, covering 47,399 square miles. South Korea's portion of the Peninsula occupies 38,375 square miles. The population of South Korea is 45,948,811, while North Korea has 24,317,004 people.

The first president of South Korea, who led the country from 1948 to 1960, was Syngman Rhee, who proved to be a dictator. A military coup in 1961 brought to power General Park Chung Hee. South Korea was under martial rule for two years. Park was then elected president in 1963, 1967, and 1971.

In 1972, the constitution was changed, weakening the legislative branch of government and giving the president more power. Park was again elected president in 1978. In 1979, Park was assassinated. General Chun Doo Hwan took control and again established martial law.

Military rule ended in 1981, and in the following years there were violent demonstrations. Chun agreed to the direct election of the president by the people rather than by an electoral college. In 1987, Roh Tae-woo was elected. Many people, especially students, are eager to reunify North and South Korea. Others oppose such a move.

Government

The Republic of Korea adopted its first constitution in 1948. It was changed eight times between 1948 and 1987. In 1987, after General Roh Tae-woo became president, the National Assembly approved a new constitution. The constitution calls for a president to be elected every five years. The president is limited to one term of office.

The president appoints a prime minister and 15 to 30 State council members who head the various departments of government and assist the chief executive.

The single-house legislature, called the National Assembly, has 299 seats, and its members are elected to four-year terms. Anyone over the age of nineteen may vote.

The new constitution took away the president's power to dissolve the National Assembly, and it guaranteed human rights, including the right of workers who were not in defense industries to join unions.

The president appoints the Chief Justice of the Supreme Court with the approval of the National Assembly. He appoints the other Supreme Court justices, all of whom serve five-year terms, with the approval of the Chief Justice. The Chief Justice appoints the justices of the lower courts. There are three courts of appeal that hear cases still disputed after having been tried in one of the ten district courts.

Religion

Most South Koreans follow Buddhism or Confucianism. About 20 percent of the people are Buddhists. The Buddhist religion was brought to Korea about 2,500 years ago from China. Today South Korea has more than 700 Buddhist temples.

Although people do not consider the teachings of Confucius to be a formal religion, many Koreans live by following the rules of Confucianism. Because many South Koreans were taught the values of Confucius centuries ago, and because these values still dominate the thinking of the people, women are at a disadvantage. Inheritance laws and divorce codes are heavily weighted in favor of men. The desire for male rather than female children led at one time to the practice of infanticide in South Korea.

Ancestor worship and shamanism, the belief in unseen gods and demons, also still exists as part of South Korea's culture.

Missionaries from China introduced Christianity in the seventeenth century. Christianity became popular after World War II, and today about 16 percent of the Korean population are Christians. South Korea has more than 9 million Christians, of whom more than 5 million are Presbyterian Protestants. Another 16 percent of the Christians are Catholic.

Turkish soldiers were part of the United Nations forces and took part in the Korean War. They introduced the Muslim religion, and there are now several thousand Muslims in Korea, with Muslim mosques in Seoul, Pusan, and Kwangju.

Education

South Korea has a literacy rate of over 90 percent. Primary schooling is free, but parents pay for education beyond that. The four levels of Korean education are primary school, lower secondary, upper secondary, and higher education. Technical training to prepare students for jobs in business and industry begins in middle schools. About 90 percent of South Korean children between the ages of twelve and seventeen attend secondary school.

A primary school has six grades. Classes usually start at 9:00 A.M. and end at 3:00 P.M. Students attend five and one half days a week. A class may have as many as fifty-four students. Typically there are six class periods a day with each class lasting 40 minutes. There is a ten-minute break between periods.

On Monday mornings, most Korean primary schools begin the week by gathering for a weekly assembly. This is called *Cho-hoe*, which means morning meeting. Each teacher is present with her class, and the principal gives students some important words to think about during the week ahead. The students also sing the Korean national anthem and perhaps a school song.

Beginning about fifth grade, the six daily class periods usually are devoted to Korean language, English, mathematics, science, social studies, music, art, home economics, and physical education. Some classes are offered daily while others may be taught only once a week.

Lunch is usually after fourth period. A typical school lunch might be *tokbokki* (rice cake seasoned with red pepper), fried wonton, milk, and mandarin oranges. Students may eat the school lunch or may bring their lunches from home.

Students in South Korean schools help to keep their schools clean. Every day, some students have cleaning duties and they also take turns helping to serve lunch. On spe-cial occasions, there are parties at school. There are also clubs such as folk dancing clubs.

On the way home from school, students may stop at a book rental store. Most of the rental books are comics.

There are more than 200 two-year and four-year colleges and universities but there is a lot of competition for acceptance. Ewha University is a large women's university.

Immigrants

From the late 1500s to the late 1800s, China dominated Korea, and only a few Koreans traveled outside of the country. But in 1882, Korea entered into a treaty of friendship and trade with the United States. The Treaty of Chemulpo allowed the United States to send diplomats, merchants, and missionaries to Korea and permitted Koreans to travel to the United States. Several dozen Christian students from Korea came to the United States during the period 1890 to 1905.

Widespread immigration of Koreans to the United States began in 1905. There had been a drought in Korea followed by floods. The rice crop was ruined and people did not have enough to eat. Many Koreans immigrated to Hawaii, which at that time was an American territory, to work in either the pineapple or sugar fields. These early immigrants had to work hard and they were poorly paid, but conditions were still better in Hawaii than they were back in Korea.

Before long, some Koreans came to California to work on farms. Christian churches were often the center of life for small groups of Korean immigrants. The first church established on the mainland in 1905 was the Korean Methodist Church of San Francisco. Some Korean immigrants started small businesses such as fruit and vegetable markets or opened laundries. At first, the Korean immigrants to the mainland United States were mostly men, but soon families joined them or the men sent for Korean brides.

Many Koreans who remained in the United States settled in the Los Angeles area. By the 1930s, Korean Americans operated more than sixty businesses in Los Angeles including shops, herbal stores, and trucking companies.

Some people in the United States did not like Koreans and other Asians coming into the United States. They felt that Koreans were taking jobs that were needed by other

U. S. citizens. In 1924, the United States government passed an Oriental Exclusion Act that prevented Asian workers from coming into the United States. This law was not canceled until World War II.

Fearing that Japanese in California would assist Japan during the war between Japan and the United States, many Japanese were sent to stay in internment camps. Some Koreans were also sent to these camps because they "looked like" Japanese.

After the war, the Asians in these internment camps were released, and much, much later, the U. S. government apologized for its actions.

After the Korean War, many South Koreans came to the United States. Some women came as "war brides." Congress enacted a law allowing Americans sent to Korea to bring their Korean-born wives to America. Between 1951 and 1964, 28,000 Korean war brides immigrated to the United States.

After World War II, there were also many Korean orphans. Some were children whose fathers were American soldiers who had been stationed in Korea. Others were children whose Korean parents had been killed in the war. It is estimated that Americans adopted 50,000 Korean orphans between 1978 and 1989.

After 1965, immigration laws were changed, and the new laws made it easier for Koreans to enter the United States. About 35,000 Koreans emigrated each year. Between 1981 and 1990, 338,800 Koreans immigrated to the United States. During 1991 to 1995, another 95,900 came.

Many of these new Korean immigrants have been professional or business people and work in the United States and Canada as doctors, teachers, and merchants. Many more Koreans come to attend colleges and universities.

Two-thirds of the Korean immigrants to Canada came to Toronto, Montreal, and Vancouver. In the United States, the immigrants tended to settle in Los Angeles, New York, and Chicago. It is easier for Koreans to find jobs in big cities and to locate other Koreans to be with.

Korea Town, or *Little Seoul,* is the name given today to a section of Los Angeles along Olympic Boulevard. In the four-mile stretch, there are hundreds of Korean shops, restaurants, offices, churches, and temples. It is a center for southern California's more than 300,000 Korean immigrants.

Language

South Koreans speak Korean, with the Seoul dialect being the one most frequently used. Korean is a member of the Altaic family of languages and is related to Manchurian and Mongolian. Although it is not related to Chinese, it has borrowed many words from the Chinese. The Korean language has also borrowed words from Japanese and English.

South Koreans write in *hangul,* which is an alphabet developed in 1443. Hangul is used for most of Korean writing, but Chinese characters are still used for names of people and places.

The Arts and Sciences

Both North and South Korea share a rich tradition in the arts and sciences. Early Korean poets wrote about the natural beauty of the country and life in the court. Korea's most famous female poet was Hwang Chini, who lived in the 1500s and wrote love poems.

There is a long history of Korean folklore. One of the folktales that is best known is the story of two brothers, Hungbu and Nolbu, and how they treat each other. This story goes back to the mid-eighteenth century, when it was sung as part of a classic repertoire called *p'ansori.* These stories were performed in courtyards for rural aristocrats. They are still performed today by Korean musicians and singers.

Members of the upper classes wrote short lyric poems known as *sijo.* A scholar might write a sijo for a special occasion. Among common people, *pansori,* or ballads, were popular. Contemporary Korean poets, such as Kim Chi-ha, denounce government corruption in their works.

Painting is an ancient and respected Korean art. Early examples of Korean art are the frescos on the walls of tombs from the Koguryo dynasty. Later paintings include portraits, landscapes, and decorative screens. Popular subjects include flowers, animals, and birds. Many of these paintings have a delicate and misty quality. The oldest Buddhist painting in the world is Korean.

Some painters in Korea, such as Kim Whan-ki, do work that is a modern adaptation of a traditional theme.

226 • Keeping the Traditions

Pak Saeng-kwang painted masks in one of his 1985 paintings to represent ancient Korean folk art.

There are also many Korean sculptures that are admired. A great Buddhist monument exists at the famous grotto, *Sokkuran,* near Kyongju. Most of the sculptures were done in stone, although some are bronze, wood, and clay.

There are rich clay deposits, and Korean pottery is world famous. Artisans invented a method of inlay on pottery that was then glazed and fired. The product, called *celadon,* was gray green with a translucent glaze. During the Koryo period (A.D. 935–1391) celadon was highly regarded. Antique celadon is almost priceless.

Korea's musical tradition includes ballet, folk songs and dances, and royal court music. Native Korean music uses stringed and wind instruments and drums. Two types of zithers that are used are the 6-stringed *komungo* and the 12-stringed *kayagum.* The *changgo* (hourglass drum) is another popular instrument.

Koreans also were innovative in the sciences. One of the oldest astronomical observatories in the Far East was built in A.D. 647 in the ancient Silla capital of Kyongu. Very early charts of the movements of stars and planets were made here.

The ground plan of the cave temple, Sokkuram, which was built around A.D. 750, demonstrates an advanced understanding of mathematics, engineering, and architecture.

In 1277 a Korean Buddhist monk invented a type of glass tile that led to the development of ceramics manufacture.

Although Johann Gutenberg of Germany is credited with the invention of the printing press, Koreans were printing books with metal type in 1234, almost 200 years before Gutenberg. They also invented a Korean phonetic alphabet in the fifteenth century, *hangul,* which eventually allowed the masses access to learning. And Koreans are credited with the first set of encyclopedias ever printed. The 112-volume work from the fifteenth century was put on display in the Library of Congress in Washington, D.C.

During the fifteenth century, Koreans made more inventions, including a spinning wheel, astronomical instruments, surveying instruments, the sundial, and a clock that not only gave the time of day but indicated the seasons and when the sun and moon would rise and set.

Rainfall has been carefully measured in Korea ever since the reign of King Sejong (1419–1450), when a rain gauge was invented.

Food

During much of Korea's early history, there were four distinct classes of people: nobility, intellectuals, common people, and the lowest class. Each had its traditions that influenced dietary customs. Even today, the royal court cuisine uses many ingredients, and special seasonings and follows elaborate cooking procedures. The home-style cooking of more than half the people in Korea, however, is less complex and elegant.

For both groups, breakfast and dinner are more formal affairs than lunch, which is a light meal. Although business entertainment may be done in restaurants, most meals, including birthday and weddings feasts, are traditionally held at home.

It is common in Korea for family members to sit on the floor and eat from a low table using chopsticks and small bowls. Spoons are used for eating soup.

One common dish eaten almost daily is *kimchi,* which is probably the most universal dish served in Korea. Each family has its own recipe, combining vegetables with spices and other strong flavored foods. Common vegetables used in making kimchi are radishes, leeks, cucumbers, turnips, cabbages, and Chinese parsley, while the spices used might be red pepper, garlic, or sesame. Kimchi is sometimes stored in large crocks that are sunk in the ground.

A Korean meal might include the following: beef and radish soup, beans with rice, sheets of dried seaweed, boiled fish, short-necked clams, tofu, *pulkogi* (seasoned, barbecued beef), and kimchi made from Chinese cabbage. A simple meal might consist of rice, soup, kimchi, and one or two special foods.

For a special occasion, the meal might start with *kujolpan.* Several cooked meats and vegetables are served on a platter along with thin pancakes. The diner rolls the meats and vegetables into a pancake. This might be served in a nine-part dish with the vegetables and meats in eight covered trapezoidal boxes designed to fit around a center octagonal box holding the thin pancakes.

There are many outdoor food stalls in Korea in cities such as Seoul. Some are scattered throughout the city while others are clustered in markets such as the East Gate Market in Seoul. At these stands you can buy food such as cuttle-fish, potatoes, baked chestnuts, noodles, fruits, vegetables, and rice porridge with red beans. You might also buy American food such as hamburgers and fried chicken. There are also large supermarkets.

One Korean food that might seem familiar to students in the United States are *Kebabs*. If there is sufficient adult help, and if the season is right for an outdoor grill, students might enjoy the following:

Korean Kebabs (Sanjeok Kooi)

1 pound round steak

6 thin green onions

Basting sauce:

4 tablespoons soy sauce

2 tablespoons sugar

3 tablespoons minced green onion

1 1/2 tablespoons minced garlic

1 tablespoon toasted, ground sesame seeds

2 tablespoons sesame oil

dash of pepper

Slice the beef into small pieces about 2 inches long. Sprinkle basting sauce over the beef. Cut green onions the same size as the beef. Alternate threading beef and onion onto a skewer. Grill the skewers outdoors until cooked. While cooking, continue to baste with the basting sauce. Serve hot. Serves 4.

Recreation

Soccer is probably the most popular sport in South Korea. There are professional teams that compete in a pennant race each year. About twenty years ago, professional baseball leagues were started. Just like in the United States, people in South Korea have their baseball heroes. In addition to professional teams, these games are also played in high schools and colleges. Even younger students may stop after school to play baseball or soccer in a sports field.

Women and girls as well as men and boys play vol-leyball and have done well in international competition.

Wrestling is a traditional Korean competition. *Ssirum* is the ancient Korean form of wrestling. Many children in Korea (as well as in the United States) take lessons in *Taekwondo,* which is a Korean form of karate. Instructors in Taekwondo can be found in cities throughout the world.

Like most countries of the world, people in Korea play board games. One of these games, called *yut,* is played with four sticks and is similar to backgammon. Chess *(janggi)* is also popular. On school playgrounds, there are swings and seesaws.

Other popular sports are skiing, skating, swimming, tennis, table tennis, golf, archery, and boxing. Many Koreans enjoy hiking, mountain climbing, hunting, and fishing.

One famous Korean is Sammy Lee, who was born in California, the son of Korean immigrants. In 1948 in London, he won an Olympic Gold Medal for platform diving and the Bronze Medal for springboard diving. He also won the Gold Medal for platform diving at the 1952 Olympics held in Helsinki.

South Korea was host to the 1988 Olympic Games in Seoul. The Koreans built a stadium that seats 100,000 people, as well as other sports facilities.

Customs and Traditions

The first three days of the New Year are part of a big celebration in South Korea. Some celebrate the first three days in January while others celebrate according to the lunar or Chinese calendar.

Many people dress in colorful folk costumes and give New Year's gifts. Korean women spend much time preparing food for New Year's Day offerings to ancestors as well as to living members of the family. It is a time of special honoring of parents and grandparents. *Sal* (rice wine) and *ttokkuk* (rice dumpling soup) are often served.

Around April 5, Koreans celebrate *Hansik,* or Grave Visiting Day. In the morning, food and wine are carried to ancestral graves, and the graves are cleaned up.

For the First Full Moon of the Year, Koreans drink wine, which is supposed to prevent deafness. Then during the day, they visit twelve houses, eating food at each of them. A special rice dish is featured.

Koreans celebrate Buddha's birthday in early May. This is a national holiday. The colorful festival is sometimes called the Feast of Lanterns. All across the country, lanterns are hung in Buddhist temples. In Seoul, hundreds of thousands of people take part in a parade carrying lighted lanterns.

Children's Day occurs on May 5. This is a special day to honor children. Families typically plan excursions to parks and playgrounds.

Near the beginning of June, there is a celebration called *Tano* Day. Among rural people, this is a major holiday. It is a day of praying for good harvests. Another holiday on June 15, that is celebrated in rural areas is Farmers' Day. Farmers get together and help each other with their work, but there is also music and dancing.

Families also hold special celebrations. When a son is one hundred days old, the family prepares a great feast and invites guests to the celebration. The baby is placed by a table on which a variety of objects are placed. On the basis of what the baby touches first, predictions are made about his life.

A family also holds a special celebration when someone reaches a sixty-first birthday. A normal life span is considered to be sixty years, and when someone is sixty-one, that person begins a new cycle. A great feast with many dishes is formally served.

Suggested Activities

Writing

1. Three Korean Americans stand out as important leaders who wanted freedom for Korea. These three are Syngman Rhee (1875–1965), Ahn Chang-ho (1878–1938), and Pak Yong-man (1881–1928).

   Invite six students to work in pairs and research these men and the part they played in the struggle for Korean independence. Have each pair write a paper detailing what they learned. The paper should include a bibliography.

Reading

2. A group of interested students could read several versions of the Cinderella story and then discuss them, pointing out how details were changed to reflect the culture represented by the story. Among stories that might be considered are: *Kongi and Potgi, A Cinderella Story from Korea,* adapted by Oki S. Han and Stephanie Haboush Plunkett (Dial Books for Young Readers, 1996); *The Golden Sandal: A Middle Eastern Cinderella,* by Rebecca Hickox (Holiday House, 1998); *Smoky Mountain Rose: An Appalachian Cinderella* by Alan Schroeder (Dial Books for Young Readers, 1997); *The Turkey Girl: a Zuni Cinderella* by Penny Pollock (Little, Brown, 1996); and *Jouanah: A Hmong Cinderella,* by Jewell Reinhart Coburn and Tzexa Cherta Lee (Shen's Books, 1996).

Vocabulary

3. A special bulletin board can be prepared during a unit of study on Korea. As students read books and articles on Korea, they should be alert to Korean words and add both the Korean and English equivalent on 3 x 5-inch cards on the bulletin board.

   Here are some words for a beginning: *cho-hoe*—morning meeting, *kimchi*—pickled, spiced vegetable *Chom jaengi*—wise person, *halmoni*—grandmother, *haraboji*—grandfather, *ttalgi*—strawberries, *mun*—gate, *sa*—temple, *kung*—palace, and *toegi*—rabbit.

Math

4. A pair of students might want to study currency of ancient people and share with the class their sources of information and what they learned. What did old money look like? How was its value established? Ancient Korean money, for example, was called *nyung*. It was made of copper and had a hole in its center so that it could easily be carried on a cord.

Social Studies

5. Many Koreans follow the teaching of Buddha or Confucius. Ask a group of students to study Buddhism and Confucianism and share what they learn in an oral report. In addition to print resources, students might

want to use the World Wide Web. A possible site for them to explore is http://www.sogang.ac.kr/~burns/cult96/s940067.html, which contains information on Buddhism and the Korean people. Another site with leads to Korean Buddhism is http://www.human.toyogakuen-u.ac.jp/~acmuller/Buddhism-Korean.html. For information on Confucionism in Korea, students might visit http://www.iworld.bet/Korea/text/f89.html.

Geography

6. Invite a pair of students to find the answers to the questions that follow and report what they learn to the class. How far is Seoul from the city or town in which you live? If you were to visit Seoul, how would you get there? Is there more than one way to travel there? How long would it take? How much would it cost? What route would you follow and what cities would you find along the way?

Music

7. The music educator in your building could prove helpful in finding and sharing Korean music with your students. One source is the 2VHS/Book Set, order # ARTS-1 from Multicultural Media, RR#, Box 6655, Granger Road, Barre, Vermont 05641. This set was produced by the National Center of Korean Traditional Performing Arts. The program is divided into three parts, focusing on traditional vocal styles, instrumental music, and over sixty types of instruments. A 25-page booklet is included.

Art

8. Calligraphy, or brush writing, is an art in Korea. Try to locate someone in your community who does calligraphy and who is willing to come to visit the class and demonstrate. Follow up the visit with an appropriate thank you letter.

Drama/Movement

9. A pair of interested students, assisted by a media specialist, could research the masked dancers of Korea and report what they learn to the class. Historically, common people used masked dances to criticize the upper classes. They would portray corrupt monks, greedy merchants, and quack doctors in song, dance, pantomime, and dialogue. The performers wore colorful costumes and expressive masks.

Dress

10. *Hanbok* is the traditional Korean dress. Koreans used to wear hanbok every day and some older Koreans still do. But younger people usually now wear hanbok only on special holidays. Korean women often wear a long, full skirt (*chima*) gathered to a bodice and topped by a short jacket (*chogori*). A traditional costume for a man is long pants (*baji*) topped with a sleeveless vest and covered with a long coat called a *turumagi*.

Working with an adult volunteer or a media specialist, have two students search for pictures of Koreans in native dress. Then, with permission, they should photocopy these pictures or borrow the books to bring to class to show other students typical Korean dress.

Cooking

11. Ginger candy would be a good dessert to offer at a special class party.

Ginger Candy (Saeng Pyeon)
5 ounces fresh ginger
5 ounces sugar
1/2 teaspoon cinnamon
1/2 cup minced pine nuts

Pare the ginger and then boil it in a small saucepan of water for 4 minutes. Drain and mince.

Place the ginger, sugar, and cinnamon in a heavy pan and cook over low heat. Stir constantly. When the mixture is sticky and any liquid has evaporated, remove the pan from the heat and let it cool until just warm to the touch. Take a small piece of the mixture and roll it into a round ball. Then roll the ball in minced pine nuts and set it on a serving tray. Repeat.

Culminating Activity

12. A group of students, working with a pair of adult volunteers, might want to do research and then hold a

debate for the class on the topic: Should South and North Korea be re-unified? Yes or No. Students should point out the pros and cons of recreating a unified Korea and should list the factors that keep the two countries apart and point out both the benefits and dangers involved in any reunification effort. The debaters should read accounts in magazines and newspapers of recent student demonstrations for reunification.

Suggested Reading

Gay, Kathlyn and Martin Gay. *Korean War*. New York: Twenty-First Century Books, 1996.

Han, Suzanne Crowder. *The Rabbit's Escape*. New York: Henry Holt, 1995.

Han, Oki S. and Stephanie Haboush Plunkett. *Kongi and Potgi: A Cinderella Story from Korea*. New York: Dial Books, 1996.

———. and Stephanie Haboush Plunkett. *Sir Whong and the Golden Pig*. New York: Dial Books, 1993.

Jaffe, Nina. *Older Brother, Younger Brother: A Korean Folktale*. New York: Viking, 1995.

Jewett, Eleanore M. *Which Was Witch? Tales of Ghosts and Magic from Korea*. New York: Viking Press, 1954.

Kubota, Makoto. *South Korea*. Milwaukee, Wisc.: Gareth Stevens, 1987.

Kwon, Holly H. *The Moles and the Mireuk: A Korean Folktale*. Boston, Mass.: Houghton Mifflin, 1993.

Lye, Keith. *South Korea*. New York: Franklin Watts, 1985.

Mayberry, Jodine. *Koreans*. New York: Franklin Watts, 1991.

McMahon, Patricia. *Chi-Hoon: A Korean Girl*. Honesdale, Pa.: Boyds Mills Press, 1993.

McNair, Sylvia. *Korea*. Chicago, Ill.: Childrens Press, 1986.

Ok, Cho Joong. *Home Style Korean Cooking in Pictures*. Tokyo, Japan: Japan Publications, 1981.

Riordan, James. *Korean Folk-tales*. New York: Oxford University Press, 1994.

Rodgers, Mary M., ed. *South Korea . . . In Pictures*. Minneapolis, Minn.: Lerner Publications, 1989.

The United Kingdom

A Legend from England

As you read this re-telling of a Cornish Legend, you are sure to be reminded of *The Shoemaker and the Elves*. The two stories have much in common. Another version of this story can be found in *The Little People's Pageant of Cornish Legends* by Eric Quayle.

The Three Piskie Threshers

Once, in a little village near Penzance in Cornwall in the southernmost part of England, there lived a poor farmer and his wife. The wife was a fine seamstress, and the farmer worked hard from sunup to sundown every day. Although they were very poor, they were content.

The farmer was busy this spring season threshing grain by hand. He would go to his barn each morning and labor all day long. This was hard work, and he usually managed to fill only two sacks with grain each day. But one morning when the farmer went to the barn, he was amazed at what he found. There were eight sacks of grain lined up neatly against one of the walls. The farmer counted them, scratched his head, and counted them again.

Then he hurried back to his wife in the cottage. "Wife," he said, "I do believe that we were visited by piskies during the night."

"Nonsense," she said. "No one has seen piskies in these parts for years. What makes you think such a foolish thing?"

The farmer took his wife out to the barn and showed her the eight bags of grain.

"Now do you believe me?" he asked. "I only filled two sacks."

"I do not," said his wife. "You must have worked extra hard yesterday and filled these bags yourself. Perhaps you were so tired that you've forgotten all about it."

The farmer was not convinced. So that night, he slipped out of bed and quietly went to the barn. As he approached, he could hear sounds—clickity, clackity, clackity, click, click, click. There was silence for a moment. Then again the farmer heard clickity, clackity, clackity, click, click, click.

Mystified, the farmer peeked through a window in the wall. He was amazed to see inside three tiny piskies, dressed in ragged suits of green, working hard. Each used a flail to beat the sheaves of grain. Their flails went up and down so fast that the farmer could barely see them. The chaff floated off, and the piles of grain looked like little mountains of gold.

The farmer silently crept back to his cottage where he awakened his wife. He took her to the window and asked her to listen. She could hear the distant sounds of threshing and stared in wonder at her husband. "Is it true then?" she asked. "Are there piskies in our barn?"

"True enough," said the farmer.

That night the farmer and his wife listened at the window. They heard loud squeaking sounds as if the piskies were quarreling over who would get the suit. Finally the squeaks stopped, and the sounds of threshing were heard.

The next morning when the farmer and his wife awakened, they rushed out to the barn and found eight more sacks of grain. They were so happy at their good fortune that they tried to think of some way to thank the little piskies.

It was the wife who came up with a plan. "Since you say they're dressed in tatters, why not give them each a new suit of clothes?"

"A good idea," the farmer agreed, and he quickly set off for Penzance. When he came back, he carried a handsome bolt of green cloth.

The wife got busy with her scissors, needle, and thread. That evening she stopped to bake some Cornish pasties for their dinner. By nightfall, she had finished one little suit of clothes. It looked grand indeed.

The farmer took the suit to the barn and set it out on a three-legged stool for the piskies. He pinned a note on it that his wife had written. It said, "Another suit tomorrow."

That night the farmer and his wife listened at the window. They heard loud squeaking sounds as if the piskies were quarreling over who would get the suit. Finally the squeaks stopped, and the sounds of threshing were heard—clickity, clackity, clackity, click, click, click.

In the morning, the farmer and his wife rushed to the barn. The little suit was gone, and they found five sacks of grain waiting for them. "Hmmm," said the farmer. "Yesterday there were eight sacks and today there are only five. Still, that's a lot of work that I don't have to do."

That day, in addition to her chores, the wife cut and sewed another suit of clothes for the piskies. As before, the farmer took it to the barn and left it on the stool. The wife had pinned a note to it that read, "Another suit tomorrow."

That night at their bedroom window, the farmer and his wife heard more loud squeaking, and finally the sounds of threshing, clickity, clackity, clackity, click, click, click.

In the morning when the farmer and his wife went to the barn, they found the second suit of clothes was gone. There were three sacks of grain waiting by the wall.

"Hmmm," said the farmer. "Yesterday there were five sacks and today there are only three. Still, it's a lot of work that I don't have to do."

That day the wife finished the third suit of clothes. Her husband took it to the barn. That night, he crept near the barn and hid, hoping to see the piskies again. When he heard squeaking noises inside, he peeked through the barn window.

There were two little men dressed in their fine new suits. The third piskie picked up the new suit, held it out in front of him, and then twirled in a circle before taking off his old clothes and pulling on his new suit. Then the three piskies joined hands and danced and sang a strange little song. Suddenly, as the farmer watched, they flew into the air and disappeared.

The next morning the farmer and his wife were sad when they went to the barn and found that none of the grain had been threshed.

"I'll just have to finish the rest myself," said the farmer.

The wife looked around the barn. She was disappointed that the little piskies had left. Then she noticed a leather purse on the three-legged milking stool. Its strings were tied tight.

She picked it up and handed it to the farmer, but his hands were shaking so that he couldn't open it.

Carefully the wife untied the knot, and tipped the purse. A golden shower of coins tumbled to the floor. The farmer and his wife fell to their knees, picking up the coins one by one and crying tears of joy.

Now they would be able to buy things they had never been able to afford—a spinning wheel for the wife, new boots, and a brand-new plow for the farmer. Through her tears of joy, the wife said, "Bless the little people."

Background Information

As a nation of immigrants, the United States is indebted to many countries for the richness and variety of its culture. No other part of the world, however, has contributed as much to the American scene as the United Kingdom.

The British Isles lie off the northwest coast of Europe between 50 and 60 degrees north latitude and at 0 degrees longitude. The English Channel, the Strait of Dover, the North Sea, and the Atlantic Ocean bound these islands. The islands enjoy a cool to mild temperature.

There are two main islands, Great Britain and Ireland, and many smaller islands. There are two independent nations in the British Isles. Great Britain, the largest island, is made up of England, Scotland, and Wales. Along with Northern Ireland, they make up the United Kingdom of Great Britain and Northern Ireland, with a population of 58,610,182. They cover an area of 94,251 square miles. The capital of the United Kingdom is London, England.

The second independent nation in the British Isles is the Republic of Ireland, which is discussed in another chapter.

Great Britain has cities and factories, but it also contains farmlands, forests, heathlands, moorlands, mountains, and peat bogs. Among its natural resources are coal and iron, which were heavily mined in the nineteenth century after the development of steam power.

England

England is 50,056 square miles in area. The eastern portion, known as East Anglia, is a low region of fertile land. Wheat, sugar beets, potatoes, and other vegetables are raised here.

The South Coast has mostly farmland. There are orchards, grape vines, hop fields, and flocks of sheep. The southern coast also has beaches that welcome summer tourists.

The West Country has pasture land and barren heaths. This area contains the monoliths of Stonehenge. Devon has pretty coastal towns. And Cornwall (Kernow) is famous for its beaches. Once it was known for tin mining and it still produces China clay.

The Home Counties include the suburban areas around the city of London. London is the capital of England and the center of government for the entire United Kingdom. The river Thames runs through this city which has over 7 million people. London is home to the Bank of England and the Stock Exchange.

In the central portion of England is the second largest city in Britain, Birmingham. It is a business center and also a center for industry. Automobiles, bicycles, and machine tools are manufactured here. Britain's industry developed in the low plateaus near Nottingham and Leicester. In this section of the country there are potteries, breweries, and the port city of Liverpool. More than 100 years ago, ships from Liverpool took cloth from factories to all parts of the world.

Nottingham, Stoke-on-Trent, Greater Manchester, and Sheffield border the Peak District. This area has moorland and craggy rocks and is popular with hikers and climbers.

The Lake District in northwest England, north of Lancashire, is mountainous and filled with lakes. Many of these lakes, including Lake Windermere, are popular for boating. Climbers attempt various peaks in the area.

The Northeast County of Durham is on a coal field and also contains the moorlands of the Pennine hills. Newcastle was an important shipbuilding port, and to the north of it is Northumbria, where sheep farming and forestry are the main forms of agriculture.

Scotland

Scotland is 29,794 square miles in area. People in Scotland have many customs different from those of Northern Ireland, England, and Wales. Some Scots in the north and the west speak *Gaelic*, a Celtic language. Others, in the Borders region, speak Scots, which is a form of English. And many speak standard English with a distinct accent.

Edinburgh, the capital of Scotland, has 2 universities. It is a center for medicine, banking, law, insurance, and tourism. It is also home to the Edinburgh Festival, where artists, actors, musicians, and comedians come from all over the world to take part.

Highland games are held where competitors dance and participate in tossing a heavy pole called the *caber*. Bagpipes are commonly played at various games and ceremonies.

Glasgow, on the River Clyde, is Scotland's second largest city and the third largest city in the United Kingdom. It was once famous for its manufacturing and shipbuilding activities, but those industries have declined. Current industries include textiles, food and beverages, and printing.

Scotland has cattle in the highlands and rich farmlands in the Central lowlands. The Grampian Mountains divide the highlands from the lowlands. In the highland plateau, there are lakes called lochs. Loch Ness is the most famous because it is supposed to contain a prehistoric monster. Ben Nevis, the highest mountain in Britain at 4,406 feet, is nearby.

Aberdeen is an oil-processing town for North Sea oil. The islands of Jura and Islay are famous for their whiskey. The Isle of Aran is known for its woolen knitwear.

In the northwest highlands there are small farms of 5 to 10 acres where oats and potatoes are grown. Chickens are raised here also.

Wales

Wales is 7,967 square miles in area. It is surrounded on three sides by the sea. It is a hilly and mountainous country known for its mining and sheep raising. At one time, the coalmines in the south were very important, but they have been partly replaced by new industries. Wales has two official languages. The Welsh are Celtic, and many people in the north and west speak Welsh, *Cymraeg* as their first language. Others speak English.

The capital city of Wales is Cardiff (Caerdydd), which is a shopping and service center, and is the home of a variety of food processing plants. Another major city in south Wales is Swansea (Abertawe). The Severn Bridge over the River Severn just north of Bristol is a major connecting road link between England and Wales.

Welsh people are famous for their poetry and their choral singing. Singers and poets compete at festivals that are called *eisteddfodau*. A similar festival called a *Feis* is often held in Ireland. The National Eisteddfod is held in a different place each year. Most of the competitions are held in the Welsh language, but at the International Eisteddfod held in Llangollen, many of the competitors do not speak Welsh. The Eisteddfodau are part of a long tradition among Celtic peoples to hold a festival in the summer, bringing everyone together in peace.

Northern Ireland

Northern Ireland is made up of the six northeastern counties of Ireland: Antrim, Armagh, Down, Fermanagh, Londonderry, and Tyrone, together with the county boroughs of Londonderry and Belfast. It covers 5,459 square miles. Northern Ireland was established by the partition of Ireland following the Government of Ireland Act of 1920. Its border with the Republic of Ireland is 250 miles.

Scots colonized most of Northern Ireland during the seventeenth century, and Scots settlers continued to move in during the eighteenth century. About two-thirds of the population is Protestant and one-third Roman Catholic. The largest Protestant group is represented by Presbyterians.

Northern Ireland is primarily agricultural, with most farms being under 30 acres. Oats, hay, and potatoes are common crops, with wheat and barley confined to the relatively dry lowlands. Grass seed and seed potatoes are grown for export. Chicken, cattle, sheep, and pigs are also raised.

Inland and sea fisheries are of considerable value. A small amount of coal is mined. Much of the industry within 30 miles of Belfast involves textiles.

Northern Ireland has a history of violence between Catholics and Protestants that has never been resolved. A stormy relationship continues among the Republic of Ireland, Northern Ireland, and Great Britain. However, in 1998, the Belfast accord was approved in a referendum in Northern Ireland and the Republic of Ireland.

The Accord sets up an Assembly of 108 members, 6 from each of Northern Ireland's 18 British parliamentary constituencies. It is hoped that the Assembly will gradually take over from the British government responsibilities in all areas except security and prison policies. To assure that neither Protestants nor Catholics impose their will, controversial issues must either have a "weighted majority" (at least 60 percent approval) or "parallel consent" (at least 50 percent of both the Catholic and Protestant blocs).

The top post in the new government is a "first minister," who will be Protestant and a "deputy first minister," who will be a Catholic. The Assembly as a whole must endorse decisions made by the ministers.

The Accord also sets up a North-South Ministerial Council so that ministers from the Irish Republic and Northern Ireland will meet on mutually agreed areas of common interest including agriculture, tourism, environmental protection, welfare fraud control, and transportation.

History

Celtic people, called *Britons,* from Central Europe settled in Britain and in Ireland. Then around 43 B.C. the Romans made southern Britain a part of the Roman Empire but failed to conquer Scotland. They built roads and cities and erected walls to keep out the northern Picts and Scots. After 400 years, the Roman Empire began to weaken, and Roman armies left Britain.

Three Germanic tribes invaded after the Romans left. The Angles settled in the east, the Saxons farther west and in the midlands, and the Jutes in the south coast. In A.D. 865, the Vikings from Norway and Denmark invaded the British Isles but were eventually driven out, although raids continued.

In 1066, William, Duke of Normandy, defeated the Anglo-Saxons. Other barons and lords challenged the power of the king. In 1215, King John signed a document known as the Magna Carta, setting out rules for governing the country.

In time, many of the overseas possessions of the British Empire became independent. Some joined the Commonwealth, headed by the ruling queen or king, and in 1973, Britain joined the European Union.

Government

The United Kingdom of Great Britain and Northern Ireland is a constitutional monarchy. The ruling king or queen performs the ceremonial role of head of state. But the government works on a system of parliamentary democracy. Elections are held at least every five years, and all citizens over eighteen who are on the electoral roll can vote. The political party that wins the most seats in parliament forms a government.

The prime minister, who is the leader of the party in power, has similar duties to those of the president of the United States. The prime minister appoints a cabinet. Ministers represent different government departments such as health and education. This cabinet serves much as the cabinet of the President of the United States.

Bills are debated and passed in the House of Commons, which is a body similar to the House of Representatives in the United States. Then the bills go to the House of Lords. The House of Lords is not a representative or elected group like the Senate is in the United States. The number of members of the House of Lords was greatly decreased in 1999. Its members include the two archbishops and other bishops, lords with inherited titles, and peers appointed for life in recognition of their public service. The House of Lords debates the bills sent to it by the House of Commons and generally agrees to their passage. Then the king or queen gives assent to the bills before they become law.

The United Kingdom does not have a written constitution but relies on common law, which has built up since the eleventh century, and on statute law, which is legislation passed by Parliament. Citizens are also subject to laws passed by the European Community.

From the above brief description, it is easy to tell that although it is a monarchy, the United Kingdom contributed a great deal to the structure of our government in the United States. Even before the first settlers landed after their long journey on *The Mayflower,* they drew up a short document known as The Mayflower Compact, which each man signed showing a willingness to abide by a common set of rules.

Early settlers swore their allegiance to the English king, but even after demanding their independence and setting up a new nation, they continued to support a representative type of government.

Most criminal cases in England and Wales are tried in local courts. More serious cases go to the crown courts, which are presided over by a judge and a jury of twelve citizens.

In Scotland, minor cases are tried in police courts or magistrates' courts. Serious cases go to the sheriff courts, where the sheriff can call in a jury.

In Northern Ireland, the inferior courts deal with minor civil and criminal matters. County courts, which deal with civil and criminal matters, are held in twenty-three towns. Petty sessions courts are presided over by one magistrate, or in some cases, two are called in to adjudicate.

Although they are not set out in a written Constitution in the United Kingdom, there are three branches of government: the legislative, the executive, and the judicial. Our government has these same three branches, which provide checks and balances of power.

The United Kingdom is still ruled by a queen today, and all sovereigns of the United Kingdom must also head the Church of England. Although kings and queens in the United Kingdom have great wealth and some power, the chief executive officer is the prime minister.

Changes in government in the United Kingdom are presently going on. Both Scotland and Wales in 1997 voted to establish their own Parliament. And the agreements set up in the Belfast Accord are in the early stages of what may be the settling of important differences that have existed for a very long time among the Republic of Ireland, Northern Ireland, and Great Britain.

Religion

The official religion of Great Britain is Christianity. The Church of England and the Church of Wales are both Anglican. In Scotland, the Presbyterian Church is the official church.

But other Protestant religions and Catholicism are also practiced. There are Methodists, Baptists, Congregationalists, Unitarians, Quakers, Jehovah's Witnesses, Seventh Day Adventists, Christian Scientists, and other active groups including the Salvation Army. Jewish people practice Judaism and worship in synagogues. Muslims worship in mosques and follow Islam. Sikhs and Hindus worship in temples.

The Church of England dates back to Henry VIII (1509–1547). His wife gave Henry VIII a daughter, but not a son, so Henry VIII applied to the Pope to annul the marriage. When the Pope refused, Henry VIII left the Roman Catholic Church. Parliament drafted legislation making Henry VIII supreme governor of the Church of England. At first the Church of England followed the Catholic rituals closely, but it has changed over time.

Education

Education in the United Kingdom is free and compulsory for children between the ages of six and sixteen. The typical school day runs from 9:00 A.M. to 4:00 P.M. There is a national curriculum in these state schools. This system is similar to the one common in the United States, except that in the U.S. there is no national curriculum.

In both England and Wales, public school is divided into primary for children ages six to eleven, and secondary for students aged eleven to sixteen. There are also nursery schools for those below the age of six run by private foundations or local education authorities.

There are several examinations during the years of schooling. Achievements tests are given at ages seven, eleven, thirteen, and sixteen. The General Certificate of Secondary Education is taken at age fifteen or sixteen. The Advanced ("A") Level Exam is taken at age seventeen or eighteen.

In addition to state schools, there are public schools, which are private and for which students pay a fee. Some of these are boarding schools while at others the children live at home and attend school by day. Some churches also run schools.

In Scotland, children take the Scottish Certificate of Education at age sixteen. At seventeen, they take the Higher Examinations in a number of subjects. Some students remain in school until they are eighteen and then can take the Sixth Year Studies exams, which are similar to the British "A" Level Exams.

In Northern Ireland, primary and secondary education is provided in grant-aided schools. Children eleven and under attend primary schools. Then those who qualify for a scholarship attend grammar schools, which provide an academic secondary education. Those who do not qualify for grammar schools attend intermediate schools, where the emphasis is on more technical subjects. There are also teacher training schools and Queen's University in Belfast.

Entrance to Great Britain's universities is competitive based on a student's "A" level exams or equivalent.

Immigrants

"New England" is that northeast portion of the United States where early settlers originally came from the United Kingdom. There were many causes—political, religious, and economic—that led to this colonization. Trading companies got charters from the crown to give Great Britain outlets abroad. A group of Separatists revolted against the other creeds in Britain, insisting that the Bible was the only test of faith. These were among the first to emigrate.

Most of those early inhabitants brought with them many of the features of their life in the "old country" with its deeply rooted traditions. After all, when the Pilgrims set sail from England in 1620, London, the capital of the United Kingdom, was already 1,577 years old.

But this was only one wave of immigration. When religious bickering broke out, when there was fighting between groups trying to get control of the crown, when there was famine and economic hardship, people left their homes and came to America.

When George I of Hanover was on the British throne in 1715, a group of Scots, called *Jacobites,* proclaimed James Edward king in Scotland. When this threat to the throne failed, many Jacobites were shipped to plantations in America. Such occurrences were common throughout British history.

Language

Perhaps the most important contribution early settlers brought with them was a language, English, which continues as the dominant language used in the United States today. Usually one of the first things that immigrants from other countries do on coming to the United States is to learn to speak English. Today, more than 450 million people in the world speak the English language. English has the largest vocabulary of any language.

Although many people speak English, they may speak it with an accent. In England, natives can make a pretty good guess if the English person speaking to them is from the city of London, from the north, or from Cornwall. Differences are even more pronounced when the speaker is Scottish, Welsh, or Irish. And the accent of an American can be picked out immediately.

In 1611, James I of England (who was also James VI of Scotland) authorized a translation of the Bible, the King James version, which is still used by many religious groups and is noted for the beauty of its English language.

The Arts and Sciences

The United Kingdom has shared with the world many famous writers, painters, musicians, philosophers, architects, and scientists whose works are highly valued. Of these, arguably the most famous is William Shakespeare. During the summer, there are open-air performances of plays by Shakespeare in London's Regent Park.

His plays are also commonly enjoyed throughout the United States. Several states, including Colorado and Oregon, have well known Shakespeare Festivals where veteran actors and directors come for the summer and perform three or four plays. Over a period of years, these festivals present all of Shakespeare's histories, tragedies, and comedies.

Because we share the same language, the great playwrights, poets, and novelists from the United Kingdom are very familiar to people in the United States. They include John Milton, John Donne, Ben Jonson, Jonathan Swift, Alexander Pope, Henry Fielding, Samuel Taylor Coleridge, George Gordon, Lord Byron, William Blake, William Wordsworth, John Keats, Elizabeth Barrett Browning, Alfred, Lord Tennyson, Jane Austen, Charles Dickens, Emily Brontë, Thomas Hardy, Rudyard Kipling, and Dylan Thomas.

In the field of philosophy, major contributors include: Englishman John Locke, Irishman George Berkeley, and Scotsman David Hume. All these philosophers stressed the importance of observation and experience in learning about the world. Locke's ideas on natural rights and the just limits of government influenced many of the leaders of the American revolution and framers of the Constitution of the United States of America.

Painters also flourished in Great Britain, including John Constable, J. M. W. Turner, William Hogarth, and Thomas Gainsborough.

Among the famous names in the field of architecture are Inigo Jones, Christopher Wren, John Wood the Younger, and Norman Foster.

In the sciences, Great Britain is proud of the contributions of many people. William Harvey discovered how blood circulates in the human body. Isaac Newton discovered laws of gravity. John Dalton began modern atomic theory in chemistry. Michael Faraday discovered electromagnetic induction. Charles Darwin put forth the theory of evolution, and Charles Parsons invented the steam turbine engine.

Among famous musicians from the United Kingdom are: William Byrd, Henry Purcell, Thomas Arne, Arthur Sullivan, W. S. Gilbert, Gustav Holst, Edward Elgar, Ralph Vaughn Williams, Arthur Bliss, William Walton, Michael Tippett, and Benjamin Britten. Even though George Frederick Handel was born in Germany, the bulk of his writing was done in England.

British pop stars, such as the Beatles, are world famous. In Wales and Scotland there are many folk singers. National orchestras, ballet, and opera companies perform classical music, ballet, and opera. Many towns have their own local music and drama festivals.

Food

Great Britain is not known for elaborate cooking. A typical English breakfast includes eggs, bacon, sausages, and tomatoes. The main meal, dinner, may be served at mid-day or in the evening. It typically includes meat, chicken, or fish with vegetables. On a big family occasion, the traditional meal might be roast lamb with mint sauce, roast potatoes, cauliflower, carrots, and gravy. At Christmas, a roast goose may be the main dish. Lunch or supper are lighter meals, with soup, salad, and sandwiches.

Perhaps the most famous of British meal customs is afternoon tea. This is usually served at 4:00 P.M. and often includes sandwiches, cookies, or cakes. The Duchess of Bedford established this practice during the 1840s.

Scones are a popular English food. Below is a recipe you might wish to try.

Scones

4 cups all-purpose flour

2 tablespoons sugar

1 tablespoon baking powder

2 teaspoons baking soda

1 teaspoon salt

$1/2$ cup cold butter, cut up

$1/2$ cup currants

2 egg yolks

$1\,1/3$ cups plus 1 tablespoon of half-and-half cream

Combine flour, sugar, baking powder, baking soda, and salt in a large bowl. Cut butter into flour mixture until it resembles coarse cornmeal. Mix in the currants.

In a separate bowl, beat together eggs and cream. Add wet mixture to dry mixture. Don't overwork. Pat out dough into a rectangle about one inch thick on a floured surface. Cut into 12 triangles. Bake on an ungreased baking sheet in a pre-heated 350°F oven about 25 minutes. Cool on a rack.

Just as we speak in the United States of "Southern Cooking," "Western Barbecues," or "New England" clambakes, regions in the United Kingdom are famous for certain foods. Stilton is famous for its cheese, and Yorkshire is known for its puddings. The Cornish have meat and potato pies known as *pasties*. Wales is known for *laverbread*, which is seaweed fried with oats and bacon. In Scotland, a dish called *haggis* is made with sheep or calf organs and oatmeal. Fish and chips are popular everywhere.

British pubs are famous. These are public houses where people come to meet, talk, eat, and drink. There are over 70,000 public houses in England and Wales and several thousand more in Scotland. Favorite games played in pubs are darts, billiards, and dominoes.

Recreation

Many of the sporting events that we enjoy in the United States are also played in England. Soccer, probably the most popular game throughout the world, is called Association football in Great Britain. Division games are played every week from mid-winter until May.

Rugby football (sometimes called rugger or Union football) is more like American football than soccer. England, Scotland, and Wales have their own teams. Playoffs take place in January between England, Scotland, and France in odd-numbered years, and between England, Wales, and Ireland during even-numbered years.

Cricket is a popular summer sport as is tennis. Many enthusiasts in the United States tune their television sets to watch the famous tennis tournaments held in Wimbledon.

Horseracing is also popular. Just as the Kentucky Derby is a big event in the United States, the Derby held at Epsom Downs and the Grand National, run at Liverpool, are the most famous horse races in Great Britain. An annual rowing regatta takes place in Henley, and Cowes is famous for its sailing regatta.

Many people also take part in the field sports of hunting, shooting, and fishing. Others have gardening as a major hobby.

Customs and Traditions

Our life in the United States today is enhanced by many of the customs and traditions that have origins deep in the United Kingdom's past. New Year's Day is celebrated everywhere. In Scotland, January 1 is called *Hagmanay.* You may have sung or listened to others sing *Auld Lang Syne* on New Year's Eve. Robert Burns, a famous Scottish poet, wrote the words to the song.

Easter egg hunts and egg rolling are particularly famous in Lancashire, England. The tradition of egg rolling or Pace-Egging may symbolize rebirth and the renewal of life after a dark winter. Children roll brightly colored and artistically painted hard-boiled eggs. Easter egg hunts continue to be held all over the United States. Perhaps the most famous egg hunt in the United States is hosted each year by the President on the White House lawn.

The old-fashioned Easter Parade of fine clothes and Easter bonnets dates back to 1829 in Battersea Fields on the outskirts of London, England, where a duel was set between the Marquess of Winchester and the Duke of Wellington. Members of London society, dressed in their finery, flocked to the scene to witness the duel.

Eventually this district was cleaned up and named Battersea Park. In 1858, Queen Victoria paid it a state visit, wearing, of course, a new spring bonnet and gown. Now in addition to people in their finery, ornamental floats following a theme are on display.

The Notting Hill Carnival is a street festival of floats, stalls, and music celebrating West Indian culture. Since 1966, it has been held in north London on Easter Monday. This Afro-Caribbean affair features steel bands and Caribbean food specialties.

Just as we do in the United States, the British celebrate April Fools' Day, the first day of April, by playing practical jokes on one another. May Day, the start of summer, is often celebrated with a Maypole. Women dance around the pole holding ribbons that they wind and unwind as they dance.

In the United States, we celebrate Halloween on October 31, the eve of All Saints' Day. Children wear costumes, carve jack-o'-lanterns, bob for apples, and go trick-or-treating throughout the streets. Many people in the United Kingdom also celebrate Halloween and go trick-or-treating.

All Hallows in the ancient Celtic calendar marked the beginning of true winter. In various parts of England this holiday is called Punky Night, Nut-Crack Night, or Apple and Candle Night. The "punkies" are candle lanterns carved by children from large mangel-wurzels hollowed out and windowed, with a candle placed inside to make a lantern. Children knock on doors, hoping for coins.

Guy Fawkes Day is celebrated on November 5. It commemorates Guy Fawkes, who tried to blow up the Houses of Parliament in 1605. There are often bonfires and fireworks.

The Sunday nearest to November 11 is celebrated as Armistice Day, marking the date of the end of World War I. Ex-servicemen march in a procession led by the queen and wreaths are laid on the War Memorial in Whitehall. Red paper poppies are sold to benefit war veterans. Most towns and cities in the United States celebrate Armistice Day or Memorial Day, and at one time, red poppies were commonly sold in the United States, too.

During the Christmas season, there are special carol services and nativity plays in the United Kingdom. There are street decorations and decorated Christmas trees. In most families, Father Christmas fills stockings children leave by the chimneys, and presents are exchanged. Turkey or goose is served followed by Christmas pudding.

Farmers in Great Britain take their best animals to agricultural shows similar to the county and state fairs held throughout the United States. Animals win ribbons and prizes. The Royal Show, which lasts for several days, is held every summer.

Northern Ireland's oldest country fair is called Oul Lammas. It is held every summer in Bally Castle. In addition to many farm animals on display, there are stalls selling goods to the fair visitors.

Suggested Activities

Writing

1. England, Scotland, and Wales have national symbols or emblems. England uses the rose, Wales uses either the leek or the daffodil, and the Scottish emblem is a thistle. Ask a small group of students to do some research. Why were these symbols chosen? Is a special symbol used in Northern Ireland? Ask the students to share what they learn in a written report with the class.

Reading

2. Invite students to read some poetry written by one of the English poets. Ask them to choose a favorite, practice reading it aloud, and then read it to the class.

Vocabulary

3. Some words that are common in Britain are unfamiliar to Americans. Encourage students to be on the alert for "British" words. List these words on a sheet on the bulletin board with brief definitions. Here are some examples to get you started: a *lift* is an elevator; drivers fill their cars with *petrol* rather than with gasoline; high ranking police officers are referred to as *guava* or *governor.*

Math

4. British money is divided in pounds and pence, with 100 pence equal to a pound. A visitor from the United States converts American dollars into British pounds. The exchange rate between two countries varies from day to day. Ask a pair of students to find the current exchange rate for dollars and pounds and report to the class how many British pounds could be purchased for 500 dollars.

Social Studies

5. In 1973, Britain joined the European Union. Ask a pair of students to do some research on this topic and write a short paper, including a bibliography, sharing what they learn. What was the purpose of the European Union? What other countries joined? Does it still exist? Post the paper on a bulletin board.

Geography

6. Ask a small group of students to project a map of Great Britain onto a large sheet of tag board and trace it. List the major cities on the map, show the division of the different countries, and label the bodies of water around Great Britain. Post the map on a class bulletin board.

Music

7. A favorite patriotic song in the United States is *Our Country 'Tis of Thee.* The same melody is used for the famous British patriotic song *God Save the Queen.* Ask a student to find, type up, and post the words to *God Save the Queen.*

Art

8. The flags of the United Kingdom are both colorful and interesting. Students might enjoy making colored drawings of the flags of the United Kingdom. The Union Jack is a blend of English, Scottish, and Irish flags. The Welsh flag shows a red dragon on a green and white background. The English flag is the red Cross of St. George on a white

background, and the Scottish flag is the white Cross of St. Andrew on a blue background. Once the flags are finished, they might be displayed on a bulletin board.

Drama/Movement

9. Have an interested pair of students rehearse and present to the class a short excerpt from one of Shakespeare's plays.

Dress

10. There are more than 250 patterns of tartan related to specific clans in Scotland. Invite a group of students to research and find out more about tartans and kilts. They should try to find colored pictures of some of the tartan designs. Perhaps someone in the community has a scarf, kilt, or skirt featuring a specific tartan that could be brought to class and shared. In an oral report, these students should share with the class what they learn.

Cooking

11. These cookies could be prepared the night before and served at the culminating activity suggested below. "Petticoat Tails" is a recipe that was brought from France to Scotland by Mary, Queen of Scots.

Petticoat Tails

1 cup soft butter
1 cup sifted confectioners' sugar
1 teaspoon vanilla
2 $^1/_2$ cups sifted four
$^1/_4$ teaspoon salt

Mix together the butter, sugar, and vanilla. Sift together and stir in the flour and salt. Mix thoroughly and shape into a long roll. Wrap in waxed paper and chill overnight.

Cut in thin slices ($^1/_8$ inch thick), place slices on an ungreased baking sheet, and bake 9 minutes at 400°F.

Culminating Activity

12. The combined efforts of the class, along with assistance from parent volunteers, could be mobilized to hold a "high tea." One group could choose appropriate British music to be played in the background. Another group could research and then prepare the sandwiches or treats to be served. A third group could be charged with selecting and preparing a variety of teas to be served.

Suggested Reading

Campbell, Louisa. *A World of Holidays.* New York: Silver Moon Press, 1993.

Davies, Kath. *A First Guide to Great Britain.* Winchester, England: Zoe Books, 1994.

Flint, David. *Great Britain.* Austin, Tex.: Raintree Steck-Vaughn, 1997.

Fuller, Barbara. *Cultures of the World: Britain.* New York: Marshall Cavendish, 1994.

Gerrand, M. and J. Morrison. *The Lake District.* Lincolnwood, Ill.: Passport Books, 1997.

Green, Robert. *Queen Victoria.* New York: Franklin Watts, 1998.

Hogg, Garry. *Customs and Traditions of England.* New York: Arco Publishing, 1971.

Lovett, Sarah. *Kidding Around London: A Family Guide to the City.* Santa Fe, N. Mex.: John Muir, 1995.

Quale, Eric and Michael Foreman. *The Little People's Pageant of Cornish Legends.* New York: Simon & Schuster, 1986.

St. John, Jetty. *A Family in England.* Minneapolis, Minn.: Lerner Publications Company, 1988.

Singman, Jeffrey L. *Daily Life in Elizabethan England.* Westport, Conn.: Greenwood Press, 1995.

Sproule, Anna. *Great Britain.* Morristown, N.J.: Silver Burdett Press, 1991, second edition.

Steele, Philip. *Discovering Great Britain.* Winchester, England: Zoe Books, 1994.

Sutherland, Dorothy B. *Enchantment of the World: Scotland.* Chicago, Ill.: Childrens Press, 1985.

Vietnam

A Legend from Vietnam

Vietnam is rich in folktales. Because great quantities of water are needed for rice growing in the country, it is not surprising that some of these tales involve rain. In "The Toad Is the Emperor's Uncle," the title story of a book of tales, *The Toad Is the Emperor's Uncle, Animal Folktales from Viet-Nam*, told and illustrated by Vo-Dinh, Toad goes to the emperor to demand rain. This same story stands alone as a picture book, *Toad Is the Uncle of Heaven, A Vietnamese Folk Tale*, retold and illustrated by Jeanne M. Lee. It also appears in a brief form in *Vietnam* by Audrey Seah, part of the Cultures of the World Series published by Marshall Cavendish Corporation.

Uncle Toad Demands Rain

The sun beat down upon the earth fiercely for so long that ponds began to dry up, plants and animals died, and those few living things surviving on earth panted for water.

Toad had burrowed down in the mud to keep moist and cool, but he knew that soon the mud would dry and so would his skin. The pond where he lived had shrunk to a little puddle, and the fish that once happily swam about had died.

"This is intolerable," shouted Toad one day. "I am going to visit the heavenly palace of the Jade Emperor and demand that he send rain to our parched earth." And so Toad set out on his long journey.

Before long he met some bees, buzzing sadly. "Where are you going in such a hurry?" they asked Toad.

"I'm going to the Jade Emperor to demand rain," Toad said.

"We'll go with you," said the bees. "All we need is a little nectar, but the flowers have all withered and we cannot last much longer."

Toad hopped forward and the bees buzzed above him as they continued on their way. They passed a desolate farm where all the crops had died. An old rooster was crying there. "Where are you going?" he asked Toad and the bees.

"We are going to the Jade Emperor to demand rain," Toad explained.

"May I go with you?" asked the rooster. "Everything on the farm has dried up and died, and I have nothing to eat."

"Of course," said Toad, and he and the bees and the rooster continued on their way. As they climbed into the mountains toward the heavens, they came upon a dusty tiger whose tongue was hanging out of his dry mouth.

"Where are you going?" asked Tiger.

"We are going to the Jade Emperor to demand rain," Toad explained.

"This is intolerable," shouted Toad one day. "I am going to visit the heavenly palace of the Jade Emperor and demand that he send rain to our parched earth."

"May I go with you?" asked Tiger. "I have been hungry and thirsty now for days and still there is no sign of rain."

"Of course," agreed Toad, and he led the expedition all the way to the palace gates. The animals peeked inside the door of the palace and saw the Jade Emperor sitting on his throne, alone in the great room.

"You wait here," said the Toad to his friends. "I will talk to the emperor. But listen carefully. If I need you, I will call your name and then you must come quickly."

The Bees, Rooster, and Tiger waited outside the door while Toad went inside. Toad gave a tremendous hop, but instead of landing at the emperor's feet as he had intended, Toad surprised the emperor and himself by landing right in the emperor's lap.

"How dare you!" said the emperor.

"Your majesty," Toad began, "I have come . . ."

Toad got no farther. "Guards!" shouted the emperor. "Come and get this miserable Toad."

As the guards rushed into the throne room, Toad croaked loudly, "Bees! Come help."

The bees rushed into the throne room and began stinging the guards who turned, ran, and hid in a corner of the room.

Then Toad tried again to tell the Jade Emperor how rain was desperately needed on earth. He had only begun to tell his complaint when the emperor shouted again. "Thunder God! Come at once and silence this impudent Toad."

The Thunder God came rushing in amidst loud thunderclaps that crashed through the throne room.

"Rooster! Come help," shouted Toad above the noise.

Rooster came flapping into the throne room, leaped up on the Thunder God's shoulder, and crowed so loudly that the Thunder God covered his ears and went rushing into another corner of the room.

The Jade Emperor was furious. "How dare you disrupt my palace!" he shouted at Toad.

But Toad once again quietly and calmly tried to tell the emperor about the drought on earth.

Before he had gone far, the emperor called for the Hound of Heaven to come to his aid, and a huge beast slipped into the throne room and began to chase Toad.

"Tiger! Come help!" shouted Toad.

Tiger pounced into the throne room and attacked the Hound of Heaven. There was a furious battle, and it was clear that Tiger was about to sink his fangs into the Hound's throat and kill it.

"Stop! Stop!" shouted the Jade Emperor. "Uncle Toad," he said, using a term of great respect, "I beg you to call off your Tiger."

Toad puffed himself out proudly on hearing himself addressed so respectfully. "Tiger," he shouted. "Release the Hound."

Tiger stepped back and the Hound went yowling to a third corner of the throne room.

"Now, Uncle Toad," said the Jade Emperor, "what is it that you wished to tell me?"

Toad finally told his story about the great drought on earth and how everything was dying.

"Oh, dear," said the Jade Emperor. "I have been terribly careless. Let there be rain on earth this moment," he decreed.

"Thank you, your majesty," said the Toad, who was surrounded by the Bees, Rooster, and Tiger. They all bowed.

The emperor stared into the corners of the throne room and then looked back at Toad. "Uncle Toad," he finally said, "if there is a time in the future when you need rain again, you need not journey all the way to my palace. No indeed. Simply look at the heavens and croak. I will hear you, and I promise to send rain."

"Thank you," said Toad. He and his friends returned to earth where the rain fell softly upon them.

From then on, whenever a drought threatened earth, Toad simply raised his head to the heavens and began croaking. Rain always followed.

Background Information

The official name of Vietnam is the Socialist Republic of Vietnam. It is located in Southeast Asia. Vietnam's boundaries are China to the north, Laos to the west, Cambodia to the southwest, the Gulf of Tonkin to the northeast, and the South China Sea to the southeast. Vietnam has more than 1,400 miles of coastline.

Vietnam lies within the tropics in an area of warm temperatures and little seasonal change. In the south, the average temperature is 81°F, with April and May being the hottest and most humid months. The northern provinces have a cool season between December and March. In January, the coldest month, the average daily high and low temperatures in Hanoi are 68°F and 56°F, respectively. During June, the warmest month, the average high is 91°F, and the average low is 78°F.

Vietnam, like most of Southeast Asia, has a climate greatly affected by the monsoons. The dry season runs from November to April and the wet season runs from April into October.

The northern highlands, called Bac Bo, border the countries of Laos and China. This area is thinly populated, and there are many forests and jungles, although some of these have been cut for lumber or cleared for farming. Vietnam's highest peak, Fan Si Pan, at 10,312 feet, is located in these highlands. The northern region is rich in coal, tin, zinc, and lead.

Farmers in the northern and the central highlands live in small villages and grow crops by building terraces on the hillsides. The remote hilly regions of Vietnam are home to over thirty different tribes, each with its own language, dress, and customs.

The Red River Delta is between the northern Highlands and the Gulf of Tonkin. This is a major agricultural region. The Red River begins in Yunnan Province in China and flows through Vietnam into the Gulf of Tonkin. It is known as Song Hong Ha, or Mother River. The region is one of the world's most densely populated areas.

The central highlands, a region called Trung Bo, is the narrowest part of Vietnam. Tea plants and rubber trees are grown here. The French named the native peoples that live here Montagnards.

Many people in the central area of Vietnam live along the coast in fishing villages. Here thousands of boats go out from seaports to gather catches of fish. The waters in and around Vietnam provide saltwater and freshwater fish such as shrimp, crab, lobster, mackerel, and tuna. Some fish caught off the coast are sold to Japan. Others are sold in fish markets in Vietnam.

Not all of Vietnamese food fish come out of the sea. Fish farming is popular throughout Vietnam. Fish are kept in pens, which are enclosed parts of rivers and streams. Carp, catfish, and snakeheads are farmed in this way. Shrimp are farmed in the canals in the Mekong River Delta.

Nam Bo is Vietnam's southern region. This lowland area contains the Mekong River Delta. Millions of people live in this Delta or in the nearby fertile farmlands.

The Mekong River, called Nine Dragons by the Vietnamese, starts in the mountains of Tibet, runs through China, and forms part of the borders of Myanmar, Thailand, and Laos. After entering Cambodia, the Mekong divides into two main branches, the Lower River and the Upper River. In Vietnam, the Lower River flows into the South China Sea.

A chain of mountains, the Annamite Cordillera range, extends southward from the northern highlands and separates much of Vietnam and Laos. The Troung Son Mountains along the Cambodian and Laotian borders are the source of many small rivers that wind their way across the coastal lowlands that cover east-central Vietnam. There is considerable rice production in this area.

Vietnam covers 127,816 square miles, with a population of 75,123,880. The capital is Hanoi. Other major cities are Ho Chi Minh City, Haiphong, Cholon, Hue, and Danang.

Ho Chi Minh City was named after the north Vietnamese Communist leader who died in 1959. It was formerly called Saigon. Ho Chi Minh City and its surrounding areas in the Mekong Delta are home to 4 million people. Located on the southern coast, it is a major port and a center of finance and industry. Although there are an increasing number of cars, most people get around in the city by bicycle, motorcycle, motor scooter, bus, trolley, or cyclo (bicycle taxi.)

Many of the south's factories are located in Cholon, which is a suburb of Ho Chi Minh City. Many people of Chinese ancestry live in this city.

Danang is the second largest city in the south. It is a port facility and was the site of an air force base and other military installations during wartime.

Hue was the old imperial capital of Vietnam. It was home to thirteen emperors from 1802 to 1945. A walled fort surrounds much of the city, which is on the coast near the center of the country and has a population of about 260,000 people. Much of this city was destroyed in 1968 fighting.

Hanoi was the capital of North Vietnam and became the capital of the country when the north and south were united. The city is built on the banks of the Red River and is famous for its lakes and beautiful parks. About 3 million people live in the eleven districts that make up Greater Hanoi. It is the second largest city in Vietnam. Large deposits of coal are located near Hanoi.

Haiphong is a port city not far from the capital, Hanoi. It is an industrial center. Factories in the port of Haiphong process some of the region's stocks of phosphates. Haiphong has a population of about 1.5 million people.

Approximately 85 percent of the population of Vietnam are ethnic Vietnamese. Another 3 percent are Chinese, living mostly in the city of Cholon. More than fifty other peoples, including the Muong, Tai, Meo, Cambodians or Khmer, and Cham live throughout Vietnam.

More than two-thirds of the people of Vietnam work at farming, fishing, and forestry. More than half the farmers in Vietnam are women. Farming is mostly done by hand, using simple tools and devices pulled by water buffalo.

Rice is the main crop, and Vietnam is the third-largest exporter of rice in the world. Maize, sorghum, cassava, and sweet potatoes are also grown, as are many kinds of fruit, including pineapple, mango, rambutan, jackfruit, and oranges. Cash crops such as rubber, tea, coffee, soybeans, and peanuts are exported.

Many Vietnamese farmers work on farm cooperatives. They work on the cooperative's fields as well as their own plot. The size of their own plot of ground depends on the size of the family. The farmers share tools and livestock. The profits from the shared fields go to the cooperative and the government. The family keeps the rice they grow on their own plot. Each family also has a vegetable garden on drier land. They raise vegetables to eat, and they sell any extra.

Beginning in 1987, some privately owned, profit-making enterprises were allowed. And the government modified the farm collectives. Collective farming has almost disappeared in the south. Farmers were allowed to sell crops on the open market for a profit.

Hydroelectric dams in the north and the Central Highland are now a major source of electricity, and new power plants are planned in the south. These various reforms have led to some improvement in the economy.

History

The Vietnamese emigrated from southern China in prehistoric times. The first settlers in the Ma River Valley in Vietnam, southwest of what is now Hanoi, arrived about 300,000 years ago. About the fourth century B.C., the Lac Viet, who moved into and occupied most of the Red River Delta, pushed the early settlers south and southwest.

China took over Vietnam and ruled it from 111 B.C. to A.D. 939. During this time, the Vietnamese were introduced to rice growing and the use of the metal plough. Chinese religion, beliefs, food, language, arts, dress, and traditions also influenced the people.

The Vietnamese overthrew the Chinese but then came under China's control again in the early 1400s. In 1427, Vietnam again became independent from China.

During the 1500s, the Portuguese became the first Europeans to trade with the Vietnamese. Then in 1636, Dutch traders came.

From A.D. 100 to 1656, the coast of central Vietnam was part of the kingdom of Champa. The Champ people built palaces and temples, and ruins of their buildings still remain. The Lac Viets eventually defeated the people of Champa and also defeated the Khmer of Cambodia. By the mid-1700s A.D., the Vietnamese had defeated their rivals and occupied all the land that makes up modern Vietnam.

In the early 1800s, Emperor Gia Long arranged for the construction of a citadel or walled fortress in the city of Hue. The design of this citadel was similar to that of the Forbidden City in Beijing.

France invaded Vietnam in 1858 to establish a colony in Indochina. By 1883, the French controlled all of Vietnam. In 1945, at the end of World War II, a Communist named Ho Chi Minh led the people against the French and set up a new government in Northern Vietnam, with its capital in Hanoi. The French army stamped out Ho Chi Minh supporters in Southern Vietnam and continued in control in Southern Vietnam until 1954.

In 1954, after fighting between Vietminh Communist forces and the French, Ho Chi Minh and his Communist Vietnamese followers defeated the French army at the Battle of Dien Bien Phu, in the northern part of Vietnam. A Peace Conference was held in Geneva, Switzerland, and by terms of the peace treaty Vietnam was divided at the 17th parallel into North and South Vietnam.

Ho Chi Minh, the popular Vietnamese leader who had organized the National Liberation Army, became the leader in North Vietnam. He believed in Communism and thought that land should be shared equally between all the people. Ngo Dinh Diem led South Vietnam.

The Communist north and the non-Communist south came into conflict and a civil war had its beginnings in 1957. The Soviet Union supported the Communist north, and the United States supported the south.

At first, 1,600 United States troops went to Vietnam to advise and train South Vietnamese soldiers. But by 1967 there were more than half a million American troops in Vietnam.

The Vietnam war was at its height between 1965 and 1968. Neither side won decisive victories. The North relied on guerilla warfare and the south used superior weapons to stage major offensives.

The Vietnamese war was very unpopular in the United States. President Johnson looked for a way to withdraw from the conflict. When Richard Nixon became president, he announced a gradual withdrawal of U.S. troops, although the United States continued to supply weapons and training.

The United States pulled out of Vietnam two months after peace talks resulted in the Paris Agreement of January 27, 1973 and a cease-fire was signed.

But in 1974, the war was renewed between North and South Vietnam. Because South Vietnam was without U.S. support, the North Vietnamese were able to overrun the South. Then the country was unified and named the Socialist Republic of Vietnam in 1976.

The Khmer Rouge took over the government of Cambodia and made border attacks on Vietnam. Then Vietnam invaded Cambodia in 1978 and carried on that fight for ten years. Landmines were used extensively in this war. As a result of the invasion of Cambodia, a trade embargo was imposed on Vietnam. The Vietnamese left Cambodia in 1989.

A United Nations supervised peace accord in Cambodia was signed in 1991. Relations with China were also normalized at this time. In 1994, after Vietnam cooperated in efforts to locate U.S. servicemen listed as missing in action during the Vietnam War, the United States lifted the trade embargo it had imposed on Vietnam. In 1995, the United States officially recognized the government of Vietnam.

Because of all these wars, Vietnam is a poor country. In fairly recent years, the people have endured the occupation of the country by the Japanese during World War II, an anticolonial war with France from 1946 to 1954, the American bombing of the north, Communist guerilla fighting in the south during the Vietnam War, 1959–1975, and the war in Cambodia.

Now all of Vietnam is under a Communist government. At first, the government owned all property and businesses and everyone worked for cooperatives. Since the late 1980s there have been changes. New policies, called *coi moi* (openness) and *doi moi* (renovation) allow Vietnamese to own some property and earn some money.

Tourism has become a big business in Vietnam. By the year 2000, the Vietnamese government hopes for 4 million tourists annually. Foreign visitors are usually well-received and the money that they spend is a big help to the Vietnamese economy.

Government

The Vietnamese government functions along with the Communist party. The Political Bureau, with a dozen or more high level leaders, is the most powerful group in the Communist party. It issues directives to the government. Every four to six years, the almost 2 million members of the Communist party in Vietnam attend meetings and set major policies. The party's top administrator is the general secretary.

Many changes were made in the government of Vietnam, beginning in 1992 with the adoption of a new constitution. Vietnam's highest legislative body is the National Assembly, made up of 496 deputies who serve five-year terms. This National Assembly is responsible for legislative functions and selects the Council of State, which in turn appoints a prime minister who runs the government. The assembly also chooses a Council of Ministers, whose members run various government departments.

There are forty provinces in Vietnam and three independent city provinces for Hanoi, Ho Chi Minh City, and Haiphong. A province is divided into districts, each with its own people's council. These council members are elected every two years.

The Communist party runs the country's judicial system. Vietnam's legal system is derived from the French Civil Code but has been modified to fit Communist legal theory. The highest tribunal, which hears serious national cases, is the Supreme People's Courts. People's courts operate at the provincial, district, and city levels.

Religion

Buddhism is the most widespread religion in Vietnam. This includes two forms, Mahayana from China and Hinayama, which is Hinduized. Almost 90 percent of Vietnamese practice some form of Buddhism. Others follow Taoist or Confucian beliefs. Belief in a combination of these three religions is called *Tam Giao,* or Triple Religion.

Those who follow Buddhism contribute money to support the monks and the pagoda, which is the center of a community's spiritual life. Monks cannot own anything and rely on the people who visit the pagoda to supply them with food and necessities. Those who become monks start as novices and then, after study and passing examinations, can pass upward through as many as five levels.

About 10 percent of Vietnamese are Christians. Missionaries introduced Roman Catholicism into Vietnam during the 1600s. Christianity was widespread until 1975, when Communists took over the country. Some hill people practice animism or spirit worship.

Cao Dai is a faith that originated in Vietnam and which is followed by 2 million people. Followers believe in one God who has a female counterpart called the Mother Goddess. These followers accept lessons of Muhammad, Jesus, Buddha, and other teachers. The center of this faith is a temple in the town of Long Hoa near Ho Chi Minh City.

Small numbers of Vietnamese are Protestants, and others are members of the Hoa Hao sect.

Education

The literacy rate in Vietnam in 1945 was only 10 percent. Now it is estimated that 90 percent of the Vietnamese can read and write. Vietnamese value education, but parents must pay for their children to go to school. There are few school supplies, and classes of fifty students in some cases meet in a room with old tables and benches.

Children aged six to eleven go to primary school six days a week, where they learn to read, write, and do arithmetic. They study science and geography as well. Students learn how to read and write in *quoc ngu*, the Vietnamese written language. *Quoc ngu* uses English letters with special symbols to indicate tones.

Students do not receive letter grades, but each month the teacher sends home a note telling the parents where a student ranks in the class.

In crowded schools, students attend in shifts. One group comes from 7:30 A.M. to 11:30 A.M. Then there is a long break for lunch. After lunch, a new group of students comes for afternoon classes.

Schools located in agricultural areas schedule into the year long breaks during harvest time so the children can work with their families.

To be admitted to secondary schools, students must pass difficult examinations. Secondary school is essential to those who wish to go on to colleges and universities. Some students in vocational schools spend half their days in the classroom and half learning a trade such as mechanics, carpentry, or agriculture.

Immigrants

Since 1848, more than 6 million Asians have immigrated to the United States. These Asians include Chinese, Filipinos, Japanese, Asian Indians, Koreans, and Vietnamese.

After the collapse of the United States–backed government of South Vietnam in April 1975, a huge group of Vietnamese immigrated to the United States. In 1975, approximately 130,000 of these refugees entered the United States from Vietnam. By 1984, 700,000 Southeast Asian refugees had entered the U.S. It is expected that by the year 2000 the Vietnamese will be the third largest group of Asian Pacific Americans in this country.

In 1990, there were about 200,000 Vietnamese living and working in the Soviet Union and eastern European countries as "guest workers." Many of these sent money home to relatives in Vietnam.

Between 1981 and 1990, 401,400 Vietnamese immigrated to the United States. Between 1991 and 1995, another 275,800 came.

Language

Vietnamese, or *Kinh,* is the official language of the country. The Vietnamese language is spoken by 90 percent of the people. It shares its roots with the Chinese, Cambodian, and Thai languages. The Vietnamese language is composed of single-syllable words with different meanings depending on the level of pitch. The dialect spoken in the north uses six tones, while the southern dialect has five tones.

Educated people originally used Chinese ideographs in writing, and Vietnamese was only a spoken language. Then people began to use Chinese symbols to write down Vietnamese words. Each symbol represents one word. The writing system, *chu nom,* is only used now for ceremonies and traditional greetings.

A new system for writing Vietnamese was introduced in the 1600s by Portuguese and French missionaries. This new system, *quoc ngu,* uses the same letters that European systems use, the Latin alphabet. Small signs next to the letters indicate their tone. This is the common writing system used in Vietnam today. About 90 percent of the population are able to read and write *quoc ngu.*

Some of the Thai who live in Vietnam speak Thai-Kadai, French, English, and Chinese dialects. In specialized local areas, Mon-Khmer and Malayo-Polynesian are also spoken. In the hill tribes, about sixty different dialects are spoken.

The Arts and Sciences

Most Vietnamese music is sung, often accompanied by a variety of musical instruments. Musical styles include the Chinese musical tradition based on five tones and popular and classical music from Europe and North America.

Percussion instruments play an important part in the music of Vietnam and include the use of xylophones, drums, and bells. Zithers, such as the single-stringed *dan doc huyen* and the sixteen-stringed *dan tranh,* are popular. The *dan nguyet* resembles a long-necked guitar. The *dan tam* and *dan ty* are also guitar-like. Some of the flutes that are used are made from bamboo.

The oldest surviving literature of the Vietnamese, dating back to the eleventh century, is work by Dieu Nhan, a Buddhist nun who lived from 1042 to 1114.

One of Vietnam's famous authors, Nguyen Du, worked in the royal courts in the late 1700s and early 1800s. His major work, *The Tale of Kieu,* is a 3,250-verse poem and is probably the most famous piece of Vietnamese literature.

A best-selling modern author is Nguyen Manh Tuan, a novelist. A Buddhist monk, Thich Nhat Hanh, writes popular poems, novels, and folk tales. Some of these, such as *A Taste of Earth* and *Hermitage among the Sleeping Clouds,* have been translated into English. Other novels, such as *Teacher Minh* by Nguyen Cong Hoan, examine the conflicts between traditional and modern values.

Theatre in Vietnam is controlled by the government, which hires the actors. *Hat tuong* is traditional theatre adopted from Chinese opera. The stories of these dramas are myths and legends.

Hat cheo is a type of comic opera featuring funny scenes, folk songs, and dance. *Cai luong* theatre was invented in the 1920s and is musical comedy.

Puppetry is also popular in Vietnam. *Roi nuoc* is water puppetry where the stage is a small pond. The audience sits on shore and the puppeteers, standing waist-deep in water, work behind a backdrop to move the puppets around on the water by the use of strings and poles.

Shadow puppets are cut from pieces of leather. At night, a fire is lit behind a large screen of white cloth. A narrator tells the story while puppeteers hold the puppets behind the screen to cast shadows. Some shadow puppet plays have stories that last over seven nights of performances.

Lacquerware items are made from wood, painted, and then covered with a hard, shiny coating. Originally this coating was made from the sap of the *son* tree. Currently new stronger chemical finishes are used to preserve the pieces. Some items are inlaid with gold, silver, and abalone. Up to ten coats of lacquer may be added before the object is completed.

Ceramic techniques can be traced back to the rule of the Chinese from 111 B.C. to A.D. 930. During this period Vietnamese learned to create glazed pottery. Most famous today are ceramics decorated with delicate blue and white designs.

Food

The cuisine of Vietnam reflects the influence of China, France, and other countries in Southeast Asia. Vietnamese dishes tend to be flavorful but not dominated by hot seasonings. Many dishes are accompanied by platters of lettuce, fresh herbs, and raw vegetables such as carrots, cucumbers, and bean sprouts.

Food is often cooked on a clay or brick stove heated with charcoal or wood. In cities, portable stoves are set up on stands. Rice and vegetables are served with almost every meal, and pork is more popular than chicken or beef.

Soft wrappers are often used to wrap meats and vegetables before they are dipped in some kind of sauce. Just as Chinese cooks use soy sauce, Vietnamese cooks rely on a basic fish sauce called *nuoc cham.*

At a typical family meal, each person would have a bowl of rice. Other foods would be served on large dishes from which people would serve themselves using chopsticks.

In cities, there are street vendors selling food. Soups are often sold, including *pho,* a beef-noodle soup enjoyed for breakfast.

The French influence on Vietnamese cooking is evident in stands selling baguettes, croissants, crepes, and special pastries.

The northern city of Hanoi is famous for its thick soups. Chicken or pork broth is cooked with fish, eel, or crab and slices of mushrooms. The coastal cities, such as Danang, specialize in grilled seafood. People in the Mekong Delta enjoy fish, eel, snake, turtle, and frog. Hot green tea is often served with a meal.

Asparagus was brought to Vietnam by the French and quickly became a favorite food. Vietnamese often call asparagus "Western bamboo." Asparagus soup is a favorite for New Year's dinner.

Asparagus Soup (Canh mang)
1 egg
2 tablespoons cornstarch
1/4 cup water
2 10 3/4-ounce cans chicken broth
1/2 pound fresh asparagus cut into bite-sized pieces
1 chicken breast, skinned, boned, and cut into bite-sized pieces
2 teaspoons fish sauce*
*A bottled sauce made of processed fish, water, and salt

Beat the egg in a small bowl and set aside. In another small bowl, mix cornstarch and water to make a smooth paste. Set aside.

In a large saucepan, bring broth to a boil, add asparagus, and reduce to medium heat. Cover and cook for 3 minutes. Add chicken. Cook for 4 minutes or until chicken and asparagus are thoroughly cooked.

Add fish sauce and cornstarch paste, stirring well before adding. Stir about 2 minutes or until soup starts to thicken. Add beaten egg a little at a time, stirring constantly. Cook for 30 seconds. Serve hot over rice or in soup bowls with rice on the side.

Recreation

Vietnamese enjoy sports as a social activity. Professional competition in sports is rare. Gym or physical education is part of the school curriculum. Favorite sports are soccer, table tennis, volleyball, swimming, and tennis.

The Communist state encourages physical fitness. The government provides facilities at community centers and youth clubs. Boys enjoy various forms of martial arts such as judo, karate, and kungfu. A local form of martial arts enjoyed by many is *vo viet nam.* This involves the use of bamboo sticks as well as bare hands.

Older Vietnamese sometimes meet together in parks in the morning for exercises such as tai chi.

Customs and Traditions

Tet Nguyen Dan, or Tet for short, is the Vietnamese New Year and is the most important holiday of the year. Tet begins on the first new moon between January 19 and February 20. The festival lasts for a week and is a time to settle debts and arguments. It is also a time to remember ancestors whose spirits are supposed to be present during Tet.

On a baby's first birthday, a party is held and the baby is officially introduced with his or her given name. After that, individual birthdays are no longer celebrated. Everyone honors their birthday on Tet and is considered one year older on that day.

The "firecracker festival" starts at midnight on the first day of Tet with the sound of firecrackers going off. Well before the holiday, women have spent days making *banh chung,* which are sticky rice cakes wrapped in banana leaves and tied with bamboo. These are given to friends and relatives as New Year's gifts. Dragon dancers fill the streets as a traditional part of the celebration.

To get the New Year off to a good start, homes are cleaned and everyone wears new clothes. People buy flowers to decorate their homes and New Year trees to ward off evil spirits. Homes are decorated with apricot and plum blossoms and chrysanthemums.

Thanh Minh falls on the fifth day of the third lunar month. This is a day for remembering the deceased. Vietnamese visit and clean the graves of their ancestors and bring gifts of food and flowers to offer to the souls of the departed.

Most homes have altars where people pray and make offerings to their ancestors. The *Doan Ngu* festival occurs on the fifth day of the fifth lunar month. According to ancient tradition, the dead continue to live in the underworld, where they need many things for their daily life. Paper effigies and pretend money are burned as offerings to the god of death.

On the fifteenth day of the seventh lunar month, *Trung Nguyen* begins and continues for a month. During this time it is believed that souls of the dead wander the earth. People make special offerings to their ancestors.

Mid-autumn Festival in Vietnam is held during the eighth month of the lunar calendar, which usually falls in our month of September. In olden days, this festival was celebrated by grownups, who gathered on a porch to look at the beautiful full moon, eat mooncakes, and sip tea. Sometimes poems were composed in honor of the moon. Now the festival is celebrated with a Children's Day. Children walk around the streets carrying lighted lanterns. Some of the lanterns are round like the moon. Others are shaped like fish and birds.

Women bake mooncakes on the day of the festival and enter them in the mooncake contest. Grownups perform one dragon dance and children perform another. Some of the dancers form the dragon's head while others carry its tail. Musicians march in the streets beating drums and clashing cymbals.

In some villages, a songfest is held by boys and girls in the middle of a field. In their midst, a large pot is turned upside down. A rope is stretched over the top of the pot, and the ends of the rope are tied to stakes. As the singers sing folksongs, they beat the taut rope with bamboo sticks to make notes like those of a musical instrument.

Two important holidays are National Day on September 2, which marks both the anniversary of Ho Chi Minh's Declaration of Independence in 1945 and the anniversary of his death, and May 19, is celebrated as the birthday of Ho Chi Minh. On these holidays there are parades and concerts. International Worker's Day is celebrated each year on May 1.

Suggested Activities

Writing

1. In 1960, the armed forces were one of the few racially integrated groups in American society. Black soldiers had faced discrimination during World War II. African Americans who joined the military to serve in Vietnam had various reasons for joining, but among these reasons was a search for equal opportunity.

   Encourage a group of students to work with a librarian to compile a reading list and then to read and study about the treatment of minority service men and women in World War II and in Vietnam. Each student should write a paper sharing what he or she learned from this research and includes a bibliography of sources.

Reading

2. A group of students may choose to read fiction that is connected with the Vietnam War and orally share a book report with others in the reading group. Possible titles include the following: Allan Baillie's *Little Brother* (Viking, 1992) takes place in Cambodia after the Vietnamese War. Walter Dean Myers' *Fallen Angels* (Scholastic, 1988) follows the trauma faced by Richie Perry, just out of Harlem High School, who spends 1967 on active duty in Vietnam. Stella Pevsner's *Sing for Your Father, Su Phan* (Clarion Books, 1997) tells of the life of the youngest daughter in a North Vietnamese village during the 1960s and 1970s. In *My Name Is San Ho* (Scholastic, 1992) a twelve-year-old Vietnamese comes to the U.S. to live with his mother and an American marine stepfather. *Tough Choices* by Nancy Antle (Viking, 1993) shows Samantha struggling with how to act with her two brothers, one of whom is a soldier and the other a Vietnam war protestor. In *The Purple Heart* by Marc Talbert (Harpercollins, 1992) Luke tries to understand when his wounded father comes home from Vietnam.

Vocabulary

3. As students read books and study pictures about Vietnam, they will be introduced to many Vietnamese words. Invite the class members to add to a class bulletin board words in Vietnamese and English written on 3 x 5-inch cards. The following can be used as "starters": *ban*—friend, *con trai*—boy, *hoa*—flower, *kem*—ice cream, *nam*—south, *voi*—elephant, and *ca*—sing.

Math

4. Invite a pair of students to use the data below, extracted from page 9 of *Vietnam* by Ole Steen Hansen, to prepare a set of math problems for the class to solve. The students should also prepare an answer key.

1 = average temperature in degrees C° for the city of Hanoi
2 = rain in mm in the city of Hanoi

Month	1	2
January	15	22
February	17	36
March	19	45
April	23	89
May	27	216
June	29	254
July	28	335
August	28	339
September	27	276
October	24	115
November	21	48
December	18	27

Social Studies

5. An anti-war demonstration at Kent State University in Ohio in 1970 was a tragedy that made headlines. National Guardsmen fired on students, killing four and wounding nine. Working with a library media specialist, invite a pair of students to research this event in past issues of newspapers and magazines. They should prepare a paper to share with the class on this incident and include a bibliography of the sources that they used.

Geography

6. In addition to the mainland, Vietnam includes some small islands in the South China Sea called the Paracel Islands. Invite a pair of students to research these islands and write a report on their findings to share with the class.

Music

7. The hill people (sometimes called Montagnards) of Vietnam have an interesting and distinct culture. Perhaps the music specialist could locate *Music of the Montagnards* on two CDs and play these for the class. The recordings from one disc were made between 1958 and 1966, and the recordings on the second disc were made in 1996 and 1997. The set comes with a 124-page booklet with notes and photos. *Music of the Montagnards*, CNR-2741085/86, is available from Multicultural Media, RR 3, Box 6655, Granger Road, Barre, Vermont 05641.

Art

8. According to Vietnamese beliefs, it is good luck to see a dragon wandering the earth during Tet (between late January and early February). *The Kids' Multicultural Art Book* by Alexandra M. Terzian (Williamson Publishing, 1993) gives directions for making dragons from simple materials, including a paper cup, flexible straw, construction paper, tape, scissors, and a hole punch. Students might want to make colorful dragons to decorate the border of a bulletin board devoted to Vietnamese topics.

Drama/Movement

9. The retelling of the folktale from Vietnam, *Uncle Toad Demands Rain*, which appears in this chapter, lends itself to puppetry. A group of students might decide to make papier mâché puppets, record dialogue and sound effects, and prepare the tale as a puppet show, which they present to interested classes at an elementary school.

Dress

10. Ask a pair of students to search out books containing pictures of Vietnamese in traditional dress, and with permission, photocopy pictures to bring in and share with the class. Among the pictures should be some showing the cone shaped hats, called *non la*, which are woven from palm leaves and which protect farm workers from the sun. Other photographs might show the women's traditional dress, the *ao dai*, which is a long blouse slit up the sides and worn over baggy pants. Pictures should also be sought of the North Vietnamese, who often wear black or blue fabrics decorated with beautiful embroidery.

Cooking

11. With sufficient parent help, students may make and enjoy Shrimp Soup with Pineapple. Shrimp is a favorite seafood in Vietnam. This interesting dish is sweet as well as sour. The recipe given serves four.

Shrimp Soup with Pineapple
(Canh Chua Ca)

4 large garlic cloves

$1/4$ cup vegetable oil

2 tablespoons chopped green onion tops

3 cups beef broth

1 cup water

$1/4$ cup distilled white vinegar

1 (8 ounces) can pineapple chunks

1 $1/2$ tablespoons sugar

1 tablespoon fish sauce

1 teaspoon salt

$1/8$ teaspoon red (cayenne) pepper

$1/4$ teaspoon white pepper

1 (4 ounces) can button mushrooms, drained

1 small firm tomato, cut into 8 wedges

24 small shrimp (about 6 ounces), shelled & deveined

$1/4$ lb. bean sprouts

Chop the garlic into small pieces until you have 3 tablespoons. Heat oil in a small skillet and heat the garlic, frying until golden and stirring frequently. Drain on paper towels and discard the oil. Set garlic and green onion tops aside for garnish. Combine beef broth, water, and vinegar in a 3-quart saucepan. Drain juice from pineapple, adding juice to the saucepan. Set pineapple chunks aside.

Add sugar, fish sauce, salt, red and white pepper to saucepan and bring to a boil. Add pineapple chunks, tomato wedges, and mushrooms and bring to a boil again. Add shrimp. Reduce heat and simmer for 2 minutes. Divide the bean sprouts among 4 large soup bowls. Ladle soup into the bowls and garnish with green onion tops and fried garlic.

Culminating Activity

12. A wall of one of the hallways in the school might be reserved for displaying a series of six murals. These murals would depict information that students had learned during their unit of studies. Students in the class could choose on which of six mural committees they wished to work to share what they had learned about Vietnam. They would need to plan the design of the mural, sketch it, and paint it.

Possible topics might be: early Vietnam—the Champa ruins; Hue—the imperial capital; Rice farming in the Mekong Delta; a tea or rubber plantation; animals of Vietnam, including the carabao; a central Vietnamese fishing village; the Vietnam War.

Suggested Reading

Ashabranner, Brent. *Always to Remember, The Story of the Vietnam Veterans Memorial.* New York: Dodd, Mead, 1988.

Asian Cultural Centre for Unesco. *More Festivals in Asia.* New York: Kodansha, 1975.

Gay, Kathlyn and Martin Gay. *Vietnam War.* New York: Twenty-First Century Books, 1996.

Hansen, Barbara. *Barbara Hansen's Taste of Southeast Asia.* Tucson, Ariz.: HP Books, 1987.

Hansen, Ole Steen. *Vietnam.* Hove, England: Wayland Publishers, 1996.

Hills, Ken. *Vietnam War.* Bath, England: Cherrytree Books, 1990.

Jacobsen, Karen. *Vietnam.* Chicago, Ill.: Childrens Press, 1992.

Kalman, Bobbie. *Vietnam, the Culture.* New York: Crabtree, 1996.

———. *Vietnam, the Land.* New York: Crabtree, 1996.

———. *Vietnam, the People.* New York: Crabtree, 1996.

Lawson, Don. *An Album of the Vietnam War.* New York: Franklin Watts, 1986.

Lee, Jeanne M. *Toad Is the Uncle of Heaven: A Vietnamese Folk Tale.* New York: Holt, Rinehart and Winston, 1985.

Lorbiecki, Marybeth. *The Children of Vietnam.* Minneapolis, Minn.: Carolrhoda Books, 1997.

Rodgers, Mary M., Senior Editor. *Vietnam in Pictures.* Minneapolis, Minn.: Lerner Publications, 1994.

Seah, Audrey. *Vietnam.* New York: Marshall Cavendish, 1994.

Super, Neil. *Vietnam War Soldiers.* New York: Twenty-First Century Books, 1993.

Viesti, Joe and Diane Hall. *Celebrate! in Southeast Asia.* New York: Lothrop, Lee & Shepard Books, 1996.

Vo, Dinh Mai. *The Toad Is the Emperor's Uncle, Animal Folktales from Viet-Nam.* Garden City, N.Y.: Doubleday, 1970.

Winchester, Faith. *Asian Holidays.* Mankato, Minn.: Bridgestone Books, 1996.

Bibliography

Ada, Alma Flor. *Where the Flame Trees Bloom.* New York: Atheneum, 1994. Contains eleven stories based on the author's experience growing up in Cuba.

Adler, David A. *Chanukah in Chelm.* New York: Lothrop, Lee & Shephard Books, 1997. This picture book illustrated by Kevin O'Malley provides a good introduction to the make-believe town of Chelm, which is famous in Polish folklore.

Ancona, George. *Fiesta U.S.A.* New York: Lodestar, 1995. This book, with photographs, captures the spirit of four fiestas for Spanish-speaking people in the United States.

Bennett, Martin. *West African Trickster Tales.* New York: Oxford University Press, 1994. This is a lively collection of ten stories from West Africa.

Bouvier, Leon F., and Lindsey Grant. *How Many Americans? Population, Immigration and the Environment.* San Francisco, Calif.: Sierra Club, 1994. This book examines what might happen to the environment if population in the United States continues to grow.

Caduto, Michael J. *The Crimson Elf: Italian Tales of Wisdom.* Golden, Colo.: Fulcrum Kids, 1997. This book contains six traditional Italian tales.

Campbell, Louisa. *A World of Holidays!* New York: Silver Moon Press, 1993. This book describes holidays celebrated in Japan, Pakistan, Namibia, Canada, and Mexico.

Carle, Eric. *Flora and Tiger, 19 Very Short Stories from My Life.* New York: Philomel Books, 1997. This book is a collection of personal stories about Eric Carle's life in America and in Germany.

Carpenter, Frances. *South American Wonder Tales.* New York: Follett, 1969. This is a collection of twenty-two folktales.

Chambers, Catherine. *All Saints, All Souls, and Halloween.* London, England: Evans Brothers, 1997. Illustrated with color photographs, this book explores the ways in which Halloween is celebrated around the world.

Chambers, Wicke and Spring Asher. *The Celebration Book of Great American Traditions.* New York: Harper & Row, 1983. This book gives hints on creative ways to mark special occasions, including craft, party, and food ideas.

de Paola, Tomie. *The Legend of Old Befana: An Italian Christmas Story.* New York: Harcourt Brace Jovanovich, 1980. In this story, an old woman keeps searching for the Christ Child to give him the presents she has made.

———. *The Legend of the Poinsettia.* New York: G. P. Putnam's Sons, 1994. This legend explains how the poinsettia came to be through a little girl's unselfish gift to the Christ Child.

Dolan, Edward F. *America after Vietnam: Legacies of a Hated War.* New York: Franklin Watts, 1989. Discusses the aftermath of the most unpopular war the U.S. was ever engaged in.

Evans, Phil, and Eileen Pollock. *Ireland for Beginners.* Oxford, England: The University Press, 1983. Gives a brief history intermingled with cartoons.

Fitzjohn, Sue, Minda Weston, and Judy Large. *Festivals Together: A Guide to Multi-Cultural Celebration.* Gloucestershire, England: Hawthorn Press, 1993. Contains a discussion of different types of celebrations.

Garland, Sherry. *Why Ducks Sleep on One Leg.* New York: Scholastic, 1993. This large-format picture book has color illustrations of a Vietnamese tale.

Han, Suzanne Crowder. *The Rabbit's Judgment.* New York: Henry Holt, 1994. This picture book tells a Korean folktale. On each page the English words are translated in Korean and are shown in the Han-gul alphabet.

Haskins, Jim. *Count Your Way through China.* Minneapolis, Minn.: Carolrhoda Books, 1987. A simple picture book that uses a few written Chinese characters.

Haviland, Virginia. *Favorite Fairy Tales Told in Italy.* Boston, Mass.: Little, Brown, 1965. Six traditional Italian fairy tales are included in this book.

———. *Favorite Fairy Tales Told in Japan.* Boston, Mass.: Little, Brown, 1967. This book contains retellings of six popular Japanese tales.

———. *Favorite Fairy Tales Told in Poland.* Boston, Mass.: Little, Brown, 1963. This book contains six traditional Polish tales.

Hay, John. *Ancient China.* New York: Henry Z. Walck, 1973. A study of archaeology in China.

Hillyer, V. M. and E. G. Huey. *The Americas.* New York: Meredith Press, 1966. This book is part of a series, "Young Peoples' Story of Our Heritage."

Hodges, Margaret. *Brother Francis and the Friendly Beasts.* New York: Charles Scribner's Sons, 1991. This account focuses on the incidents of St. Francis's life involving birds and animals. It is illustrated by Ted Lewin.

Kitchen, Margaret. *Grandmother Goes Up the Mountain and Other Mexican Stories.* London: Andre Deutsch, 1985. Contains a series of folk tales.

Lankford, Mary D. *Christmas Around the World.* New York: Morrow Junior Books, 1995. Contains stories about the way in which Christmas is celebrated throughout the world.

Levine, Herbert M. *Immigration.* Austin, Tex.: Raintree Steck-Vaughn, 1998. This book is part of a series that gives information and discusses both sides of an issue, permitting the reader to come to a conclusion.

Long, Robert Emmet, ed. *Immigration to the United States.* New York: H.W. Wilson, 1996. Discusses refugees from the Caribbean and Central America, and Mexico, and Vietnam, and examines immigration policy.

Millman, Joel. *The Other Americans, How Immigrants Renew Our Country, Our Economy, and Our Values.* New York: Viking, 1997. Discusses the everyday working lives of different immigrants in various parts of the United States.

Mohr, Nicholasa. *The Magic Shell.* New York: Scholastic, 1995. This book tells of a young boy who moves from the Dominican Republic to New York City.

Nottridge, Rhoda. *Let's Celebrate Winter.* Hove, England: Wayland, 1994. This is one of a series of books that also includes "Let's Celebrate Spring," "Let's Celebrate Summer," and "Let's Celebrate Autumn."

Paek, Min. *Aekyung's Dream.* San Francisco, Calif.: Children's Books Press, 1988. This simple picture book shows the English and the Korean words on each page, and a young immigrant's experiences are described.

Quayle, Eric. *The Little People's Pageant of Cornish Legends.* New York: Simon & Schuster, 1986. Illustrated in color by Michael Foreman. This book contains twelve Cornish legends.

Robertson, Dorothy Lewis. *Fairy Tales from Viet Nam.* New York: Dodd, Mead, 1968. This book contains nine tales.

Rosen, Mike. *Spring Festivals.* New York: Bookwright Press, 1991. This illustrated book describes spring festivals held throughout the world.

———. *Summer Festivals.* East Sussex, England: Wayland, 1990. Illustrated with photographs, this book discusses a variety of summer festivals held throughout the world.

Rugoff, Milton, ed. *A Harvest of World Folk Tales.* New York: Viking, 1949. This is a collection of tales collected from all over the world.

Sowell, Thomas. *Migrations and Cultures, A World View.* New York: Basic Books, 1996. This is an historical and global look at a large number of migrations of people over time.

Taylor, Mark. *The Fisherman and the Goblet, A Vietnamese Folk Tale.* San Carlos, Calif.: Golden Gate Junior Books, 1971. This picture book was illustrated by Taro Yashima.

Tifft, Wilton S. *Ellis Island.* Chicago, Ill.: Contemporary Books, 1990. This book, filled with photographs, presents the history of the tiny island in New York Harbor that was the first step on American soil for millions of immigrants.

Vittorini, Domenico. *The Thread of Life: Twelve Old Italian Tales.* New York: Crown Publishers, 1995. These favorite Italian stories are illustrated by Mary GrandPre.

Vuong, Lynette Dyer. *The Brocaded Slipper and Other Vietnamese Tales.* Reading, Mass.: Addison-Wesley, 1982. Contains five fairy tales with author's notes.

Walker, Paul Robert. *Little Folk: Stories from Around the World.* San Diego, Calif.: Harcourt Brace, 1997.

Index

Acrobatics and gymnastics, 24, 26
Acupuncture, 22
Aguinaldo, Emilio, 171
Ahn Chang-ho, 228
Akbar, 110
Alberti, Leon Battista, 137
Alexander I, II, and III, Tsars, 197
Alexander the Great, 110
Alvarado, Pedro de, 158
Amazon River, 31
Amber Coast, 56
Ambrus, Victor G., 93
The American Immigrant Wall of Honor, xi
Anderson, Peggy King, 102
Andrade, Manuel J., 53
Angel, Ann, 189
Anne Frank, Beyond the Diary, 89
Antilles islands, 55
Antle, Nancy, 253
Aquino, Benigno, 171
Aquino, Corazon, 171
Arabs, 110
Arepa, 35
Argunov, Ivan Petrovich, 200
Arnold, Bruce, 128
Arnold, Katya, 93
Aryabyata, 112
Ashoka, King of India, 110
Asian-Americans, 21, 148, 176, 224–225, 250
Aztecs, 158–159, 164

Ba, Mariama, 213
Ba Jin, 22
Baba Yaga, 191–195
Bach, Johann Sebastian, 87
Badminton, 24
Baffin, William, 13
Baffin Island, 13
Baillie, Allan, 253
Balaguer, Joaquin, 58
Ballets Russes, 200
Bamba, Amadou, 215
Bangladesh, 115
Bank of America, 136–137
Bank of Italy, 136–137
Barlow, Genevieve, 155
Barry, David, 115
Bartok, Bela, 100, 102–103
Baseball
    Cuba, 49
    Dominican Republic, 61–62
    Japan, 151
    Mexico, 162
Batista y Zaldivar, Fulgencio, 45, 49
Batory, Stefan, King of Poland, 183
Baudelaire, Charles, 74
Bayanihan Dance Company, 173
Becerra de Jenkins, Lyll, 37
Beethoven, Ludwig von, 87, 90
Beijing, China, 18
Bell, Alexander Graham, 9
Beluga whales, 12
Benalcazar, Sebastian de, 29
Berlin Wall, 84–85, 89
Bilibin, Ivan I., 191
Bismarck, Otto von, 84
Blade of the Guillotine, 76
Bode, Janet, 25
Bogota, Colombia, 32
Boleslaw the Brave, 183

Bolivar, Simon, 33
Bombardier, J. Armand, 9
Bondar, Roberta, 9
Borski, Lucia Merecka, 179
Boru, Brian, 123, 125
Bosch, Juan, 58
Bosse, Malcolm J., 115
Bossy Gallito stories, 41
"The Bossy Rooster," 41–42
Bracero program, 160
Brahms, Johannes, 87
"The Brave Chattee-Maker," 105–108
"The Brave Cuckoo," 155–157
"The Brave Red Rooster," 93–95
Brecht, Bertolt, 87
"The Bremen Town Musicians," 79–82
Brezhnev, Leonid, 197
British Empire, 236
Brown bears, 202
Budapest, Hungary, 96
Buddhism, 20, 147, 198, 223, 228–229, 249
Bulosan, Carlos, 173
Burma, 115
Bylot, Robert, 13

Cabot, John, 6
Caesar, Augustus, 134
Caesar, Julius, 134
Camaguey, Cuba, 50
Camargo, Alaberta Lleras, 33–34
Canada
    Act of Union and independence, 6–7, 11
    actors and drama, 9, 13
    arts, 9
    authors and poets, 9
    background information, 4–6
    Canada Act (constitution and charter), 7
    chansonniers, 13
    customs, traditions, and holidays, 10–12
    education, 8
    First Nations, 6, 7, 8, 10, 11–12, 13
    food, 10, 13
    French and British control, 6–7
    geographical regions, 4
    gold rush, 12
    government, 7
    history, 6–7
    immigration, 8–9
    inventors, 9
    Korean immigrants, 225
    languages, 8, 9, 12
    multiculturalism, 14
    musicians, 9
    national parks, 13
    Ojibway creation tale, 3–4
    painters and other artists, 9
    population (by province), 12
    provinces and territories, 4
    religion, 7–8
    sciences, 9
    sports and recreation, 10
    television personalities, 9
    and United States, 4, 8–9
Canadian Shield, 4
Cao Dai, 249
"The Carabao-Turtle Race," 167–168
Caribao Festival, 175–176
Caro, Miguel Antonio, 33

Cars, 73, 88, 135
Carter, Dorothy Sharp, 53
Cartier, Jacques, 6
Casimir the Great, 183
Castro, Fidel, 45, 46, 49
Castro, Raul, 45, 46
Cathedral of Zipaquira, 32
Catherine the Great, 197
Catholic Church. *See also* Christianity, Orthodox Church
    Colombia, 34, 36–37
    Cuba, 46
    Dominican Republic, 59
    France, 70, 72
    Germany, 83–84, 85
    Hungary, 98, 101
    Ireland, 125
    Italy, 136
    Mexico, 159–160
    Philippines, 170–171
    Poland, 183, 184, 185
    and Reformation, 70
Celts, 70, 123, 125, 236
Cezanne, Paul, 73
Chagall, Marc, 200
Champlain, Samuel de, 6
Chandler, Robert, 191
Chang, Jung, 22
Chansonniers, 13
Chaplin, Charlie, 77
Charlemagne, 70, 83, 134
Charles VII, King of France, 70
Charles X, King of France, 71
Chavez, Carlos, 161
Chekhov, Anton, 199
Chernobyl nuclear accident, 202
Chiang Kai-shek, 19
Children's Magazine Guide, 50
China. *See also* Tibet
    agriculture, 17
    astronomy, 25
    background information, 17–18
    calendars, 24
    clothing, 26
    and Communist party, 19, 22
    dynasties, 18
    education, 20–21
    emigration, 21, 25
    ethnic groups, 21
    festivals, 24–25
    food, 22–23, 26
    games, 23
    geographical regions, 17–18
    government, 19
    history, 18–19
    inventions, 21–22
    and Japan, 15, 19, 146
    and Korea, 222, 223, 224, 225
    languages and transliteration, 21, 25
    literature, 22
    mathematics, 22, 25
    media, 22
    paper lanterns, 26
    pottery, 22
    provinces and other divisions, 18
    recreation and sports, 23–24
    religion, 20
    theater, 22, 26
    and Vietnam, 247–248
    Zhou bell music, 26
The Chinese American Struggle for Equality, 25

Chopin, Frederic, 186
Christianity, 20, 223–224, 237. *See also* Catholic Church, Orthodox Church
    King James Bible, 238
Chun Doo Hwan, 223
Cinderella stories, 228
City population exercise, 202
Clovis, 70
Coats-of-arms
    Cuba, 51
    Dominican Republic, 63
    Hungary, 103
    Italy, 140
    Poland, 189
Coffee, 31, 36, 38
Cohen, Barbara, 191
Colombia
    artists, 35, 38
    background information, 31–33
    clothing, 38
    drug trade, 31–32
    education, 34
    emigration, 35
    ethnic and racial diversity, 32–33
    food, 35–36, 38–39
    geographical regions, 31, 38
    government, 34
    history, 33–34
    holidays and festivals, 36–37
    language, 35, 37
    major cities, 32
    math exercises, 37–38
    Museum of Folk Arts and Tradition, 35
    music and dance, 35, 38
    Post Card Day, 39
    reading exercises, 37
    recreation and sports, 36
    religion, 34
    soups, 35, 36
    writers and poets, 35
Columbus, Bartholomew, 57
Columbus, Christopher, 57
Columbus, Diego, 57
Coming to America, 176
Commonwealth of Independent States, 195, 197–198
Confucianism, 19, 20, 223, 228–229
Constantine, 70
Copernicus, Nicolaus, 186
Cornwall and Cornish-Americans, xi
Corot, Jean Baptiste Camille, 73
Cortez, Hernan, 158–159
"Count Silver Nose," 131–133
Cover, Arthur Byron, 76
Cowning, Charles, 191
Craig, Mary, 189
Crusades, 70
Cuba
    artists, 48
    arts, 47–48
    background information, 42–44
    dance, 48, 51
    economy, 43
    education, 46–47
    emigration, 45, 47
    flora and fauna, 51–52
    food, 48–49, 51
    geography, 42–43, 51
    government, 45
    guayaberas, 51

Cuba, *continued*
  history, 44–45
  holidays, 49–50
  immigration, 47
  language, 47, 50
  music and musicians, 47–48, 51
  peso exchange rate (math exercise), 50
  provinces and cities, 43, 46
  reading exercise, 50
  recreation and sports, 49
  religion, 46
  royal palm (coat-of-arms), 51
  theater, 48
  and United States, 43, 44–45
Cuba: I Am Time, 51
Cuban Missile Crisis of 1962, 45, 50
Curie, Marie Sklodowska, 186
Curie, Pierre, 186

da Vinci, Leonardo, 137
Dakar, Senegal, 210
Dalai Lama, 20
Dalton, John, 239
Daniels, Roger, 176
Dante, 137
Danube River, 95
Darwin, Charles, 239
Daughter of the Mountains, 115
de Gaulle, Charles, 71
Debussy, Claude, 74
Del Monte, 136
Delacre, Lulu, 29, 41
Delacroix, Eugene, 73
Demi, 15
Deng Xiaoping, 19
Descarte, René, 74
Diaghilev, Sergei, 200
The Diary of a Young Girl, 89
Diaz, Dinis, 210
Diaz, Porfirio, 159
Dieu Nhan, 250
DiGeorgia, Giuseppe, 136
Diop, Birago, 205, 213
Dominican Republic
  art and artists, 60
  background information, 55–57
  Carnival, 63–64
  coat-of-arms, 63
  courts, 59
  dance, 61, 63
  education, 59–60
  emigration, 60
  ethnic mix, 58
  fashion design, 61
  flora and fauna, 62–63
  folk beliefs, 63
  food, 61, 64
  geography and climate, 55–56, 57, 63
  government, 58–59
  and Haiti, 55, 57–58, 59, 60
  history, 57–58
  holidays, 62
  language, 60, 63
  major cities, 56–57
  merengue, 61
  mourning customs, 62
  music, 60, 61, 63
  native peoples, 57, 60, 63
  population, 55
  religion, 59
  romanceros, 60
  sports and recreation, 61–62
  travel planning and costs, 63, 64
  and United States, 58
  writers and literature, 60–61
Dostoyevsky, Fedor, 199
Drake, Francis, 57
Dreamcatchers, 13
Duarte, Juan Pablo, 58

Dublin, Ireland, 123, 124

Earthquakes
  Italy, 139
  Japan, 145
  Mexico, 158, 164
  Philippines, 169
  South Korea, 221
Easter Rebellion, 124
Eastern China, 17
Ehlert, Lois, 155
Ekiguchi, Kunio, 153
El Camino de La Salsa, 51
"El Dorado and the Lake of the Moon,"
  29–31
Elizabeth I, Queen of England, 124
Ellis Island, xi
Engels, Friedrich, 87
England, 234–235. *See also* United King-
  dom
  flag, 241–242
  national symbol, 241
European Union, 241
Everyman, 90

The Fall of the Red Star, 102
Fallen Angels, 253
Fansler, Denis S., 167
Faraday, Michael, 239
Fashion design
  Dominican Republic, 61
  France, 73
  Italy, 140
Feast of San Juan, 50
Film industry
  India, 112
  Italy, 137
  Japan, 150
  Philippines, 173
  Poland, 186
Finlay, Carlos Juan, 50
Fire in the Mountains, 189
Football. *See also* Soccer
  Canada, 10
  Gaelic, 127
  rugby, 240
France
  agriculture, 69–70
  background information, 69–70
  ballet, 74
  cars, 73
  education, 72
  emigration and immigration, 72
  empire and spread of language, 73, 76
  fashion design, 73
  food, 74–75, 77–78
  fruit ornaments (art exercise), 76–77
  geography and climate, 69
  government, 71–72
  historical headdresses, 77
  history, 70–71, 76
  holidays, 75–76
  industry, 70
  kings, 70–71
  language, 73, 76
  major cities, 69
  music and composers, 74, 76
  painters, 73
  perfumes, 73
  population (math exercise), 76
  recreation and sports, 75
  religion, 72
  scientists, 73, 74
  travel planning exercise, 78
  and Vietnam, 248
  wine, 70
  writers and literature, 73–74
Franck, Cesar, 74
Francois I, King of France, 70

Frank, Anne, 89
Frederick the Great, 84
French, David, 13
French, Fiona, 143
French Revolution, 71, 76
Frere, Mary E., 105
Frobisher, Martin, 6

Gaelic, 125–126, 128
Gainde, Yousou N'Dour, 216
Galan, Antonio, 33
Galdone, Paul, 41
Galileo, 137
Galvino, Italo, 131
Gambia, 208
Gambia River, 208
Gandhi, Mohandas K., 110, 115
Ganges River, 108
Garcia Lorca Theater. *See* Great Theater
  of Havana
Garden, Nancy, 79
Gauguin, Paul, 73
George I, King of England, 238
Germany
  agriculture, 83
  art and artists, 87, 90
  background information, 82–83
  Basic Law (constitution), 85
  Bavarian clothing, 90–91
  cars, 88
  education, 85–86
  emigration and immigration, 83, 86
  food, 88, 91
  forests, 83
  geography, 82, 90
  government, 85
  history, 83–85
  holidays and festivals, 89
  and Holocaust, 91. *See also* Frank,
    Anne
  industry, 82
  inventors and scientists, 87
  Lander (states), 82, 84, 85
  language, 86–87
  literature and writers, 87
  major cities, 83
  mittelstand (small businesses), 82–83
  music and composers, 87, 90
  postwar division and reunification, 85,
    89–90
  and printing press, 87
  Prune People, 90
  recreation, 88–89
  religion, 85
  Turkish immigrants, 85, 87
  wine and beer, 83
Geza, 97
Gia Long, Emperor of Vietnam, 248
Giannini, A. P., 136–137
Gift Wrapping, Creative Ideas from Japan,
  153
Gingerbread houses, 91
Giotto, 137
Gobi desert, 17
God Save the Queen, 241
Godunov, Boris, 197
Goethe, Johann Wolfgang von, 87
Gogol, Nikolai, 199
Gomez, Maximo, 44
Gomulka, Wladyslaw, 184
Gonzalez, Lucia M., 41
Gorbachev, Mikhail, 90, 197
Goree, 210, 211, 213
Great Theater of Havana, 48
Great Wall of China, 17, 26
Grimm, Jacob and Wilhelm, 79, 87
Gupta Empire, 110
Guru Nanak, 111
Gutenberg, Johann, 87, 226

Guy, Rosa, 205
Guzman, Antonio, 58
Gypsies, 99

Habsburgs. *See* Holy Roman Empire
Haiku, 152
Haiti
  and Cuba, 44, 46
  and Dominican Republic, 55, 57–58,
    59, 60
Han, Joanne Croder, 219
Han, Suzanne Crowder, 219
Handel, George Frederick, 87, 239
Hannibal, 140
Hanno the Great, 211
Hanoi, Vietnam, 247, 253
Hansen, Terrence Leslie, 53
Haraszty, Agoston, 99
"The Hare's Liver," 219–221
Harvey, William, 239
Havana, Cuba, 43
Haviland, Virginia, 67, 79, 119, 179
Henri IV, King of France, 70–71
Henry II, King of England, 123–124
Henry VIII, King of England, 124, 237
Heo, Yumi, 219
Hidalgo, Felix Resureccion, 173
Hidalgo, Miguel, 159
Hindi, 112
Hinduism, 109–111
  festivals, 114
Hiroshima Murals, 149
Hitler, Adolf, 71, 84, 134
Ho Chi Minh, 248
Ho Chi Minh City, Vietnam, 247
Hockey, 10
Hoffman, Felix, 179
Hokusai, 149
Holocaust, 91, 97, 102, 183, 185. *See also*
  Frank, Anne
Holy Roman Empire, 97, 134
Hong Kong, 18, 21
House of Slaves, 211
Hsi Ling-shi, 22
Hudson, Henry, 6
Hughes, Monica, 143
Hugo, Victor, 73–74
Hungary
  background information, 95–97
  biographical exercise, 103–104
  coat-of-arms, 103
  and Communist party, 98
  education, 98–99
  emigration, 99
  food, 100–101
  geography and climate, 95–96, 102
  government, 98
  history, 97–98
  holidays, 101–102
  industry and agriculture, 96
  language, 99
  major cities, 96–97
  music and composers, 100
  recreation and sports, 101
  religion, 98
  reversible fur coats, 103
  revolution of 1956, 98
  scientists and mathematicians, 100
  travel planning exercise, 102
  writers, 99–100
Hurling, 127
Hurricanes and typhoons, 55, 57, 169,
  221
Hwang Chini, 225

"The Inchling," 143–144
India
  architecture, 112–113
  background information, 108–109

India, *continued*
  biographical exercise, 116
  dance, 112
  education, 111
  emigration, 111–112
  film industry, 112
  food, 113, 116
  geography, 108–109, 115
  government, 110
  history, 109–110
  holidays and festivals, 113–115
  language, 112
  literature and writers, 112
  major cities, 109
  math exercise, 115
  music, 112, 115–116
  religion, 110–111
  science and mathematics, 112
  sports and games, 113
  traditional clothing, 116
  vocabulary exercise, 115
  and western powers, 110, 112
  wildlife (Sundarbans area), 116
Inner Mongolia, 17, 25
Insulin, 9
Inuit, 6, 8
  Cat's Cradle, 10
Ireland. *See also* Northern Ireland
  common names (math exercise), 128
  education, 125
  emigration, 124, 125, 128
  famine, 124
  food, 126–127
  geography and climate, 122–123, 128
  government, 124–125
  history, 123–124
  holidays and festivals, 127
  language, 125–126
  major cities, 123
  music and composers, 126, 128
  news exercise, 128
  painters, 126, 128
  provinces, 128
  religion, 125
  scientists, 126
  sports, 127
  writers and poets, 126, 128
Irish Art, 128
Islam, 20
  Germany, 85
  India, 110, 111
  mosques, 216
  Philippines, 170–171, 177
  Russia, 198
  Senegal, 208, 211, 212, 215, 216
  South Korea, 224
Italy
  architecture, 137
  art, 137
  background information, 134–135
  cars, 135
  coats-of-arms, 140
  education, 136
  emigration, 136–137
  fashion design, 140
  filmmakers, 137
  food, 138, 140
  geography and climate, 134–135
  government, 135–136
  historical pageant activity, 140
  history, 134–135
  holidays and festivals, 138–139
  industry, 135
  language, 137, 139
  major cities, 135
  map exercise, 140
  music and composors, 137
  national anthem, 140
  religion, 136

Italy, *continued*
  science, 137
  sports, 138
  wine, 134
  writers and literature, 137
Ivan III, Tsar, 197
Ivan IV, Tsar, 183, 197
Ivanov, Alexander, 200
Ivanov, Anatoly, 191

Jadwiga, "King" of Poland, 183
Jagiello, grand duke of Lithuania, 183
James I, King of England, 124, 238
Japan
  arts, 149–150
  background information, 145
  calligraphy, 150
  and China, 15, 19, 146
  cities, 145
  dance, 150
  drama (Noh, Kabuki, Bunraku), 149–150, 153
  education, 147–148
  emigration, 148
  emperors, 146
  films, 150
  food, 150–151
  gardens, 150
  geography and climate, 145
  gift wrapping (*tsutsumi*), 153
  government, 146
  history, 145–146
  holidays and festivals, 152, 154
  house design project, 153
  industrialization, 153
  and Koreans, 146, 222
  language, 149, 153
  literature, 149, 152, 153
  music, 150, 153
  painting, 149
  religion, 147
  samurai clothing, 153
  sculpture, 149
  sensu (fans), 150
  sports, 151
  tea ceremony, 150, 154
Jaruzelski, Wojciech, 184
Jiang Qing, 22
Jimenez de Quesada, Gonzala, 33
Joan of Arc, 70
John, King of England, 236
John Paul II, Pope, 184
John III Sobieski, King of Poland, 183
Johnson, Lyndon, 248
Juarez, Benito, 159
Julius Caesar, 139
Just So Stories, 116

Kadar, Janos, 98
Karol Stoch Ban, 189
Kawabata, Yasunari, 152
Kelley, Emmett, 77
Kennedy, John F., 45
Kent State University, 254
Khrushchev, Nikita, 45, 197
The Kids' Multicultural Art Book, 254
Kim Chi-ha, 225
Kim Whan-ki, 225
Kimmel, Eric A., 41, 93, 131
King, Martin Luther, Jr., 110
Kipling, Rudyard, 116
Kitajima, Osamii, 153
Kitano, Harry H. L., 176
Kodaly, Zoltan, 100
Kohl, Helmut, 85, 90
Kongi and Potgi, 228
Korea. *See also* North Korea, South Korea
  and China, 222, 223, 224, 225
  history, 222–223

Korea, *continued*
  and Japan, 146, 222
  reunification issue, 223, 229–230
Korean War, 222–223, 225
Koumba, Amadou, 205
Krak, 189–190
Krakow, Poland, 183, 189–190
Kramskoi, Ivan, 200
Krushchev, Nikita, 45, 197
Kublai Khan, 20

Ladislas the Short, 183
Ladoga, 196
Lake Baikal, 196
Lake Enriquillo, 63
Lake Superior, 4
Landowska, Wanda, 186
Leaving Home, 13
Lebiedzinski, Piotr, 186
Lech Walesa, 189
Lee, Bruce, 24
Lee, Tsung-dao, 22
Leitzinger, Rosanne, 41
Lenin, Vladimir, 197
Limericks, 128
Lin, Maya, 22
Liszt, Franz, 100, 102–103
Little Brother, 253
Livingston, Myra Cohn, 128
London, England, 234
Lord, Betty Bao, 22
Lots of Limericks, 128
Louis of Hungary, 183
Louis the Great, 97
Louis XIV, King of France, 71
Louis XVI, King of France, 211
Louis XVIII, King of France, 71
The Louvre, 69
"The Loyal Turtle," 219–221
Lu Xun, 22
Luna, Luan, 173
Luther, Martin, 83–84, 86, 90
Lutoslawski, Witold, 186

Ma, Yo-yo, 22
MacArthur, Douglas, 146, 222–223
Machado y Morales, Gerardo, 45
MacManus, Seumas, 119
Madach, Imre, 100, 103
Magellan, Ferdinand, 170
Magyars, 97, 99
Mahabharata, 112
Mah-jongg, 23
Malczewski, Jacek, 186
Malinke proverbs, 215
"Mama Crocodile," 205–208
Mameli, Goffredo, 140
Manet, Edouard, 73
Manila, the Philippines, 170
Manley, Molly, 128
Mann, Thomas, 87
Mao Tse-tung, 19, 22
Maple syrup, 13
Marceau, Marcel, 77
Marcellino, Fred, 67
Marcos, Ferdinand, 171
Mariana Trench, 177
Marostica's living chess game, 139
Marti, Jose, 44–45
Martial arts, 24, 151, 227
Maruki, Iri, 149
Maruki, Toshi, 149
Marx, Karl, 87
Mary I, Queen of England, 124
Masks, 216
Mauryan Empire, 110
Maximilian, Archduke of Austria, 159
Mayan Route, 163
Mayans, 158, 164

Mayer, Mercer, 79
Mazowiecki, Tadeusz, 184
McDermott, Gerald, 15
Medellin, Colombia, 32
  drug cartel, 31–32
  festivals, 37
Mendeleev, Dmitri, 200
Merengue. See Meringue
Meringue, 35, 61, 63
Mexican Hat Dance, 164
Mexico
  ancient civilizations, 158
  background information, 157–158
  dance, 161, 164
  education, 160
  emigration, 160–161
  ethnic mix, 157
  fiction reading exercise, 163
  folk art, 161
  food, 161–162, 164
  geography and climate, 157–158
  government, 159
  history, 158–159
  holidays, 159–160, 162–163
  language, 161, 163–164
  major cities, 158
  murals and painting, 161, 164
  music, 161, 164
  piñata party, 165
  recipe conversion (math exercise), 164
  religion, 159–160
  sombreros, 164
  sports and recreation, 162
  and United States, 159, 160
  writers and poets, 161, 163
Mexico City, Mexico, 158
Michelangelo, 137
Middle Passage Monument Project, 213
Mieszko I, Prince of Poland, 183
Miller, Kate B., 179
Milosz, Czeslaw, 186
Mime, 77
Mindanao Trench, 177
Mitterand, Francois, 71
Moguls, 110
Moliere, 73
Molnar, Ferenc, 100, 103
Monet, Claude, 73
Moniuszko, Stanislaw, 186
Montagnards, 254
Monte, Felix Maria del, 60
Montezuma, 158–159
Morality plays, 90
Moscow, Russia, 196, 202
Mosques, 216
Mother Teresa, 115
Mount Everest, 25–26
Mount Fuji, 145
Moussa, Keur, 216
Multicultural fairs, 14
Murals
  Hiroshima Murals, 149
  Mexico, 161, 164
  Vietnam exercise, 255
Murasaki, Lady, 149
Mussolini, Benito, 134
Mutsuhito, Emperor of Japan, 146
My Name Is San Ho, 253
Myers, Walter Dean, 253

Nagy, Imre, 98
Napoleon, 69, 71, 84, 139, 197
Napoleon III, 71, 159
NATO. *See* North Atlantic Treaty Organization
Nehru, Jawaharlal, 110
New England, 238
New Kids on the Block, 25
Newton, Isaac, 239

Ng, Franklin, 25
Ngo Dinh Diem, 248
Nguyen Cong Hoan, 251
Nguyen Du, 250
Nguyen Manh Tuan, 251
Nicholas II, Tsar, 197
Nietzsche, Friedrich, 87
Nijinsky, Vaslav, 200
Niokolo Koba National Park, 215
Nixon, Richard, 248
Nobel Peace Prize, 189
Normans, 123
North Atlantic Treaty Organization, 85, 90
North Korea, 221, 222–223. *See also* Korea, South Korea
  reunification issue, 223, 229–230
Northern Ireland, 124, 125, 235–236, 237. *See also* Ireland, United Kingdom

OAS. *See* Organization of American States
Ojeda, Alfonso de, 33
Ojibway creation tale, 3–4
Old Woman and Her Pig stories, 41
Olmecs, 158, 164
Organization of American States, 58
Orthodox Church, 198
Otto III, Emperor of Germany, 183
Ovando, Nicolas de, 57

Pacific Rim, 153
Paderewski, Ignace Jan, 186
Pak Saeng-kwang, 226
Pak Yong-man, 228
Pakistan, 109, 115
Pancake breakfasts, 13
Paper, 22
Paracel Islands, 254
Paris, France, 69
Park Chung Hee, 223
Parsons, Charles, 239
Pasternak, Boris, 199
Paula Santander, Francisco de, 33
Pavlov, Ivan, 200
Pavlova, Anna, 200
Pei, I. M., 22
Pen pals, 127, 178
Perez de Barradas, Jose, 29
Perov, Vasily, 200
Perrault, Charles, 67
Peter I, Tsar (Peter the Great), 197, 199
Peter III, Tsar, 197
Pevsner, Stella, 253
The Philipinos in America, 176
Philippines
  agriculture, 169–170
  arts and artists, 173–174
  background information, 168–170
  dance, 173, 177
  education, 172
  emigration, 172–173, 177
  ethnic groups, 170
  fauna, 176
  film industry, 173
  food, 174–175
  geography and climate, 168–169, 177
  government, 171
  history, 170–171
  holidays and festival, 175–176
  language, 173, 176
  literature, 173
  major cities, 169, 170
  music, 173, 177
  national costumes (*barong tagalog* and *terno*), 177
  and New People's Army, 177
  political unrest, 177
  recreation and sports, 175

Philippines, *continued*
  religion, 171
  Star lanterns, 177
  tribal arts and crafts, 173
  and United States, 171, 172
Pick Up Sticks, 23
Pido, Antonio J. A., 176
Pilipino language, 173, 176
Pilsudski, Jozef, 183
Pinilla, Gustavo Rojas, 33
Plume, Ilse, 79
Poland
  agriculture, 182, 184, 189
  background information, 182–183
  biographical exercise, 190
  coat-of-arms, 189
  Communist era, 184
  crafts, 186
  education, 185
  emigration, 185
  film industry, 186
  folk costumes, 190
  food, 186–187
  geography and climate, 182
  and Germany, 184, 185
  Gorale, 185, 190
  government, 184–185
  history, 183–184
  holidays and festivals, 188–189
  industry, 182, 184, 189
  invasions and occupations, 183
  Jewish population, 185
  language, 186, 189
  literature and writers, 186
  major cities, 182–183
  minorities, 185
  music and composers, 186, 189
  and Nazi death camps, 183
  nonexistence (1795–1918), 183, 189
  painters, 186
  religion, 185
  and Soviet Union, 183–184, 185
  sports and recreation, 187
  theater, 186
Polanski, Roman, 186
Polybius, 211
Popular Music Foundation of the Philippines, 173
Post Card Day, 39
Potatoes, 125, 126
Price, Christine, 105
Proust, Marcel, 74
Puccini, Giacomo, 137
Pulitzer, Joseph, 99
Puppets, 23, 251, 254
The Purple Heart, 253
Pushkin, Aleksandr, 199
"Puss in Boots," 67–69

Quayle, Eric, 231
Quesada of Colombia, 37
Quetzalcoatl, 158

"The Race Over Seven Hills," 167–168
Rackham, Arthur, 79
The Rajah's Rice, 115
Ramayana, 112, 114
Rankin, Louise, 115
Ravel, Maurice, 74
Ray, Satayajit, 112
Rayyan, Omar, 131
Readers' Guide to Periodical Literature, 50
Reagan, Ronald, 184
Recipes
  Asparagus Soup (Canh mang) (Vietnam), 251–252
  Batidos (Cuba), 51
  Burfi (India), 116
  Cherry Filling/Meggyes (Hungary), 103

Recipes, *continued*
  Christmas Spice Cookies (Germany), 88
  Dominican Fruit Cocktail (Dominican Republic), 61
  Fried Egg Rolls (Lumpia) (Philippines), 174–175
  Frituras de Name (Fried Yam Cakes) (Dominican Republic), 64
  Ginger Candy (Saeng Pyeon) (South Korea), 229
  Groundnut Sauce (Senegal), 214
  guacamole dip (Mexico), 165
  Hot Ginger Tea (Salabat) (Philippines), 177–178
  Hungarian Scrambled Eggs/Tojasrantotta (Hungary), 100–101
  Indian Sweet Milk Dessert (India), 113
  Irish Soda Bread (Ireland), 126–127
  Jollof Rice (Senegal), 216
  Korean Kebabs (Sanjeok Kooi) (South Korea), 227
  Little Almond Cakes (France), 75
  Moros y Christianos (Cuba), 48, 49
  Nachos Ole (Mexico), 162
  Nin Go Cake (China), 26
  Noodles with Poppy Seed (Kluski z makiem) (Poland), 187
  Papas Chorreadas (Colombia), 38–39
  Paradel (Apple Bread Pudding) (Italy), 138
  pasta (Italy), 140
  Pesto (France), 77
  Petticoat Tails (United Kingdom), 242
  Pirog (Russia), 203
  Pirozhki (Russia), 200–201
  Pistou (France), 77–78
  Polvorones (Mexico), 164
  Poppy Seed Cookies (Poland), 190
  Pork and Cabbage Dumplings (Japan), 150–151
  Pork Pie (Canada), 10
  Scones (United Kingdom), 239
  Shrimp Soup with Pineapple (Canh Chua Ca) (Vietnam), 254–255
  Strudel/Retes (Hungary), 103
  Tang Yuan (China), 23
  Tortillas de Maiz (Colombia), 35–36
  Vinegar Dip (Philippines), 174–175
  Yellow Man (Ireland), 128
Reed, Walter, 50, 51
Renaissance, 137
Renta, Oscar de la, 61
"A Retelling of *Puss in Boots*," 67–69
"A Retelling of *The Bremen Town Musicians*," 79–82
Reymont, Wladyslaw, 186
Richelieu, Cardinal, 71
Riordan, James, 219
Rizal, Jose, 171
Robert, Charles, 97
Rockwell, Anne, 41
Rodin, Auguste, 73
Roh Tae-woo, 223
Roman Empire, 70, 83, 97, 134
Romanceros, 60
Romanies. *See* Gypsies
Romanov, Michael, 197
Ronstadt, Linda, 164
Roosevelt, Franklin Delano, 97
Rossini, Gioacchino, 137
Royal Canadian Mounted Police, 7
Rubinstein, Arthur, 186
Russia
  background information, 195–196
  ballet, 200, 203
  bears, 202
  biographical exercise, 203

Russia, *continued*
  and Communism. *See* Soviet Union
  education, 198–199
  emigration, 199
  ethnic costumes, 203
  food, 197, 200–201
  geography, 195–196, 202
  government, 198
  history, 196–198
  holidays, 201–202, 203
  icon paintings, 200, 203
  Jewish population, 199, 202
  language, 199, 202
  major cities, 196
  music and composers, 199
  painting, 200, 203
  recreation and sports, 201
  religion, 198
  sciences, 200
  time zones, 202
  writers and literature, 199–200
La Ruta Maya, 163

Saint-Saens, Camille, 74
Sakade, Florence, 143
Salt, 22
San Marino, 134
San Martin, Ramon Grau, 45
Sancocho, 61
Sanskrit, 110, 112
Santa Anna, 159
Santeria, 46
Santiago, Cuba, 43
Santiago de los Caballeros, Dominican Republic, 57
Santo Domingo, Dominican Republic, 56–57
Savonarola, 140
Schroeder, Gerhard, 85
Scotland, 235, 237, 238. *See also* United Kingdom
  flag, 242
  national symbol, 241
  tartans and kilts, 242
Sejong, King of Korea, 222, 226
Sene, Yande Codou, 216
Senegal
  agriculture, 209–210
  background information, 208–211
  clothing, 216
  dance, 213–214, 216
  education, 212
  emigration, 212–213
  ethnic groups, 208, 209, 215
  food, 210, 214, 216
  geography, 208–209, 215
  government, 212
  griot tradition (oral literature), 213
  history, 211–212, 216–217
  holidays, 214–215
  language, 213, 215
  major cities, 210
  masks, 216
  music, 213, 215–216
  peanuts, 209, 214, 215
  religion, 212
  and slavery, 209, 210, 211, 212–213
  social classes and customs, 209
  sports, 214
  writers and poets, 213
Senghor, Leopold Sedar, 212, 213
Senghor, Sonar, 216
Seoul, South Korea, 221, 229
Seredy, Kate, 93
Serraillier, Ian, 189
Shakespeare, William, 139, 238, 242
Shanghai, China, 18
Shaw, George Bernard, 128
Shinto, 147, 152

Siegal, Aranka, 102
Sienkiewicz, Henryk, 186
Sikhism, 109, 111, 113
Silk, 22
"Silver Nose," 131–133
The Silver Sword, 189
Sing for Your Father, Su Phan, 253
Sinn Fein Society, 124
Sky Woman, 3–4
Slavery, 209, 210, 211, 212–213
    and dance, 213–214
Snow Country, 153
Snowmobiles, 9
So Loud a Silence, 37
Soccer, 23, 36. *See also* Football
    France, 75
    Germany, 88
    Hungary, 101
    Italy, 138
    Mexico, 162
    Poland, 187
    South Korea, 227
    United Kingdom, 240
Solidarity, 184
Solzhenitsyn, Aleksandr, 199–200
Soseki, Natsume, 149
South Korea
    agriculture, 222
    ancient money (*nyung*), 228
    background information, 221–222
    calligraphy, 229
    dance and masked dances, 226, 229
    education, 224
    emigration, 224–225
    food, 226–227
    geography and climate, 221
    government, 223
    history, 222–223
    holidays, 227–228
    language, 225, 226, 228
    major cities, 221–222
    music, 226, 229
    painting, 225–226
    poetry, 225
    and printing press, 226
    religion, 223–224
    reunification issue, 223, 229–230
    sciences and inventions, 226
    sculpture and pottery, 226
    sports and recreation, 227
    traditional clothing (*hanbok*), 229
Soviet Union, 195, 197
    and education, 198
    and Poland, 183–184, 185
    and Vietnamese "guest workers," 250
Spanish-American War, 44
Spellman, John W., 105
The Spirit Cries, 38
St. Francis of Assisi, 139
    Basilica di St. Francesco, 137
St. John Baptiste, 8
St. Patrick, 123, 127
St. Peter, 175
Stalin, Joseph, 197, 199
Stanislas de Boufflers, Jean, 211
Stephan I, King of Hungary, 97
Steptoe, John, 205
Sternberg, George M., 50, 51
Stevenson, Robert Louis, 42
The Stonecutter, 15
The Stonecutter, A Japanese Folk Tale, 15

Strangers from a Different Shore, 176
Stravinsky, Igor, 74, 199, 202–203
Suba, Susanne, 79
Sugar industry
    Cuba, 43, 45
    Dominican Republic, 61
Sun Yat-sen, 19
Swan Lake, 203
Syme, Ronald, 37
Syngman Rhee, 223, 228
Szablya, Helen M., 102

"The Tailor Who Became King," 179–182
Taj Mahal, 109, 113, 115
Takaki, Ronald, 176
Talbert, Marc, 253
Talkaty Talker, 128
Tan, Amy, 22
Taoism, 20
Tchaikovsky, Peter, 199
Tea, 17
Terzian, Alexandra M., 254
Texas, 159
Thich Nhat Hanh, 251
Thies, Senegal, 213
A Thousand Cranes, 153
"The Three Piskie Threshers," 231–234
Three-toed sloths, 37
Tibet, 17
    food, 23
    Mount Everest, 25–26
    thangka, 22
Tinikling, 177
Toad stories (Vietnam), 243–246, 254
Tokyo, Japan, 145, 146
Tolentino, Guillermo, 174
Tolstoi, Leo, 199
Toltecs, 158
Tombolo, 139
Tons (math exercise), 215
Tough Choices, 253
Tour de France, 75
Trans-Siberian Express, 196
Treasure Island, 42
"Tricking Count Silver Nose," 131–133
"Tricking Death Twice," 53–55
Tristao, Nuno, 211
Trujillo, Rafael, 58, 59
Truman, Harry S, 223
Tsiolkovsky, Konstantin, 200
Turgenev, Ivan, 199
Turks
    in Germany, 85, 87
    in Hungary, 97
    in India, 110
    in South Korea, 224
Tusk and Stone, 115
Typhoons. *See* Hurricanes and typhoons

Uchida, Hoshiko, 143
"Uncle Toad Demands Rain," 243–246, 254
Union of Soviet Socialist Republics. *See* Soviet Union
United Kingdom
    architects, 239
    background information, 234–236
    education, 237–238
    emigration, 236–237, 238
    flags, 241–242

United Kingdom, *continued*
    geography and component countries, 234–236
    government, 236–237
    "high tea" activity, 242
    history, 236
    holidays, 240–241
    language, 238, 241
    major cities, 234, 235
    mapping exercise, 241
    music and musicians, 239, 241
    national symbols, 241
    painters, 239
    philosophers, 238–239
    pound exchange rate (math exercise), 241
    religion, 237
    scientists, 239
    sports and recreation, 240
    writers and poets, 238, 241
United States
    Asian immigrants, 21, 111–112, 148, 176, 224–225, 250
    British immigrants, xi, 236–237, 238
    and Canada, 4, 8–9
    Chinese immigration, 21, 25
    Colombian immigration, 35
    and Cuba, 43, 44–45
    Cuban immigrants, 45, 47
    and Dominican Republic, 58
    Dominican immigration, 60
    ethnic backgrounds, xii
    Filipino immigrants, 172–173, 177
    French immigrants, 72
    German immigrants, 86
    Hungarian immigrants, 99
    immigration, xi–xii
    Irish immigrants, 124, 125, 128
    Italian immigrants, 136–137
    Korean immigrants, 224–225
    Polish immigrants, 185
    racial integration and the military, 253
    Russian immigrants, 199
    Vietnamese immigrants, 250
Upon the Head of the Goat, 102

"Vasilissa and Baba Yaga," 191–195
Vasquez, Horacio, 58
Vatican City, 134, 137
    math exercise, 139
Velazquez, Diego, 44
Venetsianov, Aleksei, 200
Ventura, Sylvia Mendez, 167
Verdi, Giuseppe, 137
Verhoeven, Rian, 89
Vidal, Beatriz, 29
Vietnam
    agriculture and fishing, 246, 247
    background information, 246–247
    ceramics, 251
    and China, 247–248
    and Communism, 247, 248, 249, 252
    dragon art exercise, 254
    education, 249–250
    emigration, 250
    and France, 248
    geography and climate, 246–247, 253, 254
    government, 249
    history, 247–248
    holidays, 252–253

Vietnam, *continued*
    lacquerware, 251
    language, 250, 253
    major cities, 247
    mural exercise, 255
    music, 250, 254
    puppetry, 251, 254
    religion, 249
    sports and recreation, 252
    theatre, 251
    traditional clothing, 254
    wars, 248
    writers and literature, 250–251
Vietnam War, 248, 253
    and Kent State University incident, 254
    fiction, 253
Villa, Jose Garcia, 173
Vistula River, 182
Vivaldi, Antonio, 137
Vladimir, Prince of Kiev, 196
Volcanoes
    Italy, 135
    Japan, 145
    Mexico, 157
    Philippines, 169
Volga River, 196
Voodoo, 46

Wajda, Andrzej, 186
Wales, 235, 237. *See also* United Kingdom
    flag, 241
    national symbol, 241
Walesa, Lech, 184, 189
Wallenberg, Raoul, 97–98
Warsaw, Poland, 182–183
Weiqi, 23
West African ethnic groups, 215
"The Widow's Lazy Daughter," 119–122
Wieniawski, Henryk, 186
William, Duke of Normandy (the Conqueror), 236
William I and II, Kaisers, 84
Wine
    France, 70
    Germany, 83
    Italy, 134
"The Wishful Stonecutter," 15–17
Wolof people, 209, 211, 213, 215, 216
World War I, 71, 84, 97, 146
World War II. *See also* Holocaust
    France, 71
    Germany, 83, 84–85, 90
    Hungary, 97–98, 102
    Italy, 134
    Japan, 146
    Korea, 222, 225
    Philippines, 171
    Poland, 182, 183, 185, 189
    U.S. military, 253

Yaque del Norte River, 56
Yaque del Sur River, 56
Yellow fever, 50–51
Yeltsin, Boris, 197, 198
Yi Sung-gy, 222

Zhang Heng, 25
Zukor, Adolph, 99